K4305. L34 2015

# REGULATING SPEECH IN CYBERSPACE

The fine for this overdue item is <u>50p per day</u>.
infolib@jbs.cam.ac.uk

*Item should be returned or renewed by the time the Centre closes on:*

| | |
|---|---|
| | |
| | |
| | |
| | |
| | |
| | |
| | |
| | |
| | |
| | |

**BOOKS SHOULD NOT BE MARKED IN ANY WAY**
Charges will be made for damaged items.

Privat
on th
engin
intern
nelled
facilit
for a l
govern
touch
*in Cyt*
of thre
respon
govern
the in
for hu

EMILY
Univer
United
School
Anglia
copyrig
respon

D1427785

913L9

# REGULATING SPEECH IN CYBERSPACE

Gatekeepers, Human Rights and Corporate Responsibility

EMILY B. LAIDLAW

*University of Calgary Faculty of Law*

CAMBRIDGE
UNIVERSITY PRESS

## CAMBRIDGE
### UNIVERSITY PRESS

University Printing House, Cambridge CB2 8BS, United Kingdom

One Liberty Plaza, 20th Floor, New York, NY 10006, USA

477 Williamstown Road, Port Melbourne, VIC 3207, Australia

4843/24, 2nd Floor, Ansari Road, Daryaganj, Delhi - 110002, India

79 Anson Road, #06-04/06, Singapore 079906

Cambridge University Press is part of the University of Cambridge.

It furthers the University's mission by disseminating knowledge in the pursuit of education, learning and research at the highest international levels of excellence.

www.cambridge.org
Information on this title: www.cambridge.org/9781107626997

© Emily B. Laidlaw 2015

This publication is in copyright. Subject to statutory exception and to the provisions of relevant collective licensing agreements, no reproduction of any part may take place without the written permission of Cambridge University Press.

First published 2015
First paperback edition 2017

*A catalogue record for this publication is available from the British Library*

*Library of Congress Cataloging in Publication data*
Laidlaw, Emily B., author.
Regulating speech in cyberspace : gatekeepers, human rights and corporate responsibility / Emily B. Laidlaw.
pages   cm
Based on author's thesis (doctoral – London School of Economics, 2012) issued under title:
'Information Gatekeepers, Human Rights and Corporate Social Responsibilities.
ISBN 978-1-107-04913-0 (hardback)
1. Internet service providers – Law and legislation.   2. Freedom of expression.   3. Freedom of information.   I. Title.
K4305.L35   2015
342.08′5302854678–dc23
2015001683

ISBN 978-1-107-04913-0 Hardback
ISBN 978-1-107-62699-7 Paperback

Cambridge University Press has no responsibility for the persistence or accuracy of URLs for external or third-party internet websites referred to in this publication, and does not guarantee that any content on such websites is, or will remain, accurate or appropriate.

One of the greatest ironies of this period in history is that, just as technology remakes our world, the need to maintain the human dimension of our work, and a company's sense of its social responsibility, is growing at an equally rapid pace. Harmonising economic growth with the protection of human rights is one of the greatest challenges we face today.

> Mary Robinson, former United Nations High
> Commissioner for Human Rights[1]

The problem of maintaining a system of freedom of expression in a society is one of the most complex any society has to face. Self-restraint, self-discipline, and maturity are required. The theory is essentially a highly sophisticated one. The members of the society must be willing to sacrifice individual and short-term advantage for social and long-range goals.

> Thomas Emerson[2]

---

[1] Office of the United Nations Commissioner for Human Rights, *Business and Human Rights: A Progress Report* (2000), Preface.

[2] T. I. Emerson, *The System of Freedom of Expression* (New York: Random House, 1970), p. 10.

# CONTENTS

# PREFACE

New technologies have changed the way we communicate, challenging traditional structures of speech regulation. In the internet context, the transnational, instantaneous nature of communications makes it difficult for governments to directly control the information that enters and leaves a country. At the same time, the power of companies that control this information flow increases because the communication technologies that enable or disable participation in discourse online are privately owned. To find information, we use search engines. To share information, we use communication platforms such as Twitter. To access the internet, we need to use internet service providers (ISPs). Thus, we inevitably rely on these companies to exercise the right to freedom of expression online, and they thereby become gatekeepers to our online experience. This is problematic for a human rights system that has treated human rights as a government responsibility and has effectively privatised human rights in the digital environment.

Our reliance on these gatekeepers to exercise the right to free speech has had two effects. First, such gatekeepers have increasingly been the target of legal measures designed to capitalise on their capacity to regulate third-party conduct. This ranges from orders for ISPs to block access to copyright-infringing websites and other unlawful content, as seen in United Kingdom cases involving Pirate Bay and Newzbin2, to orders by the Egyptian government during the Arab Spring in 2011 for Vodafone to switch off mobile networks. These orders put pressure on companies, both domestically and internationally, to be advocates for users' free speech rights and to have in place governance codes that guide their conduct in this respect.

Second, in the Western world, speech regulation in cyberspace has largely been left to self-regulation, in much the same way that regulation of the internet in general has been light-touch. When Facebook decides to delete a group it deems offensive, Twitter suspends a user's account for the content of his or her tweets or Amazon decides to no longer host a site such as Wikileaks, the determination tends to be made outside the legal system of human rights. The result is a system of private governance running alongside the law, without any of the human rights safeguards one normally expects of state-run systems, such as principles of accountability, predictability, accessibility, transparency and proportionality.

When companies have chosen to address their human rights impact, the models of regulation that have resulted range from internal codes of conduct often set down through terms of service to more formalised industry self-regulatory frameworks such as the Internet Watch Foundation (IWF) to address child sexual abuse images and the Global Network Initiative to address free speech and privacy. Informal corporate social responsibility (CSR) codes and self-regulatory frameworks therefore emerge as powerful forces in shaping the right to freedom of expression online.

This book challenges the traditional conception of human rights as a relationship between citizens and state, arguing that, in the Digital Age, the experience of human rights in general, and free speech in particular, often occurs with and through private parties. This calls for a new system of human rights governance that takes account of private power yet is sensitive to the models of regulation that have emerged in the communications technology sector. This book seeks to extend the internet regulatory debate to take account of CSR, which, up until now, has either been unaccounted for in the regulatory discussion or folded too simply within the notion of self-regulation. Through a series of case studies, literature review and analysis, this book examines the sufficiency of CSR frameworks to protect and respect freedom of expression on the internet. This examination connects three fields of study: CSR, regulation (more broadly, law) and human rights. All three ask questions about where the law ends and social responsibility begins, and it is the link between these fields that grounds this book's proposal for a new governance model. This has wider relevance to the debates concerning human rights and business, regulatory theory and internet governance.

This book argues that CSR lacks the standards and compliance mechanisms needed to be a credible and sustainable framework for speech regulation in the communications technology sector. Equally, top-down legal controls are too blunt a tool for this arena. What is needed is a framework that embraces the legal dimension of human rights and its accountability mechanisms and the nonlegal moral commitment to human rights that CSR more effectively facilitates. In the internet environment, I suggest that this involves building complementarity between the various systems of regulation. Drawing on regulatory and human rights traditions, a new governance model for speech regulation is proposed, one that acts as a template for the increasingly common use of non-state-based models of governance for human rights.

The book is organised as follows. Chapter 1, 'The internet as a democratising force', examines the internet's potential to be both a tool of democracy and a tool of control, setting up for the reader the critical role played by private gatekeepers in making discourse online possible and the need for human rights-compliant governance structures to facilitate this democratic potential. In Chapter 2, 'A framework for identifying internet information gatekeepers', the gatekeepers (IIGs) studied in this book will be identified and rooted in their impact on human rights.

In Chapter 3, 'Corporate social responsibility in cyberspace', CSR theory will be examined, tracing its history and establishing its relationship with the law and human rights and how it is being used in practice. It will show that the promise of CSR in the digital environment is in deploying human rights principles to nonpublic bodies that operate largely outside the remit of traditional human rights law. Ultimately, however, the largely voluntary nature of CSR instruments makes it a problematic candidate as a governance tool for IIGs and freedom of speech.

Chapters 4 and 5 comprise case studies of the public-facing governance frameworks of two macro-gatekeepers to determine their compliance with the principles underlying Article 10 of the European Convention on Human Rights and the United Nations Guiding Principles. In Chapter 4, 'Mechanisms of information control: ISPs', I examine the role of ISPs in filtering content, in particular the role of the industry regulatory IWF. In Chapter 5, 'Mechanisms of information control: search engines', the case study examines the role of search engines in controlling information flows through search indexing and rankings.

Chapter 6, 'A corporate governance model for the Digital Age', draws together the findings of the case studies and examines their significance to the question of what role CSR has played in governing the free speech impact of internet gatekeepers, and, in this role, asking if CSR adds value to the goal of facilitating and protecting free speech online. In this chapter, an alternative governance model will be proposed to address the deficiencies identified in the book and through the case studies.

This book focuses narrowly on freedom of expression, but it is intended to have wider significance. Many issues of free speech are

accompanied by concerns of, among others, privacy, the right to education and/or freedom of association. Indeed, privacy is an important
enabler of the exercise of free speech. This book does not examine privacy
as freedom, but it is written deeply conscious of it. Thus, when appropriate, the book speaks of human rights generally, and its proposals in
Chapter 6 are geared to have this wider effect. The book is further
narrowed by its focus on the Western world, in particular the United
Kingdom. However, there is an inevitable outward focus as a result of the
transnational nature of internet communications. The governance model
proposed in Chapter 6 is offered as a template to be used to address other
human rights engaged by the activities of the gatekeepers that are the
focus of this book and to be used (modified as necessitated by domestic
laws and culture) in other countries in the Western world.

# ACKNOWLEDGEMENTS

Numerous people supported me in various ways with this book, and I would like to take a moment to thank a special few of them.

Thank you to my family for your support. Special thanks to my parents, Larry and Sharon Cochran, for their love, support and guidance throughout my academic life (and it has been a long academic life). To my husband Ted, you deserve the most thanks of anyone. Your steadfast love and support, late night proofreading and sense of humour made this possible. Finally, thank you to our two children, Tessa and Hudson, for making all of this fun.

This book builds from the work I did during my PhD at the London School of Economics and Political Science (LSE). Thank you to my supervisors Conor Gearty and Andrew Murray. You both consistently went above and beyond what was called for as supervisors and mentors, and it was a joy to work closely with you two. My PhD work was partially funded by the generous Modern Law Review Scholarship, Olive Stone Memorial Scholarship and the Research Studentship of the LSE. Thank you also to my colleagues, at various points in time, from the LSE and the University of East Anglia Law School for your years of insight. In particular, I would like to thank Alastair Mullis and Daithí Mac Síthigh for their advice, ideas and support. All errors and omissions are my own.

# ABBREVIATIONS

| | |
|---|---|
| ASA | Advertising Standards Authority |
| AUP | Acceptable Use Policy |
| BBFC | British Board of Film Classification |
| BIS | Department of Business, Innovation and Skills |
| CCI | Commonwealth Cybercrime Initiative |
| CJEU | European Court of Justice |
| CSR | Corporate Social Responsibility |
| DMCA | Digital Millennium Copyright Act 1998 |
| DTI | Department of Trade and Industry |
| EFF | Electronic Frontier Foundation |
| ECHR | European Convention on Human Rights |
| ECtHR | European Court of Human Rights |
| EHRC | Equality and Human Rights Commission |
| EICC | Electronic Industry Code of Conduct |
| FSC | Forest Stewardship Council |
| FTC | Federal Trade Commission |
| GeSI | Global e-Sustainability Initiative |
| GNI | Global Network Initiative |
| HRA | Human Rights Act |
| ICCPR | International Covenant on Civil and Political Rights |
| ICO | Information Commissioner's Office |
| ICT | Information and Communication Technologies |
| IIG | Internet Information Gatekeeper |
| ISP | Internet Service Provider |
| ISPA | Internet Service Providers Association |
| ITU | International Telecommunication Union |
| IWF | Internet Watch Foundation |
| NCP | National Contact Point |
| NGO | Nongovernmental Organisation |
| NGT | Network Gatekeeper Theory |
| NHRI | National Human Rights Institution |
| NSA | National Security Agency |
| OCSARP | Online Child Sexual Abuse Reporting Portal |

| | |
|---|---|
| OECD | Organisation for Economic Co-operation and Development |
| OfCom | Office of Communications |
| PCC | Press Complaints Commission |
| TNC | Transnational Corporation |
| ToS | Terms of Service |
| TRIPs | Trade-Related Aspects of Intellectual Property Rights |
| UDHR | Universal Declaration of Human Rights |
| VGT | Virtual Global Taskforce |
| WTO | World Trade Organization |

# TABLE OF LEGISLATION AND CASES

## Legislation/international treaties/declarations

## Cases

# The internet as a democratising force

The internet has the power to be a tool of democracy, but its potential in this respect is at risk. This is because the same technology that can be a positive force for the discursive values underlying democracy can also be a tool of control. The same technology that facilitates discourse creates opportunities for censorship of information, monitoring of online practices and the subtle shaping and manipulation of behaviour. This is not to say that the architecture of the internet does not somewhat determine how it is used,[1] but, ultimately, the internet is neutral in the face of the human agents that control its use. As Kofi Annan stated in 2003, '[w]hile technology shapes the future, it is people who shape technology, and decide to what uses it can and should be put'.[2] In this chapter, I explore the positive aspects of technology. The purpose is to identify for the reader the internet's potential and what is at stake if we do not intervene to secure the requisite freedoms into the internet's governance structure. This grounds the book's inquiry into the role of private gatekeepers in facilitating or hindering this democratic potential through their control of the pathways of communication.

Based on a theory developed by Jack Balkin, the internet's democratic potential will be argued to be rooted in its ability to promote democratic culture. Threaded through this argument will be the centrality of communication to democracy. In saying that the internet has the potential to

---

[1] See L. Winner, 'Do Artifacts Have Politics?', in D. MacKenzie and J. Wajcman (eds.), *The Social Shaping of Technology*, 2nd edn (Buckingham: Open University Press, 1999), discussing whether artefacts can have built-in politics. With regard to the internet, Lawrence Lessig famously argues that the internet's code is law: L. Lessig, *Code and Other Laws of Cyberspace* (New York: Basic Books, 1999); L. Lessig, *Code: Version 2.0* (New York: Basic Books, 2006).

[2] K. A. Annan, 'Break the technology barrier – the world information summit' (9 December 2003), at www.nytimes.com/2003/12/09/opinion/09iht-edannan_ed3_.html (last visited 16 June 2014).

be a democratising force, what will be asserted is that the internet can help facilitate deliberation and participation in the forms of meaning-making in democratic society. The distinction between the internet having potential to be a democratising force and its achieving it must be noted at the outset. Attempts have been made to prove empirically that the internet facilitates democracy, but such studies are compromised by the numerous variables present.[3] The goal of this chapter is more modestly to identify democratic culture as the type of democracy that the internet can facilitate and to explicate the characteristics of the internet that give it this potential.

This chapter sets up the broader investigation of this book into our reliance for facilitation of the internet's democratic potential on privately owned internet information gatekeepers (IIGs). The term IIG will be defined and examined in detail in Chapter 2; briefly, it means a gatekeeper which facilitates or hinders deliberation and participation in the forms of meaning-making in democratic culture. Every time we use the internet, we engage with IIGs. To find information, we use search engines. To access the internet, we need to use internet service providers (ISP). To be able to participate on message boards or social networking sites, we go through a host.[4] The role of such regulators has not yet been settled, and, as of yet, they do not have any democratic or public interest mandate[5] that assures the internet's democratic potential is being facilitated. If the internet is a democratising force, we inevitably at present must rely on these IIGs for the realisation of this aspect of its capacity. It is argued in this book that the corporate social responsibility (CSR) frameworks that currently govern the activities of IIGs are insufficient to meet their human rights obligations and that, without intervention, the continuation of their work in its current mode will hamper the ability of the internet to work as a tool of democracy.

---

[3] Michael Best and Keegan Wade attempted an empirical study of the effect of the internet on democracy from 1992 to 2002. The authors were only able to conclude that their study suggests a positive, but not absolute, link between internet penetration and democratic development. The authors also summarise other empirical studies of the internet's democratising effect that show mixed results: M. L. Best and K. W. Wade, 'The Internet and Democracy: Global Catalyst or Democratic Dud' (Research Publication No. 2005–12: Berkman Center, 2005).

[4] See discussion by Sandor Vegh, 'Profit Over Principles: The Commercialization of the Democratic Potentials of the Internet', in K. Sarikakis and D. K. Thussu (eds.), *Ideologies of the Internet* (Cresskill, NJ: Hampton Press, 2006).

[5] P. M. Shane (ed.), *Democracy Online: The Prospects for Political Renewal Through the Internet* (New York: Routledge, 2004), p. 54.

To that end, this chapter first orients the reader with a history of the rise and fall of the concept of the internet as a democratising force. It then examines the elastic concept of democracy and articulates the substance and appropriateness of democratic culture as the type of democracy most capable of facilitation by the internet. This includes an analysis of the narrower and, for our purposes, ill-fitting concept of deliberative democracy most famously discussed by Jürgen Habermas. Last, this chapter looks more closely at the ways that the internet is promoting democratic culture and the criticisms thereof, focusing on the internet's facilitation of information access and participation in politics and culture.

## 1.1. The historical context of the internet

The internet was celebrated in its infancy as a democratising force. Its decentralised structure invited anti-establishment-type rhetoric arguing that it was uncontrollable by governments and that it was a new space outside of legal institutions and territoriality.[6] 'Information wants to be free'[7] was the slogan. This optimism was reflected by the courts, particularly in the United States, with the U.S. Supreme Court noting the increasingly important role of the internet in facilitating communication in democratic society.[8] In *ACLU* v. *Reno*,[9] one opinion famously described the internet as a vast library which anyone can access and a platform from which anyone can publish, continuing that anyone 'can become a town crier with a voice that resonates farther than it could from any soapbox'.[10]

In the late 1990s, however, the reality of the internet's regulability began to crush cyberlibertarian idealism. Discussions no longer centred on the internet as a democratising force and instead were about the forces waiting to clamp down on it. With publications by Joel Reidenberg[11] and

---

[6] D. R. Johnson and D. G. Post, 'Law and borders – The rise of law in cyberspace' (1996), at www.temple.edu/lawschool/dpost/Borders.html (last visited 16 June 2014).

[7] Popularised by John Perry Barlow in 'Selling wine without bottles: economy of mind on the global net' (March 1994), at http://virtualschool.edu/mon/ElectronicFrontier/Wine WithoutBottles.html (last visited 16 June 2014), although it has been attributed originally to Stewart Brand, who stated, 'Information wants to be free because it has become so cheap to distribute, copy and recombine – too cheap to meter. It wants to be expensive because it can be immeasurably valuable to the recipient': *The Media Lab: Inventing the Future at MIT* (New York: Penguin Group, 1987), p. 202.

[8] See, most famously, *ACLU* v. *Reno* (1997) 521 U.S. 844, Justice Stevens delivering the opinion of the Court.

[9] Ibid.    [10] Ibid., pp. 852–53, 896–97.

[11] J. R. Reidenberg, 'Lex Informatica: The Formulation of Information Policy Rules Through Technology', *Tex. L.R.*, 76(3) (1998) 553.

Lawrence Lessig,[12] a new constraint was recognised. It was not just governments and laws that regulated behaviour, but those entities (inevitably private) that controlled the technology – the code writers and engineers who, as a result of their work, delineated the environment of our social life.[13] The message was that treating cyberspace as a separate place that will flourish if left alone by governments will not ensure the freedoms sought because that ignores the indirect ways that governments can regulate, as well as the ways architecture can be harnessed by private parties to constrain behaviour.

We also witnessed the increased regulation of the internet by states, which continues today.[14] Through the use of filtering and blocking technologies, countries such as China and Syria have developed tools to prevent their population accessing undesirable content. China's filtering system is complex, with the famous outer layer known as the 'great firewall of China' blocking access at international gateways and the inner layer comprising internet companies required by the government to monitor and remove objectionable content.[15] Syria prevents access to the entire Israeli.il domain, and many other states routinely filter access to websites with pornography and dissident or human rights-oriented content.[16] Sites such as www.youtube.com, are routinely blocked. For example, from 2007 to 2010, Turkey blocked access to YouTube, sparked by the posting of videos deemed offensive to the memory of its founding father Mustafa Kemal Ataturk.[17] In 2014, Turkey passed a controversial law allowing its telecommunications regulator to block access to websites without court order. As a result, in 2014, the authority blocked access to YouTube and Twitter, the latter being overturned quickly by court

---

[12] Lessig n. 1.     [13] Ibid., pp. 85–86.

[14] See R. J. Deibert et al., *Access Controlled: The Shaping of Power, Rights, and Rule in Cyberspace* (MIT Press, 2010), and the earlier R. J. Deibert et al., *Access Denied: The Practice and Policy of Global Internet Filtering* (MIT Press, 2008).

[15] See R. MacKinnon, *Consent of the Networked: The Worldwide Struggle for Internet Freedom* (New York: Basic Books, 2012), pp. 34–40.

[16] R. J. Deibert and N. Villeneuve, 'Firewalls and Power: An Overview of Global State Censorship of the Internet', in M. Klang and A. Murray (eds.), *Human Rights in the Digital Age* (London: Cavendish Publishing, 2005), pp. 121–22.

[17] The ban was briefly lifted between 30 October 2010 and 3 November 2010: A. Hudson, 'Turkey lifts its ban on YouTube-agency' (30 October 2010), at http://uk.reuters.com /article/2010/10/30/oukin-uk-turkey-youtube-idUKTRE69T1JE20101030 (last visited 16 June 2014), and I. Villelabeitia, 'Turkey reinstates YouTube ban' (3 November 2010), at www.reuters.com/article/2010/11/03/us-turkey-youtube-idUSTRE6A227 C20101103 (last visited 16 June 2014).

order.[18] Saudi Arabia now requires a licence to post content to YouTube.[19] During the protests across Africa and the Middle East in 2010 and 2011, filtering technologies were readily employed by states to block access to communication technologies that were seen as enabling and mobilising the protesters.[20]

Filtering is not limited to Asian or Middle Eastern countries. Germany blocks certain Nazi/hate websites.[21] The European Union provides the framework for national-level notice and takedown regimes for unlawful content.[22] Russia has blocked access to news sites for what the government describes as calling for participation in authorised rallies.[23] In 2014, the United Kingdom implemented an opt-in filter through agreement with four major ISPs, whereby access to content that is pornographic (though legal) is blocked unless a broadband user opts in with its provider to access such sites.[24] Naturally, much material lies at the

---

[18] C. Letsch and D. Rushe, 'Turkey blocks YouTube amid "national security" concerns' (28 March 2014), at www.theguardian.com/world/2014/mar/27/google-youtube-ban-turkey -erdogan (last visited 16 June 2014).

[19] See H. Noman, 'Saudi Arabia to impose restrictions on online content production, including on YouTube' (3 December 2013), at https://opennet.net/blog/2013/12/saudi -arabia-impose-restrictions-online-content-production-including-youtube (last visited 16 June 2014).

[20] See, for example, discussion of blocking of access to Twitter: D. Kravets, 'What's fueling Mideast protests? It's more than Twitter' (28 January 2011), at www.wired.co.uk/news /archive/2011–01/28/middle-east-protests-twitter?page=all (last visited 16 June 2014). Egypt went so far as to shut down connection to the internet nationwide in January 2011 (see M. Crete-Nishihata, 'Egypt's internet blackout: extreme example of just-in-time blocking' (28 January 2011), at http://opennet.net/blog/2011/01/egypt%E2%80%99s -internet-blackout-extreme-example-just-time-blocking (last visited 16 June 2014)). Google and Twitter created a 'Speak to Tweet' tool that enabled Twitter users to post tweets by leaving voice messages which the tool then turned into tweets: Google, 'Some weekend work that will (hopefully) enable more Egyptians to be heard' (31 January 2011), at http:// googleblog.blogspot.com/2011/01/some-weekend-work-that-will-hopefully.html (last visited 16 June 2014).

[21] Diebert and Villeneuve n. 16, p. 121.

[22] Directive 2000/31/EC of the European Parliament and of the Council of 8 June 2000 on certain legal aspects of information society services, in particular electronic commerce, in the Internal Market.

[23] Agence France-Press, 'Russia censors media by blocking websites and popular blog' (4 March 2014), at www.theguardian.com/world/2014/mar/14/russia-bans-alexei-navalny -blog-opposition-news-websites (last visited 16 June 2014), and E. Galperin and D. O'Brien, 'Russia blocks access to major independent news sites' (13 March 2014), at www.eff.org/deeplinks/2014/03/russia-blocks-access-major-independent-news-sites (last visited 16 June 2014).

[24] 'Online pornography to be blocked by default, PM announces' (22 July 2013), at www.bbc.co.uk/news/uk-23401076 (last visited 16 June 2014).

boundary of what would be blocked or material might be blocked accidentally, such as sex education sites. The government has also stated its intentions to extend the opt-in filter to extremist sites.[25] Companies such as BT have implemented such filters under the framework of parental controls, in which new users now must opt in to a variety of content, ranging from obscene content to content featuring nudity, drugs and alcohol, self-harm and dating sites.[26]

John Palfrey would describe this as comprising the second and third phases of what he frames as four phases in the evolution of internet regulation.[27] The first phase, paralleling the preceding discussion, was the phase of the *open internet*, in which the internet was seen as a separate space outside of governmental and other legal control. The second phase, from 2000 to 2005, he describes as the *access-denied phase*, in which the internet was seen by states as something to be managed; this period was therefore characterised by the use of filtering technologies. The third phase – *access-controlled*, from 2005 to 2010 – was characterised by more nuanced and sophisticated forms of control often layered on other forms of regulation. Filters were still used, but they could be targeted to particularly sensitive political events, such as the filtering of a controversial photo from the Tiananmen Square massacre leading up to the twenty-year anniversary. Additionally, it was characterised by the increasing use of private companies to regulate online content through data collection and sharing or blocking, licensing schemes to publish online, or a combination of filters combined with laws, as seen in cases like *Twentieth Century Fox Film Corp & Ors* v. *British Telecommunications Plc*,[28] where a UK court ordered ISPs to block access to file-sharing sites.

We have moved into a new phase, aptly described by one scholar as the time of the 'cyberrealists',[29] where discussions of the internet as a democratising force are re-emerging but with more sophistication and less naivety than in the past. Partly, this is due to the speed with which the internet is becoming the very things that the writers of the early 1990s forecast it would be. The internet has quickly moved from primarily

[25] G. Halfacree, 'Government extends porn filter to "extremist" content' (29 November 2013), at www.bit-tech.net/news/bits/2013/11/29/extremism-filter/1 (last 16 June 2014).

[26] S. Curtis, 'BT forces porn filter choice' (16 December 2013), at www.telegraph.co.uk /technology/internet-security/10520537/BT-forces-porn-filter-choice.html (last visited 16 June 2014).

[27] J. G. Palfrey, 'Four Phases of Internet Regulation', *Social Research*, 77(3) (Fall 2010).

[28] [2011] EWHC 1981 (Ch). See also *Dramatico Entertainment Ltd.* v. *British Sky Broadcasting Ltd.* [2012] EWHC 268 (CH) and [2012] EWHC 1152 (CH).

[29] Shane n. 5, p. xii.

being used for information access to become a participatory environment more closely mimicking the democratic participation traditional in the physical world. Although this interactivity was available on the early internet in the form of message boards and the like, they were not mainstream and did not offer the same range of tools available now. This participative environment, coined 'Web 2.0' by Tim O'Reilly,[30] is difficult to define comprehensively, although it is best captured by Stephen Fry's definition:

> Web 2.0 is an idea in people's heads rather than a reality. It's actually an idea that the reciprocity between the user and the provider is what is emphasised. In other words, genuine interactivity, if you like, simply because people can upload as well as download.[31]

It is a notion that describes the maturing internet's combination of 'aspects of the telephone, post office, movie theatre, television, newspaper, shopping mall, [and] street corner'.[32] Users are simultaneously creators and consumers of content.[33]

Indeed, it is this combination of public awareness, increasing private power and the importance of the internet to daily life that defines Palfrey's current and fourth phase of internet regulation. He calls this the *access-contested phase*, in which 'the regulation that states have imposed in the earlier phase is giving rise to strong responses from the private sector and from other states unhappy with this regulation ... Regulation online is increasingly a blend of the public and private'.[34] The key aspect of this period, he posits, will be the interplay among these various forms of regulation.

The internet will potentially become increasingly participatory as it continues to develop, thus opening up increasing possibilities for democracy. The next generation of the internet is the *semantic web*.[35] In this

---

[30] See the discussion by Tim O'Reilly about the coining of the term: 'What is Web 2.0' (30 September 2005), at www.oreillynet.com/pub/a/oreilly/tim/news/2005/09/30/what -is-web-20.html (last visited 16 June 2014).

[31] Video interview with Stephen Fry, at www.videojug.com/interview/stephen-fry-web-20 (last visited 16 June 2014).

[32] R. Rosenzweig, 'How Will the Net's History Be Written? Historians and the Internet', in H. Nissebaum and M. E. Price (eds.) *Academy & Internet* (New York: Peter Lang Publishing, 2004), p. 26.

[33] D. Rowland, 'Free Expression and Defamation', in Klang and Murray n. 16, p. 56.

[34] Palfrey n. 27, p. 992.

[35] See L. Feigenbaum et al., 'The Semantic Web in Action', *Scientific American* (Dec. 2007), reproduced with permission, at www.thefigtrees.net/lee/sw/sciam/semantic-web-in-action (last visited 16 June 2014). The vision of the semantic web was articulated by Tim Berners-

future, it is predicted that computers will be able to meaningfully read and process the data on networks such that if I input a question online, the answer is customised to me; data will be mashed together and information managed for you. Pictures you take might be linked to your calendar so that you know where and when you took them, planned travel might trigger updates of your medical file and in the booking of flights, car rentals and entertainment.[36] The World Wide Web Consortium sees the semantic web as a standardisation of two things: first, of the formats integrating and combining data and, second, of the languages used to relate data to the real world.[37] It is within this interactive environment that we can readily identify opportunities for participation in democratic culture and identify the growing power of private gatekeepers to shape discourse.

## 1.2. Which democracy for the internet?

Every communication technology from the printing press to the radio has at one time been celebrated as having a democratising force, but, in this context, few ask what is meant by democracy.[38] This is compounded by the difficulty in defining the very idea of democracy, depending so much (as it invariably does) on one's discipline or perspective. It is an elastic concept that can be approached both as an institutional construct and as an aspiration. It has cynically been described as a nonexistent[39] or as a 'vague endorsement of a popular idea'.[40] The goal here is neither to join the debate with my view of the proper definition of democracy, nor to engage in a discussion of the various forms of government in which

Lee. See 'The Semantic Web' (17 May 2001), at www.scientificamerican.com/article.cf m?id=the-semantic-web (last visited 16 June 2014).
[36] Feigenbaum, ibid.
[37] See explanation by the World Wide Web Consortium, at www.w3.org/2001/sw/ (last visited 16 June 2014).
[38] For a discussion more broadly about technology and democracy in history, see B. R. Barber, 'Three Scenarios for the Future of Technology and Strong Democracy', *PSQ*, 113(4) (1998–99) 573–75.
[39] B. R. Barber, 'Which Technology for Which Democracy? Why Democracy for Which Technology?', *IJCLP*, 6 (2001) 1, commenting '[b]ut there is no such thing as democracy. There are only a variety of forms of governments, which have a variety of characteristics that can be labelled under different groupings that define (not without controversy) distinctive forms of democracy': p. 3.
[40] R. A. Dahl, *Democracy and Its Critics* (Yale University Press, 1989), p. 2. See also R. A. Dahl et al. (eds.), *The Democracy Sourcebook* (MIT Press, 2003).

democracy is manifest;[41] rather, it is to articulate the democracy most capable of facilitation by the internet and most capable of facilitation or hindrance by IIGs.

We are living in an Information Age,[42] where access to information and participation in the circulation of information is a distinguishing feature of our world.[43] It is an era represented by a shift from the manufacturing jobs typical of an industrial society to a world in which jobs are increasingly devoted to the creation, handling or circulation of information. In this networked society, information flows dominate and shape our ways of life because of the speed and distance that information circulates[44] and our dependence on 'the production and distribution of information [as] a key source of wealth'.[45] In this information society, the internet has emerged as a key tool for the creation and circulation of information, but, more broadly, it has developed into an important mechanism for participation in democracy.

Yochai Benkler was correct in commenting that the early internet theorists' beliefs that the internet is a democratising force 'was correct but imprecise'.[46] With the costs of entry low and the architecture decentralised,[47] the internet invites mass participation at unprecedented levels. In this sense, it finds favour with Ithiel de Sola Pool's seminal work *Technologies of Freedom*, in which the author describes decentralisation of communication networks as the 'fostering' of freedom.[48] Yet, if the

---

[41] See discussion by Barber n. 39, pp. 3–4.

[42] For a discussion of the notion of information society, see R. F. Jørgensen, *Framing the Net: The Internet and Human Rights* (Cheltenham: Edward Elgar, 2013), pp. 17–18.

[43] See F. Webster (ed.), *The Information Society Reader* (London: Routledge, 2004), p. 1, which describes information as a 'distinguishing feature of our modern world'. M. Castells calls it an era of 'information capitalism': F. Webster, *Theories of the Information Society*, 2nd edn (London: Routledge, 2002), p. 100. See M. Castells, *The Rise of the Network Society*, 2nd edn (Oxford: Blackwell, 2000), and M. Castells, *The Internet Galaxy: Reflections on the Internet, Business, and Society* (Oxford University Press, 2001).

[44] M. Castells, 'An Introduction to the Information Age', in F. Webster (ed.), *The Information Society Reader*, ibid. For criticisms of Castells, see A. Halcli and F. Webster, 'Inequality and Mobilization in the Information Age', *European Journal of Social Theory*, 3 (1) (2000) 67, and N. Garnham, 'Information Society Theory as Ideology', *Loisir et Societe*, 21 (1)(1998) 97.

[45] J. M. Balkin, 'Digital Speech and Democratic Culture: A Theory of Freedom of Expression for the Information Society', *NYULR*, 79(1) (2004) 1, 3.

[46] Y. Benkler, *The Wealth of Networks: How Social Production Transforms Markets and Freedom* (Yale University Press, 2006), p. 271.

[47] Ibid., p. 212.

[48] I. de Sola Pool, *Technologies of Freedom* (Cambridge, MA: Belknap Press, 1983), p. 5.

internet is to achieve its democratic potential, it must tackle difficult problems of the Digital Divide, that the division between the haves and have-nots of the information society; concentration of the market; fragmentation of discourse and of quality control.[49] There are also problems such as the balkanisation of knowledge through the continual viewing of the same small group of websites[50] and the entrenchment of these websites at the top by the self-referencing of these sites in blogs, Twitter or on search engine results.[51] However, this does not mean that the internet does not have democratic potential, but rather that it is more complex than was previously thought. It means that how we think of notions of democracy, the public sphere and information must be tweaked to better reflect the complex and swiftly evolving internet.[52]

Under traditional conceptions of democracy, there are three types that the internet might facilitate: electoral, monitorial and deliberative.[53] *Electoral democracy* is commonly known in the internet context as 'e-government', the direct political communication between the state and its citizens. For example, countries are increasingly delivering public services and information to citizens directly through the internet by setting up websites to recruit volunteers and seek financial support for

---

[49] Although the digital divide between those with the wealth, literacy and language to access and fully enjoy the internet is a critical issue, particularly between First and Third World countries, it will not be discussed here. For more on this topic, see P. Norris, *Digital Divide: Civic Engagement, Information Poverty, and the Internet Worldwide* (Cambridge University Press, 2001), particularly chapter one.

[50] See Benkler n. 46, p. 234.

[51] In the context of search engines, see E. Goldman, 'Search Engine Bias and the Demise of Search Engine Utopianism', *YJLT*, 8 (2005–6) 188.

[52] Keeping in mind the pangloss scenario cautioned by B. Barber in examining technology and democracy, where complacency leads to a naivety about possible corruption: Barber n. 38, pp. 576–80.

[53] There are many ways that democracy can be divided for the purpose of the internet. This division was made in G. Longford and S. Patten, 'Democracy in the Age of the Internet', *UNBLJ*, 56 (2007) 5. In contrast, in a speech, Benjamin Barber simplified democracy into three types for a discussion about technology: representative, plebiscitary and deliberative; Barber n. 39, p. 3. Leni Wild divided democracy into three strands of liberal representative (the rational, autonomous individual), communitarian (participation in communities) and deliberative (participation in the dialogue); L. Wild, 'Democracy in the Age of Modern Communications: An Outline' (2008), paper for Freedom of Expression Project, Global Partners & Associates, pp. 5–6. In addition, some attempts have been made to differentiate between individual-oriented democracy and communitarian democracy, but this will not be discussed here because the internet can be both a place for individual growth and participation in the community, which duality is accounted for in J. Balkin's theory of democratic culture discussed herein. See, for example, L. Dahlberg, 'Democracy via Cyberspace', *New Media & Society*, 3(2) (2001) 157.

election campaigns.[54] States are increasingly embracing the electronic casting of votes.[55] In addition, countries are exploring ways to facilitate citizen-to-government discourse, such as the UK government's e-petition website to facilitate citizen petitions.[56] *Monitorial democracy* refers to the bottom-up, grassroots activism that can be facilitated by the internet.[57] These grassroots groups monitor political actions of governments and nongovernmental organisations (NGOs) by using the internet to organise protests and disseminate information.[58] *Deliberative democracy* refers to participation by individuals in open debate in the belief that it will lead to better decisions on matters of common concern.[59] It reflects 'the participative practice of democratic life'[60] and was said to have originated in town halls and public squares, and in pubs and coffee houses, anywhere groups came together to exchange their views on issues of the day.[61] Most commonly, it is framed as participation in the *public sphere*, a term most notably used by Jürgen Habermas and discussed further later.

While the internet can certainly contribute to all of these facets of democracy, its key contribution to democracy is as a facilitator of participation. Although participation is present in all three forms of democracy just identified, it finds its home most closely in deliberative democracy. This is because participation is experienced in cyberspace by communication (or the lack thereof through chilling effects such as surveillance and hate crimes), and deliberative democracy is at its core a communicative framework.[62] However, deliberative democracy does not quite capture the significance of participative practices on the internet either, being altogether too narrow a concept for what I have been describing here; this is an issue that will be explored in more detail shortly. An examination of deliberative democracy is necessary, however, as it has a presence in the democracy promoted here, in particular concerning the concept of the public sphere. This book, however, will frame its definition of democracy in none of the three areas we have been discussing up to now but rather in the broader notion of *democratic*

---

[54] Longford and Patten, ibid., p. 7.     [55] Wild n. 53, p. 13.

[56] See http://epetitions.direct.gov.uk/ (last visited 16 June 2014).

[57] Longford and Patten n. 53, p. 13. The e-petition example here illustrates where e-government can in fact facilitate monitorial democracy.

[58] Ibid., pp. 13–14.     [59] Ibid., p. 8.

[60] B. S. Noveck, 'Unchat: Democratic Solution for a Wired World', in Shane n. 5, p. 2.

[61] Longford and Patten n. 53, p. 8–9.

[62] L. M. Weber and S. Murray, 'Interactivity: Equality, and the Prospects for Electronic Democracy: A Review', in Sarikakis and Thussu n. 4, p. 102.

*culture*, which better embodies the participative practices we have been discussing.

### 1.2.1. Deliberative democracy

The deliberative democracy concept has two essential features for the purposes of analysis here, both of which have different potentialities and drawbacks as embodying the democratic potential of the internet. First, at its core, deliberative democracy is about valuing the rational and open exchange of opinions as the ideal way to reach understanding and agreement concerning common issues of concern.

One of its key theorists is Jürgen Habermas, who takes a normative approach in which he idealises what he has described as the rational debates that took place within bourgeois society in the coffee houses of the seventeenth and eighteenth centuries.[63] He argues that legitimate decisions are only made when preceded by a period of rational discourse that satisfies certain rules.[64] This is described as the *ideal speech* situation and requires, for example, that everyone who wishes to speak must have the opportunity to do so and that all speakers must be free from coercion.[65] Thus, the communication sought in deliberative democracy is more than simple communication: it requires that the interchange is reasoned and open, and it pushes towards the goal of publicly acceptable decisions.[66] As Vincent Price et al. state, '[w]hat makes opinion deliberative is not merely that it has been built upon careful contemplation, evidence, and supportive arguments, but also that it has grasped and taken into consideration the opposing view of others'.[67] There is a

---

[63] See J. Habermas, *The Structural Transformation of the Public Sphere*. Translated. (Cambridge: Polity Press, 1989).

[64] His theory on the ideal speech situation was developed after his work on the *Structural Transformation of the Public Sphere*. See J. Habermas, *Moral Consciousness and Communicative Action*. Translated. (Cambridge: Polity Press, 1990), and J. Habermas, *Justification and Application: Remarks on Discourse Ethics* (Cambridge: Polity Press, 1993). For Habermas, there were five conditions for ideal speech, summarised by Brian Esler as: '(1) every subject with the competence to speak and act is allowed to take part in a discourse; (2) everyone is allowed to question any assertion whatever; (3) everyone is allowed to introduce any assertion whatever into the discourse; (4) everyone is allowed to express his attitudes, desires and needs; and (5) no speaker may be prevented, by internal or external coercion, from exercising his rights laid down in (1) and (2)'; B. W. Esler, 'Filtering, Blocking and Rating: Chaperones and Censorship', in Klang and Murray n. 15, p. 99.

[65] Ibid., p. 92.    [66] Dahlberg n. 53, p. 2.

[67] V. Price et al., 'Does Disagreement Contribute to More Deliberative Opinion?', *Political Communication*, 19(1) (2002) 95, 97.

mythical tint to deliberative democracy, a nostalgic idealisation of citizens meeting to exchange reasoned political thoughts.[68] Most internet-based discourse would fail to satisfy these rules.[69]

In a 2006 journal publication, Habermas made a 'passing remark' on the applicability of his theory to the internet. He commented that while the internet provides egalitarian opportunities for communication, it fragments discourse, and, in a way that echoes the arguments of Cass Sunstein (discussed in more detail later in the chapter) said this:

> The Internet has certainly reactivated the grassroots of an egalitarian public of writers and readers. However, computer-mediated communication in the web can claim unequivocal democratic merits only for a special context: It can undermine the censorship of authoritarian regimes that try to control and repress public opinion. In the context of liberal regimes, the rise of millions of fragmented chat rooms across the world tend instead to lead to the fragmentation of large but politically focused mass audiences into a huge number of isolated issue publics.[70]

Most of the technologies discussed later in this chapter, such as blogs, social networking sites and message boards, are not decision-making tools, but are rather solely tools for discourse.[71] And most of the social norms or terms of service that govern behaviour on such sites would fail Habermas's rigid rules of discourse.[72] Deliberation also excludes many forms of communication that the internet is particularly good at facilitating, such as poetry, humour and satire. Such communications are meaningful to what I have been calling here democratic culture.[73]

---

[68] P. E. Agre, 'The Practical Republic: Social Skills and the Progress of Citizenship', in A. Feenberg and D. Barney (eds.), *Community in the Digital Age: Philosophy and Practice* (Oxford: Rowman & Littlefield Publishers, 2004), p. 204. Agre lists the problems of deliberative democracy as follows: it is inaccurate even about how the old 'town meetings' worked, ignores the amount of strategic work that goes into preparing for a public forum meeting and ignores the fear of public speaking of many potential participants: ibid.

[69] See, however, the view of A. M. Froomkin in 'Technologies for Democracy', in Shane n. 5, p. 4.

[70] J. Habermas, 'Political Communication in Media Society: Does Democracy Still Enjoy an Epistemic Dimension? The Impact of Normative Theory on Empirical Research', *Communication Theory*, 16 (2006) 411, 423, footnote 3.

[71] Froomkin n. 69, p. 14.

[72] A thorough discussion of this issue is outside of the scope of this chapter, but see part V of M. Froomkin's article: A. M. Froomkin, 'Habermas@Discourse.Net: Towards a Critical Theory of Cyberspace', *HLR*, 116(3) (2003) 751.

[73] A. Pinter and T. Oblak, 'Is There a Public Sphere in This Discussion Forum?', in Sarikakis and Thussu n. 4, p. 156.

The second element of deliberative democracy is 'the institutional arena'[74] in which such rational communication takes place. This is the concept of the public sphere for which there has been considerable discussion with regard to the internet's democratic potential.[75] The internet might not necessarily facilitate the type of discourse deliberative democracy envisions, but, by offering spaces for such discourse, it might be said to play, in an institutional sense, a democratising role. Granted, rational communication might be a precondition to the public sphere, but equally one first needs a space in which deliberative communication might take place.[76] In this sense, it might be better to describe the internet as creating a new public space, as contended by Zizi Papacharissi, one which does not yet constitute a public sphere.[77]

The public sphere, as Habermas describes it in *The Structural Transformation of the Public Sphere*,[78] is a 'network for communicating information and points of view'.[79] It is a metaphorical space where individuals gather to participate in rational discourse on issues of the day. Through this role, it is seen as a vehicle for societal integration.[80] In modern society, as social organisation took on a larger scale, the mass media became viewed as 'the chief institutions of the public sphere'.[81] It became their role to express the varying viewpoints of

---

[74] Dahlberg n. 53, p. 168.

[75] In a modern account, P. Dahlgren conceptualises it as consisting of three dimensions: the structural dimension, focused on institutional characteristics of ownership, regulation, laws and finance; the representational dimension, focused on media output in the form of broadcasts, newsletters and so on; and the interactive dimension focused on individuals' interactions with both the media and between themselves: P. Dahlgren, 'The Internet, Public Spheres, and Political Communication: Dispersion and Deliberation', *Political Communication*, 22 (2005) 147, 148–50.

[76] This is also discussed in Chapter 5 regarding the need of access to a forum of communication in order to engage in freedom of expression; see also E. Barendt, *Freedom of Speech*, 2nd edn (Oxford University Press, 2005), p. 274.

[77] Z. Papacharissi, 'The Virtual Sphere: The Internet as a Public Sphere', *New Media & Society*, 4(1) (2002) 9, 22–23.

[78] Habermas n. 63.     [79] Habermas quoted in Pinter and Oblak n. 73, p. 99.

[80] See discussion in the Introduction of C. Calhoun (ed.), *Habermas and the Public Sphere* (MIT Press, 1992), and Pinter and Oblak n. 73, p. 108. Habermas's theory has been criticised as naive and undemocratic, idealising coffee houses that were limited to educated male property owners; however, Habermas did view the modern public sphere as being transformed by its continual expansion to include more participants. While this influx of participation also led to the public sphere's degeneration, Habermas concluded that the structure of modern society means we cannot close up the sphere again: Calhoun, ibid., p. 3.

[81] Peter Dahlgren quoted in M. Feintuck and M. Varney, *Media Regulation, Public Interest and the Law* (Edinburgh University Press, 2006), p. 15.

the day and keep the public informed. In Habermas's view, the modern public sphere has collapsed in comparison with this earlier period, and he has sought to revive it by placing discourse firmly at its centre.

The internet might be an answer to Habermas's call for a reinvigorated public sphere by, as Michael Froomkin describes it, 'draw[ing] power back into the public sphere',[82] because it uniquely offers a participatory environment unavailable with traditional media. It is a shift from the mass-media public sphere, where relevance was decided by a select few constrained by space (for newspapers) and time (radio and television) and fed to the masses in a one-to-many structure, to a many-to-many structure in which groups of individuals can simultaneously be contributors and consumers of their culture. At the same time, cultural technologies such as the telephone, television and cinema have been multiplying, and 'our identities increasingly come to be constructed by, and expressed through, what we consume'.[83]

By opening up a discourse tool to mass participation, it also has the potential to facilitate the creation of communities; democracy is partly something experienced, which is done through the social organisations that educate citizens on how to engage socially and politically.[84] Before the internet, full democratic participation was hamstrung by the sheer inability of bringing together numerous people in one place for rational discussion.[85] With the removal of spatial and temporal bounds, and the freedom to participate anonymously or pseudonymously, the internet facilitates town-hall-type gatherings and the creation of communities that might not have otherwise formed. Although internet communities are hard-pressed to compete with the strength of a real-world community, this may change as the younger digital generation ages. The internet can be a way to create a community despite distance and borders.[86]

We must be mindful not to stretch Habermas's theory of the public sphere too far. In a 2010 interview, Habermas opined that the internet is not, in itself, a public sphere. He describes the internet as a 'centrifugal

---

[82] Michael Froomkin uses this phrasing. See Froomkin n. 69, p. 8.

[83] H. Mackay et al., *Investigating the Information Society* (London: Routledge, 2001), p. 2.

[84] M. Klang, *Disruptive Technology*, unpublished PhD thesis, p. 13.    [85] Ibid.

[86] D. Johnson and B. Bimber, 'The Internet and Political Transformation Revisited', in Feenberg and Barney n. 68, p. 248.

force' for disparate communications and discussion, but one which cannot, on its own, produce any public spheres:[87]

> But the web itself does not produce any public spheres. Its structure is not suited to focusing the attention of a dispersed public of citizens who form opinions simultaneously on the same topics and contributions which have been scrutinised and filtered by experts.[88]

However much the internet might reinvigorate the public sphere by activating public participation, it is difficult to argue that the internet itself qualifies as a public sphere. Increased access to information does not automatically translate into a more informed or participatory citizenry. The internet, it is argued, is best viewed not as one public sphere, but as multiple spaces, some public, some private, with multiple public spheres akin to Peter Dahlgren's description of the public sphere as a 'constellation of communicative spaces'.[89] The internet's distributive architecture prevents centralised control over communication and, in so doing, 'decenters the public sphere'.[90] In this way, it fits with Habermas's modified public sphere model, which focuses more on thematic spheres and communication networks:

> The public sphere can best be described as a network for communicating information and points of view (i.e. opinion expressing affirmative or negative attitudes); the streams of communications are, in the process, filtered and synthesized in such a way that they coalesce into bundles of topically specific public domains.[91]

Structurally, new types of public spheres are emerging, such as e-governments, advocacy domains, cultural and social domains and the journalism domain.[92] Rather than compare the public sphere to Habermas's utopian model, perhaps it should be compared to the media public sphere. In such a comparison, internet users are not passive consumers of information picked, crafted and presented by the mass media, but instead have the opportunity to be empowered participants in their democratic life. Anyone can be a publisher, and anyone can access

---

[87] S. Jeffries, 'A Rare Interview with Jürgen Habermas', *The Financial Times* (30 April 2010), at www.ft.com/cms/s/0/eda3bcd8-5327-11df-813e-00144feab49a.html (last visited 16 June 2014).
[88] Ibid.
[89] Pinter and Oblak n. 72, p. 148. See also discussion of Jørgensen n. 42, p. 87. Others have called for a relaxation of the requirements of the public sphere: J. Bohman, 'Expanding Dialogue: The Internet, Public Sphere, and Transnational Democracy', in Shane n. 5, p. 49.
[90] Ibid., p. 51.    [91] J. Habermas, *Between Facts and Norms* (MIT, 1996), p. 360.
[92] Dahlgren n. 75, p. 153.

an abundance of information and ideas unavailable in the tailored mass-media environment.[93] Conceiving of the internet in this way embodies the broader definition of democratic culture promoted here. This participative environment also helps transform traditional notions of democracy into a network model, where power and participation are decentred and experienced across various sectors, such as social, political and civil society networks.[94] This also mimics the shift seen on a global scale and in other fields, such as financial regulation and commerce, from more structured forms of regulation to decentred models of governance, discussed more in Chapter 3. Mobile access to the internet, for example, has linked cyberspace with the physical world in a way that fuses these two worlds and facilitates action-oriented public spheres, as seen with the Arab Spring demonstrations.[95] The kernel of deliberative democracy is its emphasis on the participative part of democratic life and, most particularly, participation in the public sphere.

### 1.2.2. Democratic culture

Jack Balkin argues that the internet has changed the social conditions of speech such that its central purpose is the promotion of what he terms democratic culture.[96] Democratic culture refers to the following:

> [It] is more than representative institutions of democracy, and it is more than deliberation about public issues. Rather, a democratic culture is a culture in which individuals have a fair opportunity to participate in the forms of meaning making that constitute them as individuals. Democratic culture is about individual liberty as well as collective self-governance; it is about each individual's ability to participate in the production and distribution of culture.[97]

This approach to democracy is framed in terms of democratic participation rather than democratic governance, meaning that it is a form of

---

[93] This is suggested by Y. Benkler n. 46, pp. 10, 185, 212–14. And see Y. Benkler, 'From Consumers to Users: The Deeper Structures of Regulation Toward Sustainable Commons and User Access', *Fed. Comm. L.J.*, 52 (2000) 561, 562.

[94] See discussion in Jørgensen n. 42, p. 19.

[95] Ibid., p. 85. See Y. Benkler et al., 'Social Mobilization and the Networked Public Sphere: Mapping the SOPA-PIPA Debate' (July 2013), The Berkman Center for Internet & Society Research Publication Series No. 2013–16 (July 2013): it defines the networked public sphere as 'a complex ecosystem of communication channels that collectively offer an environment that is conducive for communication and the creation of diverse organizational forms': p. 5.

[96] Balkin n. 45, p. 1.    [97] Ibid., pp. 3–4.

social life that underlies culture and exists beyond the confines of representative democracy. It focuses more broadly on culture, on the forms of meaning-making in society, because it includes within its ambit nonpolitical expression, popular culture and individual participation. It is democratic because anyone can participate regardless of race, age, political ties or economic status. This participation is of value because it creates meaning for culture, promotes a sense of self and encourages active engagement in the world.[98] Thus, in this book, when it is said that the internet is a democratising force, the substance of what is being asserted is that the internet can help facilitate deliberation and participation in the forms of meaning-making in democratic society.

Balkan's theory finds its roots in *semiotic democracy*, a term coined by John Fiske with regard to television to describe active public participation in creating and circulating meaning and pleasure.[99] Although television is a one-to-many medium, its viewers are on equal footing with the producers and are invited to ascribe meaning to what is seen. The viewer, in effect, becomes part of the discursive practice by taking pleasure in making meanings and participating in the creation of social identities.[100] Using this theory, Balkin asserts that the internet has changed 'the social conditions of speech', bringing to the forefront previously less important features of speech and necessitating a revisiting of free speech theory.[101] The internet, he concludes, accentuates the cultural and participatory features of freedom of expression.[102]

Freedom of expression, like the internet's topology, can be described as an interconnected network; a system of cultural and political interactions, experienced at both individual and collective levels.[103] Information and communication technologies (ICTs), largely owned by private companies, allow for participation in such interactions in a way previously

---

[98] Ibid., pp. 3–4, 35–38. He states, '[a] democratic culture includes the institutions of representative democracy, but it also exists beyond them, and, indeed undergirds them. A democratic culture is the culture of a democratized society; a democratic culture is a participatory culture': p. 33.

[99] J. Fiske, *Television Culture* (London: Routledge, 1987), pp. 236–37.

[100] Ibid., pp. 236–39, 311. For a discussion of the growth of semiotic democracy's popularity in scholarship and a proposal to extend the framework to semiotic disobedience, see S. K. Katyal, 'Semiotic Disobedience', *Wash. U. L. Rev.*, 84(2) (2006) 489.

[101] Balkin n. 45, pp. 1–3.    [102] Ibid., pp. 1–3, 33–34.

[103] Ibid., pp. 3, 5, referencing T. I. Emerson, *The System of Freedom of Expression* (New York: Random House, 1970). Emerson describes such as a system as having four key values: (1) self-fulfilment; (2) advance of knowledge and discovery of truth; (3) participation in decision making; and (4) stability of the community: pp. 6–8.

unimagined. It is also appropriative in the sense that participants can borrow from, manipulate, build on or simply co-opt existing cultural resources.[104] This interaction expands what is meant by democracy beyond the political to the cultural. What democratic culture does is broaden our conception of what it means for the internet to have democratic potential, and it recognises that democracy is as much something experienced as it is a political structure; it is a way of life inextricably tied up with community and culture.

Democratic culture also recognises the importance of freedom of expression to democracy and to human rights. Democracy has always been embodied in the practices of communication,[105] and freedom of expression has consistently been identified by the courts as central to democracy. In *Lingens* v. *Austria*, the European Court of Human Rights (ECtHR) famously commented that freedom of expression 'is one of the essential foundations of a democratic society'.[106] Habermas's theories concerning deliberative democracy cannot be applied seamlessly to the internet environment. However, his work tying together democracy and human rights by identifying the link as communication is persuasive.[107] Human rights, he articulates, is the enabling condition, the language, for legitimate and democratic decision making. He summarises:

> The internal connection between popular sovereignty and human rights that we are looking for consists in the fact that human rights state precisely the conditions under which the various forms of communication necessary for politically autonomous law-making can be legally institutionalised.[108]

Freedom of expression and access to a wide range of information sources has been described as the 'lifeblood of democracy'.[109] In an information

---

[104] Balkin n. 45, pp. 4–5.

[105] C. R. Kedzie and J. Aaragon, 'Coincident Revolutions and the Dictator's Dilemma: Thoughts on Communication and Democratization', in J. E. Allison (ed.), *Technology, Development, and Democracy: International Conflict and Cooperation in the Information Age* (Albany: State University of New York Press, 2002), p. 107.

[106] (1986) 8 EHRR 407, paras 41–42.

[107] J. Habermas, 'Human Rights and Popular Sovereignty: The Liberal and Republican Versions', *Ratio Juris*, 7(1) (1994) 1.

[108] Ibid., pp. 12–13.

[109] *R* v. *Secretary of State for the Home Department, ex parte Simms* [2000] 2 AC 115 (HL) (per Lord Steyn). He goes on to state, '[t]he free flow of information and ideas informs political debate. It is a safety valve: people are more ready to accept decisions that go against them if they can in principle seek to influence them'. See C. Walker and R. L. Weaver (ed.), *Free Speech in an Internet Era* (Durham: Carolina Academic Press, 2013) for a discussion in the internet context.

society, the importance of communication rights as a type of human right is accentuated because of the central role played by information in wealth and development:[110] '[I]n the deliberative process, information plays a central role along with achieving equality of access to it. Equality of access to information and an unrestricted means of access are fundamental to a more ambitious practice of discourse'.[111]

This right is more comprehensive than is often understood. Most human rights instruments explicitly or implicitly include the right to receive information in the right to freedom of expression. This can be clearly seen in Article 19 of the Universal Declaration of Human Rights (UDHR), which states:

> Everyone has the right to freedom of opinion and expression; this right includes freedom to hold opinions without interferences and to seek, receive and impart information and ideas through any media and regardless of frontiers.[112]

Similar language is used in the European Convention on Human Rights (ECHR)[113] and German Basic Law.[114]

Many states, such as Estonia, Finland, France, Greece and Spain, have legislatively recognised internet access as a fundamental right.[115] In 2003,

[110] R. F. Jørgensen (ed.), *Human Rights in the Global Information Society* (MIT Press, 2006), p. 119.

[111] Antje Gimmler quoted in Froomkin n. 72, p. 867. There were calls in the 1980s by Paul Sieghart (member of the UK Data Protection Committee) for an International Convention on the Flow of Information. He argued that 'one of the fundamental human rights should be access to as much accurate, complete, relevant and up-to-date information as everyone needs for the free and full development of their personality, the enjoyment of their lawful rights and the performance of their lawful duties, and protection from the adverse consequences of the misuse of information by others': quoted in G. J. Walters, *Human Rights in an Information Age: A Philosophical Analysis* (University of Toronto Press, 2001), p. 19.

[112] Universal Declaration of Human Rights 1948. The International Covenant on Civil and Political Rights 1966 uses similar language in Article 19.

[113] European Convention for the Protection of Human Rights and Fundamental Freedoms 1950, Article 10.

[114] Basic law for the Federal Republic of Germany (as amended 1990), Article 5. In 1946, at the first session of the UN General Assembly, it was stated that freedom of 'information' was a fundamental right, describing it as a 'touchstone of all the freedoms to which the United Nations is consecrated': quoted in Jørgensen n. 110, p. 54.

[115] Estonia sets out a universal right to Internet access in its Telecommunications Act, Article 5. In June 2009, France's Constitutional Council recognised the importance of internet access in its decision concerning the constitutionality of the HADOPI law: Decision no. 2009–580 of 10 June 2009 (France Constitutional Council), re Act furthering the diffusion and protection of creation on the internet, at www.conseil-cons titutionnel.fr/conseil-constitutionnel/root/bank_mm/anglais/2009_580dc.pdf (para. 12).

the Committee of Ministers of the Council of Europe adopted a Declaration affirming the importance of freedom of expression on the internet.[116] Since 2010, we have seen a paradigm shift at an international level in the recognition of human rights in cyberspace. Access to the internet as a fundamental right received the United Nations (UN) stamp of approval in a report by Frank La Rue, the Special Rapporteur on the promotion and protection of the right to freedom of opinion and expression.[117] In this report, La Rue not only recognised the importance of the internet to the exercise of free speech, but acknowledged the critical role of companies as the gatekeepers to exercising it: '[g]iven that internet services are run and maintained by private companies, the private sector has gained unprecedented influence over individuals' right to freedom of expression and access to information'.[118] He concluded that state use of blocking technologies was often in violation of their obligation to guarantee the right to free speech and that such measures should never be delegated to private parties.[119] This was followed up in 2012 by the UN Human Rights Council passing a resolution affirming internet freedom as a basic human right, in particular the right to freedom of expression.[120]

Recently, in *Ahmet Yildirim* v. *Turkey*,[121] the ECtHR held that blocking access to the entire sites.google.com platform breached the right to freedom of expression under Article 10 of the ECHR. This case, discussed

---

Finland has legislated a right of access to the internet by setting a right to a minimum amount of broadband in its Communications Market Act s. 60(c) (363/2011). Spain has enacted a similar provisions for broadband access: Law 2/2011 of March 4, Sustainable Economy, Article 52. Greece amended its Constitution to provide a right to information and right to participate in the information society, including facilitation of access to 'electronically transmitted information': Article 5A. For discussion of access to the internet as a fundamental right, see the work of the Internet Rights and Principles Coalition of the Internet Governance Forum arguing for such a right: http://internetright sandprinciples.org/ (last visited 16 June 2014) and Jørgensen n. 42, pp. 90–93. A BBC poll of 27,000 people in twenty-six countries found that four out of five people consider internet access a fundamental right: The BBC, 'Internet access is a "fundamental rights"' (8 March 2010), at http://news.bbc.co.uk/1/hi/technology/8548190.stm (last visited 16 June 2014) (poll available at http://news.bbc.co.uk/1/shared/bsp/hi/pdfs/08_03_10_BBC _internet_poll.pdf (last visited 16 June 2014)).

[116] Adopted 28 May 2003, at https://wcd.coe.int/ViewDoc.jsp?id=37031 (last visited 16 June 2014).

[117] Report of the special rapporteur on the promotion and protection of the right to freedom of expression, Frank La Rue to the United Nations General Assembly, 16 May 2011, at www.ohchr.org/Documents/Issues/Opinion/A.66.290.pdf (last visited 16 June 2014).

[118] Ibid., para. 44.     [119] Ibid., para. 43.

[120] UN Human Rights Council A/HRC/20/L.13, at www.regeringen.se/content/1/c6/19/64 /51/6999c512.pdf (last visited 16 June 2014).

[121] Application no. 3111/10 (18 December 2012).

in further detail in Chapter 4, concerned the order by the Denizli Criminal Court to block access to a site that insulted the memory of Ataturk, which breaches Turkish law. Due to purported technical reasons, the entire platform was ordered by the Court to be blocked rather than just the offending site. Ahmet Yildirim, an owner of one of the websites hosted by sites.google.com, brought the case to the ECtHR. The Court made several notable points concerning freedom of expression. Most relevant here, the Court confirmed that the right to free expression applies to access to the internet, which includes a right of unhindered access to it.[122] The Court found that this right applies not only to the content of information, but also to the means of dissemination.[123]

Participation in communication – in discourse – is the core of the deliberative democracy framework, but, as has we have seen, it falls short of being a democracy that the internet can facilitate because of the rigidity of the types of discourse that qualify as deliberation and the expectation that such deliberation will lead to legitimate public decisions. Instead, we should understand the internet as being multiple spaces, some of which are less-idealised public spheres. In this way, the internet's potential as a force within democratic culture reveals itself. Such spaces, although they might not show such extensive deliberation and risk being in form a 'thin democracy',[124] can be seen as 'tentative forms of self-determination and control "from below".[125] These are new forms of public spheres because the very act of visiting the spaces and engaging in discussions is a movement towards participation in democratic life, which has been waning. In this sense, they enhance community and culture as well, both of which are, as we have seen, critical to the broader definition of democratic culture embraced here.

## 1.3. Participation in democratic culture

This section examines more closely the ways that the internet facilitates participation in democratic culture. The goal is to relate this to the focus of the book on IIGs and their power to facilitate or hinder the internet's democratic potential. Viewed from the perspective of democratic culture, two forms of participation emerge as important to democracy: information access and political and cultural participation.

---

[122] Ibid., para. 31.    [123] Ibid., para. 50.    [124] Johnson and Bimber n. 86, p. 242.
[125] R. Kahn and D. Kellner, 'Virtually Democratic: Online Communities and Internet Activism', in Feenberg and Barney n. 68, p. 183.

Protection and facilitation of these participations is key to moving forward with a democratic vision of the internet. As regards information access, the reader will note our growing reliance on privately owned information guidance instruments to organise the overwhelming amount of information on the internet. With increasing participation online in politics and culture, discourse also takes place in spaces and using technologies that are privately owned, with such owners setting the terms of use and deciding what information is censored. Blocking access to information through the use of filtering technologies and control of information guidance mechanisms comprise the case studies in Chapters 4 and 5.

### 1.3.1. Access to information and participation in discourse

We are increasingly dependent on the internet in the functioning of our daily lives.[126] We use the internet to socialise with friends and family, research professional and personal issues, pay bills, create works of art and purchase consumer goods and services. The importance of the internet to the information society is reflected in the rapid increase in internet access and the importance people assign to having this access. In 2013, 86 per cent of adults and 99 per cent of sixteen- to twenty-four-year-olds in the United Kingdom had used the internet, whereas 83 per cent of households had internet access.[127] This is an increase of 22 per cent since 2007 and an increase of 58 per cent since 2002.[128] At the same time, use of mobile phones to access the internet doubled between 2010 and 2013 from 24 per cent to 53 per cent, and online shopping increased from 53 per cent to 72 per cent of adults between 2008 and 2013.[129] In the

---

[126] The Council of Europe advances this as the 'public service value of the Internet' because of 'reliance on the Internet as an essential tool for everyday activities (communication, information, knowledge, commercial transactions) and the resulting legitimate expectation that Internet services are accessible and affordable, secure, reliable and ongoing': Council of Europe, 'Building a Free and Safe Internet', Council of Europe Submission to the Internet Governance Forum Rio de Janeiro, Brazil, 2007, p. 3.

[127] Office for National Statistics, 'Internet access quarterly update, Q3 2013', at www.on s.gov.uk/ons/rel/rdit2/internet-access-quarterly-update/q3-2013/stb-ia-q3-2013.html (last visited 16 June 2014).

[128] Office for National Statistics, 'Internet access 2010', at www.statistics.gov.uk/pdfdir /iahi0810.pdf (no longer available).

[129] Office of National Statistics, 'Internet access – households and individuals, 2013', at www.ons.gov.uk/ons/rel/rdit2/internet-access-households-and-individuals/2013/stb -ia-2013.html (last visited 16 June 2014).

United States, the internet penetration rate is 86 per cent for adults, up from 14 per cent in 1995.[130]

This infiltration of the internet into our daily lives reflects the increased importance of information to the functioning of society, which forms the communicative link between Habermas and democratic culture set out earlier. The internet's importance to political participation and, more broadly, its importance to the circulation of information as valuable in itself can be seen in numerous examples around the world.[131] In the United States, sites such as www.moveon.org, www.techpresident.com and www.dailykos.com have become increasingly popular resources.[132] Moveon.org, for example, claims to have more than 8 million members. In President Barak Obama's first presidential race, he launched an aggressive internet campaign using his social networking site http://my.barackobama.com to engage with and inform supporters and volunteers. Just a few years later, the use of social media and new media became a basic component of successful political campaigns. In his 2012 re-election campaign, President Obama launched MyBO, which integrated with Facebook to allow Facebook users and communities to interact with the campaign.[133] As Rob Salkowitz comments, '[t]hese erstwhile novelties are now the minimum price of admission for a modern campaign'.[134]

The participative practices online also allow stories that may have gone unnoticed by traditional media to go viral and spread globally in the blink of an eye. This happened during President Obama's run for the democratic nomination in 2008. At a fundraiser in San Francisco in April 2008, Obama remarked unwisely that small-town Pennsylvanian voters are 'bitter'. One of the attendees blogged about the comment on the popular Huffington Post website. The story was then picked up by the

---

[130] Pew Research Center, at www.pewinternet.org/data-trend/internet-use/internet-use-over-time/ (last visited 16 June 2014).

[131] See discussion in R. L. Weaver, *From Gutenberg to the Internet: Free Speech, Advancing Technology, and the Implications for Democracy* (Durham: Carolina Academic Press, 2013), chapter IV.

[132] Others include www.mysociety.org, www.answercoalition.org and www.unitedforpeace.org (last visited 16 June 2014).

[133] See www.barackobama.com/get-involved (last visited 26 July 2011).

[134] R. Salkowitz, 'Politicians seek "new" new media for 2012 run' (21 April 2011), at www.internetevolution.com/author.asp?section_id=697&doc_id=205850&f_src=internetevolution_gnews%3Cbr%20/%3E (last visited 26 July 2011, link no longer available).

mainstream media – media, it should be emphasised, which was not permitted to attend the event.[135]

Where the technology of the internet is particularly facilitative is as a platform for mobilising social and political change. Popular sites such as change.org have supported campaigns to, for example, keep a female historical figure on a British banknote.[136] This campaign also reveals the dark underbelly of online participation, as the campaigner Caroline Criado-Perez was subject to abuse on Twitter, including threats of violence and rape. Two of the abusers pleaded guilty in 2014 to sending menacing messages.[137]

Two further events are particularly relevant here. The Occupy movement in 2011 and 2012 for social and economic change ('we are the 99%') spanned more than 700 locations worldwide.[138] Social media was the organising tool for protests and other events, linking the individuals participating in the demonstrations and providing unified communication on platforms such as Twitter. The strength of internet communications here, arguably, was the ability to communicate in real time what some researchers have called 'serendipitous'[139] events, such as the pepper spraying of seated student protesters at University of California, Davis.

Similarly, the debates in the United States concerning the controversial Stop Online Privacy Act (SOPA) and the PROTECT IP Act (PIPA) were mobilised largely through internet communications. A post on Reddit, for example, suggesting a boycott of internet registration provider GoDaddy for its support of SOPA/PIPA mobilised several users to transfer to a different registrar and even more to threaten to do so. GoDaddy quickly backed down and withdrew its support of the legislation.[140] Researchers mapped the SOPA/PIPA debates and found that

---

[135] See one story of the incident by J. Rainey, 'Barack Obama can thank "citizen journalist" for "bitter" tempest' (15 April 2008), at http://articles.latimes.com/print/2008/apr/15/nation/na-bitter15 (last visited 16 June 2014).

[136] 'We need women on British banknotes', at www.change.org/en-GB/petitions/we-need-women-on-british-banknotes (last visited 16 June 2014).

[137] Press Association, 'Two face jail over Twitter abuse of banknote campaigner' (24 January 2014), at www.theguardian.com/technology/2014/jan/24/two-face-jail-twitter-abuse (last visited 16 June 2014).

[138] *The Guardian*, 'Occupy protests around the world: full list visualised', at www.theguardian.com/news/datablog/2011/oct/17/occupy-protests-world-list-map (last visited 16 June 2014).

[139] K. Nahon et al., 'Information flows in events of political unrest', at www.ideals.illinois.edu/bitstream/handle/2142/39165/259.pdf?sequence=4 (last visited 16 June 2014).

[140] E. Kain, 'Reddit makes headlines boycotting GoDaddy over online censorship bills' (26 December 2011), at www.forbes.com/sites/erikkain/2011/12/26/reddit-makes-headlines-boycotting-godaddy-over-online-censorship-bills/ (last visited 16 June 2014). See also Benklker n. 94, p. 31.

they drew participants across a variety of sectors, from smaller technology companies, to NGOs, to individuals and traditional media, where high-traffic sites could act as an 'attention backbone' to give visibility to websites with less traffic.[141] Their conclusion was optimistic as to the potential of a networked public sphere. During this controversy, several major technology companies, including Wikipedia and Google, staged a blackout of their sites in protest against the proposed legislation. This highlights a more subtle difficulty with the role of these companies and their impact on human rights such as free speech because we expect and depend on them to be our advocates.

More dramatic examples of the power of social media are to be found in the coverage of the Arab Spring demonstrations. Everyone remembers the face of the Iranian protests of 2009: a young woman named Neda Agha-Soltan, whose death was seen as a rallying cry for the protesters.[142] Grainy, shaky cell phone video footage of her being shot and killed by militia men during a protest was taken and distributed online anonymously. The video was later awarded a George Polk prize for journalism, the first time such an award was made for anonymous work.[143] Such examples show, as Colin Maclay describes it, 'the power of new technologies to support human rights'.[144] This interactivity and access to information empowers users, arguably reinvigorating the public sphere.[145]

The more recent Arab Spring, however, demonstrates both the power of social media as a tool for democracy and the power of the gatekeepers, whether state or private,[146] to shut down these avenues of discourse. Protesters across the Middle East communicated with each other using a

---

[141] Benkler n. 95, p. 10.

[142] CNN World, '"Neda" becomes rallying cry for Iranian protests' (21 June 2009), at http://articles.cnn.com/2009-06-21/world/iran.woman.twitter_1_neda-peaceful-protest-cell-phone?_s=PM:WORLD (last visited 16 June 2014).

[143] The Huffington Post, 'Neda video wins Polk Award: Iran protest death video first anonymous winner of journalism prize' (16 February 2010), at www.huffingtonpost.com/2010/02/16/neda-video-wins-polk-award_n_463378.html (last visited 16 June 2014).

[144] Colin Maclay, 'Protecting Privacy and Expression Online: Can the Global Network Initiative embrace the character of the Net?', in Deibert, Access Controlled n. 14, p. 93. He goes on to note, 'it is equally essential to recognize the potential influence of company relationships and process on government behavior': ibid.

[145] See, for example, P. N. Howard and M. M. Hussain, 'The Upheavals in Egypt and Tunisia: The Role of Digital Media', Journal of Democracy, 22(3) (2011) 35.

[146] See, for example, Vodafone's role as gatekeeper in shutting down connectivity in Egypt: C. Rhoads and G. A. Fowler, 'Egypt Shuts Down Internet, Cellphone Services', The Wall Street Journal (29 January 2011), at http://online.wsj.com/article/SB10001424052748703956604576110453371369740.html?mod=googlenews_wsj (last visited 16 June 2014).

variety of social media platforms, such as Facebook, Twitter and YouTube, to spread information and further mobilise protesters. Egypt responded by first blocking access to social media sites and then shutting down internet connectivity entirely, as well as blocking mobile networks.[147] Google and Twitter then created a 'Speak to Tweet' tool that enabled Twitter users to post tweets by leaving voice messages which the tool then turned into tweets.[148]

As we can see, there are various dimensions to online engagement with democratic culture. Two types of participation stand out as particularly facilitative of democratic culture: social/political and appropriative.[149] Much of the earlier examples have focused on social networking. Twitter has been the most surprising tool in facilitating participation in democratic culture. What started out as a platform for celebrities and narcissists to voice the most mundane minutiae of their everyday lives has rapidly become an important tool for spreading information.

Twitter consolidates tweets through 'trending', in which the most popular topics at any given moment, 'Twitter trends', are listed in a sidebar on the right side of the webpage.[150] The Occupy movement, for example, used the hashtag #occupy; following a murder rampage in California prompted by hatred of women, internet conversations on the subject were linked with the hashtag #YesAllWomen. In so doing, Twitter is not only a tool for discourse, but it also shapes democratic culture by acting as an information manager, guiding us through Twitterverse and thereby cyberspace beyond. Similarly, a site such as

---

[147] A. Alexander, 'Internet role in Egypt's protests' (9 February 211), at www.bbc.co.uk/news /world-middle-east-12400319 (last visited 16 June 2014).

[148] Google n. 20.

[149] This puts aside an important but tangential topic of the internet's empowerment of pseydonymous and anonymous participation in online communities (keeping in mind that surveillance risks can make such participation illusory). Anon/pseudonymous communications can allow participation in spaces for sensitive personal matters, such as illness, abuse or sexual and other identity issues. We must be cautious in blindly celebration their virtues, however, as anonymity has served a darker, sometimes devastating, purpose, giving voice to discriminatory and threatening speech. For more, see, for example, D. K. Citron, *Hate Crimes in Cyberspace* (Cambridge, MA: Harvard University Press, 2014) and S. Levmore and M. C. Nussbaum, *The Offensive Internet* (Cambridge, MA: Harvard University Press, 2010).

[150] 'About trending topics', at http://support.twitter.com/entries/101125-about-trending-topics (last visited 16 June 2014). People mark something as a topic by putting a hashtag in front of it (i.e., #haitiearthquake or #confessiontime).

Facebook has 1.23 billion monthly active users,[151] and while it might appear to only be of use for gossip and keeping in touch with friends, it is increasingly being used for professional networking, political activism and educational purposes.[152] For example, the Internet Governance Forum has a Facebook Group.[153] The European Union has a space called 'EU Tube' for 'free speech and open debate'.[154] Many NGOs have groups on Facebook, such as the Institute for Human Rights and Business. Most of the interactions discussed in this chapter fall short of the demands of deliberative democracy; however, in a democratic culture, the focus is less on participation in the idealised town hall and more on valuing the very act of engaging in such 'a dialectical free-for-all'.[155] This is written conscious that there are limits to the value of such a discursive free-for-all. These spaces, and the anonymity and pseudonymity they often allow, have fuelled cybermobs and given voice to discriminatory and threatening speech.[156]

The internet also facilitates what was described earlier as the appropriative aspect of democratic culture because internet users can take part in culture by producing it and modifying it themselves.[157] Whereas under a deliberative democracy framework such activities would be dismissed as purely entertainment, under democratic culture such activities play a more central role. For example, we all remember the spate of memes parodying a pinnacle scene in the movie *Der Untergang* (Downfall) depicting Adolf Hitler ranting during one of his final days in the Berlin bunker. Voice-over parodies ranged from Hitler ranting about Hillary Clinton losing the Democratic party candidacy for

---

[151] J. Kiss, 'Facebook's 10th birthday: from college dorm to 1.23 billion users' (4 February 2014), at www.theguardian.com/technology/2014/feb/04/facebook-10-years-mark-zuckerberg (last visited 16 June 2014).

[152] I co-taught a course on information technology law at the London School of Economics where we set up a Facebook group for the students to share legal news and debate issues. Unsuccessful attempts had been made in the past to engage students online through discussion boards and the like, but when the forum was moved to Facebook participation skyrocketed.

[153] Internet Governance Forum Facebook Group, at www.facebook.com/group.php?gid=6791243882 (last visited 16 June 2014).

[154] EU Tube, at www.youtube.com/user/eutube?ob=1 (last visited 16 June 2014).

[155] Balkin n. 45, p. 43.

[156] See Citron n. 149; Levmore and Nussbaum n. 149. Lawrence Lessig has a good discussion of an early social norm resolution of a famous incident in an multiplayer game, LamdaMoo, as well as a discussion of the effects of flaming on a newsgroup he set up for one of his early cyberlaw classes: Lessig n. 1, pp. 74–82.

[157] Ibid., pp. 4–5.

president to Hitler trying to find Wally to Hitler commenting on the subprime mortgage crisis.[158] There was even a parody of the removal of the parodies from YouTube for claims of breach of copyright.[159] In addition, humanitarian organisations are increasingly using the internet to persuade and educate the public about issues. For example, mtvU, in partnership with the Reebok Human Rights Foundation and the International Crisis Group, created an online game called 'Darfur Is Dying' to highlight the atrocities in the Sudan and educate users on ways to help.[160]

The promise of the internet as a tool in furthering a democratic culture is presented here with much fanfare. This is done on purpose, to tease out for the reader what is at stake. There is incredible discursive promise to the spaces and technologies made possible by the internet environment. And one commonality threads its way through this discussion: the capacity of private companies to gatekeep the flow of information, whether as innovators, facilitators or censors. They own the spaces and technologies of discourse, the implications of which are the focus of the case studies in Chapters 4 and 5. Section 1.3.2 addresses the main concerns put forward by sceptics of the internet's democratic potential, highlighting further the power of the internet to be a force for good and bad and the critical role that these private gatekeepers inevitably play.

### 1.3.2. Concerns of fragmentation and the demise of traditional media

The expansion in the range of discourses that further democracy risks pushing the idea of democratic culture too far, to a point at which any communication can be dressed up as important to democratic culture and therefore worthy of protection. Two things must be clarified. First, while democratic culture is a more inclusive notion than deliberative democracy, it is not without limits, and what is proposed here is not a form of cyberutopianism criticised by authors such as Evgeny

---

[158] There are thousands. *The Telegraph* compiled its list of the top twenty-five: 'Hitler Downfall parodies: 25 worth watching' (6 October 2009), at www.telegraph.co.uk/tech nology/news/6262709/Hitler-Downfall-parodies-25-worth-watching.html (last visited 16 June 2014).

[159] See the Electronic Frontier Foundation's commentary: 'Everyone who's made a Hitler parody video, leave the room' (20 April 2010), at www.eff.org/deeplinks/2010/04/every one-who-s-made-hitler-parody-leave-room (last visited 16 June 2014).

[160] It was originally conceived by a group of individuals at the University of Southern California: 'Darfur Is Dying', at www.darfurisdying.com/ (last visited 16 June 2014).

Morozov.[161] These issues can often be politicised unnecessarily, distorting the debate and preventing a nuanced discussion of the policy framework, legal and otherwise, that will best move us forward. As Rick Lambers notes, '[s]uch political polarisation may leave little room for legal subtleties'.[162] Second, the limits are less about what is said in this space and more about the infrastructure that makes the communication possible, about freedom of expression in practice. In looking at how private companies can facilitate or hinder participation in democratic culture, I am examining the administrative structure of freedom of expression.

Part of the concern in an environment of endless information and communities for participation is that users go online for the 'reinforcement effect' of being political if they are political, or disengaged if they are disengaged, and most often just to be entertained.[163] Such a concern can be partly dismissed as simply reflective of the realities of democratic life in the physical world transposed online. However, the argument becomes more powerful when pushed further to a concern that the internet fragments discourse and attention.[164] One of the leading scholars expressing this view regarding the internet is Cass Sunstein.

In *Republic.com*, Sunstein describes this fragmentation as 'the daily me' (a term earlier coined by Nicholas Negroponte),[165] in which people choose to filter the information that they read, see and hear to their interests, thus avoiding ever being exposed to, for example, international news or sports, but having a steady stream of celebrity gossip and fashion news. Liberals, conservatives or neo-Nazis seek out websites, forums or blogs with like-minded people who reinforce their views of the world. In this way, discourse and community are fragmented, and we suffer a loss. Online media is therefore distinct from traditional media: if one flips on the television news, one is forced to view whatever news stories the mass media chooses to run, thus exposing oneself to opposing points of view and thereby gaining a fuller perspective.

---

[161] E. Morozov, *The Net Delusion: The Dark Side of Internet Freedom* (New York: Public Affairs, 2011).

[162] R. Lambers, 'Code and Speech. Speech Control through Network Architecture', in E. Dommering and L. Asscher (eds.), *Coding Regulation* (Cambridge University Press, 2006), p. 95.

[163] See discussion in Longford and Patten n. 53, pp. 9–10.

[164] C. R. Sunstein, *Republic.com* (Princeton University Press, 2001).

[165] Ibid., chapter one. See N. Negroponte, *Being Digital* (New York: Vintage Books, 1995), in particular chapter 12.

In his updated book *Republic.com 2.0*, Sunstein emphasises at the outset that freedom of expression is not simply freedom from censorship but that it requires affirmative steps as well. It must challenge people by exposing them to opposing points of view.[166] This is lost by the 'daily me' of internet fragmentation:

> The fundamental concern of this book is to see how unlimited consumer options might compromise the preconditions of a system of freedom of expression, which include unchosen exposures and shared experiences. To understand the nature of this concern, we will make the most progress if we insist that the free-speech principle should be read in light of the commitment to democratic deliberation. In other words, a central point of the free-speech principle is to carry out that commitment.[167]

Sunstein's concern regarding fragmentation is not the death knell to the internet's force as part of democratic culture. Rather, it is the narrower concept of deliberative democracy with which he is concerned and which is undermined by this fragmentation of discourse.

Examination of how to guard against fragmentation is an important examination, but fragmentation is not as polarising as Sunstein fears.[168] First, Sunstein's criticism here is essentially of the choices people make when they go online. Furthermore, fragmentation already occurs in the physical world by the very existence (and mushrooming) of advocacy groups and other issue-oriented organisations. In addition, a certain amount of fragmentation is part of being a member of a group, where the group might first flesh out its membership, views and bonds internally before entering the fray of the public sphere.[169] Of concern in cyberspace is whether such groups do more than associate internally, but cyberspace has also created the ability for many groups to form at all, thus bridging previously insurmountable spatial and temporal boundaries and often, through anonymity and pseudonymity, facilitating membership of the otherwise reclusive and shy.

The internet has also been criticised on a different basis by authors such as Andrew Keen[170] for creating a 'cult of amateurs' which has

---

[166] C. R. Sunstein, *Republic.com 2.0* (Princeton University Press, 2007), p. xi.

[167] Ibid., p. 177.

[168] See also Sunstein's book *Infotopia* (Oxford University Press, 2006), in which he examines these new forms of deliberation and the opportunities and risks they create. See the excellent discussion by R. Lambers n. 162, chapter four, section 2.1.3.

[169] Dahlgren n. 75, p. 152.

[170] A. Keen, *The Cult of the Amateur* (London: Nicholas Brealey Publishing, 2007). See also, more recently, the arguments of E. Morozov n. 161.

caused the demise of traditional media and ultimately harmed society. Keen's concern is that traditional media are being replaced by personal media[171], and, as a result, we increasingly rely on unreliable, amateur non-vetted posts on, for example, Wikipedia, Digg, YouTube or Twitter for our news and education. In turn, traditional media are floundering, with profits plummeting as fewer buy newspapers, and classified advertisements are alternatively posted for free online at such websites as Craigslist.[172] He cautions that traditional media are facing extinction, and, with them, 'today's experts and cultural gatekeepers – our reporters, news anchors, editors, music companies and Hollywood studios'.[173] The overriding concern arising from this 'cult of amateurs' is who will play the watchdog role.[174]

The internet is not replacing traditional media, but is instead another tool for participation in democratic culture. In terms of political participation, a study of the 2006 American midterm elections found that television was still the main source of political news at 69 per cent of respondents, trailed by newspapers at 34 per cent and the internet at 15 per cent.[175] Researchers found that use of the internet for political news doubled since the 2002 election, whereas use of television and newspapers remained static.[176] This indicates that use of one is not replacing the other; they are being used in combination. There is no doubt, however, that traditional media are facing a period of challenge and decline.[177] This is despite the fact that the media have a strong presence online and are arguably a core part of the internet's public sphere.[178] Charlie Beckett describes it as a shift from a manufacturing industry to a service economy in which '[i]t is a change in practice, from providing a product to acting as facilitators and connectors. It means an end to duplication and a focus on what value every bit of journalism production adds'.[179] Some, therefore, argue that traditional media are simply in the midst of a revolution.[180]

---

[171] Keen, ibid., p. 7.    [172] Ibid., p. 8.    [173] Ibid., p. 9.
[174] See discussion in Y. Benkler n. 46, pp. 261–66.
[175] D. Fallows, 'Election Newshounds Speak Up: Newspaper, TV, and Internet Fans Tell How and Why They Differ', *The Pew Research Center* (6 February 2007), at http://pew research.org/pubs/406/election-newshounds-speak-up (last visited 16 June 2014).
[176] Ibid.    [177] See Weaver n. 131, chapter III.    [178] Dahlgren n. 75, p. 153.
[179] C. Beckett, 'State 2.0: a new front end?' (7 September 2009), at www.opendemocracy.net /article/state-2-0-a-new-front-end (last visited 16 June 2014). Also see C. Beckett, 'SuperMedia: the future as "networked journalism"' (10 June 2008), at www.opendemoc racy.net/article/supermedia-the-networked-journalism-future (last visited 16 June 2014).
[180] See discussion in Weaver n. 131, pp. 58–59.

Furthermore, as the public becomes more mistrustful of traditional media and questions whether the Fourth Estate is in fact fulfilling its watchdog obligations, citizen journalists emerge as both partners with the media, such as the blogger about Barack Obama's comment on Pennsylvanian voters, and watchdogs of the media. While it is true that citizen journalists cannot investigate issues as thoroughly as can paid reporters with the backing of a commercial media company, on the other hand, they are not beholden to corporate interests and therefore are not influenced by corporate advertisers or the risks of litigation.[181] What is important in terms of the internet's potential in democratic culture is that citizens can participate in the discussion. The news becomes interactive.

The opportunities for participation in democratic culture opened up by the internet have also reinforced our dependence on private companies for its effective use. With the influx of information that the internet has empowered comes the issue of information overload, also known as the *Babel objection*.[182] A user is confronted with an endless array of information without the vetting of a professional media organisation as to its quality and reliability. It becomes the task of modern internet users to sort through large amounts of information and determine what is relevant and reliable. And, as we move towards a semantic web, it has become the task of innovators to create more tools for information management.[183]

Information management technologies have emerged to help guide the user through the clutter. For example, without a search engine, a user must know the URL (uniform resource locator, or webpage address) for a piece of information or a website of interest. As a result, most users rely on search engines such as Google or Yahoo! to organise the information on the internet for them.[184] Other more subtle information guidance instruments play a similar role. Google News selects and categories news

---

[181] Benkler n. 46, pp. 261–62, 265; Dahlgren n. 75, p. 151 discussing how the internet is becoming commercialised in much the same manner as traditional media. See also the controversy surrounding superinjunctions in the United Kingdom, where traditional media were prevented from printing the names of people who sought these injunctions, while simultaneously their names were being revealed and/or speculated about on Twitter: Out-Law, 'Super-injunction Twitter user in contempt of court if tweets were true' (10 May 2011), at www.theregister.co.uk/2011/05/10/super_injunctions_tweeter _in_trouble_if_its_true/ (last visited 16 June 2014).

[182] Benkler n. 46, p. 234.

[183] See the BBC, 'Luminaries look to the future web', at http://news.bbc.co.uk/1/hi/737371 7.stm (last visited 16 June 2014).

[184] See Chapter 5 for case study of search engines.

stories. Apple controls the apps available on its devices.[185] These innovations are critical to users having a meaningful experience of the internet and to facilitating the internet as a force within democratic culture.

Are we doomed to the same websites, same information and same self-reinforcing views? Some might find comfort in the internet's use as such. But this is not fatal to the internet's democratic potential. Rather, as Benkler states, the internet 'structures a networked public sphere more attractive than the mass-media-dominated public sphere'.[186] As the internet begins to permeate every aspect of our lives, it increasingly begins to reflect the real world. It increasingly becomes part of the real world. This is not an invasion of cyberspace that nullifies the internet's democratic potential, which some have argued.[187] Instead, it ushers in the same complexities and variables of the real world. Not everyone watches the news nor will everyone seek news online. However, the internet does offer new tools for participating in such discussions for those interested and an abundance of resources for any individual who might have a specific issue of interest. The hope is that digital technologies will eventually increase concern and participation in politics and culture.

## 1.4. Conclusion

The internet has the potential to facilitate participation in democratic culture by inviting widespread involvement of internet users in creating and defining the things that mean something in our democratic society. Through the increasingly interactive nature of the online experience and the endless spaces available for the creation of communities, users are able to seek out and circulate information and ideas, and build on, modify and comment on their culture. This communicative process, enabled by technology, is what makes democratic culture the type of democracy for which the internet is most facilitative.

The thread running through this chapter is the critical role that freedom of expression plays in furthering participation in democratic culture online and the therefore central role that information gatekeepers play in facilitating or hindering this expression. If the internet has the potential to be a democratising force, the other side of the coin is that it can be used

---

[185] See D. Mac Síthigh, 'App Law Within: Rights and Regulation in the Smartphone Age', *IJILT*, 21(2) (2013) 154.
[186] Benkler n. 46, p. 239.     [187] Johnson and Bimber n. 86, pp. 241–42.

as a tool to limit participation, which threatens to draw the internet away from its democratic potential. The technology itself is neutral, and its use for democratic or undemocratic purposes depends on those who control it. Since, in Western democracies, privately owned companies for the most part own the technologies that control the pathways of communication, they become the focal point for the realisation of the internet's democratic potential. This means focusing on the governance structure of the gatekeepers. This book will show that the corporate governance frameworks that currently govern many of their activities are insufficient to facilitate this potential and instead hamper the ability of the internet to work as a tool for democracy. The next chapter examines what is meant by the term *gatekeeper* and will define for reader the term *internet information gatekeeper* discussed here, proposing a human rights-driven framework for their identification.

# A framework for identifying internet information gatekeepers

The purpose of this chapter is to identify the gatekeepers that are the primary subject of this book. They will be referred to as internet information gatekeepers (IIG). We have a broad understanding of the entities that are gatekeepers and what it is about the internet that has placed them in this position. They include, for example, search engines, internet service providers (ISPs), high-traffic social networking sites and portal providers. Yet, a focused analysis of what is meant by gatekeeper in the internet context, but most particularly in the context of viewing the internet as a force within democratic culture, is needed not only to confirm that these parties are indeed gatekeepers, but also to find a method for identifying other gatekeepers and for finding the boundary between what is a gatekeeper and what is not.

The need to define what is and is not a gatekeeper is particularly acute when one attempts to draw a conceptual line between some hosts of message boards or other Web 2.0 platforms and others. What we want to avoid is imposing the same gatekeeping responsibilities on John Smith for his personal blog, where friends sometimes comment in a conveniently prefabricated comments section, that we do on the BBC for its interactive 'Have Your Say' discussions forums. Likewise, whereas such interactive sites might have many visitors, they are inherently different from gatekeepers such as ISPs, which control our very access to the internet, or search engines, which organise the information available online. Thus, an examination of what is meant by the term 'gatekeeper' not only serves a definitional purpose, but also guides the nature and extent of their legal duties.

In this chapter, first, the historical development of the term 'gatekeeper' will be traced. Second, traditional conceptions of gatekeeping

An article version of this was published in IRLCT, 43(3) (2010) 263.

will be assessed and their conceptual inadequacy for the internet explained. Third, a human rights-driven framework for identifying IIGs will be articulated, and this will set the framework for the case studies in Chapters 4 and 5.

## 2.1. From cupcakes to Yahoo!

At a general level, gatekeepers are entities whose job it is to decide what shall or shall not pass through a gate. What makes gatekeepers unique is that they usually do not benefit from misconduct, although they are in a position to prevent it because they control access to the tools, area or community required to commit the misconduct. Thus, shaping a liability regime around gatekeepers instead of those breaking the rules can at times be more effective.[1] One famous example involves oil tankers. The goal was to reduce oil spills, and the use of segregated ballast tanks and a system of crude oil washing was identified as the solution. Top-down legal controls targeting the ship owners were implemented to encourage the use of these technologies, but with little effect. So, instead, regulators targeted the gatekeepers: the insurers, classification societies and builders. The insurers required that the tankers were registered with classification societies, these societies required that the ships had segregated ballast tanks and crude oil washing, and builders therefore only built such ships. The gatekeepers here did not benefit from the use of unsafe ships. On the contrary, a more expensive and safer ship was in their interests. It was an effective regulatory solution achieving 98 per cent compliance by shifting the focus away from the perpetrators of the misconduct to the gatekeepers.[2] As John Braithwaite put it, '[w]here mighty states could not succeed in reducing oil spills at sea, Lloyd's of London could'.[3]

Gatekeeper regulation tends to emerge where a government's capacity to regulate a specific issue might be limited, but a third party gatekeeper's capacity to regulate the conduct – whether owing to resources, information or authority – might be better. Sometimes, such regulation arises simply by the nature of the activity engaged in. For example, librarians and bookstores choose which books to order and where to place them on the shelves. Still other gatekeepers emerge because of their role in shaping our social worlds. This can be seen with the media, where the gatekeeping

---

[1] J. Braithwaite and P. Drahos, *Global Business Regulation* (Cambridge University Press, 2000), p. 618.
[2] Ibid., pp. 618–19.    [3] Ibid.

metaphor has been used extensively. By selecting what news stories to run, print or discard, at which time and in which order, they act as 'surrogates or shortcuts for individual people's decisions'.[4] In contrast, management studies tend to view the gatekeeping role as facilitative,[5] whereas cultural theories in information sciences view gatekeepers in their role as representatives of their communities: 'individuals who move between two cultures to provide information that links people with alternatives or solutions'.[6]

The term 'gatekeeping' was first deployed in this way by Kurt Lewin in 1947. He used the term to describe how a wife or mother was the gatekeeper because of her role in deciding which foods are placed on the dinner table.[7] His 'theories of channels and gate keepers' used this example to illustrate how one can change the food habits of a population. The food moves through channels, such as grocery stores, to reach a dinner table. One enters the channel through a gate, and a gatekeeper makes selection decisions on what foods to accept and reject, thus controlling movement within the channel. This ranges from the store manager selecting food to sell to the mother selecting foods to prepare for dinner.[8]

The idea of gatekeeping in law can be traced to secondary liability regimes. In what continues to be the most influential work on gatekeeping, Reinier Kraakman mainstreamed Lewin's theory and teased out its roots in secondary liability, showing that the liability of accountants and lawyers for their clients and employers for their employees was, in essence, an issue of gatekeeper liability.[9] More recently, tort law has been used to pursue gatekeepers in the online environment, as seen in the use of vicarious or contributory liability to pursue peer-to-peer providers such as Grokster, Napster and Pirate Bay for breach of copyright for the

---

[4] P. Shoemaker, *Gatekeeping (Communication Concepts)* (Newbury Park, CA: Sage, 1991), p. 235. She updated her work in *Gatekeeping Theory* (New York: Routledge, 2009). See also discussions in R. A. Heverly, 'Law as Intermediary', *Mich. St. L. Rev*, 107 (2006) 108.

[5] K. Barzilai-Nahon, 'Gatekeeping Revisited: A Critical Review', *Annual Review of Information Science and Technology*, 43(1) (2009) 4–5.

[6] Ibid., p. 6. For an overview of the definitions of gatekeepers employed in various fields in academic journals between 1995–2007, see Table 10.1 of Barzilai-Nahon's review, pp. 23–31.

[7] K. Lewin, 'Frontiers in Group Dynamics', *Human Relations*, 1(2) (1947) 143.

[8] Shoemaker (1991) n. 4, pp. 5–9.

[9] R. H. Kraakman, 'Gatekeepers: The Anatomy of a Third-Party Enforcement Strategy', *J. L. Econ. & Org.*, 2 (1986) 53. See also R. H. Kraakman, 'Corporate Liability Strategies and the Costs of Legal Controls', *Yale L. J.*, 93 (1983–85) 857.

illegal downloading of music by third parties.[10] In the United Kingdom, illegal file sharing has been tackled through the use of injunctive relief targeted at ISPs, which compels the ISPs to implement systems blocking access to the offending sites.[11] Secondary liability is also at the root of the notice and takedown provisions in the Digital Millennium Copyright Act (DMCA)[12] and the intermediary liability exemptions in the Electronic Commerce Directive (E-Commerce Directive).[13]

More broadly positioned within regulatory studies,[14] gatekeepers are non-state actors with the capacity to alter the behaviour of others in circumstances where the state has limited capacity to do same. This is what Julia Black discusses in the context of decentred regulation, which she describes as a shift 'in the locus of the activity of "regulating" from the state to other, multiple locations and the adoption on the part of the state of particular strategies of regulation'.[15] This combination of capacity and duty is what Kraakman refers to in his definition of gatekeeper.

Most relevant to this book is the public law concerns created by this shift in the location of regulating away from the state. While private actors have long impacted freedom of expression, such as the editorial role of the media in selecting and arranging the stories it runs or property owners controlling speech in the spaces they own, there has arguably been a more wholesale shift away from the state to private nodes of governance concerning regulation of internet communications. As we saw in Chapter 1, this regulation can be observed, for example, when social networking providers regulate the terms of use of their platforms

---

[10] See *A&M Records, Inc. v. Napster, Inc.* 239 F 3d 1004 (9th Cir. 2001), *MGM Studios v. Grokster* 545 US 913, and *Sweden v. Neij et al.*, Stockholms Tingsrätt No B 13301–06, 17 April 2009 (lost on appeal November 2010).

[11] S. 97A Copyright Designs and Patents Act 1998 c. 48. *Twentieth Century Fox Film Corp & Ors v. British Telecommunications Plc [2011] EWHC 1981 (Ch); Dramatico Entertainment Ltd. v. British Sky Broadcasting Ltd.* [2012] EWHC 268 (CH) AND [2012] EWHC 1152 (CH). The ISPs have been using cleanfeed technology for blocking, which is discussed in more detail in Chapter 4.

[12] 1998 Pub. L. No. 105–304, 112 Stat. 2860 (Oct. 28, 1998)

[13] Directive 2000/31/EC of the European Parliament and of the Council of 8 June 2000 on certain legal aspects of information society services, in particular electronic commerce, in the Internal Market.

[14] In regulatory literature, it can be seen to be discussed in the context of 'decentred regulation' referring to the 'horizontal decentering of the state': B. Morgan and K. Yeung, *An Introduction to Law and Regulation: Text and Materials* (Cambridge University Press, 2007), p. 280. See also J. Black, 'Decentring Regulation: Understanding the Role of Regulation and Self-Regulation in a "Post-Regulatory" World,' 54 *CLP* (2001) 103.

[15] Ibid., p. 112.

and when governments capitalise on these private actors regulatory power either informally (pressured to be proxies) or formally (legal structures such as injunctions and notice and takedown).

This shift to private nodes of governance can produce an accountability glut concerning fundamental democratic values such as freedom of expression when such non-state actors take on roles, or share roles with others, which are traditionally reserved for public actors. As Jody Freeman observes, such gatekeepers are not agents of the state and expected to serve the public interest; but, additionally, they are not subject to the norms of professionalism and public service one normally finds imposed on such institutions.[16] In addition, they 'remain relatively insulated from legislative, executive and judicial oversight'.[17] The crux of the problem, as she sees it, applies equally to the issues raised on the internet:

> To the extent that private actors increasingly perform traditionally public functions unfettered by the scrutiny that normally accompanies the exercise of public power, private participation may indeed raise accountability concerns that dwarf the problem of unchecked agency discretion. In this view, private actors do not raise a *new* democracy problem; they simply make the traditional one even worse because they are considerably more unaccountable than agencies. In addition, private actors may threaten other public law values that are arguably as important as accountability. Their participation in governance may undermine features of decision making that administrative law demands of public actors, such as openness, fairness, participation, consistency, rationality and impartiality.[18]

## 2.2. The inadequacies of traditional gatekeeping online

There are two fields where the concept of gatekeeper has been most fully explored. First, there is the role of journalists and publishers as gatekeepers who select the stories and information we consume. Second, in the financial services industry, the concept of a gatekeeper has been used to describe the monitoring role of auditors, credit ratings agencies and investment bankers.[19] Whichever area is discussed, two gatekeeping roles can be identified:

1. the gatekeeper that controls access to information and acts as an inhibitor by limiting access to or restricting the scope of information; and

---

[16] J. Freeman, 'Private Parties, Public Functions and the New Administrative Law', in D. Dyzenhaus (ed.), *Recrafting the Rule of Law* (Oxford: Hart Publishing, 1999), pp. 331–35.
[17] Ibid., p. 335.   [18] Ibid.
[19] See S. Ben-Ishai, 'Corporate Gatekeeper Liability in Canada', *Tex. Int. L. J.*, 42 (2007) 443–45.

2. the gatekeeper that acts as 'innovator, change agent, communication channel, link, intermediary, helper, adapter, opinion leader, broker, and facilitator'.[20]

This recognises that gatekeepers at once can have two roles – one, inward-looking by inhibiting behaviour or access, and the other, outward-looking, shaping behaviour or perceptions. Recognising such dual purposes transfers well to the internet environment, where gate-keepers have the capacity to act both as facilitators of and impediments to participation in democracy.

Traditional definitions of gatekeeper in the literature have been narrower and therefore transfer less well to the networked environment of the internet. This is for two reasons. First, traditional definitions tend to focus on gatekeepers' capacity to prevent third-party misbehaviour. Second, the gated (a term introduced by Karine Barzilai-Nahon to refer to those on whom the gatekeeping is exercised) tend to be treated in static terms, with little attention devoted to their rights.[21] With regard to the first, Kraakman's traditional definition is narrowly focused on liability imposed on gatekeepers to prevent third-party misconduct. This is repli-cated in the financial services industry, where gatekeepers are mainly conceived as John Coffee defines them: 'an agent who acts as a reputa-tional intermediary to assure investors as to the quality of the "signal" sent by the corporate issuer'.[22] In other words, the gatekeeper acts as a proxy for corporate trustworthiness, enabling investors or the market to then rely on the corporation's disclosure or assurances. A broader defini-tion is used in the media, where the term has become a metaphor for the way the media make decisions about what stories to run or discard and when and how much attention to give to the stories once they pass through the initial gate. Most recently, Pamela Shoemaker defined such gatekeeping as 'the process of culling and crafting countless bits of information into the limited number of messages that reach people

---

[20] C. Metoyer-Duran, 'Information Gatekeepers', *Annual Review of Information Science and Technology*, 28 (1993) 111, p. 118. R. H. Kraakman breaks gatekeeping roles down to three roles: the whistle-blower, bouncer and chaperone. Whistle-blowers alert the authorities of misconduct by others, whereas bouncers refuse entry to parties engaging in misconduct and chaperones act as monitors and shapers of the behaviour of others: Kraakman (1986) n. 9, pp. 59–66.

[21] K. Barzilai-Nahon, 'Toward a Theory of Network Gatekeeping: A Framework for Exploring Information Control', *JASIST*, 59(9) (2008) 1493.

[22] J. C. Coffee, *Gatekeepers: The Role of the Professions in Corporate Governance* (Oxford University Press, 2006), p. 2.

every day'.[23] However, even such a definition is targeted to the media's role as an information publisher, and the debate is simply about the nature and extent of this gatekeeping role.

The online gatekeepers targeted here are not usually engaged in the tasks covered by such traditional definitions. The concept of gatekeepers as builders of our social reality resonates when examining the pivotal role certain online gatekeepers play in shaping our online experience, such as our reliance on ISPs simply to gain access to the internet or our reliance on search engines to sort through the clutter of information online. However, there are limits to such parallels. For example, most ISPs are not in the business of providing users with information, but rather run a business of providing access to the internet and possibly hosting services. Although media and online gatekeepers share a common gatekeeping role of information control, some online gatekeepers come to this role by a more indirect route. ISPs are not exactly CNN or the *New York Times*, but nor are they simple telecommunications carriers either.

Indeed, it is this inability to seamlessly draw comparisons between the internet and various other media models that has proved the major stumbling block to the development of a coherent and cohesive gate-keeping model in this area. Early jurisprudential and legislative debates revolved around whether to categorise intermediaries using traditional media models of print, broadcasting and common carrier. Currently in the United States, for example, under the Good Samaritan provision of the *Communications Decency Act*,[24] section 230, any service, system or access provider is shielded from liability not only for failing to act when aware or notified of unlawful content, but for any steps taken to restrict access to content. Europe has opted for a notice-and-takedown regime with the E-Commerce Directive. These regimes have been widely criticised, and it is arguable that this is, in part, because the concept of gatekeeping has not yet been sufficiently developed for the digital environment.[25]

---

[23] Shoemaker (2009) n. 4, p. 1. And see, P. Shoemaker et al., 'Individual and Routine Forces in Gatekeeping', *J&MC Quarterly*, 78(2) (2001) 233.

[24] 47 U.S.C.

[25] For a critical discussion of the European approach, see D. Mac Síthigh, 'The Fragmentation of Intermediary Liability in the UK', *JIPLP*, 8(7) (2013) 521, U. Kohl, 'The Rise and Rise of Online Intermediaries in the Governance of the Internet and Beyond – Connectivity Intermediaries', *IRLCT* 26(2) (2011) 185 and U. Kohl, 'Google: The Rise and Rise of Online Intermediaries in the Governance of the Internet and Beyond (Part 2)', *IJILT*, 21 (2) (2013) 187. See European Commission 'A Coherent Framework for Building Trust in the Digital Single Market for E-Commerce and Online Services', *COM* (2011) 942.

In addition, the static way in which the gated have been treated in traditional gatekeeping literature fails to capture the dynamic environment of the internet. This is because the roles people and institutions play online change. The technology of the internet is generative, allowing the gated to directly participate in the sharing of content and code.[26] Generativity causes one to question the one-way approach of traditional gatekeeping theory, which sees information flow from the gatekeeper out to the gated. In a Web 2.0 world (arguably now Web 3.0 world), the gated are dynamic players in creating and managing the internet environment. This means that there are an infinite number of possible gatekeepers and gated whose roles are fluid and constantly changing, operating as they do in a dynamic regulatory environment. For example, an individual who runs a blog might be gated by the terms of service of the blog host yet might also act as gatekeeper for the comments section of his or her blog. At the same time, the blog might be viewed by few readers or become so mainstream that it is read by millions.

Thus far, traditional definitions of gatekeeping have been used in internet regulation scholarship. In Jonathan Zittrain's earlier work, he identifies two kinds of gatekeepers: first, the classic kind in which gatekeepers are enlisted to regulate the conduct of third parties and, second, technological gatekeepers, in which technology is used to identify and regulate individuals.[27] His definition broadly identifies the types of business activities that move businesses into the position of gatekeepers, describing them as 'businesses that host, index and carry others' content'.[28] However, he still relies on Kraakman's definition of gatekeeping, treating them as bodies that can prevent or identify wrongdoing by third parties. Ronald Mann and Seth Belzley also adopt the Kraakman approach and focus purely on whether liability should be imposed on gatekeepers, separating this notion from responsibilities the intermediary might undertake.[29] With generativity, Zittrain reconceived the notion of how information is produced, stored, processed and consumed, and the next step is to understand what this means for our traditional conceptions of regulatory players such as gatekeepers. It is proposed here that it is not third-party misconduct that is at the heart of

---

[26] See J. Zittrain, *The Future of the Internet and How to Stop It* (Yale University Press, 2008).

[27] J. Zittrain, 'A History of Online Gatekeeping', *Harv. J.L. & Tech.*, 19(2) (2006) 253, at 255–56. See J. Zittrain, 'Internet Points of Control', *B.C. L. Rev.*, 44 (2002) 653.

[28] Ibid., p. 253.

[29] R. J. Mann and S. R. Belzley, 'The Promise of Internet Intermediary Liability', *Wm & Mary L. Rev.*, 47 (2005) 239, 265–69; also see Zittrain n. 26.

democracy-shaping gatekeepers, but rather their power and control over the flow, content and accessibility of information. How they exercise this power determines the opportunities for participation in democratic culture online.

## 2.3. Internet gatekeepers

This chapter differentiates between two types of gatekeepers: internet gatekeepers, which are those gatekeepers that control the flow of information, and IIGs, which, as a result of this control, impact participation and deliberation in democratic culture. This thread of information control is the key to understanding online gatekeeping. For the first criteria, we can turn to *Network Gatekeeper Theory* (NGT); this theory helps bring the gatekeeping concept into the networked world.

Barzilai-Nahon was driven to develop NGT because traditional gatekeeping literature ignored the role of the gated and thus failed to recognise the dynamism of the gatekeeping environment. Most relevant is the fact that not only NGT was developed specifically with the internet in mind, but it moves gatekeeping from a traditional focus on information 'selection', 'processes', 'distribution' and 'intermediaries' to 'information control':

> Finally, a context of information and networks makes it necessary to re-examine the vocabulary of *gatekeeping*, moving from processes of selection (Communication), information distribution and protection (Information Science), and information intermediary (Management Science) to a more flexible construct of information control, allowing inclusion of more types of information handling that have occurred before and new types which occur due to networks.[30]

NGT helps identify the processes and mechanisms used for gatekeeping, and it most particularly highlights information control as the thread that ties the various online gatekeepers together. NGT can only take us so far, however, because it focuses on gatekeepers who have the power to choose to be in a gatekeeping position. This can be seen in the definition of a network gatekeeper as 'an entity (people, organisations, or governments) that has the discretion to exercise gatekeeping through a gatekeeping

---

[30] Barzilai-Nahon n. 21, p. 1495. See her other work on gatekeepers in 'Gatekeepers, Virtual Communities and the Gated: Multidimensional Tensions in Cyberspace', *Int'l J. Comm. L. & Pol'y*, 11(9) (2006) 1, and, in particular, see 'Gatekeeping Revisited: A Critical Review' n. 5 and her summary of the various approaches to gatekeeping.

mechanism in networks *and can choose* the extent to which to exercise it contingent upon the gated standing'.[31] This theory, thus, can only be used as a starting point for this book because often the gatekeepers we are concerned with here do not choose to be in that position and quite often might just fall into that role by happenstance because of technology or social behaviour. For example, they might become gatekeepers as a side effect of top-down regulation such as the E-Commerce Directive or Data Protection Directive.[32] Or, they might become gatekeepers because of the popularity of their product or services, such as Facebook and Twitter. Nevertheless, NGT is useful for articulating what qualifies as a gatekeeping process and mechanism.

Under NGT, an act of gatekeeping involves a gatekeeper and gated, the movement of information through a gate and the use of a gatekeeping process and mechanism. A gatekeeping process involves doing some level of selecting, channelling, shaping, manipulating and deleting information. For example, a gatekeeping process might involve *selecting* which information to publish, or *channelling* information through a channel, or *deleting* information by removing it or *shaping* information into a particular form. Her taxonomy of mechanisms for gatekeeping is particularly useful. The mechanisms include, for example, channelling (i.e., search engines, hyperlinks), censorship (i.e., filtering, blocking, zoning), value-added (i.e., customisation tools), infrastructure (i.e., network access), user interaction (i.e., default homepages, hypertext links) and editorial mechanisms (i.e., technical controls, information content).[33]

Pursuant to NGT, therefore, online gatekeeping is the process of controlling information as it moves through a gate, and the gatekeepers are those institutions or individuals that control this process. However, just because someone is an online gatekeeper does not mean that they are an IIG in the sense that human rights responsibilities should be incurred. Traditional approaches see the gatekeeper as somehow uninvolved or the gated as being unaffected, at least in the sense that the focus is purely on

---

[31] Barzilai-Nahon n. 21, p. 1497 (emphasis added). In addition, the next aspect of her theory is salience, where she builds on the infrastructure she has just set out to understand the relationship among gatekeepers and between gatekeepers and gated. It helps identify the motivations of the gatekeepers. She identifies four attributes of network gatekeepers: political power, information production, a relationship between the gatekeeper and gated and the availability (or lack thereof) of alternatives: ibid., p. 1498.

[32] Directive 95/46/EC of the European Parliament and of the Council of 24 October 1995 on the protection of individuals with regard to the processing of personal data and on the free movement of such data.

[33] Barzilai-Nahon n. 21, pp. 1497–98.

gated *misconduct* rather than gated *rights* as well. Human rights theory helps flesh out the facilitative aspect of how gatekeepers work that is missing from such traditional approaches. By incorporating the gated's *rights* into the mix, a fuller picture emerges. Barzilai-Nahon focuses on this as the role of the gated, while Andrew Murray focuses on this as 'nodes' in a polycentric regulatory environment.[34] Add to that a human rights conception of gatekeeping emphasising the rights of the gated to, for example, freedom of expression, and we have a better picture of the complex environment within which we are tasked with identifying IIGs.

The human rights framework proposed here depends on the extent to which the gatekeeper controls deliberation and participation in the forms of meaning-making in democratic culture. As was set out in Chapter 1, democracy here is conceived of in semiotic terms, meaning that the public plays an active role in creating and circulating meaning and pleasure. Democracy has always been embodied in the practices of communication, and freedom of expression has consistently been identified by the courts as central to democracy. Thus, when it is said here that the gated have rights and are not just the sources of the misconduct, this shift in focus incorporates human rights as the driver of gatekeeper responsibility. Or, more specifically, it incorporates a gatekeeper's impact on democracy as the driver of its responsibility. The following sections expand on this concept and articulate a framework for identifying IIGs.

## 2.4. A human rights framework for internet information gatekeepers

When does a company's responsibilities go from semi-private, where no gatekeeping function is occurring, to something more, where a gatekeeping function necessitates certain responsibilities? When does an entity go from being a gatekeeper to an IIG? We can say that even individuals running their own blogs act as gatekeepers. They can accept, reject or delete comments by others. But they are not yet IIGs. It is when the space for which they intermediate becomes one that facilitates or impedes democratic discourse that the entity is a gatekeeper for participation in democratic culture as we have envisaged it in Chapter 1.

---

[34] A. Murray, 'Symbiotic Regulation', *The John Marshall Journal of Computers & Information Law*, 26(2) (2009) 207, at 210.

### 2.4.1. Internet information gatekeepers: identification

Two things are required for a framework of analysis. First, we must identify what qualifies an entity as an internet gatekeeper. Second, we must identify what elevates such a gatekeeper to an IIG. As shown earlier, for the first criteria, Barzilai-Nahon's NGT can be used. Once an entity has been identified as a gatekeeper through such an assessment, it must be determined whether the gatekeeper is an IIG.

#### 2.4.1.1. Conceptual basis of internet information gatekeepers

An IIG is conceptually different from any other online gatekeeper because it attracts human rights responsibilities. Whether human rights responsibilities should be incurred and the extent of these responsibilities depends on the extent to which the gatekeeper controls deliberation and participation in the forms of meaning-making in democratic culture. This reflects the most mainstream conception of the corporate social responsibility (CSR) model, which is that businesses are responsible for human rights within their sphere of influence. *Sphere of influence* is a concept articulated in one of the leading CSR instruments, the United Nations Global Compact:

> While the concept [of sphere of influence] is not defined in detail by international human rights standards, it will tend to include the individuals to whom the company has a certain political, contractual, economic or geographic proximity. Every company, both large and small, has a sphere of influence, though obviously the larger or more strategically significant the company, the larger the company's sphere of influence is likely to be.[35]

John Ruggie, the former Special Representative to the Secretary General on issues of human rights and transnational corporations, whose work is discussed in detail in the following chapter, has suggested that the sphere of influence approach is problematic.[36] He states that it focuses on a limited set of rights, but with expansive and imprecise responsibilities, and proposes that instead we focus on all human rights and set out business-specific responsibilities in this regard. To that end, he suggests that we focus on the potential and actual human rights impacted and

---

[35] Business Leaders Initiative on Human Rights, United Nations Global Compact and the Office of the High Commissioner for Human Rights, 'A Guide for Integrating Human Rights into Business Management I': p. 8.

[36] J. Ruggie, 'Protect, respect and remedy: a framework for business and human rights: report of the Special Representative of the Secretary General on the issue of human rights and transnational corporations and other business enterprises' (2008), at www.reports -and-materials.org/Ruggie-report-7-Apr-2008.pdf (last visited 17 June 2014), pp. 14–15.

imposes a requirement of due diligence on companies. His work is having a dramatic impact on the development of CSR and signals that there will likely be a shift away from the concept of sphere of influence.

What is proposed here, unlike Ruggie's approach, does not wholly reject the sphere of influence notion that has emerged in CSR literature. It does not, however, fall victim to Ruggie's criticisms either. The reason is that although human rights are broader than democracy-related rights, the human rights referred to in the context of this book, specifically the human rights engaged on the internet in a democratic culture, are narrow. A broader conception of democracy engages rights such as the right to vote, and it arguably depends on such rights as the right to life and prohibition of torture. However, when the term 'human rights' is used here, and when the term 'IIG' is used, the focus is on the right to freedom of expression and related rights to privacy and association. Thus, we start from the position of specifically engaged human rights, and the issue is identifying those gatekeepers that impact these rights. The resulting regulation would be, as Julia Black describes it, the 'outcome of the interactions of networks, or alternatively "webs of influence" which operate in the absence of formal governmental or legal sanction'.[37]

An IIG is an entity that, due to the role it takes on, the type of business it does or the technology with which it works, or a combination of all of these, has the capacity to impact democracy in a way traditionally reserved for public institutions. An IIG's human rights responsibilities increase or decrease based on the extent that its activities facilitate or hinder democratic culture. This scale of responsibility is reflected not only in the reach of the gatekeeper, but also in the infiltration of that information, process, site or tool in democratic culture. Although at this juncture we will not identify what those responsibilities are, it is necessary to understand that the responsibilities are a sliding scale to help identify who gatekeepers are. A typical figure of the public sphere uses concentric circles to illustrate that a business's human rights obligations are strongest to its workers, where it has the most influence, and gradually weakens as its sphere of influence decreases out to the supply chain, marketplace, community and government. A typical sphere can be seen in Figure 2.1.

For our purposes here, the model can be set up in exactly the opposite manner. It is not thought of in terms that the sphere of influence lessens as one moves to the outer circles, but rather that, as the democratic impact increase, so does ones' responsibilities. This begs an important question:

---

[37] Black n. 14, pp. 110–11.

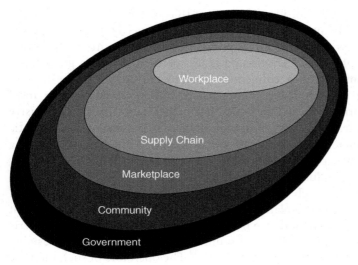

**Figure 2.1.** Sphere of influence.

how does one as a gatekeeper have a greater or lesser impact on participation in democratic culture? There are two ways: (1) when the information has democratic significance and (2) when the communication occurs in an environment more closely akin to a public sphere.

### 2.4.1.2. Characteristics of internet information gatekeepers

First, one must keep in mind the broader definition of democratic culture discussed in Chapter 1, which encompasses more forms of speech as furthering democracy than is reflected in traditional human rights jurisprudence. Freedom of expression, like the internet's topology, can be described as an interconnected network, a system of cultural and political interactions, experienced at both individual and collective levels. Information and communication technologies (ICTs) allow for participation in such interactions at a level, speed, distance and cost previously unimagined. Thus, as we have seen in Chapter 1, the democracy offered online is not restricted to the notion of deliberative democracy, but rather is the broader notion of facilitation and participation in democratic culture, which brings within its ambit cultural participations such as nonpolitical expression, popular culture and individual participation. Therefore, in assessing the impact on democracy, it is not just political discussions that are heralded and protected, but any communication which is part of meaning-making in democratic culture.

What this means for identification of IIGs is that at the far end of the scale of clearly protected speech would be overtly political speech. Historically, political speech is given a preferred position over other forms of expression.[38] Discussing issues pertaining to the governance of one's community or country are considered crucial to the healthy functioning of democracy. This can serve as a marker of the most protected form of speech for which businesses incur the most extensive responsibilities. However, nonpolitical speech that furthers democratic culture is offered more protection than might have been available in a traditional conception of democracy. This can be seen with the increasing reliance by individuals on the internet to help them cope with major life experiences. For such users, the internet not only is an information resource, but provides platforms for various communities they can visit to seek comfort and guidance from others going through similar experiences. For example, online communities have become an increasingly important resource for cancer patients.[39] The operators of such message boards, therefore, exercise significant power to exclude members and censor content. Under a traditional conception of freedom of expression, such content might be accorded less weight, yet, through the lens of democratic culture, such content is found to be more significant and its gatekeepers in a greater position of responsibility as a result.

Second, it must be remembered that the notion of the public sphere discussed here is necessarily relaxed, as shown in Chapter 1. The internet has multiple spaces, some private, some public, with opportunities to participate in forms that mimic the real world and, at other times, with opportunities to participate in new forms of communication. As we have seen, most, if not all, of these spaces would fail Jürgen Habermas's utopian model of the public sphere, but they empower participation in democratic life by creating a form of self-determination from below. Oren Bracha and Frank Pasquale talk about it in terms of the internet's structure:

> [The web's] structure results in a bottom-up filtration system. At the lowest level, a large number of speakers receive relatively broad exposure within local communities likely composed of individuals with high-intensity interest or expertise. Speakers who gain salience at the lower

[38] For a discussion of traditional speech theories, see E. Barendt, *Freedom of Speech*, 2nd edn (Oxford University Press, 2005), chapter one. Or see, for example, *Lingens* v. *Austria* (1986) 8 EHRR 407, paras. 41–42.

[39] See S. Orgad, 'The Cultural Dimensions of Online Communication: A Study of Breast Cancer Patients' Internet Spaces', *New Media & Society*, 8(6) (2006) 87.

levels may gradually gain recognition in higher-order clusters and eventually reach general visibility.[40]

Whereas this focuses on speakers, we can think of this also in terms of
those who receive information. The 'speaker' might be a blogger, and the
blogger writes in an interactive environment. It is not a one-way communication in which the writer is separate from the gatekeeper and/or
the information is received by a static gated. Rather, there are multiple
channels of communication. The writer writes, readers comment,
information is hyperlinked and, eventually, a blog might become so
well known that the conversation becomes relevant to democratic
culture, and the entity becomes a gatekeeper.

Such gatekeepers support or constrain the public sphere through the
various ways they control the information communicated in online
spaces. In a participative democracy, this is information of democratic
significance, being content going closer to the core protected by freedom
of expression discussed earlier, which by reason of (1) reach or (2) its
structure, can be described as a modern public sphere. This structure, to
adopt part of James Bohman's approach, has two dimensions.[41] First,
visitors can express their views, and others can respond. Second, the
space is inclusive in that the communication is to an indefinite audience.
Bohman adds that the interaction is in an environment of free and equal
respect, but this is perhaps rather a duty of the gatekeeper to facilitate
instead of being a quality of the structure itself. If required, it would mean
that someone was not a gatekeeper as long as the interaction was
disrespectful and unequal. For example, a blog might not be interactive
if comments are not permitted, and therefore it only engages issues as to
the right of the gated to seek and receive information; however, because
of its reach to many readers, it may take on democratic significance, thus
elevating the blogger to the level of IIG.

A visual begins to emerge as shown in Figure 2.2.

### 2.4.2. Internet information gatekeepers: a framework

We must then identify what the different levels are in the model. Barzilai-
Nahon's functional approach to gatekeepers is very useful and is partially

---

[40] O. Bracha and F. Pasquale, 'Federal Search Commission? Access, Fairness and
Accountability in the Law of Search', *Cornell L. R.*, 93 (2008) 1149, p. 1159.

[41] J. Bohman, 'Expanding Dialogue: The Internet, Public Sphere, and Transnational
Democracy', in P. M. Shane (ed.), *Democracy Online: The Prospects for Political
Renewal Through the Internet* (New York: Routledge, 2004), p. 49.

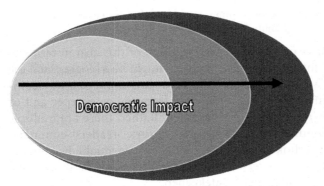

**Figure 2.2.** Internet information gatekeepers model: democratic impact.

used to flesh out the model.[42] The analysis of the democratic impact of gatekeepers is structured as a sliding scale from macro-gatekeepers down to micro-gatekeepers or vice versa. This analysis is set out in Figure 2.3.

At the top level we have macro-gatekeepers, something various authors seem to recognise using terms such as 'chokepoint', 'bottleneck' or 'super-node'.[43] Barzilai-Nahon refers to them as 'eternal' gatekeepers.[44] Bracha and Pasquale implicitly recognise these macro-gatekeepers when, in discussing the same theory of democratic culture used here, they comment, 'though speakers in the digital network environment can occasionally "route around" traditional media intermediaries, the giant intermediaries are likely to maintain significantly *superior salience* and exposure, both on and off the Internet'.[45] It is when they are of a certain size or influence or straddle several types of gatekeepers and have strong information controls that they become macro-gatekeepers. These macro-gatekeepers are not categorised on their own in any other models.

They are distinguished from the other levels because users must inevitably pass through them to use the internet and thus engage all aspects of the right to freedom of expression. This can be literal, as in the case of our reliance on ISPs for access to the internet, or figurative, as in the case of search engines on which we depend to organise the

---

[42] Barzilai-Nahon's functional approach to gatekeepers has infrastructure providers at one level, such as ISPs, authority sites at the next level, such as search providers, and administrators at the lower level such as content moderators and network administrators: n. 21, p. 1499.

[43] On the latter see A. Murray, 'Nodes and Gravity in Virtual Space', *Legisprudence*, 5(2) (2011) 195.

[44] Barzilai-Nahon n. 21, p. 1506.    [45] Bracha and Pasquale n. 40, p. 1160.

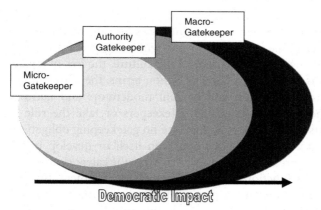

Figure 2.3. Internet information gatekeepers model: webs of influence.

information on the internet. Such bodies incur the strongest human rights obligations. In contrast, portals were once macro-gatekeepers but have since been downgraded to the next level of *authority gatekeepers*, because although central to a user's internet experience, they are no longer inevitable to it. A more recent macro-gatekeeper is mobile network providers. As mobile users increasingly move to smartphones with PC-like capabilities, mobile network providers become one of the key gatekeepers in setting the terms of access to and use of the internet.[46]

At the next level is what Barzilai-Nahon calls *authority sites*, sites which are high traffic and control traffic and information flow. They are, for example, social networking sites, portals and high-traffic sites. They, too, impact all aspects of the rights of freedom of expression. They are identified separately from other websites and macro-gatekeepers because they play a significant role in democratic culture, both in reach and in impact on culture, but their use is not an inevitable aspect of using the internet. Some started out in small capacities with no obligations and then meteorically shot to the level of authority gatekeeper – thus attracting human rights obligations – such as Facebook and Twitter.

At the base level are micro-gatekeepers, which are not well-known sources of information or discussion. They do not necessarily engage all aspects of the rights of freedom of expression. A website might engage the right to seek/receive information because it is a source of one-way

---

[46] On the issues surrounding regulation of apps, see D. Mac Síthigh, 'App Law Within: Rights and Regulation in the Smartphone Ageg', *IJILT*, 21(2) (2013) 154.

communication of information to the masses, but not the right to speak, because visitors are unable to leave comments or engage in any interactive discourse.[47] The smaller the reach, the less the right is engaged. In addition, the less the site is of significance to democratic culture, the less of a gatekeeping obligation is incurred. In Barzilai-Nahon terms, these are administrator sites such as application and content moderators and network administrators. They can be designated gatekeepers or take the role of administrator. At its most basic level, there are no gatekeeping obligations that the administrator site does not impose on itself or develop in the community. This is where there is the most fuzziness: the categorisation of a website depends on its function, and, in a dynamic environment, this can change. If one worries that, say, a particular discussion might elevate a message board's impact on democratic culture, thus instantly and temporarily inviting obligations, this would not be the case. In such a situation, it is surely up to the site to decide how to be governed. Something more sustained would be needed to move up a level from a micro-gatekeeper to a middle-level gatekeeper or from a simple gatekeeper to an IIG.

For a gatekeeper to qualify as a micro-gatekeeper, the content of the site must pertain to democratic culture, and the space must have attributes of a public sphere in either reach or structure. For example, this author's family blog would not qualify as a micro-IIG, although gatekeeping is exercised, because the information is not of democratic significance, it is read by few people and it is not structured as an interactive space. However, this author's work blog, www.laidlaw.eu, has the potential to be an IIG, although is not one yet because the information has democratic significance, is read by more people and is structured to allow user comments, although such comments require approval to be posted. A greyer example is a blog that, over time, attracts a large audience, which in turn attracts advertisements and revenue for the author. Such websites would seem to fall on a sliding scale, with success stories such as www.techcrunch.com and www.talking pointsmemo.com likely qualifying as IIGs. A clearer example of an IIG is Huffington Post. Some reader contributions have broken important stories that have been subsequently picked up by mainstream media. A website such as Huffington Post is of such democratic significance, arguably having transformed into a mainstream media organisation, and with such great reach, that it has moved up a level from a micro-IIG to be an authority gatekeeper.

The various gatekeepers are exemplified in Figure 2.4.

---

[47] This leaves aside the argument that one may have a 'right' to comment on such sites.

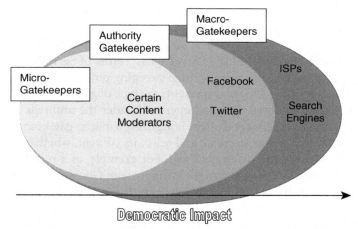

**Figure 2.4.** Internet information gatekeepers model: webs of influence (examples).

Such a model helps pinpoint the gatekeepers along the scale of responsibility to tackle certain issues such as internet filtering. In the United Kingdom, for example, a body such as the Internet Watch Foundation (IWF), the industry's self-regulatory body for addressing unlawful content, would be a macro-gatekeeper. This is because the content a UK user accesses is inevitably moderated to a degree by the IWF. The IWF will be the focus of the case study in Chapter 4. The IWF sends its members a blacklist of child sexual abuse images to be filtered, but the body also makes use of the Electronic Commerce (EC Directive) Regulations[48] to issue notices for the removal of criminally obscene content hosted in the UK. The members themselves are a mix of macro-gatekeepers, such as ISPs and search engines, and authority gatekeepers, such as Facebook and the BBC.[49] Such gatekeepers have greater impact on democratic culture and thus invite greater scrutiny as to their responsibilities. Using this model to identify the gatekeepers for filtering has an additional benefit. It reveals that the dynamics are happening largely at the outer reaches of the model, where there is the most democratic impact and thus

---

[48] 2002 No. 2013.
[49] See the IWF's website, http://www.iwf.org.uk, for further information. For critical analysis of the role and remit of the IWF, see, for example, J. Petley, 'Web of Control', *Index on Censorship*, 38(1) (2009) 78; and T. McIntyre and C. Scott, 'Internet Filtering: Rhetoric, Legitimacy, Accountability and Responsibility', in R. Brownsword and K. Yeung (eds.), *Regulating Technologies: Legal Future, Regulatory Frames and Technological Fixes* (Oxford: Hart Publishing, 2008).

inviting greater scrutiny of the regulatory arrangement between these various gatekeepers.

A contrasting dynamic involves users, bloggers and blog providers. A blog provider such as Google's Blogger service has Terms of Service that the blog owner is gated by, which can include sweeping powers to, among other things, delete the blog. Blogger represents the type of gatekeeper that, on its own, would be an authority gatekeeper but, under the umbrella of Google and the breadth of services it offers, is arguably a macro-gatekeeper. The blog writer has the power to create and select its content, whether to allow comments and whether to delete them. For example, as a result of complaints under the DMCA of copyright infringement, Google deleted a series of popular music blogs. Some of the bloggers disputed the copyright infringement claims, arguing that they had been asked to post the music by either the promotional company, record label or the artist.[50] The purpose of this example is not to analyse the issues it raises concerning copyright or the DMCA. Rather, this incident serves to highlight the value of the human rights-driven framework that is being argued for here. It also illustrates the layers of gatekeeping that simultaneously operate in the internet environment. By shifting the perspective to the gated's rights, the question becomes the significance of the blogs to democratic culture. One of the blogs might be a place, whether due to numbers or its structure, which elevates it to micro-gatekeeper and occasionally to the authority gatekeeper level. Thus, users might have a stronger right to the content of the blog, and the blogger, a stronger right against the blog provider to run his or her blog. In turn, the blog provider might have greater human rights responsibilities, and deletion of the blog requires greater regulatory scrutiny. Shifting the perspective gives a fuller account of the concerns raised by Google's deletion of these blogs.

---

[50] For news articles on the incident, see S. Michaels, 'Google shuts down music blogs without warning' (11 February 2010), at www.guardian.co.uk/music/2010/feb/11/google-deletes-music-blogs (last visited 17 June 2014), C. Metz, 'Google's "Musicblogocide" – blame the DMCA' (11 February 2010), at www.theregister.co.uk/2010/02/11/google_musicblogocide_2010/ (last visited 17 June 2014). Google had changed its policy with regard to bloggers in 2009. See Google's blog post in this regard, 'Let the music play' (26 August 2009), at http://buzz.blogger.com/2009/08/let-music-play.html (last visited 17 June 2014). See also Google's response to the incident, 'A quick note about music blog removals' (10 February 2010), http://buzz.blogger.com/2010/02/quick-note-about-music-blog-removals.html (last visited 17 June 2014). The DMCA takedown letters are archived at Chilling Effects, http://www.chillingeffects.org (last visited 17 June 2014). For the Blogger Terms of Service, see http://www.blogger.com/terms.g (last visited 17 June 2014).

## 2.5. Conclusion

The described framework targets a particular type of gatekeeper, termed IIGs, which, as a result of their control over the flow of information, facilitate or hinder deliberation and participation in democratic culture. Whether a gatekeeper has this impact and its extent is determined by the gatekeeper's web of influence, in which a gatekeeper with less impact on democratic culture incurs less responsibility or may not be an IIG at all. Sliding up the scale, we come to a gatekeeper that has a significant impact on democratic culture and incurs more responsibility. Where a gatekeeper fits on this range, as either a macro-gatekeeper, authority gatekeeper, or a micro-gatekeeper, is determined by the extent to which (1) the information has democratic significance and (2) the reach or structure of the communicative space. Although a simpler model might clearly delineate what qualifies as a gatekeeper from what does not, such a simple, categorical model would artificially hive off certain entities from the gatekeeper label. This artificiality cannot work when taking a human rights approach to gatekeeping because the human rights impact crosses categories. The consistency here is in the method for assessing gatekeeper qualities, which then provides guidance on the scale of human rights responsibilities it attracts. This scale of responsibility is further explored in Chapter 6.

Now that we have identified the gatekeepers that are the primary subject of this book, we can proceed with an investigation of CSR and the way CSR frameworks have been used to govern the activities of IIGs in terms of their human rights impact. Ultimately, the question is whether such frameworks are sufficient for the goal of facilitating the internet as a force within democratic culture. The following chapter will examine the concept of CSR and how it is being used in the human rights and internet governance fields while orienting the reader to its strengths and weaknesses. This will frame the enquiry in the case studies in Chapters 4 and 5 concerning how such CSR frameworks have fared for two particular macro-gatekeepers: ISPs and search engines.

# 3

# Corporate social responsibility in cyberspace

In the 2011 Arab uprising, the Egyptian government ordered Vodafone to turn off mobile telephone networks. What should it have done? Resist the government order? Immediately cease work in Egypt? Comply? In the end, Vodafone did comply, as well as allow pro-government text messages to be sent using its networks. Would a corporate governance framework have helped Vodafone navigate such issues as these? It was one of the key drafters of the Global Network Initiative (GNI), one of the leading corporate social responsibility (CSR) frameworks for technology companies concerning issues of human rights (discussed further later). Yet, Vodafone pulled out at the last minute. The question is, would being a member of the GNI have guided it on what to do?[1]

Similarly, at the height of the Wikileaks Saga in December 2010, surrounding the release of various confidential documents, most notably diplomatic cables, Amazon decided to cut off hosting of a key Wikileaks site.[2] This incident raises a slightly different question to the Vodafone one. Whereas there was most certainly pressure from government, there was no government order that we know of compelling Amazon to shut down the site. The question concerns what Amazon was entitled to do. Is a private company free to decide the types of speech it supports, or is

---

[1] The Global Network Initiative, at www.globalnetworkinitiative.org/ (last visited 17 June 2014). For interesting ideas on what Vodafone should have done, see the commentaries of the Institute of Business and Human Rights S. Tripathi: 'How should internet and phone companies respond in Egypt?' (4 February 2011), at www.ihrb.org/commentary/staff/internet_providers_in_egypt.html (last visited 17 June 2014), and 'How businesses have responded in Egypt' (7 February 2011), at www.ihrb.org/commentary/staff/how_businesses_have_responded_in_egypt.html (last visited 17 June 2014).

[2] E. MacAskill, 'Wikileaks website pulled by Amazon after US political pressure', at www.guardian.co.uk/media/2010/dec/01/wikileaks-website-cables-servers-amazon (last visited 17 June 2014).

there a right of access to certain forums and platforms of communication even if privately owned? Who should decide such matters?

Although the focus of this book is on the activities of these gatekeepers in the United Kingdom and more widely Europe, these incidents help frame the issues for discussion. All of these questions are rooted in three fields of study: CSR, regulation (more broadly law) and human rights. All three fields of study ask questions about where the law ends and social responsibility begins, and it is in this perilous land of in-between that internet gatekeepers operate.[3] The question underlying this chapter – and indeed this book – is whether CSR has the capacity to be the structural regime for governance of digital human rights. To delve into this issue, the concept of CSR and how it relates to human rights and the law must be examined. What is revealed is a lacuna in governance concerning internet information gatekeepers (IIGs), where human rights laws, regulation and current CSR regimes do not quite apply to what they are doing, even though IIGs are at the centre of the internet's democratising force. The promise of CSR, it will be shown in this chapter, is as a bridge between the extralegal dimensions of human rights and the rule-making nature of the law.

As a term, CSR is mired in conceptual disagreements plaguing its development as an academic field. This led the editors of *The Oxford Handbook of Corporate Social Responsibility* to comment, '[it] has become a major area of research despite a degree of ambiguity and disagreement that might ordinarily be expected to lead to its demise'.[4] Researchers have not agreed on a common definition of the term, nor whether a company should even have social responsibilities, much less what the core principles of such responsibilities should be.[5] For example, a study by the Ashridge Business School identified 147 species of CSR.[6] This contentiousness concerning how to define CSR even played out online when contributors to Wikipedia, both supportive and critical of CSR, tried to define it. Unable to achieve any consensus, the phrase was eventually flagged for its neutrality.[7]

---

[3] It should be emphasised that these companies typically are knowledgeable about their gatekeeping role, including the activities that are clearly regulated under the law and activities that fall in the grey area triggering softer governance strategies.

[4] A. Crane et al. (eds.), *The Oxford Handbook of Corporate Social Responsibility* (Oxford University Press, 2008), p. 4.

[5] Ibid.

[6] Discussed in M. Blowfield and A. Murray, *Corporate Responsibility: A Critical Introduction* (Oxford University Press, 2008), p. 15.

[7] Crane n. 4, p. 5.

Through the years, it can be seen appearing under the terms *social responsibility, business ethics, stakeholder theory, sustainability, corporate citizenship, corporate social responsiveness, corporate social performance* and so on. Yet, despite its vagueness, CSR is emerging as its own academic field, and this can be attributed, at least in part, to the following. As Ronen Shamir comments, 'corporate global rule is already here'.[8] Consider the following statistics. Multinational companies account for two-thirds of the world's trade in goods and services and 51 per cent of the world's top one hundred world economies; 27.5 per cent of the world's gross domestic product is generated by two hundred corporations, and their combined annual revenue is greater than the 182 states that make up 80 per cent of the population.[9]

It is not only their economic power that is significant. Companies are increasingly state-like, often influencing the development of laws, as seen in their lobbying efforts to strengthen intellectual property protections of businesses in the development of trade-related aspects of intellectual property rights (TRIPS).[10] Yet there are minimal international regulatory structures in place to articulate any corresponding duties on companies for such issues as human rights.[11] A chasm has developed:

> There is a growing recognition among scholars and activists alike of the widening gap between the transnational character of corporate activity and the availability of transnational regulatory structures that may be effectively used to monitor, assess, and restrain corporations irrespective of any specific territory in which they may happen to operate at a given moment.[12]

[8] R. Shamir, 'Corporate Social Responsibility: A Case of Hegemony and Counter-Hegemony', in B. De Sousa Santos and C.A. Rodriguez-Garavito (eds.), *Law and Globalization from Below: Towards a Cosmopolitan Legality* (Cambridge University Press, 2005), p. 92.

[9] Ibid. For more such statistics see www.corpwatch.org (last visited 17 June 2014), in particular S. Anderson et al., 'Top 200: the rise of corporate global power' (4 December 2000), at http://corpwatch.org/article.php?id=377 (last visited 17 June 2014).

[10] See www.wto.org/english/tratop_e/trips_e/trips_e.htm (last visited 17 June 2014).

[11] Shamir n. 8, pp. 95–96.

[12] Ibid. John Ruggie's work will be discussed extensively below, but note here his comment that the result of this governance gap is a 'permissive environment for wrongful acts by companies of all kinds without adequate sanctioning or reparation': J. Ruggie, 'Protect, respect and remedy: a framework for business and human rights: report of the Special Representative of the Secretary General on the issue of human rights and transnational corporations and other business enterprises' (2008), at www.reports-and-materials.org/Ruggie-report-7-Apr-2008.pdf (last visited 17 June 2014), p. 3.

It is in this grey area that CSR (however it is defined) operates, not just as a public relations tool but also as a facilitative force for socially responsible governance.[13]

With this background, it is evident that a single chapter on CSR is hard-pressed to give a thorough accounting of what CSR is. The examination that follows, however, is narrowed by the purpose of the book: the examination of the viability of CSR as a framework through which the human rights obligations of IIGs can be embedded into their practices. There is no need for this chapter (or indeed this book) to seek to resolve the varying theories and approaches to CSR (and indeed whether CSR should be a theory or simply a management practice). Rather, CSR as a concept will be harnessed here to show the regulatory environment within which the business and society relationship has developed, and its focus will be tailored to its use for the promotion and protection of freedom of expression. It is further tailored by the focus on the information and communication technologies (ICT) sector in developed countries. Under this umbrella, the various conceptions of CSR can operate – voluntary and binding, indirect and direct. It is the effectiveness of these various CSR initiatives as regulatory settlements for the promotion and protection of human rights that is of interest here.

Thus, in order to manage the vagueness and expansiveness of the CSR subject matter, this chapter will be approached as follows. It will examine what CSR is as a concept, discussing its historical development and the criticisms of its use as a governance tool. Having established how the term CSR is used in this book, the chapter will then examine two conceptual problems for the analysis of IIGs: the relationship between CSR and the law, and CSR and human rights. The chapter will conclude by identifying Article 10(2) of the European Convention on Human Rights (ECHR)[14] as the appropriate standard against which to assess CSR frameworks, which forms the approach to the case studies in Chapters 4 and 5.

## 3.1. The concept of CSR

To understand CSR as a concept, we must understand the historical context of the relationship between businesses and society because this

---

[13] Shamir n. 8, p. 95.
[14] European Convention for the Protection of Human Rights and Fundamental Freedoms 1950.

gives a sense of the public's changing expectations of businesses concerning their responsibilities. For example, whereas a modern understanding of corporate responsibilities tends to focus on the paramountcy of responsibilities to shareholders, this was not always so. Indeed, early American enterprises were subject to democratic control. The state controlled the issuance of corporate charters that set out certain public interest obligations that, if a company failed to fulfil, would result in the withdrawal by the state of the charter to operate.[15] An examination of the historical context also helps us understand the regulatory framework within which businesses operate. As the reader will recall, businesses are affected by various regulatory modalities, not just the law, but also norms, markets and architecture.[16] The law, on its own, is not necessarily the most effective way to protect digital human rights.

### 3.1.1. Where CSR came from

The evolution of the relationship between businesses and society can be classified in four eras: the Industrial Revolution, the Great Depression, post-World War II and globalisation.[17] The Industrial Revolution of the eighteenth and nineteenth centuries was an era of major changes in agriculture, manufacturing, mining and transport. With the rise of the factory system came concerns regarding child and female labour, pollution, poverty and other social problems.[18] This caused civil unrest, which led to the industrial welfare movement, which sought to prevent labour abuses by improving safety and health conditions of work places,

[15] J. Richter, *Holding Corporations Accountable: Corporate Conduct, International Codes, and Citizen Action* (London: Zed Books Ltd., 2001), p. 6.

[16] Alternatively, as A. Murray and C. Scott frame it, hierarchy, community, competition and design: 'Regulating New Media', *MLR*, 65 (2002) 491.

[17] There are many different ways to categorise these phases, although the descriptions of the time seem to be consistent. I have created four, although in Blowfield and Murray n. 6, the authors only talk about three, merging the time between the wars and after World War II. Also, generalisations are made here about the social, legal and political history of varying countries. The focus is mostly on the United States and the United Kingdom, and even there we find quite divergent histories; but this is only intended to offer broad brush strokes of the state of the business-society relationship at the time, and there is enough commonality during these eras to do this. The discussion draws extensively from the often-cited work of Archie Carroll, who has examined extensively the history and theory of the concept of CSR, most recently in Crane n. 4. For another historical discussion, see M. Heald, *The Social Responsibilities of Business: Company and Community, 1900–1960* (Cleveland: Press of Case Western Reserve University, 1970).

[18] A. B. Carroll, 'A History of Corporate Social Responsibility: Concepts and Practices', in Crane n. 4, pp. 20–21

employee wages and hours and the like.[19] It was also a time of loosened regulatory oversight.[20] In the United States, the right of states to revoke charters was curtailed, and corporations were granted increasing rights, including constitutional rights of free speech.[21]

The fulfilment of the responsibility to the community at this time largely took the form of philanthropy, with business executives such as Cornelius Vanderbilt and John D. Rockefeller regularly, and quite publicly, making contributions to various charities. Although this practice of philanthropy was not new to society,[22] it was frowned on by some members of the public, who thought these businessmen were effectively 'giving away stockholders' assets without their approval'.[23] In this pre-Great Depression period, companies exercised great economic power concentrated in the hands of a few, which created an environment ripe for corruption and irresponsibility. Although the scars of World War I led people to rethink the social order and found bodies such as the International Labour Organization which were aimed at promoting social justice, this 'new capitalism' failed to take off: the period was in reality a time of deference to market control.[24]

The second era started with the Great Depression. Robert Hay and Ed Gray characterise it as the 'trusteeship management' phase, in which corporate managers were held responsible not only to shareholders but also to customers, employees and the community.[25] In this era, companies increasingly began to be seen as having social responsibilities akin to governments. In the United Kingdom, it was a period of nationalisation of major industries such as coal, railway, power and gas, reflecting a belief that the public good was best protected by state control of businesses.[26]

However it is the period after World War II, starting in the 1950s, when we see modern CSR beginning to take shape.[27] This third era, often referred to as the era of 'social responsibility', was a time of awareness

---

[19] Ibid., p. 21 It was not just technological innovation that characterised the period of the Industrial Revolution relevant to businesses and society. It was also a time of institutional innovation, such as the debut of the limited liability company: Blowfield and Murray n. 6, p. 45.

[20] Richter n. 15, p. 6–7.

[21] Ibid., p. 6–7. Other countries did not view corporations as citizens, but rather treated them as artificial legal personalities, so they could sue, hold property, be held liable and enter transactions: ibid., p. 7.

[22] One can see that this practice traces back to patrons of the arts for churches, sculptures and endowments to universities: Carroll n. 18, p. 21.

[23] Ibid., pp. 23–24.     [24] Blowfield and Murray n. 6, pp. 46–47.     [25] Carroll n. 18, p. 23.

[26] Blowfield and Murray n. 6, p. 48.     [27] Carroll n. 18, p. 25.

raising and issue spotting, where the role of businesses in society began to receive attention on issues such as the environment, race and poverty, and the main work involved trying to simply define what CSR is.[28] In the 1980s, the subject matter splintered as researchers tried to recast CSR in other theories or models, such as stakeholder theory and business ethics, with the latter growing as the public learned of scandals that led to infant formula boycotts and the controversy of companies doing business in South Africa.[29] In the 1990s, environmental concerns came to the forefront once again, and the role of a company as a 'corporate citizen' began to gain traction.[30]

The fourth era, which overlaps with the latter part of the third era, is the current era of globalisation. Experts debate how to define the term, but *globalisation* generally refers to the view that economic growth can be achieved 'by creating a global market built on free trade'.[31] The privatisation movement in the 1980s in the United Kingdom and United States, under Margaret Thatcher and Ronald Reagan, respectively, and the establishment of the World Trade Organization (WTO) in 1995, helped pave the way for globalisation.[32] In the context of CSR, this era raises

[28] It moved the subject matter away from a focus on CSR as a form of philanthropy and onto how businesses manage their social impact. The idea of CSR as a management practice was popular in the 1970s, when issues came to the public forefront such as hiring of minorities, the environment, civil rights, contributions to arts and education, truth in advertising and product defects: ibid., p. 33.

[29] Carroll n. 18, p. 36. Blowfield and Murray n. 6, p. 12. The infant formula scandal occurred in the 1970s, when Nestle was boycotted for its marketing of formula in developing countries. The advertisements pushed formula as being better for babies than breast milk. However, in these economically starved areas, many did not have access to clean water and sanitation equipment, all of which was needed to use formula, and, due to the high cost of formula many diluted the mix. Many babies are argued to have become sick and died as a result.

[30] Corporate citizenship refers to 'the role of business as a citizen in global society and its function in delivering the citizenship rights of individuals'. With the focus on the environment, terms such as 'corporate sustainability' were also used: ibid.

[31] Ibid., p. 72. See R. McCorquodale and R. Fairbrother, 'Globalization and Human Rights', *Hum. Rts. Q.*, 21(3) (1999) 735, noting it is a contested term: p. 736. In particular, see discussion in section VI on the intersection of globalisation and human rights in the communications industry. See also K. Webb (ed.), *Voluntary Codes: Private Governance, the Public Interest and Innovation* (Carleton Research Unit for Innovation, Science and Environment, 2004). Webb defines it as: 'a complex process of interdependency or convergence resulting from dramatically increasing levels of exchange in goods, information, services and capital': K. Webb, 'Understanding the Voluntary Codes Phenomenon' in ibid., p. 8.

[32] Under Margaret Thatcher in the United Kingdom and Ronald Reagan in the United States, a set of policies known as the Washington Consensus were enacted, which promoted global free trade: Webb ibid., p. 8. See also Richter note 15, p. 12.

issues concerning the responsibilities of transnational corporations (TNCs), an issue particularly relevant to this book; most macro-IIGs, such as Google and Apple, are TNCs.

The price of globalisation, however, is regulatory oversight. In fact, the current international regulatory environment resulting from globalisation is notable mostly for its lack of regulation or oversight.[33] The call for regulation of TNCs has been renewed, and this is where CSR and globalisation are intertwined. Many CSR initiatives are spurred on by concerns that arise from globalisation and relate to standards for health and safety, human rights and the environment, such as the Rio Earth Summit concerning the environment, the United Nations Global Compact and the Organisation for Economic Co-operation and Development (OECD) guidelines for multinational enterprises.[34] In the context of ICT companies, CSR frameworks such as the Electronic Industry Code of Conduct (EICC) and the GNI have gained prominence in recent years, with the former focusing on such issues as labour, health and safety and the environment, and the latter on issues of freedom of expression and privacy.[35] The GNI, in particular, will be discussed in more detail later. This era has seen a shift from governments to governance, with greater emphasis placed on soft law tactics and the inclusion of a broader array of participants in its development.[36]

Having contextualised the story of CSR with this very brief history of the relationship between business and society, a modern accounting of CSR as a concept is needed. This will frame how the concept will be used to assess the sufficiency of IIGs governance structures.

### 3.1.2. What CSR is

As we have seen from the preceding brief history, the story of the relationship between business and society has been contentious. CSR has been used to describe a variety of responsibilities from charitable to legal, in a variety of fields from the environment to labour and financial services. Various theories and definitions of CSR have developed, all with inevitably different views on what CSR is depending on the field of research informing the perspective. As Dow Votaw states, 'corporate social

---

[33] Ibid., p. 8.    [34] Ibid., pp. 13–14; Blowfield and Murray note 6, p. 88.
[35] See www.eicc.info/ and www.globalnetworkinitiative.org/ (last visited 17 June 2014).
[36] See J. Nolan, 'The Corporate Responsibility to Respect Human Rights: Soft Law or Not Law?' in S. Deva and D. Bilchitz (eds.), *Human Rights Obligations of Business: Beyond the Corporate Responsibility to Respect* (Cambridge University Press, 2013), p. 141.

responsibility means something, but not always the same thing to everybody'.[37] A universal definition is unfeasible and, for our purposes, unnecessary. Here, we are concerned with CSR in its legal and human rights context. This gives structure to what is otherwise a relatively loose concept. We draw on human rights for the theoretical framework of a company's responsibilities and look at the law to understand the ways that CSR responsibilities are different from or overlap with legal obligations.

In regulatory theory, CSR can be described as a term for the tangled web of networks that govern businesses. Yet, unlike the tendency of regulation to focus mostly on regulation by state agencies or the various forms of self-regulation, CSR is outward looking, having both a legal and social aspect to its responsibilities: '[p]erhaps the crux of the matter is ultimately *there is no such thing as corporate social responsibility, but rather a social dimension inherent in all company's responsibilities*, just as there is an economic dimension to exercising of all its responsibilities'.[38] Viewing modern CSR through this conceptual lens involves recognising the artificiality of the division before the 1950s, as we saw earlier, between the role of government in protecting social cohesion and the like and the role of business in creating wealth. In seeking responsibility[39] and not

[37] D. Votaw, 'Genius Became Rare: A Comment on the Doctrine of Social Responsibility Pt 1', *Calif. Manage. Rev.*, 15(2) (1972) 25, p. 25. The full quote is worth replicating here: 'Corporate social responsibility (CSR) means something, but not always the same thing to everybody. To some it conveys the idea of legal responsibility or liability; to others, it means social responsible behaviour in the ethical sense; to still others, the meaning transmitted is that of 'responsible for' in a causal mode; many simply equate it with a charitable contribution; some take it to mean socially conscious; many of those who embrace it most fervently see it as a mere synonym for legitimacy in the context of belonging or being proper or valid; a few see a sort of fiduciary duty imposing higher standards of behaviour on businessmen than on citizens at large'.

[38] J. M. Lozano et al., *Governments and Corporate Social Responsibility: Public Policies beyond Regulation and Voluntary Compliance* (Basingstoke: Palgrave Macmillan, 2008), p. 15.

[39] The meaning of 'responsibility' in CSR has been researched extensively. For example, A. Voilescu sees the concept of CSR as raising a 'more fundamental normative question related to the nature of responsibility itself': A. Voilescu, 'Changing Paradigms of Corporate Criminal Responsibility: Lessons for Corporate Social Responsibility' in D. McBarnet et al. (eds.), *The New Corporate Accountability: Corporate Social Responsibility and the Law* (Cambridge University Press, 2007), p. 399. Tom Campbell frames the word 'social' in CSR as having three possible meanings: obligations owed to society, a contrast between social and legal and a question of the content of the obligations to stakeholders rather than shareholders: T. Campbell, 'The Normative Grounding of Corporate Social Responsibility: A Human Rights Approach', in McBarnet ibid., p. 534. Most important for our purposes later on, responsibility carries a certain meaning in terms of business and human rights through the work of John Ruggie, the former Special Representative of the United Nations Secretary General on business and human rights.

just accountability for minimum standards, it is engaging with a more reflective and self-conscious form of self-governance.[40]

The search for a universal definition of CSR seems to be the holy grail of CSR research.[41] This is because, as Adaeze Okoye notes, the lack an accepted definition has been linked to a lack of agreement on the normative underpinnings of CSR.[42] The issue, to put it simply, is: what exactly is CSR rooted in? Okoye persuasively argues that a definition of CSR is subject to never-ending disputes concerning its meaning and that therefore a single definition is unattainable.[43] Rather, what is needed is what she calls a common reference point. This 'sets out the parameters of the debate and identifies the common basis that indicates that all such arguments relate to the same concept'.[44] The common reference point for CSR, she argues, is the relationship between business and society.[45] This approach finds company with other authors such as Michael Blowfield and Alan Murray, who approach it in this way, stating that treating CSR as an umbrella term 'captures the various ways in which business' relationship with society is being defined, managed, and acted upon'.[46] Therefore, in approaching CSR conceptually in this book, we will treat CSR as an umbrella term for the business and society relationship.

In approaching CSR in this way, self-regulation can be seen to be a narrower, targeted concept. Self-regulation is typically the method deployed to achieve the end goal of CSR, and, therefore, the two concepts are intrinsically linked. However, it cannot be said that the rules or standards used in those circumstances always encompass the wider CSR objective nor that self-regulation is the only tool to achieve this objective. For example, co-regulatory measures might be used. For human rights issues, advocacy might at times be the most appropriate CSR tool, particularly when interpretation of law or a lack thereof is at

---

[40] C. Parker, 'Meta-Regulation: Legal Accountability for Corporate Social Responsibility', in McBarnet ibid., p. 213.

[41] There are compelling theories of CSR, notably the theory of A. G. Scherer and G. Palazzo that CSR should be viewed from a Habermasian perspective in which corporations are not just subject to rules but are part of the democratic process of rule setting: 'Toward a Political Conception of Corporate Social Responsibility: Business and Society Seen from a Habermasian Perspective', *Academy of Management Review*, 32(4) (2007) 1096.

[42] A. Okoye, 'Theorising Corporate Social Responsibility as an Essentially Contested Concept: Is a Definition Necessary?', *J. Bus. Ethics*, 89 (2009) 613, p. 614.

[43] She argues that CSR constitutes an essentially contested concept (ECC), a theory that states that certain concepts by their natures, and against certain criteria, are contested. Ibid.

[44] Ibid., p. 623.　[45] Ibid.　[46] Blowfield and Murray n. 6, p. 16.

issue.[47] As will be discussed, the European Commission (EC) and the UK government now approach CSR as corporate-led responsibility underpinned by government regulation.[48]

In the area of internet and free speech (the focus of this book), a company's CSR commitment is not always framed as a set of rules, but rather as sharing of knowledge, information or, particularly in the technology industry, innovation. Google's Transparency Report, for example, provides information on government requests for content removal, requests from copyright owner for removal of search results and requests for user information.[49] Facebook provides a report link next to content to facilitate complaints of abusive content or spam.[50] Both are arguably a component of those businesses' commitment to rights. Whether their package of commitments is effective and sufficient for the promotion and protection of free speech is a question interrogated throughout this book. When done effectively, arguably, CSR is reflected in a system of regulation, whether at the level of the individual company or industry-wide,[51] because a regulatory framework better facilitates standard setting, monitoring and enforcement. This illustrates the complexity of the relationships among CSR, law and human rights, something examined in Sections 3.2 and 3.3. It also supports the argument that internet regulatory discussions should be more explicitly extended to take account of CSR and its reach beyond the law in the way it is done in the book, in particular as proposed in Chapter 6. Discussions thus far have tended to fold CSR too simply within discussions of self-regulation.

---

[47] See later discussion of Bronwen Morgan et al. on the differences between regulation and human rights, which can be extended to consider CSR, regulation and human rights: B. Morgan (ed.), *The Intersection of Rights and Regulation: New Directions in Sociolegal Scholarship* (Aldershot: Ashgate, 2007).

[48] See Section 3.2 for a fuller discussion of the European Commission and UK approaches.

[49] See Google's Transparency Report, at www.google.com/transparencyreport/ (last visited 30 October 2014). It also contributes to Chilling Effects, at www.chillingeffects.org (last visited 30 October 2014).

[50] See Facebook, 'How to report things', at www.facebook.com/help/181495968648557 (last visited 30 October 2014).

[51] This view of CSR and self-regulation is not without controversy. Benedict Sheehy, for example, argues that that CSR is a private self-regulatory system: 'Understanding CSR: An Empirical Study of Private Self-Regulation', *Monash Law Review*, 38(2) (2011) 1. He states, 'CSR articulates a publicly oriented organizational commitment placing it within society's larger normative context. Such an understanding of CSR is wholly consistent with it as a regulatory system, indeed underpins CSR as every regulatory system must have a normative foundation': ibid., p. 6.

The appropriate theoretical framework for CSR in the context of this book is human rights. There have been several human rights-based approaches to CSR instruments, notably the UN Global Compact[52] (discussed later in this chapter). All such approaches draw their theoretical framework from the Universal Declaration of Human Rights (UDHR). As noted by Tom Campbell, 'CSR is replete with human rights concepts (and vice versa)'.[53] Campbell argues that, regardless of how one approaches CSR, it arguably draws on human rights discourse, the notion that there are basic and universal standards of morality[54] that inform ones obligations as a member of society:

> When using human rights discourse to legitimate CSR (and indeed to legitimate existing and proposed human rights law), we are drawing on the moral and political discourse of human rights on which social as well as legal obligations may be founded. In this mode, human rights are those basic human interests that ought to be recognised and guaranteed by the social, economic and political arrangements in place in all human societies. What we are drawing on here is the idea of basic universal interests of overriding moral significance, rather than any existing set of international conventions or positive legal systems.[55]

As opposed to Campbell, it is not argued here that human rights discourse forms the basis of *all* social responsibilities of businesses; instead, I seek to highlight that in asking whether IIGs have any human rights responsibilities, human rights principles naturally become the theoretical underpinning of the framework. We are left with many questions; namely, how to judge whether such principles have been met. The best approach will be outlined in Section 3.5. In addition, the difficulty, Campbell rightly notes, is in articulating the nature of the human rights duties of companies and conceptually distinguishing such duties from those imposed on citizens or the state.[56] The question of how a business is responsible, for what and to whom dominates CSR research and is

---

[52] United Nations Global Compact, 'The Ten Principles', at www.unglobalcompact.org /AboutTheGC/TheTenPrinciples/index.html (last visited 17 June 2014).

[53] Campbell n. 39, p. 553.

[54] This is not engaging in a debate about the difference between ethical and moral approaches to human rights: see J. Habermas, 'Human Rights and Popular Sovereignty: The Liberal and Republican Versions', Ratio Juris, 7(1) (1994) 1.

[55] Campbell n. 39, pp. 553–54.

[56] Ibid., p. 553. Campbell is of the view that human rights might not be able to offer a legal framework for corporate social responsibility, offering instead a discourse framework; however, his view is limited by his approach to CSR as something voluntary: pp. 557–58.

especially problematic in the arena of digital human rights. It is this dilemma that is tested in the case studies in Chapters 4 and 5.

There are two aspects to how CSR will be approached in this book that must be untangled further. As we have seen, the operation of IIGs and their impact on democratic culture takes place at the fringes of where the law ends and social responsibility begins. There is a nexus here of CSR, law and human rights. We must therefore unpick the relationship between the law and CSR, as well as the relationship between CSR and human rights, to pave the way for more thoughtful assessment of the responsibilities of IIGs for freedom of expression.

Regardless of the theoretical approach we take to CSR, as a governance tool CSR struggles to overcome criticisms that it is weak window-dressing that only serves to deflect or delay much-needed legislative attention. In the area of internet governance, as will be shown in the case studies, some of these criticisms resonate more than others; thus, the following section will highlight some of the leading criticisms of CSR in practice. The goal is not to resolve the various criticisms of CSR. Quite the contrary. The question in examining IIGs is whether the CSR frameworks that govern their activities are subject to the same weaknesses identified regarding CSR frameworks in general and whether this renders such frameworks incapable of protecting and respecting freedom of expression.

### 3.1.3.  Critiques of CSR

There are four main critiques of CSR.[57] The first argument says that CSR is anti-business because it stifles the primary purpose of business, which is to serve the shareholders' interests. This would be the Milton Friedman argument that corporate responsibility hampers a company's ability to maximise profits.[58] Under this argument, some go so far as to assert that CSR is against the law because it constitutes a breach of fiduciary duty of

---

[57] In general, see Blowfield and Murray n. 6, chapter 13, and the discussion in Crane n. 4, chapter two. Another approach is that of D. Doane in 'The Myth of CSR: The Problem with Assuming That Companies Can Do Well While also Doing Good Is That Markets Don't Really Work That Way', *SSIR*, 3(3) (2005) 23. See also the work of J. Balkan, in particular his book *The Corporation: The Pathological Pursuit of Profit and Power* (London: Constable and Robinson Ltd., 2005), although better known for the accompanying documentary of the same name arguing that corporations have the personalities of psychopaths.

[58] See M. Friedman, *Capitalism and Freedom* (University of Chicago Press, 1962); Blowfield and Murray n. 6, pp. 342–44.

the owners to the shareholders to maximise their profits: 'CSR can be seen in this context not so much as management proudly going beyond legal obligation, but, in effect, as management going beyond its legal powers (acting *ultra vires*) or even breaching its fiduciary duty to the owners'.[59] This has been generally dismissed as an oversimplification of the law,[60] but we must be mindful of not stretching corporate responsibilities too far, particularly concerning potential positive duties on companies to facilitate freedom of expression.

The second argument is the exact opposite, arguing that CSR is pro-business, favouring the needs of business over the needs of society. As with the first argument, this one is based on the idea that the role of business in society is in need of realignment, but it then disagrees as to the causes of this imbalance and the way to solve it. This argument sees CSR as too weak to protect the public good.[61] For example, Enron had a code of conduct to prevent corporate crime, but because the culture of Enron was geared primarily to increasing the price of stock, the code was ignored or overrode, with executives aiming instead for the bottom line and relying on legal advice that told them what they were doing was lawful.[62] There are many variations within this argument – that CSR needs a better framework, that it is not enough, that it has been captured by business interests and so on – but the essence is the same. One aspect of this will be teased out further, and this is the idea that CSR has been captured by business interests.

This argument proposes that businesses used to engage in philanthropy, but now CSR is treated as something to be managed by their public relations departments.[63] This 'social branding', as Ivan Manokha describes it, involves associating a company's products or services with 'morally good' notions, thus creating an emotional attachment for

---

[59] D. McBarnet, 'Corporate Social Responsibility beyond Law, through Law, for Law: The New Corporate Accountability', in McBarnet n. 39, p. 23.

[60] Ibid., see Chapter 1 in this regard.    [61] Blowfield and Murray n. 6, pp. 345–49.

[62] This legal advice, as we know, turned out to be flawed: C. Pitts and J. Sherman, 'Human Rights Corporate Accountability Guide: From Laws to Norms to Values', Working Paper No. 51, Corporate Social Responsibility Initiative (December 2008), pp. 15–16.

[63] Shamir n. 8, pp. 100–103. There is also a less-discussed issue in the area of CSR, which is an extension of the idea that CSR has been captured by business interests. Referred to as market-oriented NGO (MaNGO), it describes bodies such as the International Chamber of Commerce (ICC) and other NGOs that are sponsored by business but have the air of independence more often associated with civil society entities. Although they may appear disinterested, what they do is 'disseminate and actualize corporate-inspired versions of "social responsibility"': ibid., p. 105.

consumers to the product (by buying the product, they feel that they, too, are helping the environment or protecting human rights) and thus attracting brand loyalty and boosting sales.[64] Here, CSR is a 'project' or 'marketing device', thus commoditising social responsibility and concealing the deeper issues underlying this uneasy relationship between business and society.[65]

Google's philanthropy site, www.google.org, for example, aims to use technology to address 'global challenges',[66] such as mapping deforestation or tracking flu trends.[67] Is this corporate responsibility or mere social branding? For the purposes of the beneficiaries of these activities, does it matter? Google also has a crisis response project managed through this site. After the devastating earthquake and tsunami in Japan in 2011, Google launched a tool to help find missing people.[68] This might be both philanthropy and branding at work. To those who are looking for a missing loved one, this question is largely irrelevant. If the perspective is shifted away from the beneficiaries, however, it is arguable that what appears to be philanthropy is a distraction from the real activity in question, namely, the collection and storage of large amounts of user data through its search service,[69] which is what enables this philanthropic activity. In this way, google.org is a promotional device for justifying the collection of user data for its search service.

The third argument is that CSR is too narrow, excluding from its remit key elements of the business-society relationship such as flexible work hours, minority rights and issues of wage disparity between executives and employees. Here, CSR is often faulted for not being a formalised

---

[64] I. Manokha, 'Corporate Social Responsibility: A New Signifier? An Analysis of Business Ethics and Good Business Practice', *Politics*, 24(1) (2004) 56. Also I. Manokha, 'Business Ethics and the Spirit of Global Capitalism: Moral Leadership in the Context of Global Hegemony', *Journal of Global Ethics*, 2(1) (2006) 27. And see discussion in Shamir n. 8, p. 103.

[65] Ibid., p. 109.

[66] Google.org, at www.google.org/index.html (last visited 17 June 2014).

[67] Google.org Flu Trends, at www.google.org/flutrends/about/how.html (last visited 17 June 2014). There were arguments that Google Flu trends was faster and just as accurate as the CDC, but some research questions this: Science Daily, 'Google flu trends estimates off, study finds', at www.sciencedaily.com/releases/2010/05/100517101714.htm (last visited 17 June 2014).

[68] Person Finder 2011 Japan Earthquake, at http://japan.person-finder.appspot.com/?lang=en (last visited 27 July 2011, link now deactivated).

[69] See J. van Hoboken, *Search Engine Freedom: On the Implications of the Right to Freedom of Expression for the Legal Governance of Web Search Services* (Amsterdam: Kluwer Law International, 2012), pp. 323–24. More generally, P. Bernal, *Internet Privacy Rights: Rights to Protect Autonomy* (Cambridge University Press, 2014), chapters 4 and 5.

codification of law, which tends to expect CSR to be the same thing as more traditional command-and-control legal measures and also misunderstands the incapacitating effect of globalisation on a government's power to act. That said, the argument is not against CSR per se, but against the limited range of issues CSR currently addresses, although this is changing. The issues covered by the ISO 26000 Guidance Standard on Social Responsibility,[70] for example, are extensive, although this does not necessarily translate into internalisation of the commitment in a company's governance structure. The provisions on freedom of expression provide little more than a commitment to Article 19 of the UDHR, which provides minimal practical guidance to a company such as Twitter on how to navigate free speech issues.[71]

The fourth argument is that CSR simply does not achieve what it sets out to achieve. This is a catch-all criticism, with elements of all three of the criticisms just described. In reference to the UN Global Compact (discussed later), where only 3 per cent of TNCs have signed up, one author commented, '[i]n what realm of life other than the strange world of [corporate responsibility] would a 2–3 per cent take-up rate be considered to be a success?'[72] At the heart of it is a question of progress, asking whether CSR actually impacts corporate behaviour. This is a difficult argument for proponents of CSR to rebut because the link between CSR policies and real-world impact can be difficult to prove.[73] What can be shown is increased membership in CSR initiatives, such as the UN Global Compact or industry initiatives such as the Forest Stewardship Council for responsible forest management. What is more difficult to establish is whether the end goal of the CSR initiative, such as protection of the environment or workers conditions, is enabled by CSR or whether it simply detracts or delays from other efforts to regulate firm behaviour.

These criticisms highlight what we saw earlier; that perhaps we haven't moved much beyond simply trying to define what CSR is as a field of research. Whether these criticisms resonate concerning governance of speech by IIGs will be examined in the case studies in Chapters 4 and 5. However, to address these critiques in the context of IIGs, two conceptual problems require further examination. The first to be addressed is the

---

[70] It can be viewed at www.iso.org/obp/ui/#iso:std:iso:26000:ed-1:v1:en (last visited 10 June 2014).

[71] This is drawn from one of the final drafts of the ISO 26000; the content is no longer available.

[72] Blowfield and Murray n. 6, p. 353.     [73] See discussion ibid., p. 353–57.

relationship between CSR and the law to tease out differences between purely voluntary responsibilities and legal obligation and when the two overlap. The second to be examined is the relationship between CSR and human rights and how state and businesses human rights responsibilities operate in the context of international human rights law and policy.

## 3.2. CSR and the law

One of the main conceptual problems for CSR is its relationship with the law, and this ultimately becomes a question of the legal nature of voluntary codes because many CSR frameworks are voluntary in nature. The struggle to understand this and then determine whether CSR is consequently sufficient as a governance structure is threaded through the critiques of CSR, as we saw earlier. Voluntariness is particularly significant in the area of internet governance, where voluntary codes are a key governance tool of the type of companies that qualify as IIGs.[74]

Within Europe, there is confusion whether to treat CSR as something purely voluntary. The European Commission used to root its approach in voluntarism, pushing for multi-stakeholderism, with governments taking on more of a supportive than legislative role and companies being positioned as the 'principal actors'.[75] At that time, the European Parliament favoured regulatory mechanisms.[76] The European Commission and European Parliament are now aligned in their approach, drawing from the Commission's 2011 Communication on *A renewed EU strategy 2011–14 for Corporate Social Responsibility*.[77]

In this Communication, the Commission advocates a mixed approach combining corporate-led responsibility underpinned by government

---

[74] This is illustrated in the case studies in Chapters 4 and 5. See also J. G. Palfrey, Jr., 'Reluctant Gatekeepers: Corporate Ethics on a Filtered Internet', in *Global Information Technology Report* (World Economic Forum: 2006–2007), and U. Gasser, 'Responsibility for Human Rights Violations, Acts or Omissions, Within the "Sphere of Influence" of Companies', *Working Paper Series* (December 2007).

[75] For history of EU approach, see Voilescu n. 39. The EU has published a significant number of papers on the subject maters. See the following reports: Green Paper, 'Promoting a European Framework for Corporate Social Responsibility', *COM* (2001) 366; *European Multi-Stakeholder Forum on CSR: Final Results and Recommendations* (29 June 2004); Communication, 'Implementing the Partnership for and Jobs: Making Europe a Pole of Excellence on Corporate Social Responsibility', *COM* (2006) 136.

[76] See discussion in Voilescu n. 39, pp. 382–86.    [77] *COM* (2011) 681.

activity. CSR is still described as something voluntary, but it adds a government role that reflects the broader notion of accountability.[78] However, the language used to describe the government's role is vague and only serves to muddy its role:

> Corporate social responsibility concerns actions by companies over and above their legal obligations towards society and the environment. Certain regulatory measures create an environment more conducive to enterprises voluntarily meeting their social responsibility.[79]

This indicates a movement to something less than voluntary while still using the language of voluntariness. The government's role appears to be to set the course for companies' voluntary obligations through the use, where appropriate, of regulatory measures. This might embed what Peter Utting calls *articulated regulation*, wherein different regulatory approaches come together in ways that are complementary or mutually reinforcing.[80]

This is a more robust engagement with CSR, one better reflecting the complexity of the regulatory and social environment in which businesses operate. However, more clarity is needed on the kinds of complementary regulation that would satisfy this vision and retain flexibility on the part of companies. By intertwining public and private arenas of regulation, there must be awareness, at minimum, of the implications of this to areas of the law, such as human rights, where the legal framework has long depended on a division between public and private spheres. Despite this, the Commission's focus remains on companies leading in the area of CSR, defining CSR as 'the responsibility of enterprises for their impacts on society'.[81]

The United Kingdom historically promoted a voluntary approach to CSR backed by soft regulation, with management of CSR taking place through the Department of Business, Innovation and Skills (BIS).[82]

---

[78] See P. Utting, 'Rethinking business regulation: from self-regulation to social control', Technology, Business and Society Programme Paper Number 15, United Nations Research Institute for Social Development (2005).

[79] Communication n. 77, para. 1.     [80] See Utting n. 78.

[81] Communication n. 70, para. 3.1.

[82] Created in 2009 after the disbandment of the Department of Business, Enterprise and Regulatory Reform (BERR), which was also created on the disbandment of another department, the Department of Trade and Industry in 2007. CSR, as defined by BIS is 'essentially about companies moving beyond a base of legal compliance to integrating socially responsible behaviour into their core values, in recognition of the sound business benefits in doing so'. See now archived http://webarchive.nationalarchives.gov.uk/+/http://www.berr.gov.uk/whatwedo/sectors/sustainability/corp-responsibility/page45192.html/ (last visited 16 July 2014).

Joseph Lozano described the UK regime as business in the community model, where government acts as the promoter and facilitator of CSR. Although human rights were not a focus of the UK government's approach to CSR, human rights issues more recently have infiltrated their considerations,[83] although the focus remained on conduct of businesses overseas until 2012–2013.[84]

In September 2013, the United Kingdom launched an action plan on business and human rights designed to guide businesses on how to incorporate human rights into their operations.[85] It seeks to implement the UN Guiding Principles, a framework on human rights and business created through the stewardship of John Ruggie, discussed in detail later in this chapter. It is a significant step, with the government publishing the strongest language to date on the responsibilities of businesses and human rights: '[t]he Government strongly believes that the promotion of business and respect for human rights should go hand in hand'.[86]

Relevant to the discussion of CSR and the law is how the government frames its relationship with business.[87] It uses language of support, describing its role as to 'help' companies implement the Guiding Principles. It underpins this support with soft mechanisms such as the provision of a business and human rights toolkit and training courses, as well as harder mechanisms such as consideration of human rights in awarding export licences and procurement contracts.[88] The EC model of corporate-led responsibility underpinned by government regulation or other support is clearly now present in the UK approach to CSR.

As this shows, it would be wrong to conceive of CSR, as it is now deployed, as purely extralegal.[89] CSR embraces elements of both: '[i]f CSR is self-governance by business, it is nonetheless self-governance that has received a very firm push from external social and market forces.

---

[83] See HM Government, *Corporate Responsibility Report* (BERR, February 2009). Compare it to HM Government, *Corporate Social Responsibility* (DTI, May 2004) where there was no mention of human rights.

[84] See also discussion in Lozano n. 38, pp. 93–100, and other chapters in this book for various other models of CSR used in other countries.

[85] HM Government, *Good Business: Implementing the UN Guiding Principles on Business and Human Rights* (September 2013).

[86] Ibid., Foreword.    [87] Ibid., section 3.    [88] Ibid.

[89] As S. Picciotto states, '[c]odes entail a degree of formalization of normative expectations and practices. Even if they are not laws, they may have indirect legal effects': 'Rights, Responsibilities and Regulation of International Business', *Columbia Journal of Transnational Law*, 42 (2003) 131, p. 145.

From the start "voluntary" CSR has been socially and economically driven'.[90] These social and economic factors show that CSR can be driven by many things – governments, NGOs, consumers, investors and branding. Such drivers can take legal and nonlegal forms. Utting contends that there has been a shift from softer approaches focused on voluntariness to harder approaches focused on accountability, what he describes as the 'ratcheting-up of voluntary initiatives'.[91] This ratcheting-up can be observed in the United Kingdom and is characterised by monitoring, reporting, certification schemes and codes of conduct, as well as by support through law and policy.[92] This complicates the regulatory picture, blurring the lines between traditional notions of CSR as purely voluntary and the law. There are thus two levels to CSR as it is used in relation to the law, which will be elaborated on herein. At the first level is what I term *pure-CSR*, which refers to solely the use of voluntary codes as a governance tool. At the next level are the indirect ways that CSR can influence the development of the law and the law can encourage CSR-type responsibilities.

The main difference between voluntary codes and public law legal regimes is that the latter apply to everyone, whether or not they agree to be bound by the regimes, whereas it is the opposite with voluntary codes. Voluntary codes are based on consensus, so it is difficult to compel companies to abide by the codes, yet such companies might free-ride off the legitimacy and goodwill such codes create.[93] This can create a race to the bottom, where companies operate in jurisdictions with the least regulatory oversight on matters of social concern such as the environment, human rights or health and safety regulation in order to compete with other firms that have chosen the same route. In addition, if the codes are poorly drafted, this will cause frustration and misunderstandings and attract negative publicity. It might even slow the adoption of needed laws to govern the area or create barriers to trade. Often, the creation of the code is spurred by efforts of industry to stave off government regulation,[94] something Aurora Voiculescu calls 'interactive voluntarism'.[95] In

---

[90] McBarnet n. 59, p. 12; see also pp. 14–22.   [91] Utting, n. 78, p. 6.   [92] Ibid., pp. 5–8.

[93] K. Webb and A. Morrison, 'The Law and Voluntary Codes: Examining the "Tangled Web"' in n. 31, pp. 109–10.

[94] As discussed in Chapter 4, this is the reason for the creation of the Internet Watch Foundation. This can also be seen with the Press Complaints Commission.

[95] 'Interactive voluntarism' is where purportedly self-regulatory regimes often originate from the government, or, if they don't, they are overseen or underpinned in some way by regulatory interventions: Voilescu n. 39, p. 373.

addition, voluntary codes risk 'muting' real political struggles on important social issues behind the mask of management allocation of duties,[96] effectively internalising public interest issues.

However, voluntary codes are not wholly incompatible with the public interest; rather, they can be a method for operationalising policy objectives.[97] Such codes can be a method for putting into place policy objectives in a way that the law cannot because companies might commit to standards that are beyond their legal requirements. Furthermore, the voluntary nature of the commitment embraces the wider notion of responsibility at the core of CSR, encouraging firms to internalise the policy objectives rather than aim for base compliance.[98] Kernaghan-Webb, in his book *Voluntary Codes*, summarises the main advantages and disadvantages of voluntary codes as follows:

> Compared with laws, the main advantages of voluntary rule systems centre around their flexibility and lower costs, speed in developing and amending rules, avoidance of jurisdictional concerns, potential for positive use of market, peer pressure, internalization of responsibility, and informality. Compared to laws, typical drawbacks of voluntary codes include generally lower visibility, credibility, difficulty in applying the rules to free riders, less likelihood of rigorous standards being developed, uncertain public accountability, and a more limited array of potential sanctions.[99]

The relationship between the law and voluntary codes therefore can be seen to be dynamic. They often work together to achieve positive results, with the law affecting the development of codes and vice versa.[100] The law might enable the development of codes by creating the framework or tools for the drafting of the code. The law in this respect might also act as a constraint on the nature of the rules set out in a code, setting limits on acceptable behaviour as much as enabling it.[101] For example, creative commons licensing is an alternative regime for copyright protection, one in which the copyright owner, working within the regime of copyright and contract law, licenses out his or her work pursuant to an alternative and voluntary set of rules.[102] The licensing scheme can be seen here to piggyback the law.

---

[96]  Webb n. 31, p. 14.    [97]  Ibid.    [98]  Ibid.
[99]  Ibid., p. 27. He classifies CSR differently from the approach here, however. He sees CSR as a type of private governance, one that emphasises an *aspect* of action by companies to 'organise their affairs': ibid., p. 12.
[100]  Ibid., p. 27.    [101]  Webb and Morrison n. 93, pp. 100–101.
[102]  Creative Commons, at http://creativecommons.org/ (last visited 17 June 2014).

Codes can also affect the creation and interpretation of laws. For example, voluntary codes might be referred to in the drawing up of legal requirements.[103] Carola Glinski distinguishes between two types of corporate self-regulation: '*published* codes of conduct, guidelines or agreements on the one hand; and *internal* regulation in contracts, management handbooks or simply through the internal organisation by multinational enterprises of their environmental and safety management on the other hand'.[104] This does two things. First, it creates for the market legitimate expectations in, for example, contracts law, misleading advertising or reasonable consumer expectations under sales law. Second, it establishes a standard against which courts and tribunals assess conduct.[105] Thus, voluntary codes can be referred to in a tort case to determine the standard of care or have contract law implications for breaches thereof by industry members.[106]

Recently, in Canada, in *Choc* v. *Hudbay Minerals Inc.*,[107] the Court refused to strike out three related claims against the mining company Hudbay Minerals for alleged human rights abuses of security personnel working for its subsidiaries in Guatemala: namely, shooting, killing and gang-raping the plaintiffs. The decision is precedent-setting concerning the liability of Canadian companies for the acts of its foreign-based subsidiaries. Relevant here is consideration of the Court of CSR codes. Amnesty International as intervenor argued that CSR commitments of Hudbay, as well as the Canadian government, formed the basis of a direct duty of care on the part of Hudbay to the Plaintiffs. In this case, Hudbay had apparently stated that the *Voluntary Principles on Security and Human Rights* 'guided their corporate conduct'.[108] Amnesty International cited the Canadian government's endorsement of the leading CSR instruments such as the UN Guiding Principles, the OECD Guidelines for Multinational Enterprises and the above-mentioned

---

[103] See examples in Webb and Morrison n. 93, pp. 141–43. For example, a CSR code on hockey helmets standards has been incorporated into law in Canada in the Hazardous Products Act R.S.C. 1985, c. H-3, s. 43. See discussion A. Morrison and K. Webb, 'Bicycle Helmets and Hockey Helmet Regulations: Two Approaches to Safety Protection' in Webb n. 31.

[104] C. Glinski, 'Corporate Codes of Conduct: Moral or Legal Obligation?', in McBarnet n. 39, p. 121.

[105] Ibid., pp. 121–35.

[106] See discussion in Webb and Morrison n. 93. See *Kasky* v. *Nike*, 45 P. 3d 243 (Cal. 2002), where a false statement in a report on working conditions arising from a code of conduct was evidence of false advertising.

[107] 2013 ONSC 1414.     [108] Ibid., para. 33.

principles on security as, in effect, defining the framework for a duty of care: '[a]s such, Canadian courts should have no difficulty in recognizing these principles and drawing upon international norms and standards of conduct in considering whether a Canadian corporation owes a duty of care in the circumstances of this case'.[109]

We can see two levels to a potentially developing duty of care at work here, both drawn from CSR instruments. First, Hudbay's commitment to codes establishes the voluntary commitment of a particular business to a level of duty of care. Second, the commitment of the Canadian Government sets the reasonably expectation of companies concerning standards of conduct. In this way, the normative framework that has been historically at work in fields such as human rights as applied to governments (as seen in the UDHR) now works to set the standard of conduct of companies through other legal mechanisms, such as tort law. The Court recognised the policy argument as not clearly unsustainable (the requirement to have a claim struck out).[110] At the time of writing, this case is ongoing and will be important to follow concerning the relationship between CSR codes and legal liability.

Doreen McBarnet summarises the complex relationship as follows:

> Legal doctrines and processes are being used by NGOs [nongovernmental organisations] as part of their strategy, and market forces are being stimulated and facilitated by legal measures. At the same time, of course, much of the momentum for legal intervention has come from the CSR movement and from the change of culture it reflects and promotes.
>
> How is law being brought into play? Governments are fostering CSR through indirect regulation, old legal rights are being put to new uses, and private law – tort and contract law – are being used, tort law to extend the legal enforceability of CSR issues, contract law to give CSR standards the weight of legal obligation.[111]

CSR-type considerations are increasingly being incorporated into corporate legislation and judicial decisions. For example, the UK government indirectly regulated it by introducing legislation that required disclosure of whether social, environmental and ethical considerations (basically CSR considerations) were taken into account in investment decisions concerning pension funds.[112] Although these considerations were not legally required, the disclosure of whether they were or were not considered led to an increase in the number of pension funds that took

---

[109] Ibid., para. 36.    [110] Ibid., paras. 71–75.    [111] McBarnet n. 59, p. 32.
[112] Occupational Pension Schemes (Investment, and Assignment, Forfeiture, Bankruptcy etc.) Amendment Regulations, 1999 No. 1849, regulation 11A.

companies' CSR policies into account.[113] As of October 2013, the
Companies Act 2006 (Strategic Report and Directors' Report)
Regulations requires that listed UK companies report on human
rights issues in their annual reports, including on any human rights
policies and the effectiveness of these policies.[114] Defamation reform
in the United Kingdom resulted in a clause in the Crime and Courts
Act that, in determining whether to award exemplary damages against
a news publisher, the Court will take into account, among other
things, whether there were any internal compliance procedures in
place and whether they were adhered to.[115] Two Canadian cases
have held that the legal requirement that company directors consider
the best interests of the corporation meant taking into consideration
their responsibility to stakeholders as well.[116] The US Congress
amended its Sentencing Guidelines for Organizational Defendants
'to require that boards of directors ensure that their companies have
cultures that facilitate *ethical* conduct as well as legally compliant
conduct'.[117]

Christine Parker explores this relationship asking 'how is it possible for
the *law* to make companies accountable for going *beyond the law*?'[118] In
her answer she employs the concept of meta-regulation, which in governance literatures is 'seen as increasingly about "collaborations", "partnerships", "webs" or "networks" in which the state, state-promulgated
law, and especially hierarchical command-and-control regulation, is not
necessarily the dominant, and certainly not the only important, mechanism of regulation'.[119] Brought within this term is the concept of

---

[113] McBarnet n. 59, p. 32. This kind of indirect regulation is at the heart of gatekeeper
regulation, as seen in the oil tanker example discussed at the beginning of Chapter 2.
[114] 2013/1970, s. 414C(7).   [115] Crime and Courts Act 2013 c. 22, s. 35.
[116] Pitts and Sherman n. 62, p. 9, referring to *Teck Corporation Ltd.* v. *Millar* [1972] 33 D.L.
R. (3d) 288 and *Peoples Department Stores* v. *Wise* [2004] 3 S.C.R. 461.
[117] Pitts and Sherman ibid., p. 16. These Guidelines were enacted in order to create
uniformity in the sentencing of companies for crimes carried out by its employees.
They were designed using principles of due diligence to prevent corporate crime: ibid.,
pp. 10–11.
[118] Parker n. 40, p. 207.
[119] Ibid., p. 210. Colin Scott defines it thus: 'businesses should be required to take steps
geared to acting with social responsibility, but without a detailed specification in the law
as to what those steps should be'. C. Scott, 'Reflexive Governance, Meta-Regulation, and
Corporate Social Responsibility: The Heineken Effect', in N. Boeger et al. (eds.),
*Perspectives on Corporate Social Responsibility* (Cheltenham, Eward Elgar, 2008),
pp. 174–75.

regulation of other regulators, such as oversight of regulatory bodies by boards or accreditation agencies.[120]

Parker was interested in how the law can encourage CSR, and Colin Scott extends her work by looking at how non-law stimuli can act in a meta-regulatory capacity to encourage CSR. Scott cautions that legal responses, such as requiring reporting, risk being regarded by companies as just another obligation, whereas pressure from the market or community (referring to the Scott and Murray model of regulatory modalities)[121] might encourage companies to take a more fundamental look at how they conduct business.[122] He cites, for example the UK advertising industry self-regulating through its Advertising Association since 1962, which was partly spurred by the publication of an influential 1957 book by Vance Packard, *The Hidden Persuaders*.[123] The threat here was posed by the publication of a book, which incentivised the companies to act. His point is that public shaming, boycotts and similar avenues of action, all have the effect of incentivising firms to change behaviour so that they have the community's approval to operate.[124] Thus, from a regulatory theory perspective, the question is how the various regulatory modalities can be used to encourage CSR-type initiatives, rather than as simple minimal accountability mechanisms.

Utting frames the dynamic in broader terms as articulated regulation, discussed briefly earlier, in which, rather than focusing on bringing together different regulatory players (co-regulation), the focus is on bringing together different regulatory approaches in complementary and synergistic ways (articulated).[125] Through this, we can move beyond the voluntary versus binding debate. He identifies the line between voluntariness and the law as having significant potential for regulatory intervention. The key is to find ways for emerging private systems of regulation to be complementary, or to find the link between confrontational approaches (i.e., protests) and collaborative ones (i.e., stakeholder dialogue). For example, protests and naming and shaming can drive take-up of stakeholder-driven initiatives. In terms of law and voluntariness, many of the methods discussed herein, such as legislation requiring reporting on CSR policies or government threats of regulation if CSR codes are not committed to are forms of articulated regulation. This feeds

---

[120] Parker n. 40, pp. 210–11.   [121] Murray and Scott n. 16, p. 491.
[122] Scott n. 119, pp. 177–78.   [123] Ibid., p. 179.   [124] Ibid., pp. 175–78.
[125] See Utting, n. 78.

into the idea that there needs to be greater awareness of the regulatory environment at work for any given industry or organisation.

It is within this complex dynamic that we turn to human rights and see the potential and drawbacks of CSR to operationalise human rights objectives in the internet environment. When looking at CSR and the law, we learn that the line between voluntariness and the law is not as neatly defined as it initially appears, and the two intersect and feed off each other. Ultimately, however, the law pulls CSR in the direction of rule-setting. When looking at CSR and human rights, the Section 3.3 will show that they have a lot in common. Both have legal and extralegal dimensions with a common underpinning of morality. This has allowed human rights to become the basis of many CSR initiatives, discussed later. At the same time, however, human rights law applies directly to states, not to private companies. CSR thus becomes a powerful link between human rights and the law in the private sphere, with much promise but also certain undeniable weaknesses. The question is whether the weaknesses are insurmountable for governance of IIGs.

## 3.3. CSR and human rights

The debate about whether companies are required to be responsible for human rights standards and, if so, the extent of this responsibility, has been a popular topic of discussion. In the internet context, the transnational, instantaneous nature of internet communications makes it difficult for governments to directly control the information that enters and leaves a country, whereas, at the same time, the power of internet gatekeepers, which do control this information flow, increases. This is problematic for a human rights system that has treated human rights as a government responsibility[126] and has 'forced a reconsideration of the

---

[126] For example, the United Kingdom's Human Rights Act 1998 Ch 42 is only directly binding on 'public authorities': s. 6. Although the BBC may arguably be a public authority because it is created by Royal Charter (see discussion in H. Fenwick & G. Phillipson, *Media Freedom under the Human Rights Act* (Oxford University Press, 2006), pp. 607–608), companies such as Google and Microsoft would fall clearly outside traditional conceptions of public authority. Canada more narrowly applies its Canadian Charter of Rights and Freedoms 1982 c. 11 to Parliament, provincial legislatures, and federal and provincial governments: s. 32. Note, however, that Amnesty International views the Universal Declaration of Human Rights as applicable to companies as 'organs of society', as referenced in the Preamble: see P. Frankental and F. House, 'Human Rights – Is It any of Your Business?' (2000) *Amnesty International*, p. 8.

boundaries between the private and public spheres'.[127] This blurring of the public–private divide is the fissure in which CSR has been flourishing.

What is the link between CSR and human rights? It is a common underpinning of morality in a framework with legal and extralegal dimensions. Lozano identified four dimensions to what he calls the 'process' of CSR.[128] The first is 'explicit' CSR, in which CSR is formalised in things such as codes and statements; the second is the 'negative' aspect of CSR, in which minimum levels are set by, for example, procedural rules or sanctions, where certain activities are identified as improper. These are the two areas where regulation can influence their development. The other two processes are 'tacit' CSR, in which we see the intangible elements of CSR such as in a company's history, culture, organisation and the like, and 'propositional' CSR, which is the facilitative and shaping aspect of managing CSR. These latter two are less susceptible to regulation, showing that regulation cannot cover all areas or all aspects of CSR.[129] There is an aspect to CSR where morality holds a business to account in a way that regulation cannot. Lozano sets it out in Figure 3.1.

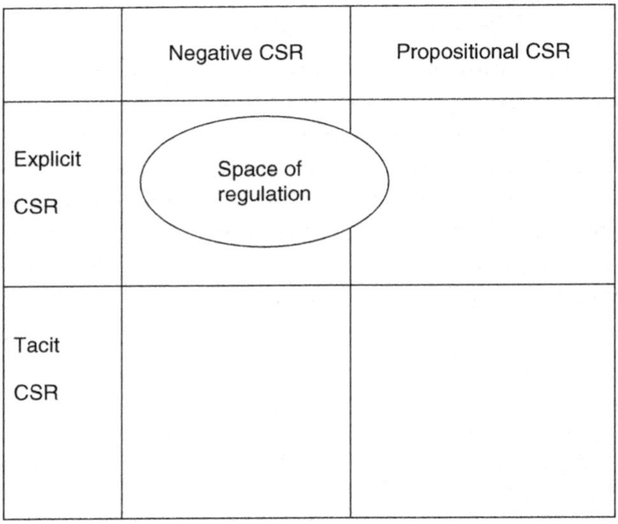

|  | Negative CSR | Propositional CSR |
|---|---|---|
| Explicit CSR | Space of regulation |  |
| Tacit CSR |  |  |

Figure 3.1.  Lozano's CSR grid.[130]

---

[127]  P. Muchlinski, 'The Development of Human Rights Responsibilities for Multinational Enterprises', in R. Sullivan (ed.), *Business and Human Rights: Dilemmas and Solutions* (Sheffield: Greenleaf Publishing, 2003), p. 37.
[128]  Lozano n. 38, p. 12.    [129]  Ibid., pp. 12–13.    [130]  Ibid., p. 13.

Complementary work is being undertaken by Bronwen Morgan concerning the related topic of the intersection of human rights and regulation. Whereas human rights tends to be aspirational and focused on mobilising social change, regulation tends to be instrumental and focused on targeted methods for achieving a particular public interest.[131] The intersection, she posits, is that regulation emerges as the machinery for monitoring and enforcing human rights. In much the same vein, this book examines the administrative structure of freedom of expression in the digital environment. It just so happens that the administrative structure largely takes the form of CSR.

Human rights are both positive and negative rights. They require states to avoid engaging in certain conduct, but they also require states to take positive steps to enable human rights to be protected.[132] In the arena of freedom of expression, this requires states to maintain a system of free expression by protecting individuals and groups from infringement by third parties, as well as by promoting and encouraging freedom of expression through such things as, perhaps, the provision of facilities, regulation of communication mediums, education and ensuring information availability.[133]

This push and pull becomes difficult when we attempt to articulate the responsibilities of companies. It becomes more difficult in the arena of freedom of expression, where one is confronted with the question of whether a company is required simply to avoid infringing such rights or whether it is required to also take positive steps to enable their protection, thus raising further issues concerning what this would involve. Thus, when looking at Lozano's figure, the push-pull dynamic of human rights can almost be directly laid across the four aspects of CSR or vice versa. There are the regulatory elements to human rights, but also extralegal, moral aspects to it. These moral aspects find parallels with the tacit and propositional aspects of the CSR grid. Human rights, it must be remembered, is not terrain limited to lawyers, although they might like it to be

---

[131] See Morgan n. 47. Morgan frames the overlap between human rights and regulation as at the first stage (naming, blaming and claiming) and the second stage (rule-making, monitoring and enforcement): ibid., chapter one.

[132] See discussion by J. Donnelly *Universal Human Rights in Theory and Practice*, 2nd edn (Cornell University Press, 2002), pp. 30–31. He discusses how all human rights have a positive and negative aspect, even the quintessential negative right not to be tortured because it requires the positive dimension of control, training and supervision of police forces: ibid., p. 30.

[133] See generally T. I. Emerson, *The System of Freedom of Expression* (New York: Random House, 1970), p. 4.

Table 3.1. *Crossover of CSR and human rights*

| Human Rights | CSR |
| --- | --- |
| Direct state duties to protect human rights | N/A |
| Indirect state duties to protect human rights – facilitation of business responsibility through law, standard setting | CSR/law nexus variously described as 'hardening' or 'ratcheting-up' of CSR. |
| Voluntary codes | Pure-CSR |

so. It is as much a moral framework as a legal one. Thus, the outward-looking aspect of CSR finds commonality with the morality of human rights, as well as finding commonality with regulatory elements.

Under this patchy framework, CSR is broad-reaching, encompassing both hard and soft laws.[134] As we have seen, CSR encompasses both indirect legal obligations (CSR influencing the law and vice versa) and pure-CSR (voluntary codes). Under human rights, this would include two things: the positive obligations that are sometimes imposed on states to protect against human rights abuses by non-state actors and voluntary human rights codes that try to harness a moral commitment to human rights where activities fall outside the reach of the law or at the fringes of it. This can be seen in Table 3.1.

Governments might fulfil their positive legal duties by passing national legislation binding companies to human rights responsibilities, such as through health and safety legislation and media regulation. At an international level, various guidelines act as nonbinding frameworks to hold businesses to account (not necessarily as a matter of law).[135] They include, for example, the UN Global Compact and the OECD Guidelines. They cannot be said to originate with companies, but they rely on their cooperation to be successful. At an industry level, some companies develop codes of practice that incorporate human rights considerations, such as the GNI. Companies have also addressed human rights in their internal governance frameworks, such as in their

---

[134] Muchlinski n. 127, pp. 35–38
[135] See generally here, Monash University Castan Centre for Human Rights Law, *Human Rights Translated: A Business Reference Guide*, p. xii.

codes of conduct or terms of use for the services or products they provide.[136]

The various CSR initiatives all tend to draw their legitimacy from the UDHR. This approach can be seen in, for example, the UN Global Compact, the Global Sullivan Principles and SA8000 (www.sa-intl.org/). The UDHR was adopted by the UN General Assembly in 1948, has been elaborated on in a variety of international treaties[137] and forms the basis for most codifications of human rights.[138] The reference in the UDHR's preamble to the responsibility of 'organs of society' as well as states for its promotion has often been cited as a basis for holding businesses responsible for human rights.[139] However, the UDHR itself is not legally enforceable.[140] Rather, it has moral force and 'floats above all local and regional contingencies and is a statement of more or less abstract moral rights and principles'.[141] As a 'moral anchor',[142] it has become the language of international human rights and, because of this moral force, has become the language for framing corporate responsibilities for human rights in CSR instruments.

---

[136] See, for example, Facebook's 'Community standards', at www.facebook.com/communitystandards (last visited 19 February 2014) and Twitter's 'The Twitter rules', at https://support.twitter.com/articles/18311-the-twitter-rules (last visited 19 February 2014).

[137] Most notably the International Covenant on Civil and Political Rights and its two Optional Protocols, and the International Covenant on Economic, Social and Cultural Rights (collectively referred to as the International Bill of Rights). The International Bill of Rights effectively forms the ethical and legal foundation of the developing system of international human rights: R. K. M. Smith, *International Human Rights* (Oxford University Press, 2007), p. 38.

[138] J. Morsink, *The Universal Declaration of Human Rights: Origins, Drafting & Intent* (Philadelphia: University of Pennsylvania Press, 1999) p. xi. Although the UDHR is not legally enforceable, it has been argued that it is so widely accepted that it is now part of the general principles of law, although not customary international law; however, some argue that some of the rights can in fact be regarded now as a codification of customary law. In addition, many states have not adopted the International Covenants, and therefore the UDHR is the only applicable international human rights instrument. see discussion in Smith n. 137, section 4.1.

[139] See Frankental and House n. 126.

[140] In contrast, the International Covenants are binding on states. The Covenants set up a Human Rights Committee to which the states must submit reports on the measures taken to give effect to the Covenants. The Committee also can make recommendations and issue comments. There is a controversial First Optional Protocol to the Covenant, which provides in Article 1 that an individual may petition the Committee. The United Kingdom and the United States have not ratified this protocol. The Committee's reports have strong moral force because they are annexed to its annual report to the UN General Assembly: Smith n. 137, section 4.2.3.

[141] Morsink n. 138, p. xi.   [142] Ibid., p. xii.

At an international level, any hard law obligations that exist are imposed on states through international human rights laws. There is discretion as to how states fulfil their human rights obligations.[143] These obligations trickle down to businesses because of the states' obligations to protect against human rights abuses by third parties. This occurs because human rights instruments not only require states not to perpetrate human rights abuses, but also require states to ensure the enjoyment of these rights.[144] For example, the International Covenant on Civil and Political Rights (ICCPR) requires that a state 'respect and ensure' that human rights are not violated.[145] Some international human rights instruments expressly state that nation states should take steps to hold companies liable for their abuses, such as the Optional Protocol to the Convention on the Rights of the Child on the sale of children, child prostitution and child pornography.[146] Thus, at a national level, one can see many examples of hard-law human rights obligations imposed indirectly on companies. One can even see it in employment legislation with regard to provisions to regulate minimum wage, nondiscrimination and hours of work.[147]

However, there is incoherence because states often sign on to human rights obligations but do not implement them in a way that binds businesses or, more commonly, agencies that directly shape business practices. For example, securities regulators 'conduct their work in isolation from and largely uninformed by their Government's human rights agencies and obligations'.[148] In addition, corporate law shapes what companies do, but, up until now, it has been viewed as distinct from human rights. The companies themselves operate with relatively little knowledge of human rights and their potential responsibilities in this regard. A study by Twentyfifty Limited found that most companies see

---

[143]  J. Ruggie, 'Business and human rights: towards operationalizing the "protect, respect and remedy" framework' (2009), at www2.ohchr.org/english/bodies/hrcouncil/docs/11ses sion/A.HRC.11.13.pdf (last visited 21 November 2014), p. 7. The duties of states extraterritorially, however, are unsettled in international law, and the incoherence that exists at national levels infiltrates the international level as well. See discussion in J. Ruggie, *Just Business: Multinational Corporations and Human Rights* (New York: W.W. Norton & Company, 2013) about the US Alien Tort Statute 28 U.S.C. 1350 and recent case of *Kiobel v. Royal Dutch Petroleum Co* (2013) 133 S. Ct. 1659.

[144]  Ruggie (2009) ibid., p. 6.    [145]  Article 2.

[146]  J. Ruggie, 'State obligations to provide access to remedy for human rights abuses by third parties, including business: an overview of international and regional provisions, commentary and decisions' (Addendum) (2009), at www.reports-and-materials.org/Ruggie -addendum-15-May-2009.doc (last visited 4 August 2011), p. 3.

[147]  See, for example, the Equality Act 2010 c. 15.    [148]  Ruggie (2009) n. 143, p. 8.

human rights as an issue of risk management and only see human rights as being about employment rights, particularly as concerning their operations overseas. More work is needed, this report argued, in guiding workers on what their day-to-day obligations are.[149]

Most international human rights law is concerned with obligations on states to provide remedies for the abuse of human rights by businesses and others. Such frameworks do not easily apply to IIGs, which are often not the wrongdoers but gatekeep the wrongdoing of others. The writers of the blog www.killbatty.com, which advocated the killing of gays and lesbians, was based in Jamaica and hosted by Google in the United States. If the bloggers were UK based, they would potentially be in breach of a variety of local hate speech laws.[150] Google, however, which acted as the blog's host, under UK law would not be liable as long as it was not apparent the content was unlawful or Google disabled access to it once it became aware.[151] This is because Google makes available the platform for the speaker, but is not the speaker itself.

For such a situation, there is little guidance in international human rights law. This can be contrasted with a situation in which an internet gatekeeper is engaging directly in the potentially unlawful conduct, such as collecting user data and/or sharing it with third parties, because they are then the wrongdoer. However, when the IIG is acting in a pseudo-judicial capacity in deciding whether to take down material accused of being hate speech, it is not directly engaged in the unlawful activity. Thus,

---

[149] Twentyfifty, *The Private Sector and Human Rights in the UK* (October 2009), pp. 3–4.

[150] See, for example, the Public Order Act 1986 c. 64, Part III and Racial and Religious Hatred Act 2006 c. 1. Racist, abusive comments on social media, such as Facebook and Twitter, have tended to be prosecuted in the United Kingdom under, for example, the Public Order Act s. 4A, s. 127 of the Communications Act 2003 c. 21, s. 1 of the Malicious Communications Act 1988 c. 27 or the Protection from Harassment Act 1997 c. 40. For more on this, see J. Rowbottom, 'To Rant, Vent and Converse: Protecting Low Level Digital Speech', *CLJ*, 71(2) (2012) 355.

[151] The Electronic Commerce Directive (Directive 2000/31/EC of the European Parliament and of the Council of 8 June 2000 on certain legal aspects of information society services, in particular electronic commerce, in the Internal Market) provides a safe harbour from liability for certain intermediaries in certain circumstances. In the case of hosts, they lose the safe harbour if they did not know, nor was it apparent, that the information was unlawful, or if they obtained such knowledge, provided they acted expeditiously to remove or disable access to the content: Directive, Article 14; Regulations. The Directive was implemented into UK law through the Electronic Commerce (EC Directive) Regulations 2002 No. 2013. The safe harbour for intermediaries is further explored in Chapter 4. In this incident, where the blog was based out of Jamaica but hosted by Google in the United States, Google initially refused to take it down, instead posting a banner warning of the content; it later took it down as a breach of its terms of service.

in the context of internet governance of gatekeepers, the focus becomes increasingly on bespoke codes, whether industry or internally drawn.

In this grey area of governance of internet gatekeepers, the work of John Ruggie emerges as particularly important, albeit controversial, because it seeks to bridge the governance gap between the human rights impact of businesses and the historical focus of human rights laws on states. An attempt was made by the UN to apply state-like human rights obligations to companies with the 2003 draft *Norms on the responsibilities of transnational corporations and other business enterprises with regard to human rights*[152] (Norms). It was the controversy surrounding these Norms that led to the appointment of John Ruggie by the UN.[153]

As previously discussed, Ruggie is the former Special Representative of the Secretary-General of the UN on the issue of human rights and business. From 2005 to 2011, he undertook multiple multistakeholder consultations and research projects, and he received input from a wide variety of sectors on the issue of how to frame the nature of businesses' responsibilities for human rights.[154] His mandate was much broader than the focus of this book. He tackled the entire subject matter of business and human rights to help tease out a framework for moving forward.[155]

Ruggie's work was carried out in three stages, with the first being identification and clarification of existing standards and practices concerning human rights and businesses.[156] In 2008, he unveiled his 'Protect,

---

[152] United Nations Sub-Commission on the Promotion and Protection of Human Rights, 'Draft Norms on the Responsibilities of Transnational Corporations and Other Business Enterprises with Regard to Human Rights' (2003), E/CN.4/Sub.2/2003/12.

[153] John Ruggie described the Norms as 'engulfed in its own doctrinal excesses', concluding that they had 'so co-mingled the respective responsibilities of States and companies that it was difficult if not impossible to disentangle the two': Ruggie n. 143, p. 16. Some view the Norms positively, however, mainly for re-energising the business and human rights debate: See discussion in D. Kinley et al., '"The Norms Are Dead! Long Live the Norms!" The Politics behind the UN Human Rights Norms for Corporations', in McBarnet n. 39, pp. 459–465.

[154] See his work and associated reports and commentaries at www.business-human rights.org/SpecialRepPortal/Home.

[155] It has formed the conceptual framework for such frameworks as the Global Network Initiative (www.globalnetworkinitiative.org/) (last visited 17 June 2014), the Draft ISO 26000 Standards (www.iso.org/iso/catalogue_detail?csnumber=42546) (last visited 17 June 2014), and it has been embraced by the European Commission, n. 77, and the UK government, n. 85.

[156] J. Ruggie, 'Guiding principles on business and human rights: implementing the United Nations "protect, respect and remedy" framework' (March 2011), at www.business-hu manrights.org/media/documents/ruggie/ruggie-guiding-principles-21-mar-2011.pdf (last visited 17 June 2014), pp. 3–4.

Respect and Remedy' framework (hereinafter the Framework).[157] He then worked towards recommendations on how to operationalise this framework, cumulating in his final report in 2011 on guiding principles (Guiding Principles).[158] The UN Human Rights Council endorsed the Guiding Principles in June 2011, entrenching Ruggie's framework and principles as 'the authoritative global reference point for business and human rights'.[159]

In the context of this book, Ruggie's work is particularly useful in three ways. First, the Guiding Principles help tease out that there are conceptual differences between the human rights obligations of the state and businesses, although how to apply this in practice is a matter of considerable difficulty. Second, the Guiding Principles help integrate pure-CSR codes into the process of assessment and create a taxonomy of governance characteristics to look for in a voluntary regime. Third, the Principles emphasise the importance of access to a remedial framework.

Ruggie cautions that there is no 'silver bullet solution', concluding that (1) there should be no limited list of human rights for which businesses are responsible (2) nor should businesses' responsibilities be the same as states. Under the three pillars of the Framework he proposes, a state's duty is to protect, respect and fulfil human rights by putting in place laws and policies to give effect to this obligation. A company's responsibility is instead to respect human rights, by which he means acting 'with due diligence to avoid infringing on the rights of others and to address adverse impacts with which they are involved'.[160] The duty to respect also includes the obligation to not be complicit in human rights abuses.[161] The third pillar is remedial, stating that those whose rights have been negatively impacted must have access to a forum of remediation to address this impact.

The state's obligation is legal in nature, drawn directly from international human rights law, which already frames the nature of states duties, as set out earlier. The corporate responsibility to respect, however, is something different. It is defined by social expectation, framing human

---

[157] Ruggie (2008) n. 12.    [158] Ruggie (2011), n. 156.

[159] UN News Centre, 'UN Human Rights Council endorses principles to ensure businesses respect human rights' (16 June 2011), at www.un.org/apps/news/story.asp?NewsID=38742&Cr=human+rights&Cr1= (last visited 17 June 2014).

[160] Ruggie (2011) n. 156, p. 4.

[161] Ruggie (2008) n. 12, p. 20. Ruggie defines complicity as 'indirect involvement by companies in human rights abuse – where the actual harm is committed by another party, whether state agents or nonstate actors, but the company contributes to it': Ruggie, *Just Business* n. 143, p. 98.

rights as the baseline for a company's social licence to operate. The obligation is therefore often nonlegal and separate from, although complementary to, the state's obligation to protect.[162] The notion of a social license to operate is admittedly vague and one that has received a significant amount of criticism.[163] Furthermore, the line between social expectation and more structured systems of governance can be fine. For example, Ruggie acknowledges that endorsement of the Guiding Principles by the UN pulls the notion of corporate responsibility to respect beyond mere social expectation into the system of public governance.[164] This finds parallels with the notion of ratcheting-up or hardening of CSR instruments. Ruggie summarises the three pillars of his framework as follows:

> Each pillar is an essential component in an inter-related and dynamic system of preventative and remedial measures: the State duty to protect because it lies at the very core of the international human rights regime; the corporate responsibility to respect because it is the basic expectation society has of business in relation to human rights; and access to remedy because even the most concerted efforts cannot prevent all abuse.[165]

If we look closer at this notion of corporate responsibility to respect, it draws its content from internationally recognised human rights.[166] Its scope is broad, including any 'actual or potential adverse human rights impacts by an enterprise's own activities or through the business relationships connected to those activities'.[167] The regulatory structure through which companies respect human rights is mostly nonlegal in nature. Companies can occasionally be charged in court, but most often will be subject to negative public opinion.[168] It is not, however, simply encouragement of voluntary codes. This is because he roots this duty to

---

[162] Ibid., p. 100.

[163] R. McCorquodale, for example, argues that the term is unclear because we do not know the society that is the benchmark of expectation, the vulnerability of it to manipulation by corporations and the difficulty in assessing whether there has been compliance: '[i]n order to base such an important distinction between a state's obligations and a corporation's obligations in relation to human rights on the nebulous idea of a social licence to operate and on vague social expectations is deeply unsatisfactory': R. McCorquodale, 'Corporate Social Responsibility and International Human Rights Law', *Journal of Business Ethics*, 87 (2009) 385, p. 392. See also discussion of C. Lopez, 'The "Ruggie Process": From Legal Obligations to Corporate Social Responsibility?', in Deva and Bilchitz, n. 36, in particular pp. 65–69, discussing the weaknesses in the normative basis of social responsibility.

[164] Ruggie, *Just Business* n. 143, pp. 101–102.    [165] Ruggie (2011) n. 156, p. 4.

[166] Ruggie, *Just Business* n. 143, p. 100.    [167] Ibid., p. 100.

[168] Ruggie (2008) n. 12, p. 16.

respect in a system of due diligence in which companies are tasked with managing their human rights risks.[169] He states, '[t]o discharge the responsibility to respect human rights requires that companies develop the institutional capacity to *know* and *show* that they do not infringe on others' rights'.[170]

As a first step, companies must set in place human rights policies that identify the company's expectations of their employees, business partners and those with which they are linked. The policy should be publicly available and embedded into the work of the company through operational procedures.[171] In addition, the duty to respect includes a process of due diligence and a forum for remediation, the latter being the third pillar of the conceptual framework being discussed. A basic due diligence process would include human rights impact assessments. These involve companies identifying their actual and potential human rights impacts; acting on these findings; monitoring and tracking their performance in this regard, including adjusting their responses with changing risks and communicating such matters to the public.[172] Ruggie notes '[b]usinesses routinely employ due diligence to assess exposure to risks beyond their control and develop mitigation strategies for them, such as changes in government policy, shifts in consumer preferences, and even weather patterns'.[173]

In the case of IIGs, by the nature of what they do, they tend to fall into a grey category, one Ruggie adverted to in his research but did not form the focus of his work. He identified companies that take on public functions as different from other companies on which human rights duties are imposed. Although Ruggie reminds us that corporations are 'specialized economic organs, not democratic public interest institutions',[174] in his later research, he identifies a special class of public interest company that might invite additional corporate responsibilities beyond the duty to respect human rights.[175] IIGs, in particular macro-IIGs such as ISPs and search engines, have characteristics of public companies in

---

[169] Ibid., p. 9. See the criticisms of R. McCorquodale that Ruggie integrates the use of the term from human rights law and business management practices, where the terminologies have different meanings: McCorquodale n. 163, pp. 392–93.

[170] Ruggie, *Just Business* n. 143, p. 99.    [171] Ruggie (2011) n. 156, pp. 15–16.

[172] Ruggie (2008) n. 12, p. 19. The operational framework is articulated in Ruggie (2011) n. 156, pp. 16–20.

[173] Ruggie (2009) n. 143, p. 14.    [174] Ruggie (2008) n. 12, p. 16.

[175] Ruggie (2009) n. 143, p. 17. As an example of a private company with public functions, he offers prisons that have become privatised and the rights of prisoners remaining unchanged from this privatisation.

Table 3.2. *Crossover of CSR, human rights and the Guiding Principles*

| Human Rights | CSR | Guiding Principles |
| --- | --- | --- |
| Direct state duties to protect human rights | N/A | Protect |
| Indirect state duties to protect human rights – facilitation of business responsibility through law, standard setting | CSR/Law nexus variously described as 'hardening' or 'ratcheting-up' of CSR. | Protect/Respect |
| Voluntary codes | Pure-CSR | Respect |

determining public access to a critical communication medium, making them arguably more akin to a public interest institution. Through the lens of human rights, this ultimately is a question of whether the government has an obligation under its human rights responsibilities to direct the obligations of these IIGs.

Building on our understanding of the term *CSR* as used in this book and on how this relates to law and human rights, the Guiding Principles help untangle the differences between these obligations. Using his protect and respect language, we can see in Table 3.2 that sometimes the state's positive duties and a company's duty to respect link up. This helps cement our understanding of what CSR means in the context of human rights and for the purpose of governance in the digital environment. What it doesn't do is help identify a standard against which to judge conduct, in which Section 3.5 will help clarify the way forward.

Turning to the third pillar of Ruggie's Framework and his recommendation that remediation services be provided particularly resonates concerning IIGs because, at present, there is little in the way of remedial mechanisms available to users who feel their rights have been impacted by the activities of these companies.[176] The Guiding Principles identify three types of remedial mechanisms: judicial, state-based nonjudicial and non-state-based.[177] Regardless of the type, the key is a mechanism

---

[176] The need for complaints mechanisms to resolve disputes with online gatekeepers was identified by me in previous research: E. B. Laidlaw, 'Private Power, Public Interest: An Examination of Search Engine Accountability', *IJLIT*, 17(1) (2009) 113.

[177] This was initially proposed in Ruggie (2008) n. 12, p. 21. It was elaborated on in Ruggie (2011) n. 156, p. 22.

whereby people with grievances can routinely raise a complaint and seek a remedy.[178] As a result, all three mechanisms are quite formalised in nature, reflecting the adjudicative nature of any remedial mechanism, even mediation-based ones. Examples provided include courts, labour tribunals, the OECD National Contact Point (NCP) through BIS or National Human Rights Institutions (NHRI) such as the United Kingdom's Equality and Human Rights Commission (EHRC).[179]

Judicial mechanisms are self-explanatory as the obligation of states to ensure effective judicial remedies for human rights abuses committed in their jurisdictions or territories. The duty includes an obligation to make the public aware that such remedial services are available.[180] State-based nonjudicial mechanisms are entities, such as NHRIs, which potentially have the capacity to handle complaints, although their role has been mainly to monitor and make recommendations concerning human rights matters. The challenges with developing NHRIs in the United Kingdom to address internet governance matters is discussed in Chapter 6. Non-state-based mechanisms are operational-level systems whereby complaints can be made directly to the company. Ruggie sees this as the most underdeveloped aspect of the grievance process. This is particularly important because, done well, such a process would enable a company to address problems before they escalate to cases of abuse.[181] Key to the Guiding Principles are the criteria that must be present for any nonjudicial grievance mechanism to be effective. Such procedures should be legitimate, accessible, predictable, equitable, transparent, rights-compatible and based on findings from consultations with stakeholders.[182]

Drawing from the Guiding Principles, a skeletal framework for analysis of the governance of IIGs emerges. The Guiding Principles help bridge the gap between those that see CSR as purely voluntary and those that seek direct imposition of human rights laws on businesses akin to the state duties. In so doing, the requirement of due diligence acts as a checklist of attributes to look for in voluntary and quasi-voluntary regimes, the details of which will be discussed in Section 3.5. In this way, the Guiding Principles can be seen as a launching point and language for discussion of a framework for specific fields of business.

---

[178] Ibid., p. 22.
[179] Ibid., p. 22. See last section of the report for a discussion of the EHRC.
[180] See discussion ibid., section III.   [181] Ibid., p. 25. Ruggie, *Just Business* n. 143, p. 104.
[182] Ruggie (2011), n. 156, p. 26.

The Guiding Principles, however, raise just as many questions as they answer; therefore, their use is limited to this skeletal framework. This is because where the Guiding Principles are weak concerns the very question this book seeks to explore: in seeking to protect the free speech rights of the internet-using public, what can be expected of companies? This is an issue that plagues most regulatory structures with a social focus, where there is a challenge in defining when and how a regulatory structure is deemed as working successfully.[183] This in turn impacts the legitimacy of the regulatory body.[184] It is magnified in the case of the Guiding Principles because of the questionable nature of the normative foundation for the responsibility to respect.[185]

The Guiding Principles have been criticised for failing to be specific enough, for failing to move beyond a theoretical framework of 'protect, respect and remedy' to something operational and for conflating and confusing human rights duties.[186] David Bilchitz argues convincingly, among other things, that Ruggie's framing of corporate responsibility as one of social expectation hampers not only the development of norms in international law, but also turns the corporate role into one of nicety:

> [T]he question arises whether, in terms of the Framework we have a right to demand that corporations respect human rights or whether this is simply a matter of expectation that they will be 'generous' or 'decent'. If it is the latter, then we have eliminated the sense in which corporations truly have obligations for the realisation of human rights and their actions in this area would merely become a matter of their benevolence. This is inconsistent with the logic of human rights, which entails duties upon those who have the capacity to violate them or assist in their realisation.[187]

Justine Nolan asks a slightly different question in the context of assessing the Guiding Principles soft-law nature: what is the particular code's 'power or authority to drive improved adherence to human rights standards'?[188] This allows a nuanced examination of that code's relationship

---

[183] See T. Prosser, *The Regulatory Enterprise: Government, Regulation, and Legitimacy* (Oxford University Press, 2010), pp. 2–4.

[184] Ibid.    [185] Lopez, n. 163, p. 66.

[186] See discussion in Joint Committee on Human Rights, *Any of Our Business? Human Rights and the UK Private Sector* (First Reports of Session 2009–10), vol. I, p. 36. Such criticisms have traction when the framework is assessed as a stand-alone framework: see McCorquodale n. 163, p. 385.

[187] D. Bilchitz, 'A Chasm between "Is" and "Ought"? A Critique of the Normative Foundations of the SRSG's Framework and the Guiding Principles', in Deva and Bilchitz, n. 36, p. 120.

[188] Nolan, n. 36, p. 145.

with existing law. The difficulty, she identifies, is that the most effective soft laws have what she calls an 'element of bindingness':[189] they tend to complement hard laws for the source of the law or for enforcement mechanisms. The Guiding Principles, she notes, are 'amorphous and not grounded in legal obligation',[190] but the context in which they were developed, namely through the UN and now endorsed by the UN Human Rights Council, moves the Guiding Principles up the scale of soft law towards something more binding.[191]

The result is that the concept of corporate responsibility to respect creates polarising reactions: either it allows too much room for companies to avoid their responsibilities while appearing compliant, or it gives them the necessary flexibility to know and show their responsibility. It remains to be seen whether the Guiding Principles evolve to become an international standard or norm. At the moment, they are best described as an emerging framework. What we should remember is that when Ruggie embarked on his work in 2005 the debate about human rights and business had stalled with the divisive views on binding versus voluntary obligations for business. It was his work that has helped move the conversation forward by taking account of the transnational, multigovernance environment within which businesses operate and human rights are governed, although, as the criticisms just described showed, some argue that the Guiding Principles are a move backward because of their lack of specifically enforceable human rights obligations.

Indeed, at the time of writing, these criticisms are gaining momentum. In 2014, the Human Rights Council adopted a proposal by Ecuador, which was supported by more than 600 NGOs (although notably lacking large organisations such as Amnesty International)[192] to establish a working group to negotiate a treaty imposing international human rights obligations on transnational corporations.[193] It is therefore unclear what the future holds for the Guiding Principles, although for the moment it is the core paradigm for business and human rights. As Ruggie points out, the day after this vote, the Human Rights Council voted to extend the

---

[189] Ibid., p. 157.   [190] Ibid.   [191] Ibid., p. 158.

[192] See Global Movement for a Binding Treaty, at www.treatymovement.com (last visited 31 October 2014).

[193] Human Rights Council, 'Elaboration of an international legally binding instrument on transnational corporations and other business enterprises with respect to human rights' (A/HRC/26/L.22), at http://daccess-dds-ny.un.org/doc/UNDOC/LTD/G14/064/48/PDF /G1406448.pdf?OpenElement (last visited 31 October 2014).

mandate of the expert working group working on promoting the Guiding Principles.[194]

There is more going on here, however, and that is the difficulty the various CSR instruments face in being a complete tool for addressing the free speech issues being raised by the activities of the IIGs. The following section offers a broad view of the CSR initiatives at work in the arena of internet governance of IIGs. It will show that there is a governance gap concerning their activities, with all the instruments not quite applying to or providing concrete guidance concerning companies' responsibilities for freedom of expression online. This is so even when the Guiding Principles are used as the baseline for a CSR regime.

## 3.4. Setting the stage: CSR in the field

The leading international CSR instruments are, to name a few,[195] the UN Global Compact and the OECD Guidelines. At a European level, in 2013, the EC published human rights guidance for the ICT sector (as well as for the oil and gas and the employment and recruitment sectors).[196] This project marks an evolution in the business and human rights landscape from generalised international instruments to government-backed voluntary frameworks specific to the needs of particular industries. Industry CSR instruments for ICTs include, for example, the GNI, the EICC, the Global e-Sustainability Initiative (GeSI) and, the most recent

---

[194] J. Ruggie, 'The past as prologue? A moment of truth for UN business and human rights treaty', at www.ihrb.org/commentary/past-as-prologue.html#_edn2 (last visited 31 October 2014).

[195] Others include Agenda 21, Beijing Declaration, CERES principles, Principles for Responsible Investment and Social Accountability 8000: Blowfield and Murray n. 5, p. 14. Also, see the International Standards Organization, particularly its environmental management standards and quality management standards, at www.iso.org/iso/home .htm (last visited 17 June 2014); AccountAbility 1000S (AA1000S), at www.account ability.org/ (last visited 17 June 2014); the Global Reporting Initiative, at www.global reporting.org/Pages/default.aspx (last visited 17 June 2014) and standards through the International Labour Organisation, at www.ilo.org/global/lang-en/index.htm (last visited 17 June 2014). At one time, the list would have also included the Draft Norms on the Responsibilities of Transnational Corporations and Other Business Enterprises with Regard to Human Rights, but this has largely been superseded by the Guiding Principles.

[196] For the ICT guide, see European Commission, *ICT Sector Guide on Implementing the UN Guiding Principles on Business and Human Rights* (drafted by Shift and the Institute for Human Rights and Business).

addition, the Telecommunications Industry Dialogue on Freedom of Expression and Privacy (Industry Dialogue).[197]

What one finds in reviewing the international initiatives is that (1) with the exception of the OECD Guidelines, they are usually voluntary; (2) they all frame the duty of companies to 'respect' human rights, sometimes adding 'promote' to the list of duties; and (3) there is little, if any, elaboration provided on the duties regarding freedom of expression (or privacy for that matter), and sometimes they are not mentioned at all. For example, the world's largest and most embraced CSR initiative is the UN Global Compact, which was launched in 2000 at the instigation of then Secretary General Kofi Annan. It is a multistakeholder effort of governments, business, labour, civil society and UN agencies to create a voluntary framework. Currently it has more than 10,000 companies from more than 145 countries as members.[198] It is operationalised by the signature of a company's CEO committing to support its principles.[199] One of the main problems faced in the arena of internet governance is that, despite the Global Compact's supposed popularity, it is not popular with ICTs. A review of the membership list reveals that there are no UK or US ICT members as of yet.[200] In addition, the Global Compact illustrates the difficulty in using generalised frameworks as governance regimes for human rights such as freedom of expression because it offers no concrete guidance on companies' obligations. Rather, it is couched in generalised obligations such as the following:

1. Businesses should support and respect the protection of internationally proclaimed human rights; and
2. make sure they are not complicit in human rights abuses.[201]

---

[197] Frameworks for other industries include, for example, the Kimberley Process to stem the trade of conflict diamonds, at www.kimberleyprocess.com (last visited 17 June 2014); the Global Sullivan Principles guiding businesses dealing with apartheid South Africa, at www1.umn.edu/humanrts/links/sullivanprinciples.html (last visited 17 June 2014) and the Forest Stewardship Council setting forest management standards, at www.fsc.org/ (last visited 17 June 2014).

[198] See www.unglobalcompact.org/HowToParticipate/Business_Participation/index.html (last visited 13 March 2014).

[199] The UN Global Compact Office, *Corporate Citizenship in the World Economy* (October 2008).

[200] See www.unglobalcompact.org/ParticipantsAndStakeholders/business_associations.html (last visited 13 March 2014).

[201] See www.unglobalcompact.org/AboutTheGC/TheTenPrinciples/index.html (last visited 17 June 2014). Note that the Compact elaborates on the nature of the human rights involved but does not mention freedom of expression in Business Leaders Initiative on Human Rights, United Nations Global Compact and the Office of the High

The OECD Guidelines are similarly vague concerning companies' responsibilities for freedom of expression.[202] The Guidelines are different from other frameworks in that states commit to the framework and set up an NCP, which manages promotions, queries and complaints concerning the Guidelines at a national level.[203] In the United Kingdom, it is managed through BIS. The Guidelines, in the end, are still simply guidelines to businesses. The United Kingdom frames it as extralegal: 'recommendations for responsible business conduct that adhering governments encourage their enterprises to observe wherever they operate'.[204] The Guidelines were updated in May 2011 to incorporate the Guiding Principles.[205] In defining the responsibilities of companies, the Guidelines make clear that they exist independently of government:

> A State's failure either to enforce relevant domestic laws, or to implement international human rights obligations or the fact that it may act contrary to such laws or international obligations does not diminish the expectation that enterprises respect human rights. In countries where domestic laws and regulations conflict with internationally recognised human rights, enterprises should seek ways to honour them to the fullest extent which does not place them in violation of domestic law.[206]

Although the new OECD Guidelines improve on the earlier version by incorporating Ruggie's conceptual and operational recommendations, we still face the hurdle of defining what it means to respect freedom of speech on the internet, on which the OECD Guidelines provide no further clarification. This is no surprise from an instrument that is

Commissioner for Human Rights, 'A Guide for Integrating Human Rights into Business Management I'.

[202] OECD Guidelines for Multinational Enterprises, at www.oecd.org/document/28/0,3343 ,en_2649_34889_2397532_1_1_1,00.html (last visited 17 June 2014). There are also efforts to create CSR standards through the International Standards Organization. ISO 26000, launched in late 2010, draws heavily from the work of John Ruggie. This author does not have access to the final version, although information is, at www.iso.org/iso /discovering_iso_26000.pdf (last visited 5 August 2011). The Draft ISO 26000 focused on the responsibilities of a company with regard to freedom of expression only to the extent that the company should not censor its employees. It is more developed concerning privacy: Draft International Standards ISO/DIS 26000, *Guidance on Social Responsibility*, pp. 29, 50–57.

[203] The thirty OECD member countries plus eleven nonmember countries are adherents to these Guidelines, and oversight is managed by the Investment Committee: www.oecd .org/about/0,3347,en_2649_34889_1_1_1_1,00.html (last visited 17 June 2014).

[204] See www.gov.uk/uk-national-contact-point-for-the-organisation-for-economic-co-oper ation-and-development-oecd-guidelines-for-multinational-enterprises (last visited 13 March 2014).

[205] OECD Guidelines n. 202.    [206] Ibid., Commentary 38 on Human Rights.

pitched so broadly. On freedom of expression, it only offers one point that, given the timing of the publication, is clearly influenced by the Arab Spring. It 'encourages' enterprises to:

> Support, as appropriate to their circumstances, cooperative efforts in the appropriate fora to promote Internet Freedom through respect of freedom of expression, assembly and association online.[207]

It is difficult to imagine how this would have guided Vodafone in its decision whether to comply with Egyptian government demands to disconnect mobile phone access or, for example, guide ISPs in the United Kingdom concerning the content it blocks. This is the only reference to freedom of expression in the OECD Guidelines.

Unlike the UN Global Compact, however, the OECD Guidelines have a remedial framework. The NCP manages complaints through a process of mediation and can make findings of a breach by a company where appropriate, issuing a statement detailing the nature of the finding and making recommendations to bring the company's practices in line with the Guidelines.[208] The remedial structure is criticised however as being toothless.[209] For example, in one investigation into Vedanta Plc regarding its mining operations in Orissa, India, Vedanta simply refused to participate in mediation, and the UK NCP did not have any powers to compel it beyond expressions of disappointment.[210] Ruggie suggests giving them more weight by, for example, withholding access to government procurement and guarantees where a negative finding is made against a company.[211] However, without properly elaborated responsibilities concerning freedom of expression, a remedial framework has no hope because there are no standards against which to then judge the activities of a company (or, for that matter, the companies to judge themselves). This puts in doubt the sufficiency of any of the international frameworks to address the free speech impact of IIGs.

The European Union's initiative to develop sector-specific guidance on human rights began to take shape with the Commission's publication of a new CSR strategy in 2011. In this strategy, the development of sector-specific guidance was listed as one of its priorities. Work on the ICT

---

[207] Ibid., section B.I, p. 18.     [208] See BERR n. 204.

[209] Joint Committee on Human Rights n. 86, pp. 28–29. Other complaints were that the UK NCP was not independent from government and there was a lack of sufficient guidance for companies on the standards they were to meet: ibid., p. 28.

[210] Ibid., pp. 28–29.

[211] Ruggie (2009) n. 143, p. 24. Ruggie views the OECD Guidelines as potentially an important remedial mechanism at a national level: ibid.

Sector Guidance (the Guidance) was led by the Institute for Human Rights and Business and Shift, took place over the course of 1.5 years and involved several public consultations and more than seventy-five multistakeholder interviews.[212] The result is a weighty guide that seeks to address the whole of the sector from telecommunications to web-based services to software, electronics and manufacturing.[213] The varying needs of the sectors, what it describes as the ICT 'ecosystem',[214] proved to be one of the greatest challenges for the drafters. The Guidance operates much as the industry-level initiatives detailed later because its focus is solely on implementation of the corporate responsibility to respect and does not consider, therefore, wider issues of its relationship with the rule of law.

The ICT Guidance identifies four common challenges: the pace of change being faster than regulators ability to respond, the struggle to respect freedom of expression and privacy for businesses operating in rights-oppressive states, the challenge in managing the legality of government requests for information about customers, and the difficulty in identifying human rights breaches in the supply chain in areas where labour laws are either absent, weak or poorly enforced.[215] Despite the breadth of the guide, the focus is still relatively narrow, focusing only on a company's obligation to avoid harm to human rights.[216] This side steps a key aspect of what is so pressing and elusive about the business impact on human rights, and that is the problem of identifying what qualifies as a human rights issue problematised further by the self-regulatory nature of the environment.

In line with its purpose, the Guidance does not seek to resolve bigger questions on the role of business in governing human right issues, but this is not a weakness of the guide. The purpose of the guide is practical, and, in this respect, it is a success. The Guidance identifies six elements to meet the responsibility to respect: a policy commitment, assessment of potential and actual impacts, integrating findings and acting to prevent or mitigate impacts, tracking impacts, communicating impacts and remediation. The greatest weakness of the Guidance is the fact that it tries to be one guide for the entire ICT industry, and this leads to issues not being engaged with in the depth and nuance needed. The GNI notes this in its Comments on a draft of the Guidance stating, 'by grouping

---

[212] This author was interviewed in the development of the Guidance and participated in one of the roundtable discussions in Brussels, Belgium.
[213] The Guidance, n. 196, p. 6.    [214] Ibid., p. 8.    [215] Ibid., p. 10.    [216] Ibid., p. 11.

together issues with fundamentally different dynamics, the usefulness of the guidance diminishes'.[217] This is a valid criticism. In the context of freedom of expression, for example, the Guidance discusses government requests to remove or block specific content and notes that '[t]his is an area in which discussions about the most appropriate approaches are on-going'.[218]

Where the Guidance excels is as an ideas bank for approaches to difficult situations and a framework to standardise a company's approach to human rights problems. The greatest value of the Guidance is in capturing the life cycle of a human rights issue and translating that into useful ideas on how a business committed to meeting its responsibilities might do so. It is not, however, a research document interrogating the very nature of the business and human rights dilemma in this sector. Since this is an EC guide, the impact of this in law also remains to be seen. If a company commits to following this guidance and drafts a code therefrom, can it be sued by an affected party for breaching the terms of its voluntary code?

At an industry level, there are four main international initiatives for ICTs concerning human rights: the EICC[219], the GeSI[220], the GNI and the Industry Dialogue.[221] The EICC can be dismissed outright because although it deals with human rights, it does not deal with freedom of expression. The focus of the EICC is on labour, health and safety and the environment. There is no mention in the document of freedom of expression.[222] Yet it is important to mention the EICC because in the US Congressional hearings on 'Global Internet Freedom', membership in the EICC was cited most often by companies as the reason they were not

---

[217] GNI, 'Comments from the GNI on the Draft Guidance for the ICT Sector on the Corporate Responsibility to Respect Human Rights', at http://globalnetworkinitia tive.org/sites/default/files/GNI%20comments%20on%20EC%20draft%20ICT%20gui dance.pdf (last visited 17 June 2014), p. 3.

[218] The Guidance, n. 196, p. 44.

[219] See Electronic Industry Code of Conduct, at www.eicc.info/eicc_code.shtml (last visited 17 June 2014). The first version was created by a group of companies in 2004. It is influenced by the main CSR standards, such as the ILO Standards, and leading industry standards, such as the Ethical Trading Initiative.

[220] http://gesi.org (last visited 17 June 2014).

[221] www.telecomindustrydialogue.org (last visited 13 March 2014).

[222] However, freedom of association is provided for: see Electronic Industry Code of Conduct n. 219, A.7.

members of the GNI.[223] Similarly, GeSI is focused narrowly on ICT social and environmental sustainability.[224]

The GNI is particularly in point for this book as it is a CSR framework for ICT companies specifically concerned with freedom of expression and privacy and created as an alternative to direct regulation.[225] The GNI is a multistakeholder creature of companies, civil society, investors and academics. Discussions of the GNI began in 2006 when ICTs in the United States were receiving considerable attention from the government and public concerning their human rights-impacting activities. Two particular incidents helped push formation of the group. First, Yahoo! handed over information about one its email account holders to the Chinese authorities, thereby exposing the identity of a Chinese journalist and leading to his arrest and imprisonment for ten years. Second, Google launched a version of its search engine in China that censored search results (it has since stopped this practice).[226]

For several years, there was a lack of take-up by ICT companies in the GNI, and membership stalled with its founders Google, Yahoo! and Microsoft.[227] As all three offer search engine services as a component of their business, the GNI will be discussed in particular in the search engine case study in Chapter 5. Vodafone was one of the drafters of the GNI, but pulled out just before it was launched, citing as the main reason for its decision the focus of the GNI on internet providers rather than on its core business of providing telecommunication services (it has since joined the Industry Dialogue).[228] The focus of the GNI on internet

[223] See the letters on Senator Dick Durbin's website under 'Related Files': http://durbin.sen ate.gov/public/index.cfm/pressreleases?ID=c3078a7d-bfd9-4186-ba86-2571e0e05ec8 (last visited 17 June 2014).

[224] See http://gesi.org/About_ICT_sustainability (last visited 13 March 2014).

[225] See J. Palfrey, 'Testimony on Internet Filtering and Surveillance' at http://jpalfrey.and over.edu/2008/05/20/testimony-on-internet-filtering-and-surveillance/ (last visited 31 October 2014).

[226] See L. Downes, 'Why no one will join the Global Network Initiative' (30 March 2011), at www.forbes.com/sites/larrydownes/2011/03/30/why-no-one-will-join-the-global-net work-initiative/ (last visited 17 June 2014). For why Google decided to stop censoring its search results in China, see Google, 'A new approach to China' (12 January 2010), at http://googleblog.blogspot.com/2010/01/new-approach-to-china.html (last visited 17 June 2014).

[227] See www.globalnetworkinitiative.org/participants/index.php (last visited 17 June 2014).

[228] See discussion, C. Marsden, 'Corporate responsibilities in times of civil unrest: the case of Egypt and Vodafone' (July 2011), at www.networkedcranfield.com/doughty/Docume nt%20Library/Hot%20Topics/Corporate%20Responsibilities%20in%20Times%20of% 20Civil%20Unrest%20the%20case%20of%20Egypt%20and%20Vodafone.pdf (last vis ited 17 June 2014).

providers, as well as the availability of the EICC as a purported alternative to the GNI have been some of the main reasons put forward by companies for not joining the Initiative.[229] By 2011, it appeared that the GNI might be a short-lived experiment in multistakeholder governance of human rights.

As of 2014, the future of the GNI is questionable. Since 2011, its membership has expanded marginally, with the addition of Evoca and Websense in 2011, Procera Networks in 2013 and the most important addition, Facebook, in 2013.[230] The addition of Facebook was an enormous boost to the organisation because it had been resistant to joining for a long time. Facebook initially held observer status for one year, meaning it did not submit its operations to a human rights audit, but, in 2013, it joined the GNI as a full member.[231] LinkedIn joined the GNI in 2014.[232]

The 2013 revelations leaked by National Security Agency (NSA) contractor Edward Snowden of mass online surveillance by governments, in particular by what is known as the Five Eyes alliance of the United States, United Kingdom, Canada, Australia and New Zealand, has impacted the legitimacy of the GNI, although the extent of the impact is as of yet unknown. The revelations seem to have had the twin result of, on the one hand, legitimising the GNI by making clear the need for a governance framework on human rights for ICT companies and, on the other hand, exposing the weaknesses of such voluntary frameworks – in particular the effectiveness of the auditing system, discussed in more detail later. After all, GNI members Google, Yahoo!, Microsoft and Facebook were identified as some of the key companies that collected and shared customer data with the NSA pursuant to secret court orders. In none of these situations was the GNI specifically consulted, although the GNI has long been alert to such issues;[233] nor, it appears, were these activities revealed

---

[229] See link to letters n. 223. For a history of the GNI, see Colin Maclay, 'Protecting Privacy and Expression Online: Can the Global Network Initiative Embrace the Character of the Net?', in Deibert, *Access Controlled*, n. 14.

[230] See www.globalnetworkinitiative.org/participants/index.php (last visited 13 March 2014).

[231] See www.globalnetworkinitiative.org/news/facebook-joins-global-network-initiative (last visited 13 March 2014).

[232] See http://globalnetworkinitiative.org/news/linkedin-joins-global-network-initiative (last visited 29 May 2014).

[233] See I. Brown and D. Korff, 'Digital Freedoms in International Law: Practical Steps to Protect Human Rights Online' (June 2012) (report commissioned by the Global Network Initiative).

through the GNI human rights audits (Facebook, however, as a new member will not be audited until 2015).[234] The secret nature of these companies' data sharing with governments made a mockery of the human rights audit process, so much so that GNI founder, the Electronic Frontier Foundation (EFF), resigned from the organisation. The EFF advised:

> [U]ntil serious reform of the US surveillance programs are in place, we no longer feel comfortable participating in the GNI process when we are not privy to the serious compromises GNI corporate members may be forced to make. Nor do we currently believe that audits of corporate practice, no matter how independent, will uncover the insecurities produced by the US government's – and potentially other governments' – behaviour when operating clandestinely in the name of national security.[235]

The GNI made the following statement on the matter in the 2013 Independent Assessment of Google, Microsoft and Yahoo:

> Protecting the free expression and privacy rights of Internet users around the world – the goal behind the creation of GNI – has never been so vital. It was not possible, however, to assess the way in which GNI companies respond to U.S. national security requests because of the restrictions under U.S. law that prohibit the companies from disclosing any information related to such requests. This strengthens our belief that legal and policy reform is necessary and advocacy for increased transparency and other changes will be a greater part of our work in future.[236]

The goal of the GNI is broadly to protect and advance freedom of expression and privacy in the ICT sector. It describes what it is doing as 'defining shared standards'[237] for the ICT sector. There are three core documents: the Principles; the Implementation Guidelines; and the Governance, Accountability and Learning Framework, as well as a Governance Charter.[238] As a governance framework, it is promising because it attempts to operationalise the broader Principles into detailed guidance to companies, a transition that most CSR initiatives have struggled to do, if at all. Furthermore, the presence of a Governance

---

[234] See Governance, Accountability and Learning Framework 'New participating companies', at http://www.globalnetworkinitiative.org/governanceframework/index.php (last visited 14 March 2014).

[235] See 'GNI resignation letter', at www.eff.org/document/gni-resignation-letter (last visited 14 March 2014).

[236] *Independent Assessment* (2014), at http://globalnetworkinitiative.org/sites/default/files/GNI%20Assessments%20Public%20Report.pdf (last visited 28 May 2014).

[237] See www.globalnetworkinitiative.org/faq/index.php#50 (last visited 17 June 2014).

[238] They can be found, at www.globalnetworkinitiative.org/ (17 June 2014).

Framework to hold the body to account is an aspect of corporate governance power that has sorely needed attention.

A distinguishing feature of the GNI is its requirement that members periodically undergo a human rights audit. Such an assessment is in keeping with the idea of human rights audits suggested in the Guiding Principles and is particularly valuable in a pure-CSR framework such as the GNI. The first set of audits were completed in January 2014.[239] The Independent Assessment examined founding companies Google, Microsoft and Yahoo!. It assessed cases of government requests in the areas of search, email and photo and video sharing services. The report concluded that these companies were making a good faith effort to comply with the GNI Principles. The Independent Assessment will be discussed in more detail in Chapter 5.

The GNI suffers from the kinds of criticisms with which, as we have already seen, this whole field of CSR is familiar, with one side arguing that it does not go far enough to protect human rights, and the other side saying it does not offer enough flexibility.[240] Amnesty International, for example, in deciding late in the drafting process not to join the GNI, described the final framework documents as 'a degree of progress in responding to human rights concerns – [but] they are not yet strong enough to allow Amnesty International to endorse them'.[241] More concerning is the lack of take-up of the regime, in particular the glaring absence of companies such as Twitter and telecommunications companies as members, thus highlighting the risks associated with purely voluntary regimes. However, the regime is quite young; but, in the context of the internet, where things develop at rapid-fire pace, the lack of take-up by now risks the subject matter moving on from what the GNI has to offer.

---

[239] See http://globalnetworkinitiative.org/news/gni-report-finds-google-microsoft-and-yahoo-compliant-free-expression-and-privacy-principles (last visited 13 March 2014).

[240] See various responses available at www.business-humanrights.org/Documents/GlobalNetworkInitiative-responses (last visited 17 June 2014). See, in particular, Reporters Without Borders criticisms: 'Why reporters without borders is not endorsing the global principles on freedom of expression and privacy for ICT companies operating in internet-restricting countries' (28 October 2008), at http://en.rsf.org/why-reporters-without-borders-is-28-10-2008,29117.html (last visited 17 June 2014), and the Electronic Frontier Foundation concerns (although it endorses the GNI), at www.eff.org/files/filenode/gni/signon_letter.txt (last visited 17 June 2014).

[241] B. Johnson, 'Amnesty criticises Global Network Initiative for online freedom of speech' (30 October 2008), at www.guardian.co.uk/technology/2008/oct/30/amnesty-global-network-initiative (last visited 17 June 2014).

As a governance structure, it is a positive starting point for framing the business and human rights discussion in the internet environment. However, there are legitimate criticisms of the framework's scope and focus. Some of the main concerns revolve around the independent assessment process of compliance with the GNI Principles. The main criticisms are that the audits might be vulnerable to bias because the companies select their assessors, and the companies might withhold damaging information. There have been more general criticisms that the governance framework does not adequately take account of data collection, retention and sharing practices, in particular procedures for handing sharing of customer data with government authorities.[242]

At a fundamental level, these criticisms translate into concerns that the GNI is simply not accountable enough.[243] The greatest strength of the GNI, on the other hand, is its promotion of the use of Ruggie-styled human rights impact assessments, which has the potential to embed human rights considerations into a company's structure at an operational level. The criticisms, however, illustrate the struggle in finding the line between a flexible governance structure that gives considerable leeway to companies in how to implement the framework and a targeted and structured regulatory regime that delineates precisely the conditions under which a company can be said to be complying with the rules.

Many of these criticisms predate the Snowden revelations and now take on a special significance. Certainly the NSA surveillance programme compelled companies to collect and share data in a way that challenges the sufficiency of corporate due diligence to address human rights issues. The auditing system is dependent on a company being open and honest about how it protects rights and about the extent of its limitations to do so. The secret government orders meant that companies could not even report the existence of these orders, much less allow an assessment of the extent to which companies were compelled versus elected to share data. That said, strengthening a framework like the GNI would require government involvement in ratcheting-up their enforceability, and, given the circumstances, it seems farcical to suggest this would provide an avenue to greater rights protection. The greatest value of the GNI in these circumstances was arguably as an advocate representing its members' commitment to free speech and privacy. In this role, it called for

---

[242] The EFF n. 235.    [243] See discussion Maclay n. 229, pp. 98–100.

government to allow greater transparency concerning the data that companies were compelled to share.[244]

The GNI, as it stands, can only take us so far in analysing the issues raised in this book. This is for two reasons. First, at the moment, there is no remedial mechanism through the GNI, a mechanism that the case studies will show to be crucial for human rights compliance of IIGs and one that also (as we have seen) forms the critical third pillar of the Guiding Principles. Concerns have been expressed that there will be an overwhelming number of complaints to field by the GNI with limited resources to handle them.[245] At the time of writing, the GNI is piloting a complaints procedure with the help of Shift, a nonprofit organisation.[246] Second, the GNI's strength is in helping companies in their conduct in countries where local laws conflict with international human rights principles. For example, free speech responsibilities are focused on situations where the government makes demands on businesses: '[p]articipating companies will respect and protect the freedom of expression of their users by seeking to avoid or minimise the impact of government restrictions on freedom of expression'.[247] The GNI also states:

> Participating companies will respect and protect the freedom of expression rights of their users when confronted with government demands, laws and regulations to suppress freedom of expression, remove content or otherwise limit access to information and ideas in a manner inconsistent with internationally recognized laws and standards.[248]

Strictly speaking, such provisions apply to all countries which might engage in human rights-oppressive conduct, and Western states are by no means operating in perfect compliance with international human rights law.[249] The GNIs response to mass surveillance by Western governments has shown its willingness to apply its Principles to any government infringing on rights. However, the reality is that the GNI is not geared to dealing with situations in which the government has simply

---

[244] See http://globalnetworkinitiative.org/news/transparency-national-security-and-protecting-rights-online (last visited 13 March 2014).

[245] Maclay, n. 229, pp. 100–101. See also GNI Governance Charter, clause 8: https://globalnetworkinitiative.org/charter/index.php#84 (last visited 13 March 2014).

[246] See discussion in its Annual Report 2012, at http://globalnetworkinitiative.org/sites/default/files/GNI%20Annual%20Report%202012.pdf (last visited 13 March 2014), p. 7.

[247] See www.globalnetworkinitiative.org/principles/index.php#18 (last visited 17 June 2014).

[248] Ibid.          [249] See Chapter 4 case study.

encouraged companies to sort it out for themselves,[250] which largely defines the governance landscape of IIGs in the United Kingdom and most Western states concerning free speech matters. It is with this grey area that this book is particularly concerned.

The Industry Dialogue, as the name indicates, applies to telecommunications operators and vendors. There are currently nine members, including companies such as Vodafone, Orange and Nokia Solutions and Networks, although it is missing key companies such as BT. At the time of writing, the Industry Dialogue is in early days. It was launched in 2013 and is in the midst of a two-year collaboration with the GNI to create 'a common platform to exchange best practices, learning, and tools'.[251] Near the end of the collaboration, a review process will be triggered to assess the future of the relationship.[252] Historically, the telecommunications industry was reluctant to join the GNI. Given its creation of its own framework, it appears this reluctance was never overcome. The collaboration creates potential for standardisation of approaches to human rights across ICT industries, but allows for industry-specific responses to particular problems.

Like the GNI, the Industry Dialogue is built on the Guiding Principles and focuses on privacy and freedom of expression.[253] It also has the benefit of drawing from the EC's ICT Guidance. Therefore, it covers the life cycle of a human rights matter: from policy commitments and raising awareness, to impact assessments and due diligence, to mitigating risks of government demands and to remedial mechanisms.[254] What is most striking about the first draft of the Guiding Principles is that it includes a section delineating what members believe governments should do concerning human rights, including '[defining] with care the balance between freedom of expression and privacy and other legitimate societal needs, such as national security, public safety, law enforcement and

---

[250] The GNI is inspired by the Sullivan Principles, a code of conduct for businesses engaged in apartheid South Africa, which is telling: Maclay n. 229, p. 92. See discussion in A. Wales, *Big Business, Big Responsibilities* (Basingstoke: Palgrave Macmillan, 2010), chapter six.

[251] See www.telecomindustrydialogue.org/about (last visited 13 March 2014).

[252] See https://globalnetworkinitiative.org/content/frequently-asked-questions-about-gni -and-telecommunications-industry-dialogue (last visited 13 March 2014).

[253] See n. 251.

[254] See http://www.telecomindustrydialogue.org/content/guiding-principles (last visited 13 March 2014).

protection of children. This is not the role of companies'.[255] It remains to be seen how the Industry Dialogue develops.

This review highlights a lacuna in governance. Human rights laws, regulation and current CSR regimes don't quite fit with what IIGs are doing. Yet IIGs are at the centre of the internet's democratising force. These instruments and laws simply circle them, not quite applying and not quite guiding them. There is promise in some of these instruments for further development to address the human rights impact of IIGs, and that is something explored in Chapter 6. In addition, when we proceed with the case studies to examine these issues in specific contexts, we must be mindful of two things. First, in not quite applying to the activities of IIGs, the international CSR guidelines, both general and industry-specific, focus their attention more on domestic initiatives. Second, it puts increasing pressure on companies' internal governance structures to be human rights-compliant.

We are left still with a gap, which is a standard against which to judge whether a particular CSR regime has sufficiently discharged a business or state's human rights responsibilities. In the case of the state, human rights laws directly apply to assess whether positive duties are required to satisfy its obligations, in particular for the purposes here, Article 10 of the ECHR. It will be shown in Section 3.5 that the ECHR and related jurisprudence is the appropriate standard for assessment of both indirect and voluntary CSR regimes in Europe, helping to identify when CSR is enough to protect and respect freedom of expression online.

## 3.5. Measure human rights compliance: Article 10

As outlined in Section 3.3, the case studies draw from the Guiding Principles and examine the public-facing governance frameworks of ISPs and search engines in the context of the wider regulatory environment in which they operate. The following questions are asked:

(a) What is the regulatory environment in which the IIGs operate?
(b) What are the due diligence processes; namely, is there guidance on human rights policies, monitoring and tracking of performance and mitigation strategies?

---

[255] The Telecommunications Industry Dialogue on Freedom of Expression and Privacy, Guiding Principles, version 1 (March 6 2013), at www.telecomindustrydialogue.org/sites /default/files/Telecoms_Industry_Dialogue_Principles_Version_1_-_ENGLISH.pdf (last visited 17 June 2014), p. 4.

(c) What are the nature of the human rights obligations set out in the policies?

(d) What remedial structures are there, if any? Do they have any of the characteristics identified as important in the Guiding Principles of legitimacy, accessibility, predictability, equitability, rights-compatibility, transparency and engagement with stakeholders?

The Guiding Principles serve an evidentiary purpose. They identify regulatory measures one looks for in the assessment of a framework, but they are not enough, on their own, to provide guidance, particularly with regard to IIGs, regarding the standards against which human rights are judged. For example, what are an ISP's obligations with regard to a duty to respect freedom of expression when it hosts a chat room and there is a complaint that some of the comments are defamatory? In this aspect, an ISP is acting in a pseudo-judicial capacity and assessing conflicting human rights without a clear legal obligation regarding human rights. The Guiding Principles criteria for, in effect, a human rights audit, asking if there have been implementation of monitoring or mitigation strategies or the like, is evidence of a commitment to human rights but does not help an ISP grapple with its responsibilities in a scenario such as this, nor does it advise a company how to be human rights-compliant in the current legal minefield within which such businesses operate. The Guiding Principles ask if there is a remedial structure, but, in this scenario, the question is: how do we then assess the human rights compliance of that remedial structure once in place?

As we have seen, the global CSR frameworks such as the UN Global Compact and the OECD Guidelines show very little guidance regarding the obligations of businesses with regard to freedom of expression, except in referring to the UDHR. The UDHR is aspirational. It provides guidance on the responsibilities of those parties that interfere with freedom of expression, and its principles of proportionality and necessity helped guide the drafting of the ECHR and codification of most human rights frameworks in the world. However, its force is moral not legal, and therefore a body of jurisprudence grappling with its application in the field is not available in the same way as with specific codifications of human rights. An IIG faced with the scenario just mentioned finds little comfort or guidance from the UDHR on what it means to respect human rights. However, guidance is available from the wide body of law and policy in European human rights jurisprudence. Specifically, Article 10 principles articulate the necessary criteria for a human rights-compliant institution.

Article 10 provides:

(1) Everyone has the right to freedom of expression. This right shall include freedom to hold opinions and to receive and impart information and ideas without interference by public authority and regardless of frontiers. This article shall not prevent States from requiring the licensing of broadcasting, television or cinema enterprises.

(2) The exercise of these freedoms, since it carries with it duties and responsibilities, may be subject to such formalities, conditions, restrictions or penalties as are prescribed by law and are necessary in a democratic society, in the interests of national security, territorial integrity or public safety, for the prevention of disorder or crime, for the protection of health or morals, for the protection of the reputation or the rights of others, for preventing the disclosure of information received in confidence, or for maintaining the authority and impartiality of the judiciary.[256]

The regulatory aspect of freedom of expression can be seen as 'rules' of communication:[257]

1. Is the interference prescribed by law?
2. Does it have a legitimate aim (national security, territorial integrity or public safety, for the prevention of disorder or crime, for the protection of health or morals, for the protection of the reputation or the rights of others, for preventing the disclosure of information received in confidence or for maintaining the authority and impartiality of the judiciary); and
3. Is the interference with the right to freedom of expression necessary in a democratic society; meaning that the 'interference [must] correspond to a pressing social need and, in particular, that it is proportionate to the legitimate aim pursued'.[258]

---

[256] ECHR, n. 14.

[257] D. Tambini et al., *Codifying Cyberspace* (London: Routledge, 2008), pp. 294–95.

[258] *Olsson* v. *Sweden* (A/250) (1994) 17 EHRR 134, para. 67. See also *Sunday Times* v. *United Kingdom* (No 1) (A/30) (1979–80) 2 EHRR 245, which goes through the criteria for assessing whether an infringement under Article 10 meets the criteria under Article 10 (2). See also *Sunday Times* v. *United Kingdom* (No 2) (13166/87) (1991) 14 EHRR 229. A related question under the ECHR is whether the framework complies with Article 6's right to a fair trial in the determination of civil rights and whether it complies with Article 13's right to an effective remedy, but those are beyond the scope of this book.

The application of ECHR principles to private or semi-private regulatory bodies is not new. The activities of media regulatory bodies are measured against the free speech standards of the ECHR.[259] A certain amount of caution must be exercised, however, in such an assessment. The law here is unclear as to 'the degree of "horizontal protection" offered by the ECHR for example (i.e. protection of speech rights against private bodies by controlling the restrictions placed on freedom of expression) has yet to be defined'.[260] In addition, these case studies' interest in the administrative aspect of freedom of expression has not been tested in the courts.[261] For example, when examining voluntary codes, it is a difficult task to determine whether the framework is prescribed by law as required under Article 10(2):

> At one end of a continuum, purely voluntary ethics codes of single companies are clearly not law, but at the other, codes that are encouraged through a legislative framework but administered by an industry association may be considered for these purposes to be law.[262]

Finally, we are concerned here with fleshing out the legitimacy of CSR frameworks, and we can draw principles from ECHR jurisprudence to set minimum standards.[263]

An Article 10 analysis helps identify when a pure-CSR versus legal framework is sufficient, with the Guiding Principles helping to flesh out the kinds of criteria to look for in voluntary frameworks and remedial mechanisms. This in turn helps pinpoint where on the scale of responsibility (as the term was used in Chapter 2 to describe the nature of IIG responsibilities) a particular issue of free speech fits. For example, an Article 10 analysis might reveal that voluntariness is adequate to address a problem or might reveal that, in fact, the state has positive duties to facilitate free speech that have or have not been discharged. The Article 10 rules would necessarily be loosened for voluntary regimes where there is no actual legal obligation engaged, but would help identify the line between legal and pure-CSR obligations.

---

[259] Tambini n. 257, p. 282.    [260] Ibid., p. 285.

[261] The lack of a remedy, however, has been the subject of court scrutiny. In the case of *Peck* v. *United Kingdom* (44647/98) (2003) 36 EHRR 41, the ECtHR questioned whether the lack of a remedy of damages being available from the PCC rendered the body non-compliant with the ECHR under Article 13.

[262] Tambini n. 257, p. 282.    [263] Deibert, *Access Denied* n. 14, p. 33.

## 3.6. Conclusion

It is against this backdrop of CSR that we proceed with the case studies on governance of filtering by ISPs and search engines in the United Kingdom. Some preliminary issues can be noted from the outset. The notable absence of much elaboration on the duties of companies regarding freedom of expression in the international initiatives discussed herein perhaps highlights the inability of CSR to protect those human rights. Pure-CSR for these issues might just not be adequate, and, at minimum, the government might have positive duties to, for example, oversee a regulatory framework. Yet this chapter also shows that CSR has an important function in being the bridge between the legal and extralegal dimensions of law and human rights. It is more flexible and better able to harness a moral commitment from corporations and thereby be internalised at an operational level in a way that the law struggles to achieve. This better encapsulates the moral underpinning of human rights and has more promise in addressing the human rights impact of businesses.

In examining the viability of CSR to govern IIGs, two overriding problems will be addressed. First, the human rights engaged by the internet, particularly freedom of expression, are less clear-cut and involve more weighing of one right against another than other areas for which CSR has been more fully developed, such as the environment and labour. The literature thus far, while acknowledging the responsibility of businesses to promote freedom of expression, has hesitated to critically examine what this means. Second, the case studies might reveal that IIGs, rather than being in a position to directly perpetrate abuses, by virtue of their being gatekeepers act in what could be described as a kind of pseudo-judicial capacity. This is arguably an inappropriate role for such companies, given the free speech impact of such decisions. Ultimately, the question is whether the CSR frameworks that currently govern many of the activities of these information gatekeepers are sufficient to provide the standards and compliance mechanisms needed to protect and respect freedom of expression online.

# 4

# Mechanisms of information control: ISPs

On 5 December 2008 the Internet Watch Foundation (IWF), the main body governing filtering of unlawful content in the United Kingdom, received a complaint on its hotline about a Wikipedia page. The complaint was about an entry for the rock band the Scorpions, specifically, the entry for their 1976 album *Virgin Killer,* which featured the album's cover: an image of a naked ten-year-old girl with a smashed-glass effect covering her genitalia.[1] This album and its cover, whilst controversial, are available for sale online and in shops.[2] The IWF promptly added the webpage to its blacklist of alleged child sexual abuse content, which it then distributed to its members, made up of – broadly speaking – the internet industry. These members then blocked access to the Wikipedia page. No one told the Wikimedia Foundation, the owners of Wikipedia, either before or after the webpage was blocked. In fact, Wikipedia only found out its page had been blocked[3] when the blocking methods used by the internet service providers (ISPs) caused other problems, such as slower connection speeds to Wikipedia and difficulty editing the site.[4] A few days later, and under significant public pressure, the IWF changed

---

[1]  See, for example, the wired article on this: C. J. Davies, 'The hidden censors of the Internet', *Wired Magazine* (June 2006), at www.wired.co.uk/wired-magazine/archive/2009/05/features/the-hidden-censors-of-the-internet.aspx?page=all (last visited 17 June 2014).

[2]  See, for example, www.amazon.co.uk/Trance-Virgin-Killer-Scorpions/dp/B000VR0F4S/ref=sr_1_6?ie=UTF8&qid=1320763078&sr=8-6 (last visited 17 June 2014).

[3]  J. Petley, 'Web Control', *Index on Censorship*, 38(1) (2009) 78, p. 89. See article of Out-law arguing that the IWF should not have changed its mind: Out-law.com, 'Why the IWF was wrong to lift its ban on a Wikipedia page' (11 December 2008), at www.out-law.com/page-9653 (last visited 17 June 2014).

[4]  Petley ibid., p. 90. The technical aspect of the Wikipedia controversy was explained by Richard Clayton as follows: www.lightbluetouchpaper.org/2008/12/11/technical-aspects-of-the-censoring-of-wikipedia/ (last visited 11 June 2014). See R. Clayton, 'Failures in a hybrid content blocking system', at www.cl.cam.ac.uk/~rnc1/cleanfeed.pdf (last visited 27 June 2014).

its mind and removed the webpage from its blacklist. This incident drew attention (however briefly) to a body that, up until then, had operated with relatively little public scrutiny or oversight, and yet it has significant control of our expressive opportunities online. A decision by the IWF to add URLs to its blacklist is a decision on what information we can and cannot access on the internet. It begs the question: what human rights responsibilities does an organisation such as the IWF have?

Going forward in this book, we have three intersecting ideas identified in the first three chapters: first, that the internet has the potential to be a facilitative force in democratic culture; second, that for this potential to be fulfilled we are reliant on privately owned gatekeepers, in particular a type of gatekeeper identified in Chapter 2 as an internet information gatekeeper (IIG); and three, governance of these gatekeepers has thus far largely taken the form of corporate social responsibility (CSR). The following two chapters are case studies of particular macro-IIGs and the gatekeeping role they play in facilitating or hindering participation in democratic culture. The significance of the findings in these cases studies to the viability of CSR as a governance tool for IIGs will be examined in Chapter 6, where the case will be made for a new corporate governance model to address digital human rights.

This chapter examines the role of ISPs in governing filtering of content, in particular the role of the industry regulator the IWF. In the following case study, the more subtle role of search engines in controlling and shaping information flows will be examined. In each of these case studies, the basic questions asked, with varying degrees of emphasis, are: (1) how do these gatekeepers impact participation in democratic culture (more narrowly freedom of expression); (2) how is their impact presently regulated; and (3) is this governance structure sufficient for the protection and respect of freedom of expression online?

An examination of filtering mechanisms, and the role of the gatekeepers in deciding what is filtered using these mechanisms, is a particularly appropriate case study for this book. Filtering of internet content brings to a head deep legal, political and theoretical divisions concerning how the internet should be governed, in particular issues surrounding the traditional public–private governance divide and how this should be accounted for in the digital environment. It also raises fundamental questions about how to administer a system of freedom of expression in the information society, particularly to facilitate the internet's democratic potential. We have a tool that can block access to unlawful content, but it can equally block access to lawful content, and, as we saw with the Wikipedia incident, much of the content in dispute lingers at the edges of social or legal acceptability. The use of such mechanisms can be framed as a necessary tool to navigate the internet unscathed or as a censorship mechanism. Ultimately, it functions as both – it just depends on who controls it and what they do with it. In the United Kingdom, these tools are largely controlled by ISPs, a particularly significant macro-IIG as identified in Chapter 2 because of their role in making access to the internet even possible.

This chapter examines the frameworks that currently govern filtering of content in the United Kingdom to determine whether they are sufficient to provide the standards and compliance mechanisms needed to protect and respect freedom of expression online. What will be shown in this case study is that filtering in the United Kingdom is largely carried out by ISPs, and the primary private body in the UK that determines the content these ISPs filter is the IWF. A separate but related issue, which will not be explored in this chapter, is the increasing use of blocking technologies to combat illegal file sharing for the protection of copyright. It is suggested that the examination here can inform that discussion.

The focus of this chapter is necessarily on the IWF and how it is governed. This makes for a particularly interesting case study because it involves a story, one which I hope, rather optimistically, we are only in the middle of. I published an article examining the human rights compliance of the IWF's regulatory structure in 2012.[5] This led to a meeting with the representatives of the IWF to discuss my key points. The IWF accepted one of my major recommendations, which was performance of a human rights audit, a notion that, as the reader will know from Chapter 3, is becoming integral to the administration of businesses whose activities in any way brush up against human rights. This audit, on which I consulted, was performed by Lord Macdonald of River Glaven. At the time of writing, the IWF has reviewed the audit and accepted some of its measures. The IWF is also currently facing a significant expansion in its remit, inviting re-scrutiny of its regulatory arrangement. This makes for an interesting case study here because it not only illustrates the impact of private governance structures on free speech, but also affords the opportunity to examine the strengths and weaknesses of audits at mending some of the problems identified.

---

[5] E. Laidlaw, 'The Responsibilities of Free Speech Regulators: An Analysis of the Internet Watch Foundation', *IJILT*, 20(4) (2012) 312.

Structuring this chapter is therefore a challenge. It will be organised as follows. It will first discuss the wider context of ISP filtering and democracy and how it is regulated in Europe and the United Kingdom. It will then home in on the IWF and examine the body as it was before my article was published and the audit was conducted. The chapter will conclude with an analysis of the audit.

## 4.1. Filtering and democracy

Most filtering involves a combination of internet protocol (IP) blocking and domain name server (DNS) tampering[6]. Both types of blocking are effective and easy to implement, but they risk overblocking because all of the content hosted on, for example, www.youtube.com will be blocked, rather than the specific page with the offending content. Since ISPs generally maintain the DNS servers for their customers, they are usually tasked with carrying out this type of filtering, which they do by configuring the servers so that the wrong IP address is returned, such as 1.1.1.1. The most advanced type of filtering is URL filtering. This is also the most accurate because specific webpages can be blocked, but it is expensive to set up and maintain. Whatever method of filtering is used – be it proxies, IP addresses or hybrids thereof – 'to be reliable [such filtering mechanisms] must be at a *choke point* – a location that all communication must go through'.[7] Normally, the chokepoint is an ISP. If a state strictly controls connection to the internet, then it is possible to set up the filtering mechanisms at international gateways; however, this is more difficult for certain types of filtering such as DNS tampering. Thus, ISPs are at the centre of the filtering debate.

In addition, the regulatory and legislative landscape means that the impetus to carry out the act of filtering can come from many directions. The filtering can be state-mandated, as seen in countries such as China, the Middle East or even Australia, or under threat of legislation as in the United Kingdom, or it might be entirely at the behest of industry or an

---

[6] For explanation of IP address, IP blocking and DNS blocking in general, see R. Faris and N. Villeneuve, 'Measuring Global Internet Filtering', in R. Deibert et al. (eds.), *Access Denied: The Practice and Policy of Global Internet Filtering* (MIT Press, 2008).

[7] S. J. Murdoch and R. Anderson, 'Tools and Technology of Internet Filtering', in ibid., p. 65. It is more expensive to set up and maintain as 'the requests intercepted by an HTTP proxy must be reassembled from the original packets, decoded, and then retransmitted, the hardware required to keep up with a fast Internet connection is very expensive': ibid., p. 63.

individual ISP. Consider some of the examples of the use of filtering technologies. The Canadian ISP Telus blocked a pro-union website during a labour dispute with its employees.[8] The Australian government explicitly outsources filtering to ISPs via legislative mandate in the Australian Interactive Gambling Act.[9] Former New York Attorney General Eliot Spitzer threatened intermediaries such as PayPal and credit card-issuing banks with criminal sanctions if they did not institute a framework for the refusal of transactions associated with internet gambling.[10] In the United Kingdom, the IWF has been repeatedly pressured to expand its remit to filter such content as terrorism-related material and legal pornography,[11] and ISPs have been enlisted by the courts to block access to file-sharing sites.[12] The UK government also has an agreement with major ISPs to block access to legal pornographic content, which users must opt-in to gain access to.[13]

The European Court of Human Rights (ECtHR) and Court of Justice of the European Union (CJEU) have considered the legality and obligations concerning blocking measures in a series of (mostly) unrelated cases. In *Ahmet Yildirim* v. *Turkey*,[14] a case to be discussed in more detail later, the ECtHR held that blocking of access to the entire Google sites, a hosting service, because one of the websites it hosted insulted the memory of Ataturk, infringes the right to free expression under Article 10 of the European Convention on Human Rights (ECHR). The CJEU in *Scarlet* v. *SABAM*[15] followed by

---

[8]  T. Barrett, 'To censor pro-union website, Telus blocked 766 others' (4 August 2005), at www.labournet.net/world/0508/canada2.html (last visited 17 June 2014).

[9]  2001 no. 84. See discussion, T. McIntyre and C. Scott, 'Internet Filtering: Rhetoric, Legitimacy, Accountability and Responsibility', in R. Brownsword and K. Yeung (eds.), *Regulating Technologies: Legal Future, Regulatory Frames and Technological Fixes* (Oxford: Hart Publishing, 2008), p. 121.

[10]  T. J. McIntyre, 'Intermediaries, Invisibility and the Rule of Law', *BILETA Conference Paper* (2008), p. 5.

[11]  See, for example, H. Mulholland, 'Government targets extremist websites' (17 January 2008), at http://guardian.co.uk/politics/2008/jan/17/uksecurity.terrorism (last visited 17 June 2014).

[12]  *Twentieth Century Fox Film Corp & Ors* v. *British Telecommunications Plc [2011] EWHC 1981 (Ch); Dramatico Entertainment Ltd.* v. *British Sky Broadcasting Ltd. [2012] EWHC 268 (CH) AND [2012] EWHC 1152 (CH).*

[13]  Prime Minister David Cameron (speech), 'The internet and pornography: Prime Minister calls for action' (22 July 2013), at www.gov.uk/government/speeches/the-internet-and -pornography-prime-minister-calls-for-action (last visited 17 June 2014).

[14]  *Application no. 3111/10* (18 December 2012).

[15]  *Scarlet Extended SA* v. *Société belge des auteurs, compositeurs et éditeurs SCRL* (2011) Case C-70/10.

*Sabam* v. *Netlog*[16] held that an ISP cannot be ordered to install a general filtering system unless safeguards are put in place, such as limiting the period for which it would apply and to whom it would apply. In contrast, the ECtHR in *Delfi AS* v. *Estonia*[17] issued the perplexing judgment that Delfi, the publisher of an article online, was liable for the insulting and threatening comments posted by readers despite the fact that Delfi removed the comments on the same day that the complaint was made. At the time of writing, this case has been referred by the ECtHR to the Grande Chamber.

It thus comes as no surprise that the use of filtering technologies to censor content, whether by the state or private parties, attracts significant attention from policy makers concerned not only about the human rights implications of the use of such technologies, but also more generally with the legitimacy of that form of governance.[18] They reveal what T. J. Mcintyre and Colin Scott describe as a 'deeper problem' with filtering: they are 'a very efficient mechanism for implementing rules, but not so good when it comes to standards',[19] which is where it crosses over with the human rights concerns of this case study. Such governance concerns translate in human rights to a concern not only over censorship as such, but also over the privatisation of censorship. By filtering access to a particular website or page, the information flow is interrupted, and particular information is then selected for removal from public consumption. As a result, participation in democratic culture, as speaker or listener, is obstructed. This becomes particularly problematic because the technology is prone to under- and overblocking, and there is a risk of function creep with any such system.[20]

This is even more problematic because the decision on who and what is permitted to participate in democratic discourse is privately determined, thus leading to what Damian Tambini et al. describe as 'a trend towards the deconstitutionalisation of freedom of speech'.[21] What may be perceived as freedom becomes a way of avoiding constitutional obligations. For example, in the United States, with its tradition of negative treatment of freedom of expression, self-regulation of broadcasting means that a decision by a broadcaster not to carry alcohol advertising

---

[16] *Belgische Vereniging van Auteurs, Componisten en Uitgevers CVBA (SABAM)* v. *Netlog NV* (2012), Case C-360/10.
[17] (2013) (Application no. 64569/09).   [18] McIntyre and Scott n. 9, p. 109.
[19] Ibid., p. 117.   [20] See, in general, discussion in ibid.
[21] D. Tambini et al., *Codifying Cyberspace* (London: Routledge, 2008), p. 275.

does not even engage First Amendment protection.[22] The idea that customers have a choice, have alternatives available to them, is illusory because it is not easy for a customer to simply choose to use a different ISP, particularly when all the ISPs block the same content; nor are users particularly aware of the terms on which content is blocked.[23] In this deconstitutionalised world, 'proxy censors'[24] operate without human rights obligations of proportionality and due process but exercise considerable power over the exercise of participation in democracy:

> Unlike an official determination, which assesses damages or penalties tailored to the prospect of public harm, censorship by proxy is an unavoidably blunt instrument. Private censorship takes place at low levels of visibility. It is neither coordinated nor reviewed. Often, neither speakers nor listeners will know that the message has not been conveyed, and there is no way to determine how dialogue has been deformed.[25]

There are knock-on effects of such privatisation because the censorship need not always be steered by government. Bloggers might self-censor to avoid problems of access to their content. In addition, intermediaries often are dependent on advertising for their financial revenue and are vulnerable to pressure by advertisers to carry or not carry certain content. Thus, the power of censorship, rightly or wrongly, shifts to 'powerful blocs of customers'.[26] For example, Yahoo! shut down a series of chat rooms with purported child sex content as a result of pressure from advertisers who withdrew their adverts.[27] Facebook, after years of complaints and withdrawal of advertising support, began taking down rape joke groups.[28] This broadens the regulatory modalities to include the community, including businesses and users, a concept familiar to human rights where publicly shaming human rights offenders is often the only tool available when the laws reach is limited. For the purposes here, it shows that ISPs become the focal point of powerful political forces from

---

[22] Ibid., p. 276. In fact, filtering software provided voluntarily by content providers was viewed as the 'panacea' for reconciling concerns regarding free speech and the protection of children: ibid., p. 276.

[23] S. F. Kreimer, 'Censorship by Proxy: First Amendment, Internet Intermediaries, and the Problem of the Weakest Link', *U. Pa. L. Rev.*, 155 (2006–2007) 11, p. 35.

[24] Ibid.     [25] Ibid., pp. 27–28.     [26] Ibid., p. 30.     [27] Ibid., p. 30.

[28] See initial coverage with L. Davies, 'Facebook refuses to take down rape joke pages' (30 September 2011), at www.theguardian.com/technology/2011/sep/30/facebook-refus es-pull-rape-jokepages (last visited 17 June 2014), then the change in policy in M. Bennett-Smith, 'Facebook vows to crack down on rape joke pages after successful protest, boycott' (29 May 2013), at www.huffingtonpost.com/2013/05/29/facebook-rape -jokes-protest_n_3349319.html (last visited 17 June 2014).

governments, consumers and business, and, without a strong governance framework any commitment to human rights, for which they have no direct legal obligation, risk being compromised. The question is then how filtering by ISPs is governed and whether the governance framework has the necessary human rights safeguards built into it to address the risks and concerns associated with the impact of filtering on participation in democracy.

## 4.2. Regulation of filtering in a European and UK context

Despite cases such as *Sabam, Yildirim* and *Delfi*, the regulatory environment governing the filtering of content by ISPs in Europe tends to be light touch.[29] The European Commission (EC) and the Council of Europe have produced an endless array of papers and guidelines and spurred the creation of networks, all commenting on the state of internet governance. The Council of Europe, for example, has been very active in shaping regulation of the information society with the issuance of soft-law guidelines on human rights for ISPs and online games providers.[30] More recently, the EC published a comprehensive guideline for the Information and communication technologies (ICT) business community.[31]

In 2008, the Committee of Ministers of the Council of Europe issued a Recommendation concerning the promotion of free speech and information with regard to filtering (Recommendation).[32] In this Recommendation,

---

[29] The push has been for multistakeholder involvement: see discussion of historical context in C. Walker and Y. Akdeniz, 'The governance of the Internet in Europe with special reference to illegal and harmful content', at www.cyber-rights.org/documents/CrimLR_ya_98.pdf (last visited 17 June 2014), p. 6. See Communication from the European Commission, *Internet Policy and Governance Europe's role in shaping the future of Internet Governance* COM/2014/072.

[30] The Council of Europe guidelines on human rights for internet service providers and online games providers. See 'Human rights guidelines for internet service providers', at www.coe.int/t/informationsociety/documents/HRguidelines_ISP_en.pdf (last visited 17 June 2014); and 'Human rights guidelines for online game providers', at www.coe.int/t/informationsociety/documents/HRguidelines_OGP_en.pdf (last visited 17 June 2014). 'Soft law' has specific meaning in European law as a nonbinding legal instrument that is followed as a matter of informal practice by member states, such as a Recommendation: Tambini n. 21, p. 5.

[31] European Commission, *ICT Sector Guide on Implementing the UN Guiding Principles on Business and Human Rights* (drafted by Shift and the Institute for Human Rights and Business).

[32] Council of Europe, *Recommendation CM/Rec(2008)6 of the Committee of Ministers to member states on measures to promote the respect for freedom of expression and information with regard to internet filters* (March 2008).

it is recognised that internet filters can promote the confidence and security of internet users, but cautions for awareness 'that the use of such filters can impact on the right to freedom of expression and information, as protected by Article 10 of the European Convention on Human Rights'.[33] The Recommendation places responsibility on Member States to adopt standards that promote such rights, including the rather weak responsibility to 'bring ... these guidelines to the attention of all relevant private and public sector stakeholders'.[34] In the Guidelines attached as an appendix to the Recommendation, the Committee crucially recommends that users should be informed of filters and have access to a grievance mechanism, something that will be notable in the analysis of the IWF later in this chapter. The Guidelines state:

> Users' awareness, understanding of and ability to effectively use Internet filters are key factors which enable them to fully exercise and enjoy their human rights and fundamental freedoms, in particular the right to freedom of expression and information, and to participate actively in democratic processes. When confronted with filters, users must be informed that a filter is active and, where appropriate, be able to identify and to control the level of filtering the content they access is subject to. Moreover, they should have the possibility to challenge the blocking or filtering of content and to seek clarifications and remedies.[35]

The EC went so far as to state in its White Paper on European governance that co-regulation might not be appropriate for cases engaging fundamental rights,[36] stating that co-regulation, 'is only suited to cases where fundamental rights or major political choices are not called into question'.[37] The significance of such a statement and it being accorded little weight in the practice of internet regulation highlights the dilemma of current internet regulation. The technology is so new, so changing, and the issues so vexing that multiple stakeholders are participating in discussions of what to do, and the effect is information overload. This is not to say that multistakeholderism is a blight on the progress of internet governance. Indeed, multistakeholderism offers the promise of a well-rounded and represented discussion of internet governance issues,

---

[33] Ibid.    [34] Ibid.

[35] Ibid., Guidelines. For further discussion of the Recommendation, see Y. Akdeniz, 'To Block or Not to Block: European Approaches to Content Regulation, and Implications for Freedom of Expression', *CLSR*, 26 (2010) 260, pp. 267–69.

[36] E. Lievens, et al., 'The Co-Protection of Minors in New Media: A European Approach to Co-Regulation', *U.C. Davis J. Juv. L. & Pol'y*, 10 (2006) 98, p. 147.

[37] European Commission, 'European Governance: A White Paper', COM(2001) 428 (25 July 2001), p. 21.

but the downside is that it is slow, voluminous, and produces little in the way of practical results.[38]

For UK ISPs, this provides the political and legal context of their operation. It means that they are constantly affected by policy discussions and recommendations on a social and political level but that, as a legal matter, these are only discussions and as such have no legal bite. ISPs, therefore, if they wish, can operate in a manner that effectively disregards these discussions. This state of affairs is compounded with regard to human rights, where, as we have seen, the international human rights regime is constantly grappling with its lack of legal force.[39] However, there is one piece of legislation that does regulate some of the responsibilities of ISPs for filtered content: the Electronic Commerce Directive (E-Commerce Directive)[40] implemented into UK law through the Electronic Commerce (EC Directive) Regulations (E-Commerce Regulations)[41] (hereinafter discussed in terms of the Directive).

The Directive harmonises the circumstances under which an intermediary is exempt from liability for unlawful content communicated by a third party. Depending on the laws of the Member State, such content for the most part concerns defamatory content, content which breaches intellectual property laws, obscene content, terrorism-related content and content which stirs up religious or racial hatred.[42] The Directive's term for the intermediary with which it deals is 'information society service' (ISS), a broad term meaning, 'any service normally provided for remuneration at a distance, by means of electronic equipment for

---

[38] For an excellent discussion of the IGF from a regulatory perspective, see R. H. Weber, *Shaping Internet Governance: Regulatory Challenges* (Berlin: Springer-Verlag, 2010).

[39] Even the International Covenant on Civil and Political Rights 1966, which is monitored and enforced by the UN Human Rights Committee (UNHRC), has weaker enforcement mechanisms. The UNHRC can only issue a 'view', which is of normative force rather than being an international court making binding decisions.

[40] Directive 2000/31/EC of the European Parliament and of the Council of 8 June 2000 on certain legal aspects of information society services, in particular electronic commerce, in the Internal Market.

[41] 2002 No. 2013.

[42] Since the Regulations were brought into force, the United Kingdom has passed two regulations applying the E-Commerce Regulations to certain types of content: the Electronic Commerce Directive (Terrorism Act 2006) Regulations 2007 No. 1550, applying it to content that violates the Terrorist Act 2006 (Terrorism Regulations), and the Electronic Commerce Directive (Hatred against Persons on Religious Grounds or the Grounds of Sexual Orientation) Regulations 2010 No. 894 (revoking and replacing the Electronic Commerce Directive (The Race and Religious Hatred Act 2006) Regulations 2007 No. 2497), applying the Directive to hatred on the grounds of race, religion or sexuality (Hatred Regulations).

the processing (including digital compression) and storage of data, at the individual request of a recipient of the service'.[43] The services covered by this definition are currently unsettled in the law, although it would tend to include ISPs and search engines.[44]

The nature and extent of the safe harbour provided to an ISS depends on the ISS's intermediary role: mere conduit, cache or host.[45] If an ISS is a mere conduit, it is exempt from liability provided it did not initiate the transmission, select the receiver thereof nor select or modify its contents.[46] However, if the ISS *caches* the material, meaning temporarily stores information in order to make the internet work more efficiently, which ISPs do, the circumstances under which an ISS will be exempt from liability are more limited. The ISS will not be liable unless the ISS has actual knowledge that the information at the initial source of the transmission was removed or access disabled, or a court or administrative authority has ordered its removal or disablement and the ISS fails to remove or disable access expeditiously.[47]

The most controversial issue is the limitations placed on the safe harbour of 'hosts' of third-party content, which would typically describe some of the activities of ISPs. Under Article 14, 'hosts' covers 'the storage of information provided by a recipient of the service'.[48] This includes the provision of server space to store websites, newsgroups and so on. Hosts are exempt from liability if they did not know, nor was it apparent, that the information was unlawful, or if they expeditiously remove or disable access to the content once they gain such knowledge.[49] Recital 46 states that such removal or disabling of access to content 'has to be undertaken in the observance of the principle of freedom of expression and of procedures established for this purpose at national level'.[50]

The Directive does not regulate the notice-and-takedown procedures. Rather, it is left to member states to implement, although the Directive

---

[43] See n. 40, the Preamble, cl. 17.

[44] See discussion of implementation of the Directive in Member States concerning specific services, such as search engines, auction sites and user-generated content, in T. Verbiest et al., 'Study on the liability of internet intermediaries', Markt/2006/09/E (November 2007), at http://ec.europa.eu/internal_market/e-commerce/docs/study/liability/final_report_en .pdf (last visited 4 November 2014).

[45] E-Commerce Directive n. 40, Articles 12–14. For general discussion of strengths and challenges of the E-Commerce Directive see, for example, Verbiest n. 44; Akdeniz n. 35, p. 266–67; R. Julia-Barcelo and K. J. Koelman, 'Intermediary Liability in the E-Commerce Directive: So Far So Good, but It's Not Enough', *CLSR*, 16(4) (2004) 231.

[46] E-Commerce Directive, ibid., Article 12.    [47] Ibid., Articles 12–13.

[48] Ibid., Article 14.    [49] Ibid.    [50] Ibid., Recital 46.

encourages the development of self-regulatory procedures by the internet industry.[51] Article 16 specifically provides that member states should encourage industry to create voluntary codes for the implementation of, amongst others, the safe harbour provisions in Articles 12–14.[52] Member states have varied in their implementation approaches across the spectrum of codified to self-regulatory measures.[53] The United Kingdom implemented Article 14 verbatim in Regulation 19 of the E-Commerce Regulations but provides specific criteria for actual notice in Regulation 22[54] and codifies specific responses for content that is terrorism-related or intended to stir up hatred on the grounds of religion or sexual orientation.[55]

In practice, the safe harbour provisions of the Directive mean that if an ISP, or more specifically an ISS, is advised that content is unlawful, it would be wise to remove the content regardless of the legitimacy of the complaint or risk losing the protection of the Directive's safe harbour. This has resulted in legitimate accusations that it privatises censorship.[56] UN Special Rapporteur Frank La Rue expressed concern with such frameworks stating that '[t]he Special Rapporteur believes that censorship measures should never be delegated to a private entity, and that no one should be held liable for content on the internet of which they are not the author. Indeed, no State should use or force intermediaries to undertake censorship on its behalf'.[57]

The concern here is not with challenging the legitimacy of the E-Commerce Directive, although there is much to be concerned

---

[51] Ibid., Recital 40 and Article 16. See discussion in Akdeniz n. 35, p. 266.

[52] E-Commerce Directive n. 40, Article 16.   [53] See Verbiest n. 44, Part 2.

[54] Actual knowledge is set out in Regulation 22 of the E-Commerce Regulations n. 41 as notice via the contact options on its site, and the content of the notice includes details of the sender's name and address, location of the information in dispute and details concerning its unlawful nature.

[55] See note 42.

[56] See C. Ahlert et al., 'How "liberty" disappeared from cyberspace: the mystery shopper tests internet content self-regulation', at http://pcmlp.socleg.ox.ac.uk/sites/pcmlp.socleg .ox.ac.uk/files/liberty.pdf (last visited 17 June 2014), pp. 11–12, where they discuss the problems with the notice-and-takedown regime, namely the lack of guidance for ISPs on how to assess a complaint and the risk of unfair competition because of claims of unlawful content made by competitors in bad faith. See also Tambini n. 21, p. 8.

[57] Report of the special rapporteur on the promotion and protection of the right to freedom of expression, Frank La Rue to the United Nations General Assembly, 16 May 2011, at http://www.ohchr.org/Documents/Issues/Opinion/A.66.290.pdf (last visited 16 June 2014), para. 42.

about.[58] Unlike the IWF, the Directive was at least enacted through a democratic process. However, the Directive does have significant implications to an assessment of the human rights compliance of a body such as the IWF because these private forms of governance are the focus of this book. The Directive makes ISPs vulnerable to organisations such as the IWF because ISPs, at least when they act as hosts of content, are in a challenged position to refuse to block content once that content is accused of being unlawful. As Julian Petley notes,

> [The E-Commerce Directive] does indeed take a certain amount of pressure off ISPs, but it also renders them extremely vulnerable to pressure from corporate interests, law enforcement agencies and self-regulatory bodies such as the Internet Watch Foundation, who have only to allege that material is illegal for ISPs to become understandably nervous about carrying it. And if they then decide to take it down, they effectively become a regulatory agent, thus to a significant extent *privatizing* the process of online censorship.[59]

It results in a strange scenario in which the censorship is framed as a 'democratic expression of the public will'.[60] After all, no one wants to be characterised as sympathetic to child pornographers and paedophiles. However, the end result is a circumvention of governmental, police or judicial oversight. They are kept 'out of the loop',[61] with the result that 'the IWF conveniently circumvents the need to justify censorship in a court of law'.[62]

The IWF, in this respect, has historically been inconsistent in its rhetoric, at times describing its blacklist as 'voluntary' to ISPs[63] and at

---

[58] The European Commission held consultations on the Directive and produced a Communication that addressed concerns with the scope and application of the safe harbour provisions. The Commission suggests a horizontal framework for notice and takedown across Europe to standardise procedures: European Commission 'A Coherent Framework for Building Trust in the Digital Single Market for E-Commerce and Online Services', *COM*(2011) 942. For a broader discussion of the state of intermediary liability, see slides from E. Laidlaw, 'Unraveling Intermediary Liability', presented at *British and Irish Law, Education and Technology* (2014), at www.laidlaw.eu/2014/06/unraveling-in termediary-liability/ (last visited 17 June 2014).

[59] Petley n. 3, p. 83. Emphasis in original.

[60] S. Starr, 'Internet Freedom', *New Humanist*, 117(1) (2002), p. 2.      [61] Petley n. 3, p. 88.

[62] Starr n. 60, p. 2.

[63] It has said this many times. For example, in its 2006 Annual Report, it discusses the blacklist as something ISPs choose to do: Internet Watch Foundation, *Annual and Charity Report 2006*, p. 5. On their website, the organisation describes the process with the blacklist as something it passes on to its members that 'have chosen to make use of this list to protect their customers', at www.iwf.org.uk/public/page.148.htm (last visited 17 June 2014).

other times as a matter of legal duty. On its website, it describes the process as follows:

> Once informed, the host or internet service provider (ISP) is duty bound under the E-Commerce Regulations (Liability of intermediary service providers) to remove or disable access to the potentially criminal content, expeditiously.[64]

In the face of journalist questions, Sarah Robertson, the IWF's former head of communication, commented, 'We just provide a list of URLs'.[65] While technically true, this is not an accurate statement on the law nor is the statement on its website. Once a host is notified of unlawful content, it risks losing its exemption from liability under the E-Commerce Directive if it chooses not to block that content, so while it may appear that an ISP has a choice or chooses to block the content, the reality is that, in its capacity as a host, it is vulnerable to bodies such as the IWF who make allegations of unlawful content, and such bodies are built around this knowledge.

The question then is what is the IWF and how did it become so constituted that it is the body in the United Kingdom that determines the online material that is blocked? This requires an investigation of the IWF at both an internal level through assessment of its regulatory structure and governance documents and at an external level by comparing claims of the IWF's free speech impact against reality. A fundamental issue with the IWF is that it has evolved to the point that it is unclear exactly what it is in law. Is the IWF a public authority and thus directly bound by the Human Rights Act (HRA)?[66] Or is it a purely self-regulatory body whose human rights responsibilities are none other than what it voluntarily undertakes?[67]

### 4.2.1. The IWF

The IWF is as an industry-funded regulatory body with charitable status. It has broad membership from the internet industry, including ISPs, mobile operators, search engine and content providers, filtering

---

[64] See www.iwf.org.uk/public/page.103.549.htm (last visited 12 May 2014).
[65] Davies n. 1.    [66] 1998 Ch 42.
[67] For another case study on the IWF concerning its role as censor, see C. Marsden, *Internet Co-Regulation: European Law, Regulatory Governance and Legitimacy in Cyberspace* (Cambridge University Press, 2011), pp. 68–178.

companies and licensees such as Cisco and MTN Group.[68] It is held out as a model, receiving praise from the Government,[69] other regulatory bodies such as Nominet[70] and the Office of Communication (Ofcom),[71] and influencing the creation of similar models abroad.[72] It has partnership agreements with the International Telecommunication Union (ITU) and the Commonwealth Cybercrime Initiative (CCI) to deliver an Online Child Sexual Abuse Reporting Portal (OCSARP), making its analysts available to assess content reported by individuals in countries which have signed up for it.[73] Its main functions are to process reports from the public regarding suspected criminal content and to compile a blacklist of internet content it deems potentially criminal. This is then filtered by its members. In its 2012 Annual Report, the IWF advised that more than 98.6 per cent of the UK population with broadband connection gained access to the internet through an IWF member ISP.[74] A decision of the IWF on what goes on the blacklist is effectively a decision as to what content is blocked in the United Kingdom for the average user. Thus, this seemingly nondescript private regulatory body wields considerable power.

The IWF's remit, set out on its website, is to minimise the availability of three types of content: (1) images of child sexual abuse hosted anywhere, (2) criminal obscene adult content hosted in the United Kingdom, and (3) nonphotographic child sexual abuse content hosted in the United Kingdom.[75] Until April 2011, the remit also covered incitement to racial

---

[68] See www.iwf.org.uk/public/page.148.438.htm (last visited 17 June 2014).

[69] See Lord Carter, *Digital Britain final report* (June 2009), at http://webarchive.nationalar chives.gov.uk/+/http://www.culture.gov.uk/images/publications/digitalbritain-finalrepo rt-jun09.pdf (last access 17 June 2014).

[70] Nominet has given the IWF a Nominet Internet Award several times. See www.iwf.org.uk (last accessed 17 June 2014).

[71] Ofcom, 'Identifying appropriate regulatory solutions: principles for analysing self- and co-regulation' (10 December 2008), at http://stakeholders.ofcom.org.uk/binaries/consul tations/coregulation/statement/statement.pdf (last accessed 17 June 2014), 9.

[72] For example, see Canada's 'cleanfeed': Cybpertip!ca, at www.cybertip.ca/app/en/ (last accessed 17 June 2014).

[73] Internet Watch Foundation, *Annual and Charity Report 2013*, at www.iwf.org.uk/account ability/annual-reports/2013-annual-report (last visited 27 June 2014), p. 5.

[74] Internet Watch Foundation, *2012 Annual and Charity Report*, at www.iwf.org.uk/account ability/annual-reports/2011-annual-report (last visited 27 June 2014), p. 21.

[75] See www.iwf.org.uk/public/page.35.htm (last visited 17 June 2014). The IWF repeatedly describes the content it targets as potentially illegal, rather than simply illegal explaining that '[w]e refer to content as *potentially* criminal because a definitive legal judgment is a matter for the Courts': www.iwf.org.uk/public/page.103.549.htm (last visited 17 June 2014).

hatred content hosted in the United Kingdom; however, such content has now been redirected to the police body True Vision.[76] The IWF views itself as a tool for CSR, stating that 'being a member of the IWF offers many benefits including evidence of corporate social responsibility'.[77]

To satisfy its remit, it works together with industry and government to combat online abuse, but its main job is threefold. First, it operates the anonymous hotline for the reporting of illegal content. In 2013, the IWF reported that it received 51,186 complaints from the public, of which it acted on 26 per cent of them.[78] It draws from this material for its second main function, which is the operation of a notice-and-takedown regime covering all potentially criminal content within its remit, not just child sexual abuse images. Under this regime, it advises ISPs and hosting companies of any potentially criminal content, as well as provides such data to law enforcement authorities in the United Kingdom and abroad to assist them with their investigations. Third, specifically with regard to child sexual abuse images hosted outside the United Kingdom, it maintains a dynamic blacklist of URLs, which it passes to its members to be blocked.[79] The IWF advises that the list usually contains approximately 500 URLs.[80] It describes its role in blocking content as follows:

> We consider blocking to be a short-term disruption tactic which can help protect internet users from stumbling across these images, whilst processes to have them removed are instigated.[81]

The blacklist is available to national and international law enforcement agencies and to International Association of Internet Hotlines (INHOPE) hotlines.[82]

It has been proposed that the IWF remit be expanded so that it takes a more proactive, investigatory role, where its analysts will browse the internet for child sexual abuse content.[83] In addition, as peer-to-peer is

---

[76] See www.iwf.org.uk/about-iwf/news/post/302-incitement-to-racial-hatred-removed-from-iwfs-remit (last visited 17 June 2014). See True Vision, at www.report-it.org.uk/home (last visited 17 June 2014).

[77] See www.iwf.org.uk/members (last visited 17 June 2014).

[78] Annual and Charity report 2013, n. 60, p. 10.

[79] See www.iwf.org.uk/public/page.103.htm (last visited 17 June 2014).

[80] See https://www.iwf.org.uk/members/member-policies/url-list (last visited 14 May 2014).

[81] Ibid.

[82] See www.iwf.org.uk/public/page.148.438.htm and www.iwf.org.uk/public/page.196.htm (last visited 14 May 2014).

[83] See Lord Macdonald of River Glaven, QC, 'A human rights audit of the Internet Watch Foundation', at www.iwf.org.uk/accountability/human-rights-audit (last visited 17 June 2014).

increasingly used by consumers of child sexual abuse content to share images, it has been proposed that the IWF begin investigating such content through surveillance of these P2P file-sharing networks. This will be discussed in Section 4.5.

The remit of the IWF – indeed the very existence of the IWF – has been controversial from the start. The IWF was founded in 1996 by the internet industry in cooperation with the Home Office and the police and under direct threat that if the internet industry did not regulate itself, the government would legislate.[84] In October 1996, 'Safety Net', the predecessor of the IWF, was born under the design of Peter Dawe, who co-founded and headed one of the United Kingdom's first commercial ISPs, Pipex.[85] In 2000, after three years in operation, it was restructured and relaunched and, importantly, endorsed by the government and the then Department of Trade and Industry (DTI) now called the Department of Business, Innovation and Skills (BIS).[86]

This restructure served the laudable purpose of making the body more transparent and accountable to the public. It streamlined governance to a single Board, and, in an effort to make it more independent of the industry that created it, the Board was then required to have a majority of and be chaired by nonindustry member(s).[87] It also started publishing its Annual Reports. However, it was also at this time that the IWF began to shift its role by expanding its remit, starting with criminally racist content.[88] The IWF also started banning entire newsgroups, even though the majority of the content in the newsgroups was legal. This led to the resignation of several board members, many of whom had played an integral role in the founding of the IWF. One of those who resigned, Malcolm Hutty, at the time described the IWF as becoming a 'child protection lobby'.[89]

Three key things happened that pushed the ubiquity of the IWF's blacklist. First, in 2002, the IWF released the blacklist to its members and any others who paid a licensing fee. Then, in 2003, BT developed the technical system known colloquially as Cleanfeed, but officially called BT

---

[84] See www.iwf.org.uk/public/page.103.552.htm (last visited 17 June 2014).

[85] G. Sutter, '"Nothing New under the Sun": Old Fear and New Media', *IJLIT*, 8(3) (2000) 338, p. 370.

[86] Petley n. 3

[87] See 'Introduction to the IWF' on former IWF Chair Roger Darlington's website, at www.rogerdarlington.co.uk/iwf.html#Introduction (last visited 17 June 2014).

[88] Ibid.

[89] W. Grossman, 'IWF: what are you looking at?' (25 March 2002), at http://archive.today /s6MY3 (last visit 17 June 2014).

Anti-Child-Abuse Initiative,[90] to block access to content on the IWF's blacklist by its users. BT made the critical decision to make Cleanfeed available for use by other ISPs, which most have. Third, ISPs were pressured to follow BT's lead, and any effort to resist this pressure was laid to rest when the government said that unless 100 per cent of the industry regulated itself, the Government would legislate.[91] Thus, the IWF's blacklist became standardised across the UK internet industry, and, as a result, effective control was consolidated under one roof.

Cleanfeed looks at individual URLs rather than simply domain names. It is a hybrid system, one that 'redirects traffic that might need to be blocked to a proxy cache, which then takes the final decision'.[92] What this means is that the destination port and IP address of traffic is examined, and, if it is suspect, it is redirected to a web proxy, which examines whether the URL sought is one on the IWF blacklist; if so, access is blocked.[93] The blacklist is held on the server in encrypted form.[94]

Cleanfeed has been criticised for failing to deal with child pornography distributed via peer-to-peer and instant messaging,[95] arguably now the more popular approach to distribution of child pornography. It has also been accused of being open to what are called 'oracle' attacks in which users can find out the sites on the blacklist.[96] In addition, since the IWF does not dictate the filtering technology used, while most ISPs use Cleanfeed, it is not the case that all of them do, and the system used for filtering in these instances is unknown.[97] Finally, not all ISPs advise users that the site they are attempting to access is blacklisted, returning instead a 404 (page unavailable) error page.[98] The IWF has recommended in its Blocking Good Practice that users are advised access has been denied (returning instead an error 403 page). However, this is not standardised at the moment. The 2013 Annual Report advises that the IWF is running a pilot in which large ISPs and mobile operators have volunteered to test the effectiveness of displaying splash pages.[99] What is clear, however, is that some ISPs are not transparent concerning the sites that are blocked,

---

[90] Clayton n. 4, p. 2.    [91] See discussion McIntyre n. 10, pp. 10–11.
[92] Clayton n. 4, p. 1.    [93] Ibid., pp. 4–5. See diagram on p. 5.    [94] Ibid., p. 4.
[95] McIntyre n. 10, p. 11.    [96] Clayton n. 4.
[97] The IWF states that, '[w]hile the IWF facilitates this blocking initiative through the provision of a URL list and does not stipulate which blocking method is used, we do provide good practice guidance regarding the way in which blocking is conducted': www.iwf.org.uk/services/blocking (last visited 17 June 2014).
[98] Academic research indicates this to be the case: Clayton n. 4, p. 4.
[99] Annual Report 2013, n. 73, p. 5.

and there is no standardisation of approaches across the industry. The question is from where the IWF derives its legitimacy.

### 4.2.2. The ISPA and internal codes of conduct

The UK ISP Association (ISPA) is the country's trade association for ISPs. It was established in 1995 and has more than 200 members, including, BT, Virgin Media, Vodafone, Google and Yahoo!.[100] Membership is voluntary, but most companies are members of the Association. The ISPA defers to the IWF with regard to filtering of unlawful content. Members of the ISPA are bound by its Code of Practice:[101] Section 5 sets out the procedure for handling the IWF blacklist. It explicitly states that membership in the IWF is not mandatory; however, it makes clear that the ISPA cooperates with the IWF and that its procedures in this regard *are* mandatory for ISPA members:

5.1 ISPA membership does not automatically confer IWF membership. Members are encouraged to consider direct IWF membership.
5.2 ISPA co-operates with the IWF in its efforts to remove illegal material from Internet web-sites and newsgroups. Members are therefore required to adhere to the following procedures in dealing with the IWF.[102]

The ISPA mandates that members must provide a point of contact to receive IWF notices and that they must remove webpages or UseNet articles which the IWF deems and notifies them are illegal child abuse images.[103] The Code only requires members to take 'careful consideration'[104] of all other types of IWF notices and recommendations. In addition, if a member cannot technically remove the material, it is required to tell the IWF why.[105] The effect of this provision is to mandate that ISPs take down any content on the IWF blacklist, whether they are members of the IWF or not. The IWF thus becomes something other than voluntary. Rather, legitimisation by the ISPA makes the IWF the

---

[100] See http://www.ispa.org.uk/about-us/ (last visited 12 May 2014) and http://www.ispa .org.uk/members/ (last visited 12 May 2014). The ISPA describes its main job as acting as a representative voice for the industry to governmental bodies. The UK ISPA helped establish EuroISPA, the European federation of Internet Service Providers Associations. EuroISPA acts as a representative body of industry at the EU level.

[101] See ISPA, *Code of Practice*, at www.ispa.org.uk/about-us/ispa-code-of-practice/ (last visited 12 May 2014).

[102] Ibid.    [103] Ibid., cl. 5.    [104] Ibid., cl. 5.6.    [105] Ibid., cl. 5.4.

industry's standard-setting body for content filtering in the United Kingdom.

The ISPA and its members have also drafted 'Best Common Practice' (BCP) documents, which are nonbinding ISPA recommendations, and 'Backgrounders', which are informational documents for users.[106] Of relevance here are two documents. In a Backgrounder on Content Liability, the ISPA confirms that it operates a notice-and-takedown procedure in which, if it is notified of illegal material by the IWF or law enforcement agencies, it removes it.[107] The BCP on Blocking and Filtering of Internet Traffic states that the ISPA must notify its customers of the nature of filtering it undertakes, which involves informing the customer of 'the form of filtering and the general criteria used to filter but need not provide a complete set of details, particularly where they are subject to change'.[108] In practice, the threshold to meet this criterion is extremely low, as can be seen in the proffered example: '[w]e block access to the IP addresses that host those web sites which IWF informs us publish child abuse images that are illegal to possess'.[109]

Indeed, in an examination of the terms of service (ToS) and acceptable use policies (AUP) of leading ISPs, it was found that they use almost this exact language and simply refer and defer to the IWF. The internal codes of conduct of the top UK ISPs based on the number of customers was reviewed. ISPreview compiled a list of the top ten ISPs as of May 2014 based on the companies' public results on subscriber size. It listed the top five as BT (PlusNet), Sky Broadband (BSkyB, O2, BE Broadband), Virgin Media, TalkTalk (AOL, Tiscali, Pipex) and EE (Orange and T-Mobile).[110] For example, PlusNet's AUP advises it is a member of the IWF[111] but does not provide any information on what or if it blocks. Virgin's Internet Security Team advises that they block access to sites the IWF asks them to but provides no other information.[112]

---

[106] See www.ispa.org.uk/about_us/page_559.html (last visited 23 August 2011). No longer available.

[107] See www.ispa.org.uk/press_office/page_58.html (last visited 23 August 2011). No longer available.

[108] ISPA, 'Best current practice on blocking and filtering of internet traffic', at www.ispa.org.uk/home/page_327.html (last visited 23 August 2011), cl. 2(1). No longer available.

[109] Ibid., cl.3.

[110] ISPreview, 'Top 10 UK ISPs', at www.ispreview.co.uk/review/top10.php (last visited 12 May 2014).

[111] See www.plus.net/support/security/abuse/internet_watch_foundation.shtml (last visited 12 May 2014).

[112] See http://help.virginmedia.com/system/selfservice.controller (last visited 12 May 2014).

BT's information on its filtering practices and its relationship with the IWF is even more difficult to find. It has a Human Rights Policy, which acknowledges the difficult position it is placed in to balance freedom of expression against competing rights.[113] With regard to child sexual abuse images, in 2011 it stated, '[t]hrough our involvement with the Internet Watch Foundation, BT receives a daily list of child abuse sites which are then blocked, preventing customers from accidentally accessing them'.[114] It uses softer language now to describe its policy: 'We have continued to work in partnership with the UK Council for Child Internet Safety (UKCCIS), the Child Exploitation and Online Protection Centre (CEOP) and the Internet Watch Foundation (IWF) to educate parents on practical ways to protect their children'.[115]

It becomes clear, therefore, that key policy decisions concerning filtering are made by the IWF. The IWF becomes a policy chokepoint on filtering in the United Kingdom and therefore emerges as an IIG in its own right separate from ISPs. The attention is thus turned to the operation of the IWF to determine its human rights compliance and, consequently, its role in facilitating or hindering participation in democratic culture.

### 4.3. An analysis of the human rights compliance of the IWF

The reader will recall from Chapter 3 that CSR, as it is used in this book, has a voluntary as well as indirect legal component, and part of the work is in teasing out the legal versus voluntary elements of the body that is the focus of analysis. We draw here from Article 10 of the ECHR to ask, first, whether the body is in fact a public authority and thus directly bound by the HRA and, if not, whether the state has positive obligations under Article 10 that it has or has not discharged. If there are no such legal obligations, we examine the IWF as a form of pure-CSR, drawing from Article 10 principles, more loosely because it is not legally binding, and looking to the criteria in the Guiding Principles as a guide. We ask:

---

[113] See https://www.btplc.com/betterfuture/betterbusiness/betterfuturereport/PDF/2002/HumanRights2002.pdf (last visited 14 May 2014), pp. 7–8.

[114] See www.btplc.com/Responsiblebusiness/Ourstory/Sustainabilityreport/section/index.aspx?sectionid=8eb1a1fe-a1b3-4fee-b438-de3cb33be585 (last visited 23 August 2011). Link no longer available.

[115] See www.btplc.com/betterfuture/betterbusiness/betterfuturereport/report/BB/cust/Child.aspx (link no longer available).

(a) What are the due-diligence processes? Namely, is there guidance on human rights policies, monitoring and tracking of performance and mitigation strategies?
(b) Do the policies on human rights include negative and positive obligations? What is the nature of the obligations?
(c) What remedial structures are there, if any? Do they have any of the characteristics identified as important in the Guiding Principles of legitimacy, accessibility, predictability, equitability, rights-compatibility, transparency and consultation with stakeholders?

### 4.3.1. How 'private' is the IWF?

Under the HRA Section 6, the Act is only binding on 'public authorities'. The definition of public authority differentiates between core public authorities, which are obvious public authorities such as government agencies and local authorities, and hybrid public authorities,[116] which under Section 6(3)(b) is 'any person certain of whose functions are functions of a public nature'. The question is whether the IWF might be a hybrid public authority. Under Section 6(5) 'a person is not a public authority by virtue only of Subsection (3)(b) if the nature of the act is private'.[117] What this means is that if the matter in dispute is private in nature, then it is not a situation in which the HRA applies to the body. In contrast, a core public authority would be bound by the HRA for all of its activities.[118] Thus, in examining the IWF, not all aspects of it need be public in nature, nor would all aspects of its work receive HRA oversight. The reader will note that since my article was published and the human rights audit was performed, the IWF has accepted that it is a public authority under the HRA.[119] It would seem to render the following analysis moot, but it is included because it forms the basis of an analysis that has implications beyond this narrow question.

---

[116] For a discussion of core and hybrid public authorities, see R. Clayton and H. Tomlinson, *The Law of Human Rights*, 2nd edn, vol. 1 (Oxford University Press, 2009), paras 5.13–5.48. Note that courts and tribunals are public authorities, leading to the indirect horizontal effect of the HRA: see *Campbell* v. *MGN Ltd* [2004] UKHL 22 in this regard.

[117] HRA, ss. 6(3)(b) and 6(5). See discussion in C. Gearty, *Principles of Human Rights Adjudication* (Oxford University Press, 2004) about earlier case law, pp. 185–91.

[118] See Clayton and Tomlinson n. 116, para. 5.08. Distinction teased out by Lord Woolf CJ in *Poplar Housing and Regeneration Community Association Ltd.* v. *Donoghue* [2002] QB 48 (CA), para. 63.

[119] Audit, n. 83, para. 7.2.

One of the leading issues of debate in UK case law is what qualifies as 'functions of a public nature' to trigger treatment as a hybrid public authority. There has been no definitive settlement on this matter; thus, it is a live issue, and a new case can at any time change the lens through which the activities of the IWF are viewed.[120] In the past, the courts have held that, given the circumstances of the cases, a parish council[121] was not a public authority, but a housing association[122] and private psychiatric hospital[123] were found to qualify as such. The most recent high-level pronouncement on the matter is the deeply divided House of Lords decision in *YL* v. *Birmingham City Council* (YL).[124]

*YL* concerned whether a private residential care home, Southern Cross Healthcare Ltd., was a hybrid public authority. The Court was divided 3:2 in favour of finding that Southern Cross was not a hybrid public authority under Section 6 of the HRA. The minority (Lord Bingham and Baroness Hale) advocated interpreting 'public function' generously, focusing on whether the nature of the function was public or private and emphasising the vulnerability of the claimant.[125] The majority (Lords Scott, Mance and Neuberger), in contrast, emphasised the fact that this was a for-profit company, operating through contracts, both private and public, with no direct public funding and no legislative oversight:

> It is neither a charity nor a philanthropist. It enters in private law contracts with the residents in its care homes and with the local authorities with whom it does business. It receives no public funding, enjoys no special statutory powers, and is at liberty to accept or reject residents as it chooses ... and to charge whatever fees in its commercial judgment it thinks suitable. It is operating in a commercial market with commercial competitors.[126]

The division in the Court was driven by starkly different policy views on the things considered by the courts in assessing whether a body is a

---

[120] See summary of early cases in Clayton and Tomlinson, n. 116, paras 5.22–5.29.
[121] *Aston Cantlow and Wilmcote with Beillesley Parochial Church Council* v. *Wallbank* [2003] UKHL 37.
[122] *Poplar Housing*, n. 118.        [123] *R (A)* v. *Partnerships in Care Ltd.* [2002] 1 WLR 2610.
[124] [2008] 1 AC 95.
[125] In particular, see Lord Bingham's opinion, paras. 4–5, 19, and Baroness Hale's at paras. 65–68: '[while there cannot be a single litmus test of what is a function of a public nature, the underlying rationale must be that it is a task for which the public, in the shape of the state, have assumed responsibility, at public expense if need be, and in the public interest': para. 65.
[126] Ibid., Lord Scott, para. 26.

hybrid public authority.[127] Thus, any cases at the borderline of hybrid public authority are very much fact driven, given the nature of the body and the circumstances of that particular case. Based on *YL*, the types of things courts look at would be the social benefit of what the business does, funding, statutory underpinning, ties to government and whether it carries out a governmental functional.[128]

We can also find guidance on the public authority status of the IWF from the judicial treatment of other media regulatory bodies. The Advertising Standards Authority (ASA), Ofcom and the British Board of Film Classification (BBFC) are all arguably public authorities under the HRA, but all three bodies have legislative underpinnings, unlike the IWF.[129] The most appropriate comparison, historically, would have been to the now defunct Press Complaints Commission (PCC), which, like the IWF, was a private self-regulatory body that operated at the encouragement of government and without any legislative underpinning.[130] When it was in operation, it was less clear that the PCC was a public authority, although a strong argument could be made. The government stated in debates concerning the HRA that the PCC undertook public

---

[127] See comments of Lord Neuberger for the majority commenting, '[t]he centrally relevant words, "functions of a public nature", are so imprecise in their meaning that one searches for a policy as an aid to interpretation': ibid., para. 128. Parliament overturned the effect of *YL* by designating care home providers contracted under a situation such as in this case as public authorities: Health and Social Care Act 2008 c. 14, s. 145. This does not have wider application, however, but gives some indication of Parliament's view on the matter.

[128] The *YL* factors have been applied with approval in subsequent case law analysing whether a particular body is a public authority. Thus far, none of these cases has helped clarify or extend the principles in *YL* in a way that would be useful in an assessment of the public authority status of the IWF. See, for example, *Barr & Ors v. Biffa Waste Services Ltd. (No 3)* [2011] EWHC 1003.

[129] Ofcom regulates broadcasting pursuant to the Communications Act 2003 c. 21. The ASA operates within a framework of community law and the director-general has the power to obtain an injunction to control misleading advertising under the Consumer Protection from Unfair Trading Regulations 2008 No. 1277. The BBFC, although a private body exercising public law functions, is brought within a system of regulation by the Home Secretary designating it an 'authority' under s. 4 of the Video Recording Act 1984 c. 39 for the issuance of video certificates. See *Wingrove v. United Kingdom* (1997) 24 EHRR 1 for a discussion of an appeal from the BBFC to the Video Appeal Committee.

[130] A natural comparison would also be to Nominet, but Nominet's status as a public authority is as untested as the IWF's, and thus attention is turned to traditional communication regulators, which have been around longer and thus received more judicial attention. As of September 2014, the PCC was controversially replaced by the Independent Press Standards Organisation (IPSO) at www.ipso.co.uk/IPSO/ (last visited 4 November 2014), although note that there remains the possibility of the government proceeding with the regulator set up by the Royal Charter.

functions.[131] Indeed, the PCC acknowledged it was a public authority in *R (Ford)* v. *The Press Complaints Commission.*[132]

In the case of the IWF, it is argued that more is going on here than a simple 'public connection', as Lord Neuberger described the activities of Southern Cross in *YL*.[133] The IWF is a product of direct government threats carrying out a function that, at its core, is governmental in nature. While there is no legislative underpinning to the functioning and legitimacy of the IWF, there can be no question that its legitimacy and role is government-driven. In addition, it has been reported that the IWF acknowledged it is a public authority under the HRA in 2001,[134] although this statement was made in minutes that are no longer available.

The IWF insists that it is a self-regulatory body operating separately from state, but the actual set-up is less clearly self-regulatory. In a Memorandum of Understanding between the Crown Prosecution Service and the Association of Chief Police Officers concerning Section 46 of the Sexual offences Act 2003, the role and remit of the IWF is described as very much an extension of government, using language such as 'support' and 'on behalf of UK law enforcement agencies' to describe its functions:

> The IWF is funded by service providers, mobile network operators, software and hardware manufacturers and other associated partners. It is supported by the Police and CPS and works in partnership with the Government to provide a 'hotline' for individuals or organisations to report potentially illegal content and then to assess and judge that material on behalf of UK law enforcement agencies. It also exists to assist service providers to avoid abuse of their systems by distributors of child abuse content and to support law enforcement officers, at home and abroad, to detect and prosecute offenders. Reports made to the IWF in line with its procedures will be accepted as a report to a relevant authority.[135]

---

[131] See Joint Committee on Human Rights, *Tenth Report* (2007), at www.parliament.the -stationery-office.com/pa/jt200607/jtselect/jtrights/81/8105.htm (last accessed 17 June 2014), footnote 11. Note, of course, that in *YL* the judges discussed the inapplicability of such documents to the question of whether a body is a public authority.

[132] *R (Ford)* v. *The Press Complaints Commission*, [2001] EWHC Admin 683, para. 11.

[133] *YL*, n. 124, para 140.

[134] McIntyre, n. 10, p. 13. This was stated in the Minutes of an IWF board meeting on 25 April 2001, reported on by Y. Akdeniz, *Internet Child Pornography and the Law* (Aldershot: Ashgate, 2008), 264, which report is no longer available to this author for review. I was able to review the minutes of then-Chair Roger Darlington, n. 87.

[135] *Memorandum of Understanding Between the Crown Prosecution Service (CPS) and the Association of Chief Police Officers (ACPO) concerning Section 46 Sexual Offences Act 2003*, p. 6.

Indeed, the language the IWF and the government use to describe the role of the IWF is mixed. The IWF describes itself as a self-regulatory body but also uses words such as 'partnership' and 'multistakeholder', indicating a co-regulatory approach halfway between the PCC and Ofcom. Professor Byron, in her child protection review, described the IWF as lying 'at the heart of the Government's safeguarding strategy'[136] for the protection of children. The IWF describes its relationship with the government as follows:

> We operate independently of Government, but are closely supported by the Home Office, the Department for Business, Innovation and Skills (BIS) and the Ministry of Justice as well as working with the Department for Education and the Department for Culture, Media and Sport (DCMS) and a number of Parliamentarians, Peers and MEPs who take an interest in our work.[137]

From this, it is unclear what the relationship between the IWF and the government is, although it can be said at minimum that there is a relationship between the two, although it is not formally provided for in a legislative document. In addition to the mutual sharing of information and resources, the IWF has in the past received funding from the UK government, although a miniscule amount compared to its operating budget.

The funding of the IWF is highly unusual and makes it difficult to draw comparisons with other media regulatory bodies. It is a registered charity, and, as a charity, it must publish its accounts. There it was revealed that the IWF's largest single donor is the European Union, although its main revenue is drawn from the subscription fees it charges to its members. Its fee structure was revamped in 2013 and ranges from very small firms paying fees of £1000 per annum to main ISPs paying £75,000 per annum.[138] It has in the past received funding from the Home Office, although the most recent reports do not list any such funding.[139] For example, in 2006, it received £14,502 from the Home Office.[140] It also received a one-off grant of £50,000 from Nominet for a research project.[141] In June 2013, BT, Sky, TalkTalk and Virgin Media agreed to

---

[136] *Safer Children in a Digital World: The Report of the Byron Review* (Crown copyright, 2008), p. 16.
[137] See www.iwf.org.uk/government/page.6.htm (last accessed 14 May 2014).
[138] See www.iwf.org.uk/members/funding-model (last visited 14 May 2014).
[139] See http://apps.charitycommission.gov.uk/Accounts/Ends98/0001112398_AC_20130331 _E_C.pdf (last visited 14 May 2014).
[140] Ibid.    [141] Ibid.

commit £1 million over four years to the IWF to combat the creation and distribution of child sexual abuse material online.[142]

Based on a narrow interpretation of public authority, the IWF might not qualify as such. However, the 'steering'[143] role of government combined with its funding structure and public function makes a strong case that the IWF is a public authority under the HRA and thus directly bound by Article 10. The case of the IWF is then quite different from that imagined. It becomes a case of a corporate governance framework developed to the point that it is brought within the rubric of state-centred human rights laws, a matter that has simply not been tested in the courts yet. It is arguable that the language of CSR here, intentionally or unintentionally, has only served to deflect attention away from this state of affairs. The evolution of this framework from a pure-CSR body to a public authority also has implications to businesses considering self-regulation because they might be fearful of exactly this result. This is explored more in Chapter 6.

However, that is not the end of the story. We are at a crossroads. If the IWF is a public authority, then we must assess whether its administration complies with Article 10(2). Even if the IWF is not a public authority, there is a strong case to be made that the state has positive obligations to the public under Article 10 concerning the governance of the IWF. This leads us in the direction of a direct application of the ECHR concerning the IWF. We cannot forget, however, the notion of the IWF as a form of pure-CSR. Even if no direct human rights obligations are engaged in a legal sense, a body such as the IWF has human rights commitments nonetheless. This leads the examination in another direction, one in which the Guiding Principles identify the characteristics to look for in the IWF's internal governance structure.

### 4.3.2. Is the IWF prescribed by law with a legitimate aim?

What qualifies as a legitimate aim is exhaustively listed in Article 10(2) as 'national security, territorial integrity or public safety, for the prevention of disorder or crime, for the protection of health or morals, for the protection of the reputation or the rights of others, for preventing the

---

[142] See www.btplc.com/BTToday/NewsList/BTjoinsforcestotackleonlinechildabuse/index .htm (last visited 12 May 2014).

[143] In McIntyre and Scott, n. 9, p. 121, the authors discuss the government's 'inherent steering capacity' with regard to the IWF.

disclosure of information received in confidence, or for maintaining the authority and impartiality of the judiciary'.[144]

There isn't any question that the IWF serves a legitimate aim – several legitimate aims – under Article 10, including the prevention of crime, the protection of reputation and, most particularly, the protection of children as reflected in the protection of health or morals or public safety. The IWF serves a valuable and notable purpose in protecting the public from exposure to child abuse images and arguably contributes to limiting access to such images or the distribution channels of paedophiles. With regard to the wider IWF remit, regulation of criminally obscene content is a legitimate aim under Article 10.

For an interference to be prescribed by law, the Court takes a wide view. For example, in *Müller* v. *Switzerland*,[145] the court held that obscenity laws, which vary depending on the views of a community at the time, were sufficiently precise to be prescribed by law. Whereas, at a minimum, there must be a specific rule or legal regime that can be pointed to,[146] it includes delegated powers and unwritten law (i.e., common law). Unfettered discretion is not prescribed by law, but if it is sufficiently delimited it is sufficient.[147] At the heart of 'prescribed by law' is the principle of legal certainty, meaning that there must be some basis in domestic law, whether statute or common law, for the conduct.[148]

In *Sunday Times* v. *United Kingdom* (No 1),[149] the Court stated it involves an examination of the quality of the law to assess its arbitrariness. This involves two criteria. First, the law must be adequately accessible. Second, a norm is not prescribed by law 'unless it is formulated with sufficient precision to enable the citizen to regulate his conduct: he must be able – if need be with appropriate advice – to foresee, to a degree that is reasonable in the circumstances, the consequences which a given action may entail'.[150]

---

[144] European Convention for the Protection of Human Rights and Fundamental Freedoms 1950, article 10(2). The issue of legitimate aim has rarely been a matter of much discussion in the case law: D. J. Harris et al., *Law of European Convention on Human Rights*, 2nd edn (Oxford University Press, 2009), p. 542.

[145] *Müller* v. *Switzerland* (1991) 13 EHRR 212.

[146] *Malone* v. *United Kingdom* (1985) 7 EHRR 14. See Harris n. 131, p. 344.

[147] See discussion ibid., pp. 344–46. See *Silver* v. *United Kingdom* (1983) 5 EHRR 347 and *Leander* v. *Sweden* (1987) 9 EHRR 433 discussed therein.

[148] See Lord Lester of Herne Hill et al., *Human Rights Law and Practice* (London: Butterworths, 1999), para. 3.14.

[149] (1979–80) 2 EHRR 245.     [150] Ibid., para. 49.

The IWF targets content which domestic law deems is illegal. Child sexual abuse images are covered by the Protection of Children Act 1978, Sexual Offences Act 2003, Memorandum of Understanding: Section 46 Sexual Offences Act 2003, the Police and Justice Act 2006 and the Coroners and Justice Act 2009. With regard to criminally obscene adult content, the relevant legislation is the Obscene Publications Act 1959 and 1964 and Criminal Justice and Immigration Act 2008 Section 63.[151] The concern is not with the content targeted by the IWF but rather with regulation of the regulator. The power the IWF exercises in determining the information we can and cannot access on the internet is vast. The exercise of this power must be prescribed by law. This requires that there are safeguards in the law to protect against arbitrary interferences by a public authority like the IWF. Such was the issue in *Halford* v. *United Kingdom*[152] concerning the interception of telephone calls.

In *Halford*, since the Interception of Communications Act[153] only applied to public communications network, and the interference occurred over a private network, there was no provision in domestic law to protect the complainant. In the context of Article 8, the ECtHR held that the lack of regulation in domestic law meant the interference was not prescribed by law, stating,

> In the context of secret measures of surveillance or interception of communications by public authorities, because of the lack of public scrutiny and the risk of misuse of power, the domestic law must provide some protection to the individual against arbitrary interference with Article 8 rights (art. 8). Thus, the domestic law must be sufficiently clear in its terms to give citizens an adequate indication as to the circumstances in and conditions on which public authorities are empowered to resort to any such secret measures.[154]

This approach can also be seen in *Ahmet Yildirim* v. *Turkey*,[155] a case particularly on point for this analysis and discussed briefly earlier. The ECtHR was tasked with assessing the lawfulness of a blocking order made by the Turkish Telecommunications Directorate (TIB). The Denizli Criminal Court of First Instance ordered the blocking of a website that insulted the memory of Ataturk. The TIB asked the court to extend the scope of the order to block access to the entire Google Sites service, which

---

[151] See www.iwf.org.uk/police/page.22.htm (last visited 17 June 2014). When incitement to racial hatred content was within its remit, it drew its authority from the Public Order Act 1986 c. 64 and the Race Relations Act 1976 c. 74.
[152] (1997) 24 EHRR 523.    [153] 1985 c. 56.    [154] *Halford* n. 152, para. 49.
[155] *Yildirim* n. 14.

hosted the offending website, because it stated that this was the only technical means to block the offending site. The Court granted the request. The application to the ECtHR was made by an academic who owns a website hosted by Google Sites and who was unable to access his site due to the block. A key aspect of this case was the fact that the court order did not apply to Yildirim, although he was impacted by it.

In *Yildirim*, the ECtHR concluded that the blocking order in question failed to be prescribed by law because it risked producing arbitrary results, and the judicial review procedures were insufficient to avoid abuse.[156] The Court was concerned with 'whether, at the time the blocking order was issued, a clear and precise rule existed enabling the applicant to regulate his conduct in the matter'.[157] Where the blocking order failed was in its reach. Yildirim's site and Google Sites did not fall within the scope of the applicable law because the legality of their content was not at issue in the case before the Criminal Court. Furthermore, the law did not provide for the kind of wholesale blocking ordered, nor was Google notified it was hosting an illegal site.[158] The Court also took issue with the extensive powers of the administrative body TIB.[159] Although the Court concluded that prior restraint is not necessarily incompatible with the ECHR, it needed to be tightly controlled to avoid abuse of power.[160] The question is what legal framework would satisfy such prior restraint. One of the things the Court noted was the fact that the Criminal Court did not investigate whether less far-reaching blocking measures could be taken and merely accepted TIB's statement that such wholesale blocking was required. In the view of the ECtHR, this was a shortcoming in domestic law. As a result, the law failed to meet the foreseeability requirement of the ECHR.[161]

As will become evident in the following section concerning the proportionately of the IWF's governance structure, the IWF's operation is largely secret with very little oversight of its operation. This can be seen with the inclusion of obscene content in the IWF's remit. The test under the Obscene Publications Act is subjective, asking whether the material will tend to deprave and corrupt those likely to be exposed to it.[162] It is inherently tied up with the views of the community of that time and is a problematic standard to apply at the best of times by a jury of one's peers in the formal setting of a court. It is far more subjective and arbitrary

---

[156] Ibid., paras. 67–69.    [157] Ibid., para. 60.    [158] Ibid., para. 61.    [159] Ibid., para. 63.
[160] Ibid., para. 64.    [161] Ibid., paras. 67–69.
[162] Obscene Publications Act 1964 c. 74, Section 1.

when assessed by an individual in a back room without the prospect of any judicial oversight and ultimately risks the imposition by a private body of its employees' moral views on the wider public. Although traditional media, particularly broadcasters, have long grappled with the standard of offensiveness, this has not made the issue any less vexing or difficult to manage, and the IWF is distinguishable from such bodies for the largely private nature of its operation.

Drawing from *Halford* and *Yildirim*, there is nothing in domestic law nor internal to the IWF's governance structure that protects the public from arbitrariness in how the IWF exercises its power. It is unchecked. Without any such protection, the law cannot be said to be adequately accessible or foreseeable, two other aspects to the concept of prescribed by law. This will become particularly apparent when, later in this chapter, we explore the process by which website owners are/are not advised their site is on the blacklist and the process of appeal. The result is that the IWF, as a public authority, is arguably operating without any legal basis. Even if the IWF is not a public authority, there should be concerns with a body which exercises such a powerful role in administering our right to freedom of expression and yet fails to show evidence that its operation is not arbitrary. Such characteristics of transparency, accountability and proportionality are considered key to any good regulatory system, public or private.

Whereas the current remit of the IWF serves the legitimate aim of preventing disorder and crime and protecting health or morals, its administration is not prescribed by law. Indeed, the strength of its aim has helped mask its lack of legal basis because people fearful of being branded sympathetic to child pornographers either do not speak up or are quickly quieted, thus deflecting attention away from the failure of the IWF to carry out its work in a manner prescribed by law. The next question is whether the interference is necessary in a democratic society, keeping in mind that this question does not arise if the operation of the IWF is found to lack legal basis.

### 4.3.3. Necessary in a democratic society

*Handyside* v. *United Kingdom*[163] clarified the meaning of the term 'necessary in a democratic society', explaining that 'necessary' "is not synonymous with "indispensible" . . . neither has it the flexibility of such

---

[163] (1979–80) 1 EHRR 737.

expression as "admissible", "ordinary", "useful", "reasonable" or "desirable".[164] Rather, it is a question of proportionality, meaning that there was a pressing social need for the interference and that the interference strikes a 'fair and proportionate balance between the means chosen to satisfy it and the individual's freedom of expression'.[165] Thus, a court considers some of the following in its assessment:

- What is the importance of the right?[166]
- Is there a rational connect between the objective and the measures taken – is it arbitrary, unfair or based on irrational considerations?[167]
- The means chosen must be no more than is necessary to satisfy the objective.
- The more severe the interference, the more it must be justified.[168]

The analysis of whether the measures taken by the IWF are necessary in a democratic society can be categorised per the importance of the right, the remit of the organisation and the proportionality of the measures taken.

Freedom of expression 'is one of the cardinal rights guaranteed under the Convention'.[169] Any exceptions to this right must be interpreted narrowly.[170] The blacklist acts as a blanket restraint on speech, the most extreme act of censorship for which the most justification is needed because, for all practical purposes, it removes from public access the information at issue. The availability of the information via alternate means, whether because a user is knowledgeable in how to route around filters or the information is available, for example, in a different format such as print, does not make it anything other than censorship. Indeed, prevention of access does not need to be foolproof: 'a censor need not stamp out information entirely to effectively rig the market of ideas'.[171]

The IWF has attempted to alleviate such concerns by describing the blacklist as voluntary. At a conference soon after the Wikipedia incident, then IWF CEO Peter Robbins commented, '[the Wikipedia image] was added to a list we give to service providers who voluntarily undertake to block access to those types of images'.[172] He further defended the incident, stating, '[n]obody in the 12 years or so that we have been

---

[164] Ibid., para. 48.     [165] Harris n. 144, p. 444.     [166] Ibid., pp. 351–52.
[167] Lord Lester of Herne Hill n. 148, para. 3.10.
[168] Ibid. Note that ECHR jurisprudence is ultimately tied up with the notion of margin of appreciation, a notion generally inapplicable here.
[169] Harris n. 144, p. 443.     [170] Ibid., p. 443.     [171] Kreimer n. 23, p. 40.
[172] Westminster eForum (comments of Peter Robbins) (transcript), *Taming the Wild Web? – Online Content Regulation* (London: 11 February 2009).

operating has had any real reason to complain about anything that we may have done'.[173] The reality, however, as we have seen is that removal of such content is far from voluntary for members through the ISPA Code of Practice, government and social pressure and, when they act as hosts, through the risk of losing the exemption from liability under the E-Commerce Directive. Such regulation, combined with a private self-regulatory body acting as monitor and notifier of unlawful content, leaves IWF members with no option other than to remove all content it is advised is illegal. The result is that a single private body makes almost all of the decisions for the United Kingdom on the content which is blocked from access.

This can be contrasted with other countries such as Canada where its Telecommunications Act forbids ISPs to block access to content. Instead, such blocking is administered by a government regulatory body, the Canada Radio-Television Telecommunications Commission (CRTC).[174] Although an industry body, www.cybertip.ca has been modelled on the IWF, and the body itself does not make decisions concerning the content that is added to the blacklist, instead forwarding it to law enforcement authorities.[175] Some countries rely on lists provided by law enforcement agencies.[176] As Lilian Edwards argues,

> This censorship [using Cleanfeed-style technology] needs no laws to be passed, no court to rule, with the publicity that entails. It only needs the collaboration, forced or otherwise, of ISPs. ISPs are not public bodies; their acts are not subject to judicial review. Nor are they traditional news organizations; their first concern (quite properly) is for their shareholders and their own legal and PR risks, not for values like freedom of expression.[177]

As we have seen with the Wikipedia incident, it highlights the risks when the IWF overblocks. It was followed up early in 2009 with the blacklisting of images on the Wayback Machine, which led some ISPs such as Demon

---

[173] Ibid.

[174] Telecommunications Act (S.C. 1993, c. 38), s. 36. See discussion J. Bayer, 'Liability of internet service providers for third party content', *Victoria University Wellington Working Paper Series*, 1 (2008), pp. 1–109, 57–58. There is discussed the application of Richard Warman to the CRTC to exempt ISPs from the prohibition of voluntary blocking so that they could block access to foreign hate sites that were harassing him.

[175] See www.cybertip.ca/app/en/works (last accessed 17 June 2014).

[176] Ian Brown, 'Internet self-regulation and fundamental rights', *Index on Censorship*, 1 (201) 98.

[177] Lilian Edwards, 'From Child Porn to China, in One Cleanfeed', *Script-ed*, 3(3) (2006), pp. 174–75, at 175.

Internet to mistakenly block the entire archive.[178] In both incidents, neither owners of Wikipedia or the Wayback Machine nor users were advised of the blocking. In addition, in May 2008 access to Flickr was degraded by some IWF members such that users could not upload photos. This was a result of the IWF blacklisting a single Flickr account.[179]

The argument might be advanced that this is not the kind of speech that goes to the core of the right to freedom of expression. It is not political. It does not further democracy. Far from it, the material is not only unlawful, but the specific material on the blacklist is the lowest form of speech, if it can be categorised as such – child sexual abuse images. This argument might be compelling, except for the fact that we don't actually know what is being censored. Indeed, in 2009, Wikileaks published the blacklists of blocked child pornographic content for Finland, Denmark, Italy, China, Thailand and Australia revealing a significant amount of content unrelated to child pornography was being blocked (except Denmark), including political content.[180]

Three things, in particular, are striking about the IWF's impact on freedom of expression. First, the blacklist and notices sent to members are kept secret. The list is sent in an encrypted format to members, 'which are subject to similarly secret terms of agreement regarding their employees' access to the list'.[181] Members can add a URL to the list and no one would know. Although it is true that there are very good reasons why the blacklist is kept secret because we don't want to 'provide a roadmap to paedophiles',[182] this does not obviate the need for a democratic, transparent and accountable governance structure. If anything, it makes the need for due process more critical.

Second, website owners are not necessarily advised when their site has been added to the blacklist or added to a list sent to ISPs for takedown.

---

[178] C. Metz, 'IWF confirms Wayback Machine porn blacklisting' (14 January 2009), at www.theregister.co.uk/2009/01/14/iwf_details_archive_blacklisting/ (last accessed 17 June 2014).

[179] Information on file with author. For forum discussion, see www.flickr.com/help/for um/en-us/72110/ (last accessed 17 June 2014).

[180] See discussion and sources in Akdeniz, n. 35, pp. 265–66.    [181] Davies n. 1.

[182] McIntyre n. 10, p. 13. Note that Australia's blacklist for child pornography, held by its communications regulator, was leaked in 2009 and revealed that several non-child pornography-related sites were included on the blacklist such as poker sites, Wikipedia entries, bus companies and Google and Yahoo! groups: D. Pauli, 'Australia's Web blacklist leaked' *Computer World* (19 March 2009), at www.computerworld.com.au/article/296 161/australia_web_blacklist_leaked/ (last accessed 14 June 2014).

The IWF simply states '[n]otifying the website owner of any blocked URL is the responsibility of the Hotline or relevant law enforcement agency in the country believed to be hosting the content'.[183] Third, users are not always told they are attempting to connect to a site that has been blocked but are rather served an error page.[184] After the Wikipedia incident, the IWF revisited its policies and created a Blocking Good Practice guide,[185] which recommends that its members are more transparent concerning the content that is filtered. The reader will note that it is framed as a recommendation rather than a condition of membership in the IWF. Thus, as it stands, there is no standardisation in the industry concerning transparency of content that is filtered, although, as it stands, six major ISPs have agree to use such splash pages.[186]

Third, the IWF is at significant risk of function creep. The IWF's remit has expanded from its initial focus on child pornography to now include criminally obscene content and, for a while, racial hatred content, thus leading commentators such as Petley to state, 'ill-defined bodies such as this are all too prone to mission creep whereby, without any proper public discussion, they quietly expand the range of their activities – usually under pressure from government'.[187] There have been calls to expand the IWF's remit to regulate terrorist content[188] and violent and unlawful content.[189] As will be discussed, the IWF now proactively seeks out child sexual abuse content and is considering tackling peer-to-peer content.

At the same time, as we saw in Section 4.2, the internet industry as a whole is under extreme pressure to address all sorts of undesirable content: euthanasia websites, suicide websites, pro-eating disorder

---

[183] See www.iwf.org.uk/public/page.148.htm (last visited 17 June 2014).

[184] See McIntyre n. 10, p. 13. This lack of transparency is mimicked across Europe: see Alhert n. 56, pp. 14–16.

[185] See www.iwf.org.uk/services/blocking/blocking-good-practice (last visited 17 June 2014).

[186] Annual Report 2013 n. 73.      [187] Petley n. 3, p. 87.

[188] In a January 2008 speech, Home Secretary Jacqui Smith indicated support for further expansions of the IWF's remit, in which she stated that the government was in talks with the communications industry to regulate terrorism in the same manner that child pornography is handled, commenting, '[w]here there is illegal material on the net, I want it removed'. H. Mulholland, 'Government targets extremist websites' (17 January 2008), at www.guardian.co.uk/politics/2008/jan/17/uksecurity.terrorism (last visited 17 June 2014).

[189] ISPreview, 'UK government seeking to expand website blocking remit through IWF' (9 June 2011), at www.ispreview.co.uk/story/2011/06/09/uk-government-seeking-to-expand-website-blocking-remit-through-iwf.html (last visited 17 June 2014).

websites (known as 'pro-mia' and 'pro-ana' sites), glorification of terrorism and, the elephant in the room, illegal file sharing. Increasingly, there are discussions, such as in Sweden, of extending the use of filters for child pornography to illegal file sharing.[190] Recent cases in the United Kingdom have mandated that ISPs use Cleanfeed to block access to particular file-sharing sites,[191] and the UK government has moved to a mandatory opt-in filter for all types of pornography.[192] Italy requires the blocking of access to online gambling, and Norway proposed blocking access to a sweeping array of sites that allow such things as gambling, flag desecration, peer-to-peer illegal file sharing and communication of hate speech.[193] Such regimes enlist intermediaries as proxies[194] to do the dirty work of censoring content. The IWF has shown itself to be resistant to expansions of its remit, but it puts considerable pressure on the governance structure to have the safeguards in place to address such challenges.

There is an evident theme running through this examination, and it is as follows. In the face of a significant interference with the right to freedom of expression, in particular where a certain amount of secrecy is necessary, extraordinary care must be taken to build safeguards into the body's governance structure. Although the aims of the IWF are legitimate, the use of blacklists and notifications of unlawful content in a way that necessarily leads to what in human rights terms is an act of censorship is a significant interference with the enjoyment of freedom of expression. In cases of filtering alleged child sexual abuse images, it acts as a blanket restraint on speech. For such an interference to be proportionate, it must be narrowly tailored so that it interferes with the right no more than is necessary.

A review of IWF governance documents reveals minimal constraints on what the IWF do with its considerable power. The IWF has a 'Code of Practice', but it is not a policy document. Policies concerning its charity status, financial risk, police liaison guidelines and, most importantly, concerning the supply of the blacklist to members are not dealt with in the Code.[195] Rather, it is focused on the notice-and-takedown

---

[190] See discussion McIntyre n. 10, pp. 8–9.   [191] See cases n. 12.   [192] Cameron n. 13.

[193] R. Deibert et al. (eds.), *Access Denied: The Practice and Policy of Global Internet Filtering* (MIT Press 2008), pp. 188–89.

[194] See Kreimer n. 23.

[195] W. Grossman, 'IWF reforms could pave way for UK net censorship: who is watching the watchers?' (29 December 2006), *The Register*, at www.theregister.co.uk/2006/12/29/iwf_fea ture/page3.html (last visited 18 June 2014).

procedure and the obligations in this regard of IWF members vis-à-vis their membership in the IWF. It does not address the members' relationship to the public.[196] Although a third party can notify the IWF of a breach of the Code by one of its members,[197] this is not helpful in practice to addressing any concerns about the rightful filtering of a URL because the IWF would not find a that member breached the Code in removing material that the IWF itself blacklisted.

The IWF is relatively transparent concerning the process by which images are assessed. The people compiling the blacklist are trained by the police, although we do not have any further information on what that training entails. They are 'periodically inspected and audited by eminent independent experts',[198] but we do not (as at 2012) have access to these reports.[199] They assess the images in line with the UK Sentencing Guidelines Council's Definitive Guideline of the Sexual Offences Act 2003.[200] The IWF URL List Policy and Procedures[201] identifies the following considerations, which are taken into account when assessing an image:

a.  Previously unseen images.
b.  History and how widely the image is disseminated.
c.  Nature of the image.
d.  Nature of the website featuring the image.
e.  Number of images associated with the URL.
f.  Jurisdictional legal disparity.[202]

In addition, the IWF considers the potential problems caused by addition of the URL to the blacklist to internet users, licensees, increased availability of the image and the impact on the website owner's reputation.[203] If the removal of the URL would cause one or more of those problems, the IWF advises it does not put the URL on the blacklist while 'actions are taken to seek the removal of source of that content',[204] which, if not removed, leads to a referral of the matter to the IWF Board.

---

[196] IWF Code of Practice, at www.iwf.org.uk/members/funding-council/code-of-practice (last accessed visited 18 June 2014). See in particular ss. 8–10.

[197] Ibid., s. 8.1.     [198] See www.iwf.org.uk/public/page.148.htm (last visited 18 June 2014).

[199] See later discussion for audit report access requests. See Section 4.4 discussing the current availability of such audits: www.iwf.org.uk/accountability/independent-inspec tion (last visited 25 June 2014).

[200] See www.iwf.org.uk/police/page.105.htm (last visited 18 June 2014).

[201] See www.iwf.org.uk/services/blocking/iwf-url-list-policy-and-procedures (last visited 14 May 2014).

[202] Ibid.    [203] Ibid.    [204] Ibid.

The IWF policy concerning newsgroups has changed. From 2001 until 2010, it compiled a list of newsgroups that ISPs are 'recommended' to not host because they 'regularly' contain child sexual abuse content, meaning that 1 per cent of the images viewed were such content. The IWF assured that the system for monitoring these newsgroups and analysing the statistics had been independently reviewed, but there is no information on the independent review.[205] The new policy is more vague as to the process concerning newsgroups. Whereas the focus is on alerting members to specific posts, which they can then remove, the IWF retains a monitorial role concerning newsgroups as a whole and makes use of the limitations to the exemptions from liability for ISSs in the E-Commerce Directive by issuing notices to ISPs. It simply no longer calls it a recommendation or notice but rather the provision of 'data' to the ISPs and newsgroup providers.[206]

It must then be determined whether the IWF approach is not only successful but necessary to deter child sex abuse and other unlawful behaviour. Other frameworks, such as Operation Pin,[207] illustrate creative and effective approaches to tackling child pornography which are human rights-compliant. Operation Pin was launched by the Virtual Global Taskforce (VGT)[208] in 2003 with the specific goal of deterring paedophiles from looking at child sexual abuse images. VGT is a collaboration of law enforcement agencies across the world. The Operation involves creating a website which falsely purports to carry child pornography but is in fact a law enforcement site. If someone enters the site or attempts to download an image, he or she is advised that it is a law enforcement site, that the person has committed an offence and that the person's details have been 'captured' and passed on to law enforcement.

In any event, paedophiles are increasingly using social networking sites, image sharing sites, free website hosting platforms and even hacked sites to distribute images.[209] Such sites, although within the purview of the IWF, are more difficult to uncover. For example, the IWF is less likely to receive notifications on its hotline concerning a closed group on Facebook. Even

---

[205] Link no longer available: www.iwf.org.uk/corporate/page.49.231.htm (last visited May 2010).

[206] See www.iwf.org.uk/services/newsgroups (last www.iwf.org.uk/corporate/page.49.231 .htm).

[207] See discussion A. Murray, *Information Technology Law: The Law and Society* (Oxford University Press, 2010), p. 439.

[208] See www.virtualglobaltaskforce.com/what-we-do/ (last visited 18 June 2014).

[209] The IWF admitted as such in the BBC, 'Child abuse "big business online"' (13 May 2010), at http://news.bbc.co.uk/1/hi/technology/10108720.stm (last visited 18 June 2014).

more concerning are peer-to-peer sites, which are increasingly being used by paedophiles, as well as the use of Virtual Worlds, where the concern is more about role play than images.[210] These are outside the reach of the Cleanfeed blocking system, although the IWF is exploring ways to address peer-to-peer networks, as will be seen later. This is not to say there isn't a role of critical importance for the IWF, but rather, given the circumstances, that there is less justification for a non-human rights-compliant regulatory structure. It is a significant interference of the right to freedom of expression and yet does not target some of the most common methods by which paedophiles distribute images.

The end result is that IWF employees calmly slip into a pseudo-judicial role, only to be questioned if a user or website owner happens to discover the blocking. Without any structures in place to guard against misuse of power, the activities of the IWF are a disproportionate interference with the right to freedom of expression and therefore breaches Article 10(2).

### 4.3.4.  A failure of the state?

As we know, the IWF has agreed to treat itself as a public authority, but, as the reader will recall, this case study has a story to tell about the evolution of the IWF's role. Even if the IWF is not a public authority, then the human rights problems we have seen concerning the IWF's operation are arguably a failure of the state to positively protect users' right to freedom of expression. Directive 2011/93/EU,[211] aimed at protection of children from sexual abuse, exploitation and child pornography, binds states to administer blocking of child pornography online pursuant to human rights principles. Article 25 sets out the rules for blocking access to child pornography, adding:

> Member States may take measures to block access to web pages containing or disseminating child pornography towards the Internet users within their territory. These measures must be set by transparent procedures and provide adequate safeguards, in particular to ensure that the restriction is

---

[210] See the study done by cybertip.ca breaking down by website type incidents of child pornography: Canadian Centre for Child Protection, 'Child sexual abuse images: an analysis of websites by cybertip.ca' (November 2009), at www.cybertip.ca/app/en/proj ects-research#projects-research (last visited 18 June 2014). About virtual worlds, see Sky News, 'Paedophiles target virtual world' (31 October 2007), at http://news.sky.com /home/article/1290719 (last visited 18 June 2014).

[211] Directive 2011/93/EU of the European Parliament and of the Council of 13 December 2011 on combating sexual abuse and sexual exploitation of children, and child pornography, replacing the Council Framework- Decision 2004/68/JHA.

limited to what is necessary and proportionate, and that users are informed of the reason for the restriction. Those safeguards shall also include the possibility of judicial redress.[212]

As we have seen, the IWF operates without any of the safeguards identified in Article 25. In addition, the state must comply with the Charter of Fundamental Rights[213] in implementing the directive. Article 52 requires that limitations of rights are proportionate, necessary and for a legitimate aim.[214] This focus on the need for safeguards against misuse was noted by UN Special Rapporteur Frank La Rue in his report on the promotion and protection of freedom of expression, wherein he stated:

> With regard to child pornography, the Special Rapporteur notes that it is one clear exception where blocking measures are justified, provided that the national law is sufficiently precise and there are sufficient safeguards against abuse or misuse to prevent any "mission creep", including oversight and review by an independent and impartial tribunal or regulatory body. However, the Special Rapporteur calls upon States to focus their efforts on prosecuting those responsible for the production and dissemination of child pornography, rather than on blocking measures alone.[215]

In addition, unlike our American counterpart, the European tradition has been more open to positive obligations on states to ensure enjoyment of Convention rights such as the right to freedom of expression. The ECtHR has regularly intervened in cases between private individuals to ensure they 'can effectively exercise their right of communication among themselves'.[216] Whether a state has such a duty in a particular case is largely driven by questions of proportionately; namely, whether there are alternative means available for the person to engage in the expression at issue.[217] Courts attempt to balance such issues as the interests of the community against that of the individual, allocation of resources, the nature and significance of the expression and the restriction and the

---

[212] Ibid.

[213] Charter of Fundamental Rights of the European Union 2000/C 254/01, recognised as law in Article 6 of the Treaty of Lisbon amending the Treaty establishing the European Community 2007/C 306/01.

[214] Note also Article 11 of the Charter setting out the right to freedom of expression and information.

[215] La Rue n. 57, para. 71.

[216] Harris n. 144, p. 446 citing *VgT Verein gegen Tierfabriken* v. *Switzerland* (2002) 34 EHRR 4; and see generally A. Clapham, *Human Rights in the Private Sphere* (Oxford: Clarendon Press, 1993).

[217] In this regard, see *Appleby* v. *United Kingdom* (2003) 37 EHRR 38 discussed later.

rights of others.[218] Thus, in *Fuentes Bobo* v. *Spain*,[219] the Court held that Spain failed to safeguard freedom of expression when an employee criticised management during a radio programme.

In *Costello-Roberts* v. *United Kingdom*, concerning corporal punishment in a private school, the Court held that the case engaged the right to education and stated that 'the state cannot absolve itself from responsibility by delegating its obligations to private bodies or individuals'.[220] Such cases where the Court has found the state responsible for safeguarding a Convention right between private individuals tend to be cases where traditional state responsibilities have been transferred to private parties.[221] This privatisation of censorship is one of the central criticisms of the legitimacy of the IWF, operating directly under threat of government legislation and with public funding. But for the IWF, its activities would be the responsibility of the state, and in other countries it is operated in this fashion.

There is a strong analogy between denying access to a forum such as a shopping mall to engage in free expression and denying access to speak to the public or for the public to receive information through the use of blocking technologies.[222] The leading case is *Appleby* v. *United Kingdom*,[223] a decision of the ECtHR sitting as a Chamber, in which the applicants were denied permission to set up a petition stand and collect signatures in a town centre known as 'the Galleries', which was privately owned by Postel Properties Limited. In the past, other associations had been granted permission to set up stands and displays and carry out collections, such as the Salvation Army, local school choirs and a Stop Smoking Campaign.

In determining whether the state has a positive obligation in the circumstances, the ECtHR raised the following factors: general interest of community balanced against that of the individual, priorities and resources and burden on authorities.[224] The ECtHR rejected that the state had a positive obligation in this case because all ways to exercise freedom of expression were not banned. They could obtain permission from individual businesses, which they did on one occasion; the ban was only on the entranceway and passageways of the Galleries. Alternatively, they could campaign in the old town, door-to-door or though the press,

---

[218] Harris n. 144, p. 446.     [219] (2001) EHRR 50.     [220] (1995) 19 EHRR 112, para. 27.

[221] See discussion of *Costello-Roberts* in Harris n. 144, p. 21.

[222] For an analysis of the links between public spaces and virtual spaces, see D. Mac Síthigh, 'Virtual Walls? The Law of Pseudo-Public Spaces', *Int. J.L.C.*, 8(3) (2012) 394.

[223] *Appleby* n. 217.     [224] Ibid., para. 40.

radio or television.[225] The Court commented that the right to freedom of expression does not create a right to a forum to exercise it, although if 'the essence of the right has been destroyed'[226] positive obligations on the State might arise.

Unlike *Appleby*, the speech targeted by the IWF is not speech central to the functioning of democracy; however, that does not mean that such speech is not swept up in error by the blacklist or issuance of a notice of unlawful content. Once such speech is filtered, the censorship is absolute because access to the content is disabled entirely, thus destroying the essence of the right. There are no alternative options available to users or website owners analogous to the scenario in *Appleby*, and, in fact, it is this unavailability of alternatives that makes filtering of content by private parties so significant and concerning. Although users might seek to circumvent the filter or post the content elsewhere and hope it is also not blocked, this is not a reasonable alternative path for the expression. If there is no constitutional right at issue, the scenario is starkly different. It is then in essence a property issue, and private property owners have the unfettered right to effectively eject people from their 'land' and do not have to comply with any test of reasonableness in this regard.[227] Based on ECHR jurisprudence, the function of the IWF and the filtering mechanisms used by its members, there is a strong case for positive obligations on the state to ensure the IWF's human rights compatibility. The failure of the state to intervene in this regard would be a breach of Article 10(2).

### 4.3.5. Assessment as a pure-CSR body

Even if the IWF successfully argued that it is not a public authority or the state is found to have no duties concerning its operation, we are still left with a body whose operations have a significant impact on the right to freedom of expression. In such a scenario, the IWF does not have any human rights obligations as a matter of law, but it cannot be said to have no human rights responsibilities (a broader notion than the law, as will be seen). The body becomes a form of pure-CSR, and, as we saw in Chapter 3, we still draw from Article 10 principles, albeit more loosely, in assessing whether the IWF is satisfying its human rights responsibilities. As we have seen, the IWF arguably fails to be an Article 10 compliant body, but, in relaxing the application of Article 10 to the IWF as a form of pure-CSR, perhaps its deficiencies are cured by the

---

[225] Ibid., para. 48.    [226] Ibid., para. 47.    [227] Ibid., para. 22.

presence of the sort of factors highlighted as important in the Guiding Principles. Such factors are also of evidentiary value in an assessment of the IWF as a public authority. Referring back to the Guiding Principles, we must ask what the nature is of the human rights obligations set out in the IWF policies. Are there due diligence processes? Namely, is there guidance on human rights policies, monitoring and tracking performance and mitigation strategies? The broader Article 10(2) question is whether the method of governance is proportionate to the legitimate aim pursued.

In order for secret lists of censored content to be human rights-compliant, the governance structure of the body carrying out this work must be democratic, transparent and accountable. Since the IWF's restructuring in 1999, it has made efforts to make its operation more transparent. It provides an Annual Report of its operations, and its hotline, information systems and security are independently audited, although it does not say how often. The following information, for example, is available on their website: '[o]ur policies; minutes of our Board meetings; details of Trustees and senior staff; our funders; accounts; details of companies that receive the IWF URL list for implementing the blocking of indecent images of children; our complaints procedures and the Code of Practice governing our relations with industry Members are also available on our website'.[228] However, the reality is that the IWF's transparency is facile.

This is where it is particularly challenging organising this chapter because most changes spurred by publication of my article and the human rights audit relate to this aspect of the IWF's governance. For the purposes of this section, the IWF will be analysed as it was in late 2012. In Section 4.4, we will examine the latest developments of the IWF.

The Annual Reports available online only go back five years. They were reviewed to determine whether human rights are considered in the Annual Report and how. As of 2012 there were no human rights policies to assess concerning due diligence, such as monitoring and tracking performance and mitigation strategies. Indeed, not one report discusses human rights or freedom of expression. Before 2010, they read like public relations pamphlets, with several pages devoted to thanking their sponsors and the primary information communicated being the number of child abuse URLs blocked, where the content was hosted and the nature

---

[228] See www.iwf.org.uk/public/page.103.551.htm (last visited 13 May 2014).

of the content.[229] There are indications of improvement, however. The 2010 Annual Report incorporates discussions of the ways in which the IWF is attempting to be more transparent in its operations,[230] but there is still no mention of human rights.

In addition, the IWF's strategic plans for 2008–2011, 2011–2014 and 2012–2015[231] are focused on such things as the effectiveness of the IWF and its public profile, role and influence. Human rights are not mentioned as part of the IWF's strategic plan. The Annual Reports are audited by Peters Elworthy & Moore, with potential to satisfy Ruggie's criteria, but the audits only concern financial matters.[232] Equally, human rights were not discussed in any of the available Board Minutes until 2012.[233] The lack of consideration of human rights is replicated at a policy level, where human rights are not mentioned in any of the IWF policies governing its notices pursuant to the E-Commerce Regulations or the blacklisting regime. The only mention found of human rights was an assurance that the IWF has struck the right balance:

> The establishment of the IWF pre-empted the introduction of formal regulatory action and legislation of the internet industry in the 1990s and has since worked to ensure the right balances are drawn between freedom of expression and protection from criminal internet content.[234]

This perhaps reflects the wider view of the IWF, at least until 2013, that this is simply not a human rights matter. As Peter Robbins, then CEO of the IWF, commented in 2009, 'I'm against censorship. I don't see us as a censorship body. We deal with illegal content and get it taken down where we can'.[235] However, this is in stark contrast to the earlier undertaking by the IWF to be governed under the HRA.[236]

---

[229] Annual Report (2006) n. 63, pp. 12–13.

[230] Internet Watch Foundation, *2010 Annual and Charity Report*, at www.iwf.org.uk/account ability/annual-reports/2010-annual-report (last visited 18 June 2014).

[231] The Internet Watch Foundation, 2008 *Annual and Charity Report*, at https://www.iwf .org.uk/accountability/annual-reports/2008-annual-report (last visited 18 June 2014), mentions the 2008–2011 strategic plan. The more recent strategic plan 2012–2015 is available at www.iwf.org.uk/accountability/strategy (last visited 14 May 2014).

[232] Annual Report (2008), ibid.: 'We have examined the summarized financial statements for the year end. . . . Our responsibility is to report to you our opinion on the consistency of the summarized financial statements': p. 12.

[233] See www.iwf.org.uk/corporate/page.69.htm (last visited 18 June 2014).

[234] See www.iwf.org.uk/public/page.103.552.htm (last visited 18 June 2014).

[235] Grossman n. 194.

[236] Akdeniz n. 121, p. 264, which report is no longer available to this author for review.

The IWF is subject to periodic audits. It advises that its '[h]otline systems, assessment, security and processes are inspected by independent auditors such as forensic, academic and law enforcement professionals'.[237] For example, its March 2011 audit is publicly available. Human rights was not one of the terms of reference for the audit team.[238] The previous report is from 2008, and the IWF advised that it passed with 'flying colours', although the report was not published nor was it provided to the magazine *Wired* at its request.[239] The most relevant to an assessment of its human rights compliance are the four reviews of its 'role, and remit, governance and procedures'.[240] It advises that these reviews involve consultations with the government, police and 'other key stakeholders'.[241] The only one for which there is any information is the review in 1998 by KPMG and Denton Hall, which led to sweeping changes in the IWF's governance in 2000, mainly an effort for the IWF to be more independent from industry, and it did so by creating more transparency with, for example, the publishing of its board minutes and papers.[242]

The IWF refused a request to see the four audits.[243] I then sought answers to the following questions in the hopes of determining whether the IWF was audited for human rights compliance in line with the Guiding Principles:

1. Might you advise what criteria form the basis of the audits? To put it another way, on what terms is the IWF audited?
2. Have the criteria been consistent for each audit? If not, how have they changed?
3. Am I correct that there have been four audits?
4. In addition, what organisations are carrying out the audits? If you are not in a position to name the companies, might you advise what types of organisations they are?[244]

---

[237] See www.iwf.org.uk/public/page.103.551.htm (last visited 18 June 2014).
[238] See report at www.iwf.org.uk/assets/media/news/Inspection%20of%20the%20IWF%20 2011.pdf (last visited 18 June 2014).
[239] Davies n. 1. It also states this on its website: www.iwf.org.uk/public/page.103.551.htm (last visited 24 August 2011).
[240] See www.iwf.org.uk/public/page.103.551.htm (last visited 18 June 2014).     [241] Ibid.
[242] Davies n. 1.
[243] When I requested a copy of these four audits from the IWF, I was advised that they were 'unable' to send them to me and that they 'don't publish everything': email between Emily Laidlaw and Lene Nielsen, Communications Executive and Webmaster Internet Watch Foundation (25 March 2010), on file with the author.
[244] Ibid.

The IWF advised: 'I'm afraid I don't have the answers to your questions below', and then directed me to its webpages with information on the IWF's governance and accountability, Board minutes and annual reports.[245] A Freedom of Information Act[246] (FOIA) request is unavailable against the IWF because it is not a body set up by the Crown, statute, a government department, the National Assembly of Wales or a Minister. The fact that it is a charity does not matter, nor that some of the funding is from public resources. Most charities and most private companies are not covered under the FOIA. In addition, it is not listed as covered by the FOIA in Schedule I. It is available to the Secretary of State under Section 5 to designate a private body a public authority under the Act if it performs public functions or is contracted by the government to perform otherwise governmental functions. Although the Secretary of State has designated a handful of organisations under Section 5, the IWF is not one of them.[247] Since 2012, the IWF has taken strides to increase transparency. Board minutes from 2001 can now be accessed online, and, similarly, Annual Reports go back seven years. Its Hotline Inspection and Human Rights audit, discussed later, are also available online.[248]

The only available complaints procedure to address blocking of content is the IWF's. The ISPA Code of Practice does not 'adjudicate on the legality or otherwise of material accessible on the Internet'.[249] If there is a 'Complaint' that the ISPA Member has breached the ISPA Code of Practice in a way that puts into issue the legality of the internet material, then the customer or third party lodging the complaint must contact the 'originator of the material directly'.[250] In addition, if a person is unsatisfied with how a dispute has been resolved, there are available alternative dispute resolution schemes approved by Ofcom, such as Ombudsman Services Communications and CISAS.[251] However, these schemes are only available for complaints by the ISP's domestic customer, and the scope of the schemes does not cover complaints concerning internet content, such as complaints about content that has been

---

[245] Ibid.   [246] Freedom of Information Act 2000 c. 36.
[247] The Freedom of Information (Designation as Public Authorities) Order 2011 No. 2598.
[248] Annual report 2013 n. 73, pp. 25–26. See also www.iwf.org.uk/accountability/govern ance (last visited 18 June 2014).
[249] ISPA n. 101, Preamble (e).   [250] Ibid., Preamble (e) and clause 8.3.
[251] Ofcom, *Customer Codes of Practice for Handling Complaints and Resolving Disputes* (May 2005), p. 8. For example, PlusNet, Virgin Media and Orange are registered with CISAS, whereas TalkTalk and BskyB are registered with Ombudsman Services Communications: see www.ofcom.org.uk/consumer/2009/12/adr-schemes/ (last visited 18 June 2014).

blocked.[252] Thus, the only available complaints mechanism is directly with the IWF.

Using the IWF's complaints procedure, if a person 'affected by'[253] the inability to access content finds out, he or she can initiate the Content Assessment Appeals Process.[254] A 'person' is defined widely to include 'a potential victim or the victim's representative, hosting company, publisher or internet consumer who believes they are being prevented from accessing legal content'.[255] Under this process, the initial complaint is made, which might include 'details regarding your complaint or reasons for appealing a content assessment by the IWF'.[256] This complaint is treated as an appeal of the initial decision to issue a notice to remove the content or blacklist the content, even though you were never involved in or even notified of the initial decision. The appeals process works in a similar manner. Once the complaint is made, this is treated as your representations on appeal, even though, again, you are not included in the actual process:

> An IWF Director is made aware of the appeal and a record is created.
>
> The content is re-assessed (This will be undertaken by a suitably trained IWF Manager not involved in the original assessment decision).
>
> If the original assessment decision is reversed and the appeal is upheld the appellant is informed and appropriate remedial action is taken i.e. notice to takedown is repealed or URL is removed from the IWF URL List.
>
> If the original assessment decision is not reversed and the appellant wishes to continue their appeal then the content is referred to the relevant lead police agency for assessment.
>
> If the URL is likely to or has triggered a significant risk, then the URL will be temporarily removed from the IWF URL List.
>
> The police agency's decision will be communicated to an IWF Director who will act in accordance with the agency's assessment. The agency's decision is final.
>
> The appellant is informed.
>
> If the original assessment decision by IWF is reversed and the appeal is upheld appropriate remedial action is taken i.e. notice to takedown is repealed or URL is removed from the IWF URL List.

---

[252] See www.cisas.org.uk/downloads/CISAS%20Application%20pack%202013%20Final.pdf (last visited 18 June 2014). See www.ombudsman-services.org/downloads/OScommunicat ions_factsheet.pdf (last visited 18 June 2014).

[253] IWF, *Content Appeal Process*, at www.iwf.org.uk/accountability/complaints/content-as sessment-appeal-process#3 (last visited 18 June 2014).

[254] Ibid. This was revamped in July 2010, but the basic structure of the mechanism changed very little. See Annual Report (2010) n. 229.

[255] IWF *Content Appeal Process* ibid.        [256] See IWF *Content Appeal Process* ibid.

The Board will be informed whenever an assessment decision is reversed following a referral to the relevant police agency. (It is not possible for the Board to make a decision relating to assessment of images as to do so would require Board members to view content that they are not trained to assess.)[257]

The appeals process had an opportunity to be test-run by Wikipedia when the Scorpions page was blocked in 2008. The IWF described this process as follows:

Following representations from Wikipedia the IWF invoked its Appeals Procedure. This entails a review of the original decision with law enforcement officers. They confirmed the original assessment and this information was conveyed to Wikipedia. Due to the public interest in this matter our Board closely monitored the situation and, once the appeals process was complete, they convened to consider the contextual issues involved in this specific case. IWF's overriding objective is to minimize the availability of indecent images of children on the internet, however, on this occasion our efforts had the opposite effect so the Board decided that the webpage should be removed from the URL list.[258]

Although this description appears to give due consideration to the complaint, the reality of how this process is experienced by a complainant is quite different. In particular, excepting the initial complaint, the complainant takes no part in what is effectively an adjudicative process. The effect of this is to make the complaints procedure inaccessible, unpredictable and, arguably, illegitimate, as can be seen in the starkly different terms used by Wikipedia's counsel to describe the experience:

When we first protested the block, their response was, 'We've now conducted an appeals process on your behalf and you've lost the appeal'. When I asked who exactly represented the Wikimedia Foundation's side in that appeals process, they were silent. It was only after the fact of their blacklist and its effect on UK citizens were publicised that the IWF appears to have felt compelled to relent.[259]

In 2012, my conclusions on the IWF were severe:

Thus a secret blacklist of censored speech is combined with secret audits, under secret terms, subject to a secret appeals process, and insulated from a FOIA request, and we are to simply rely on assurances by the IWF that

---

[257] See www.iwf.org.uk/accountability/complaints/content-assessment-appeal-process (last visited 18 June 2014). See Appendix A for this process in picture: www.iwf.org.uk/assets /media/accountability/Content%20assessment%20appeal%20process.pdf (last visited 18 June 2014).

[258] Annual Report (2008) n. 230, p. 9.   [259] Quoting from Davies n. 1.

they balance freedom of expression properly against protection from criminal content. In the face of a significant interference with the right to free expression, where the very access to the speech is blocked, there is startlingly little information available on the process by which the interference occurs. To describe such a process as a disproportionate interference with freedom of expression is an understatement, because human rights are not built into any elements of the IWF's governance framework. An analysis pursuant to John Ruggie's criteria that a company should have a process of due diligence for human rights concerns, including monitoring and tracking of performance, the presence of mitigation strategies, and characteristics of legitimacy, accessibility, predictability, equitability, rights-compatibility, and transparency in its remedial structure, reveals that none of this is present in the IWF's governance framework.[260]

I recommended, amongst other things, that there needs to be a clear recognition of the public authority status of the IWF and a recognition of the state's human rights obligations in encouraging this regulatory arrangement.[261] I contended: 'remodelling the IWF in accordance with the Protect, Respect and Remedy Framework would go a long way in meeting the principles of proportionality and due process needed to make the IWF a human rights-compliant regulatory body, and allow it to continue its role in combating exposure to and dissemination of child sexual images and criminally obscene content'.[262]

We can also find guidance from *Yildirim*. Judge Pinto provided a separate opinion setting out when filtering decisions can be made in a way that is human rights-compliant.[263] The recommendation is for any filtering to be carried out only with clear definition as to who and what can be blocked, the geographic reach of the block and the time limit of the block. In addition, Judge Pinto recommends that decisions are reviewed against Article 10(2) in terms of proportionality and necessity, that they arise from a fair trial and with notice of the block and procedures that can be taken against the blocking.[264] Such criteria reflect much of the criticisms noted earlier and capture the Council of Europe Recommendation on filtering discussed in Section 4.2. Assessing the IWF based on this criteria not only highlights the failures of the IWF's governance thus far,

---

[260] Laidlaw n. 5, p. 343. Concerns have been expressed by other authors, such as Marsden n. 67, p. 178, R. Heverly, 'Breaking the Internet: International Efforts to Play the Middle Against the Ends: A Way Forward', *Georgetown J. of Intl. L.*, 42(4) (2011) 1083, and W. Benedek and M. C. Kettemann, *Freedom of Expression and the Internet* (Strasbourg: Council of Europe Publishing, 2013), pp. 142–44.

[261] Laidlaw ibid., p. 344     [262] Ibid.

[263] See discussion Benedek and Kettemann n. 260, pp. 143–44.     [264] *Yildirim* n. 14.

but also provides guidance on how the IWF can amend its policies and procedures to ensure filtering in the future is done in a human rights-consistent way.

## 4.4. Human rights audit and the future

Following publication of my article and my meeting with IWF representatives in 2012, Lord Macdonald conducted a human rights audit of the IWF. He consulted several individuals in preparing this audit, including this author.[265] This affords a rare opportunity at this stage in the evolution of the practice of auditing organisations for human rights. It allows a very basic question to be examined: are such audits sufficient to ensure the protection and facilitation of the right to freedom of expression? At the time of writing, we are only part way through this process. Although we have the audit and a response to the audit by the IWF, it will take time to see whether the audit prompts the kinds of changes of practice envisioned here.

The terms of reference for the audit were:

a. To give a view whether the IWF is a public authority in relation to the Human Rights Act, 1998;
b. To conduct an assessment of the governance, operational policies and operational practise of the IWF against the frameworks of the Universal Declaration, the Child Convention and the Human Rights Act 1998;
c. To advise how compliant the IWF is with the above instruments; and
d. To advise how any policies or practices may be improved to better ensure compliance with the above instruments.[266]

Lord Macdonald made five key recommendations in thematic terms. First, he recommends that the IWF limit its remit to child sexual abuse content and no longer issue takedown notices for adult pornographic content which is unlawful under the Obscene Publications Act or Section 63 of the Criminal Justice and Immigration Act. He concludes that, given the risk to rights raised by regulating this category, there are questions whether the IWF is the appropriate body to do the policing. He states:

> In these circumstances, special difficulties appear to exist in the case of a private, industry-funded body, with no in-house legal expertise, exercising judgments in areas that are very likely to engage ECHR privacy and

[265] Audit n. 83, p. 36.     [266] Ibid., para. 1.2.

free expression rights, and which require complex legal reasoning to resolve satisfactorily. It seems to me that interventions by a body like IWF into these sensitive areas may present a real risk that the finely drawn balance between our criminal legislation on the one hand, and the UK's international responsibilities under the ECHR and the Universal Declaration on the other, may be upset.[267]

The IWF has deferred a decision on this recommendation.[268]

Second, he identifies several issues with the appeals process; namely, that the IWF acts in a censorship capacity with significant powers that potentially impact users rights. He highlights that this impacts the community as a whole because infringement of such rights might operate to the detriment of the broader public.[269] He concludes that 'these implications ... mandate an appeal process that is particularly rigorous'.[270] Under the current system, the final appeal involves a referral to the police agency, and its assessment is treated as final. He proposes appointment of a judicial figure, such as a retired judge, as the final point of appeal.[271] I would argue that this process needs to be adjudicative to be human rights-compliant, a point that is not explored in the audit.

The audit also earmarks this retired judge to strengthen the IWF's governance model in other ways. He recommends the IWF be inspected every two years, which should be headed by a new chief inspector, which should be a retired judge, likely the same person. Furthermore, the Inspection team should include an expert in human rights law, and a human rights expert should be appointed to its Board.[272] The IWF has accepted all of the recommendations concerning improvements to its appeals process and appointment of human rights experts and a chief inspector.[273]

Third, Lord Macdonald concluded, and the IWF agrees, that it is a public authority for the purposes of the HRA.[274] This allows for judicial review of the work of the IWF, which injects due process into the workings of this organisation and thus mends several of the concerns identified earlier. The audit neglects to explore whether what the IWF does is prescribed by law, an issue interrogated earlier with the conclusion that the IWF is, in this respect, operating in breach of Article 10.

---

[267] Ibid., para. 3.9.
[268] See www.iwf.org.uk/accountability/human-rights-audit (last visited 14 May 2014).
[269] Audit n. 83, paras. 5.2.7–5.2.10.        [270] Ibid., para. 5.2.10.        [271] Ibid.
[272] Ibid., para. 5.3.
[273] See www.iwf.org.uk/accountability/human-rights-audit (last visited 14 May 2014).
[274] Audit n. 83, para. 7.2.

Fourth, the audit interrogates the proposed developments of the IWF's role mentioned briefly earlier in this chapter. Such developments show the risks associated with these forms of governance because they are susceptible to constant pressure to tackle more issues. In the case of the IWF, the two proposals have quite significant free speech implications. At the time of the audit, the IWF had proposed – and, indeed, as of April 2014 has begun – to proactively search for child sexual abuse images as opposed to the reactive approach with which it has operated thus far through its hotline. There is undeniable value to proactively seeking such content, but it is a tremendous resource strain and exacerbates the IWF's governance problems.

Lord Macdonald concluded that the IWF needs more funding in order to engage in this investigatory role: 'there would be real danger in government outsourcing an important law enforcement function to an industry body in circumstances where the internet industry was not prepared properly to finance that function'.[275] The IWF has received some funding from businesses for the further analysts needed (by Lord Macdonald's estimation, a doubling of current numbers). The IWF accepts the recommendation that more funding is needed,[276] but, ultimately, this is not something wholly within the control of the organisation. This move must also be done with awareness that, by actively seeking out content to block, it more actively engages fundamental rights, and therefore human rights safeguards against abuse are all the more important to its governance future.

The IWF is also exploring an expansion of its remit to investigate through peer-to-peer file-sharing networks. Lord Macdonald recommends that the IWF should not expand its role, at the moment, to address content shared via this method.[277] The IWF has deferred a decision on this matter while it undertakes consultations.[278] He cautioned that it would involve a major expansion in its role involving surveillance, thus necessitating a reworking of the IWF's recruitment and training policies.[279] Whereas an examination of the privacy implications of the IWF's expansion to peer-to-peer networks is beyond the scope of this research, a brief comment is appropriate.

---

[275] Ibid., para. 8.2.5.
[276] See www.iwf.org.uk/accountability/human-rights-audit (last visited 14 May 2014).
[277] Audit n. 83, para. 8.3.5.
[278] See www.iwf.org.uk/accountability/human-rights-audit (last visited 14 May 2014).
[279] Audit n. 83, para. 8.3.

On the issue of surveillance, we should be alarmed at the notion that a private body, even with public authority status and subject to judicial review, could carry on surveillance of file sharing without a more explicit government mandate. The proposal is not for the IWF to respond to specific user complaints of child sexual abuse images found on file-sharing sites, but rather for the IWF to gain access to such networks to proactively seek out such unlawful content. Thus, the very act of inspection entails the IWF becoming a watcher of peer-to-peer content. As Lord Macdonald notes, this would involve IWF staff making sensitive decisions about the target, purpose and scope of the surveillance similar to the role of the police.[280] Given the constant pressure the IWF is under to expand its remit, and the technology used by many members being repurposed for other issues such as copyright protection, surveillance of peer-to-peer content should not be something the IWF undertakes. Indeed, Lord Macdonald identifies this job as more properly that of the National Crime Agency, commenting, '[a]rguably, it is for a properly constituted police force, properly trained and supervised, and fully cognisant of the law, to make the many difficult judgments inherent in such investigations, particularly since the means by which they are progressed are by their nature undercover and intrusive'.[281]

This audit shows the strengths and weaknesses of auditing as the regulatory tool for human rights issues. The selection of Lord Macdonald shows a commitment on the part of the IWF to take this audit seriously. Equally, the audit, even taking account of points of disagreement, was arguably independent, thorough and quite simply useful. For example, the auditing process found that the IWF takes a cautious approach when looking at content at the margins of criminality in order to avoid infringing Article 8 and Article 10 of the ECHR.[282] This shows a sensitivity to rights issues however informally executed. This is in contrast to the recent audits of the Global Network Initiative, as will be discussed in Chapter 5.

However, in the end, such documents are only worth what the receiver makes of them. Consideration and implementation of the key recommendations are dependent on the leadership of the IWF, not only present leaders, but future leaders of the organisation who might shift the commitments of the IWF in ways that might have implications to human rights such as free speech. Such concerns with CSR were noted in Chapter 3. There are no tools to hold the IWF to account for how it

---

[280] Ibid., para. 8.3.2.     [281] Ibid., para. 8.3.5.     [282] Ibid., para. 5.1.10.

treats the audit and we dare not go down the rabbit hole of accountability mechanisms requiring audits of audit responses, none of which is desirable. We are left with public and governmental chastising or praise to regulate the legitimacy of this body.

However, Lord Macdonald's point that there is a need for speed in removing child sexual abuse images is important. A body like the IWF, because of its private and charitable status, can remove and manoeuvre in a way that the police cannot, where each image would have to go through a judicial process in advance of its takedown, which is inevitably slow and revictimizes the child the longer the image is available.[283] CSR affords a flexibility needed for the internet environment even where fundamental rights are engaged. However, such frameworks need guidance in order to facilitate their accountability mechanisms. A public–private partnership would facilitate accountability and due process in the governance structures whilst protecting human rights. Such a partnership is explored in Chapter 6 and a new corporate governance model is proposed, one that would complement the appeals mechanism proposed by Lord Macdonald here.

## 4.5. Conclusion

The goals of the IWF to tackle criminal content, in particular, child sexual abuse images, are not only laudable, but tasks of critical importance. And we can only be thankful for those IWF employees willing to work with such images on a daily basis to protect the public. However, their power is vast, going to the essence of the right of freedom of expression, and thus brings with it great responsibility. As a public authority, this involves ensuring that its governance structure complies with basic human rights principles requiring that it has a legal basis, a legitimate aim and is carried out proportionately. As we saw, the IWF of 2012 utterly failed as a human rights-compliant regulatory instrument. This was a failure of the IWF as a public authority and a failure of the state.

In the end, the story of the IWF is about the evolution of a self-regulatory framework. The reader will recall that the focus of this case study is on ISPs; and yet, the predominant analysis is of the IWF, the regulator it created, because of the central role of the IWF in determining the content that is filtered in the United Kingdom. The IWF began as a targeted self-regulatory measure of the ISP industry to address its CSR

---

[283] Ibid., para. 5.1.14.

commitment to combat child sexual abuse online, and it evolved into a public authority making it directly bound to HRA. Lessons can be learned from the evolution of the IWF framework and its relationship to the ISP industry to inform other ways that ISPs are pressured to take responsibility for online content. Increasingly in the United Kingdom, illegal file sharing is being tackled through the use of injunctive relief targeted at ISPs, which compels the ISPs to implement systems blocking access to the offending sites.[284] This more explicitly engages ISPs as proxies of the government because the filters have been court ordered, whereas the IWF's creation and membership were spurred by indirect government encouragement and threats of direct regulation.

The case of the IWF and ISPs illustrates the problems that can arise from indirect government encouragement of self-regulation when fundamental rights are engaged. It results in a situation in which there is maximum human rights impact and minimum governance. Reliance on self-regulatory frameworks without guidance on how companies can meet their human rights responsibilities results in a governance gap. Yet it is not so easy to simply task government with imposing greater responsibilities or task companies with taking it on. If a state has positive obligations in the law to ensure a body is human rights-compliant, then the state is duty bound to intervene. Yet the more involved the government, the less self-regulatory the regime. In situations in which self-regulatory regimes have been left to evolve, the more formalised such a framework and the more human rights principles are operationalised, the greater the likelihood that it will be a public authority and thus directly bound by the HRA. The very act of strengthening self-regulatory structures of free speech risks dissuading companies or industries from addressing free speech concerns for fear of incurring direct liability.

The question is whether the IWF and wider ISP industry can build human rights safeguards into their governance framework in a manner that complies with human rights principles while still retaining a self-regulatory nature. Lord Macdonald has made recommendations on how the IWF can strengthen its framework, most of which the IWF has accepted. It remains to be seen whether these changes will be effective and illustrates that the IWF is, in many ways, a test case for CSR frameworks in cyberspace.

---

[284] S. 97A Copyright Designs and Patents Act 1998 c. 48. *Twentieth Century Fox Film Corp & Ors* v. *British Telecommunications Plc [2011] EWHC 1981 (Ch); Dramatico Entertainment Ltd.* v. *British Sky Broadcasting Ltd. [2012] EWHC 268 (CH) AND [2012] EWHC 1152 (CH).* The ISPs have been using Cleanfeed technology for blocking.

The significance of this case study's findings to the viability of CSR to address digital human rights matters will be discussed in Chapter 6. It is there that I will propose an alternative corporate governance model that seeks to mend the deficiencies identified in this case study and the one that follows and to discharge the duty of the state to protect freedom of expression. With this knowledge, we can proceed to the next case study to examine the role of search engines in impacting freedom of expression, which can be more subtle and indirect than the blunt instrument of filtering by ISPs.

# 5

## Mechanisms of information control: search engines

This chapter examines a macro-internet information gatekeeper (IIG) that can have a far more subtle and indirect impact on democratic culture than filtering by internet service providers (ISPs). The indirect nature of search engines' impact on speech, however, does not equate to weakened impact. It is simply less visible. Search engines, it will be shown, are critical gatekeepers of participation in discourse online. The results that are returned when a user inputs a search query and the order of results and what is included and discarded on such results channel the nature and extent of democratic participation online.

This investigation brings to light issues surrounding the viability of corporate social responsibility (CSR) as a form of governance for digital human rights altogether different from the previous chapter. The legal and normative frameworks that regulate search engine indexing and ranking are piecemeal and conflicting, and CSR instruments have not been sufficiently developed to fill the gap. The question is why not? In this case study, a tension is revealed between the legal and CSR models of human rights that has arguably stunted the development of CSR in this area. The source of the tension is in defining *what* speech and *whose* speech we are talking about when attempting to craft search engine responsibilities for freedom of expression. A conflict is revealed among the rights of users, content providers and search providers. As a result of this conflict, the subject matter of the human rights responsibilities of search engines has thus far been circular, never moving beyond a broader discussion of free speech principles to how such principles should be operationalised. Thus, in examining the human rights compliance of search engine governance structures, this chapter also seeks to move the subject matter forward to enable operationalisation of free speech principles in a governance framework. To that end, this chapter will interrogate the free speech significance of search engines, finding that it is rooted in the broader concept of accessibility of information, which, in the search engine context, is a springboard to exercising the fundamental right to seek, receive and impart information and ideas.

Although this case study examines the speech significance of search engines in general, through examples it will focus on one particular search provider, Google. Google holds almost 90 per cent of the search market in the United Kingdom, followed by Bing at 5.49 per cent and Yahoo! at 3.29 per cent.[1] Whereas Google's market share is less in the United States, sitting at 67.6 per cent, it is still the clear market leader.[2] As of 2014, Google's global market share for search is 68.65 per cent [3] (down from 82.80 per cent in 2011).[4] Thus, an examination of search engines naturally leads one to focus on Google. In addition, search providers such as Google have diversified extensively from their initial provision of search services to include, for example, maps services (Google Maps), health services (Google Health), video sharing (YouTube), photo sharing (Picasa), blog hosting (Blogger), operating systems (Android), social networking (Google+) and applications such as email (Gmail). Although their business is diverse, the focus in what follows is on their core business of the provision of search services, namely indexing and ranking, because it emerges as a particularly key aspect to participation in expression online.

Every search engine functions differently, but modern search engines, excluding simple directories, generally work as follows.[5] A computer robot called a 'spider' or 'bot' crawls the web for content in the form of keywords or links, which are then indexed and made searchable by users.[6] The bot will return to a site regularly to look for changes. Although the algorithms are protected as trade secrets, certain basic

---

[1] StatCounter 'Search engine market share as at April 2014', at http://theeword.co.uk/seo -manchester/february_2014_uk_search_engine_market_share_stats.html (last visited 22 May 2014).

[2] See comScore, 'ComScore releases January 2014 U.S. search engine rankings' (18 February 2014), at www.comscore.com/Insights/Press_Releases/2014/2/comScore_Re leases_January_2014_US_Search_Engine_Rankings (last visited 22 May 2014).

[3] See Netmarketshare, 'Search engine market share', at www.netmarketshare.com/search -engine-market-share.aspx?qprid=4&qpcustomd=0 (last visited 22 May 2014).

[4] Netmarketshare, 'Search engine market share', at http://marketshare.hitslink.com/search -engine-market-share.aspx?qprid=4 (last visited 26 August 2011) (link no longer available).

[5] For a more detailed discussion of the functioning of search engines, see chapter three of J. van Hoboken, *Search Engine Freedom: On the Implications of the Right to Freedom of Expression for the Legal Governance of Web Search Engines* (Amsterdam: Kluwer Law International, 2012). Therein, see chapter two for a history of search engines.

[6] See www.searchenginehistory.com (last visited 22 May 2014).

functions are known about search providers' algorithms. Google uses the famous PageRank approach, in which a webpage's importance is based on its popularity in the form of votes. These votes are the number of sites linking to it[7] and, as will be discussed later, can be susceptible to manipulation. In addition to PageRank, Google uses more than 200 other 'signals', such as click-through rates, social signals, terms on the website and the freshness of content.[8] This algorithm, Google reports, is updated weekly.[9] Google search functionality has evolved in recent years. It offers Universal Search, which returns expanded results to users to include images, videos, news and books;[10] Google Instant, which returns immediate results as you type; and autocomplete, which suggests keywords for your searches.[11] The future of search is what it calls the *Knowledge Graph*, with which Google is seeking to understand the meaning behind words. The goal is for Google to understand that if you search 'casino', for example, you are referring to the movie, a casino in Las Vegas or one close to you. In this way, it seeks to understand what you mean more than what you say, thus ushering into reality the semantic web discussed in Chapter 1.

## 5.1. Search engines, democracy and free speech

From the outset, search engines' relationship with freedom of expression is muddied because although they play a critical role in facilitating effective navigation of the internet, they are not creators of content, although they might be seen as creators of the search results. Google simply makes information easier to find because even if information is not ranked on a search engine, it is still available on the internet – just more difficult to find because one would need to know the information's URL. It would be incorrect to therefore characterise the information as being deleted from cyberspace if it is unavailable on or removed from search results; rather, the link to that information is simply not indexed on that particular search result for that particular search term.

---

[7] See www.google.com/intl/en-GB/insidesearch/howsearchworks/crawling-indexing.html (last visited 22 May 2014) and http://infolab.stanford.edu/~backrub/google.html (last visited 22 May 2014).

[8] See U. Kohl, 'Google: The Rise and Rise of Online Intermediaries in the Governance of the Internet and Beyond (Part 2)', *IJLIT*, 21(2) (2013) 187, p. 3. See www.google.com/intl/en-GB/insidesearch/howsearchworks/algorithms.html (last visited 22 May 2014).

[9] Ibid.     [10] Ibid.

[11] See www.google.com/intl/en-GB/insidesearch/howsearchworks/algorithms.html (last visited 22 May 2014).

Estimates on the number of websites or webpages on the internet vary widely depending on the factors taken into account. One report states that the internet contains at least 1.8 billion pages,[12] and another estimates there to be close to 1 billion websites (as opposed to individual webpages).[13] These statistics generally reflect the visible Web (the internet that has been indexed by search engines). Beyond the internet world framed by search engines is what has been called the *Deep Web*, the unindexed and unexplored terrain of the internet.[14] The size of the Deep Web is unknown, although it is estimated (widely admittedly) to comprise trillions of webpages,[15] leading one researcher to comment that searching on the internet is like 'dragging a net across the surface of the ocean'.[16] Search engines in this environment become key gatekeepers, drawing sites from the dark web to human attention by adding them to their rankings. As James Grimmelmann aptly summarises, '[t]he reason we think of the internet not as a chaotic wasteland, but as a vibrant, accessible place, is that some very smart people have done an exceedingly good job of organizing it'.[17] Consider the amount of information Google processes. There are 5.92 billion searches worldwide per day.[18] Google is able capitalise on the data it collects from its search service (and the privacy implications this creates) to provide other services, such as crisis response for humanitarian and natural disasters, including, for example, the person finder service for tsunami-struck Japan discussed in Chapter 3.[19] The Bank of England has used internet search data to help identify economic trends.[20]

---

[12]  See WorldWideWebSize, 'The size of the World Wide Web', at www.worldwideweb size.com (last visited 22 May 2014).

[13]  See www.internetlivestats.com/total-number-of-websites/#trend (last visited 22 May 2014).

[14]  See http://deepweb.us (last visited 22 May 2014).

[15]  Ibid. Early research on the Deep Web was Michael Bergman, 'The Deep Web: Surfacing Hidden Value', *The Journal of Electronic Publishing*, 7(1) (2001) 1. This article would be out of date now. However, many research projects are attempting to gauge the size of the Deep Web and how to search it. See such research as A. Ntoulas et al., 'Downloading hidden content', at http://oak.cs.ucla.edu/~cho/papers/ntoulas-hidden.pdf (last visited 26 August 2014).

[16]  Bergman ibid.

[17]  J. Grimmelmann, 'The Google Dilemma', *New York Law School Law Review*, 53 (2008/2009) 939, p. 941.

[18]  See http://www.statisticbrain.com/google-searches/ (last visited 22 May 2014).

[19]  See www.google.com/crisisresponse/ (last visited 18 June 2014).

[20]  G. Wearden, 'Bank of England turns to Google to shed light on economic trends' (13 June 2011), at www.guardian.co.uk/business/2011/jun/13/bank-of-england-google -searches?intcmp=239 (last visited 18 June 2014).

Search engines are our guides to effective navigation of the Web. They sort through the clutter and, as Jennifer Chandler describes them, act as 'selection intermediaries' by finding information and making an assessment of what is most useful for the reader.[21] Google recognises its key role in this process stating, '[t]he Internet ... makes information available. Google makes information accessible'.[22] Search engines thus emerge as critical chokepoints on the internet acting as the link between readers and information. In so doing, they structure participation in democratic culture. They decide the information that gets on the list and the information that does not. They decide the visibility of the information by ranking some of this information higher than others. Yet their role is more complex and meaningful than equating it with a simple index akin to a telephone book. The result is that search engines create categories for consumption, thereby shaping public opinion and the direction of democratic discourse:

> They structure categories in response to users' queries, and thereby have the capacity of creating categories for grasping the world. By defining which information becomes available for each query, search engines may shape positions, concepts and ideas.[23]

This is magnified by how users use search engines. First, users tend to rely on search engines to navigate the internet. Researchers in Germany found that 75 per cent of German users relied on search engines as their primary vehicle for finding information on the internet.[24] Second, users tend to expect that search results will be reliable and relevant.[25] Third, most users do not visit beyond the first or second page of search results. One study found that 91.5 per cent of users reviewed the first page of search results, whereas the figure dropped to 4.8 per cent of users for

---

[21] J. A. Chandler, 'A Right to Reach an Audience: An Approach to Intermediary Bias on the Internet', *Hofstra L. Rev.*, 35(3) (2007) 101, p. 103. U. Kohl describes them as navigation intermediaries n. 7.

[22] K. Auletta, *Googled: The End of the World as We Know It* (London: Virgin Books, 2010), p. xi quote by Google's chief economist Hal Varian.

[23] N. Elkin-Koren, 'Let the Crawlers Crawl: On Virtual Gatekeepers and the Right to Exclude Indexing', *U. Dayton L. Rev.*, 26 (2000) 179, pp. 185–86.

[24] W. Schulz et al., 'Search Engines as Gatekeepers of Public Communication: An Analysis of the German Framework Applicable to Internet Search Engines Including Media Law and Antitrust Law', *German Law Journal*, 6(1) (2005) 1419, p. 1421.

[25] Elizabeth Van Couvering has done some empirical work in this regard: See E. Van Couvering, 'Is Relevance Relevant? Market, Science, and War: Discourses of Search Engine Quality', *J. Comput.-Mediat. Comm.*, 12(3) (2007) 866.

the second page of results.[26] Even more startling, on that first page of search results, click-through data shows that results ranked number one on Google search results receive double the amount of traffic compared to the number two ranking, with number one ranked results receiving 33 per cent of traffic, and number two ranked results receiving 17.6 per cent of traffic. Results ranked ten receive a mere 2.6 per cent of traffic.[27] One comment with regard to earlier research is particularly apposite: 'to be seen is not only to be indexed, but to be highly ranked in the search results'.[28]

The importance of search engines to participation in democratic culture is further pronounced when taking into account the importance of access to the internet in our daily lives, as set out in Chapter 1.[29] Search engines, it can be argued, make any meaningful engagement online possible. Since we use the internet for various activities such as work, shopping, education, entertainment, communication and, increasingly, to work through major life issues, search engines become intertwined with participation in democratic life both on and off the internet.[30] A soft-law recommendation on search engines adopted by the Council of Europe (CoE) (Recommendation) echoes many of these same themes.[31] The Recommendation recognises the pivotal role search engines play in the information society regarding accessibility of information, noting that:

> [They] play a crucial role as one of the first points of contact on the Internet in exercising the right to seek and access information, facts and

---

[26] See http://searchenginewatch.com/article/2276184/No.-1-Position-in-Google-Gets-33-of-Search-Traffic-Study (last visited 25 May 2014).

[27] Ibid. For earlier research on this effect, see B. Edelman and B. Lockwood, 'Measuring bias in "organic" web search', at http://www.benedelman.org/searchbias/ (last visited 18 June 2014). Sometimes he found that users' preferences were for lower ranked results, thereby combating the effect of any bias they were finding in search results, but those instances were found to be rare.

[28] E. B. Laidlaw, 'Private Power, Public Interest: An Examination of Search Engine Accountability', *IJLIT*, 17 (1) (2009) 113, p. 125.

[29] See, in particular, the discussion of Internet access as a fundamental right in Chapter 1, and see Report of the special rapporteur on the promotion and protection of the right to freedom of expression, Frank La Rue to the United Nations General Assembly, 16 May 2011, at http://www.ohchr.org/Documents/Issues/Opinion/A.66.290.pdf (last visited 16 June 2014).

[30] See S. Orgad, 'The Cultural Dimensions of Online Communication: A Study of Breast Cancer Patients' Internet Spaces', *New Media & Society*, 8(6) (2006) 87.

[31] Recommendation CM/Rec(2012)3 of the Committee of Ministers to member States on the protection of human rights with regard to search engines.

ideas, as well as other content, including entertainment. Such access to information is essential to building one's personal opinion and participating in social, political, cultural and economic life. Search engines are also an important portal for citizens' access to mass media, including electronic newspapers and audiovisual media services.[32]

Search engines are information guidance instruments, accepting user queries and, in return, helping 'listeners . . . discriminate amongst speakers'.[33] In this way, they are like the media and its power to shape world views. They are unlike the media in the sense that they are not publishers of content except for the results page; but by channelling information flows, they affect democratic discourse. Although search engines do not directly engage the right to impart or receive information, as Chandler notes, freedom of expression has a range of penumbral rights, and when looking at the digital environment and the role of intermediaries, we should consider freedom of expression more broadly in terms of its communicative role. All theories of free speech, she persuasively argues, depend on there having been established between the speaker and listener a communicative relationship, and so it follows that 'all elements of that relationship'[34] ought to be protected. Selection intermediaries such as search engines intervene in this communicative relationship as follows:

> Given the large amount of information, listeners may require assistance in making their selections, and sometimes a selection intermediary will be interposed between speaker and listener. That selection intermediary will also apply some criteria of discrimination in order to select the speech to which the listener's attention will be drawn. Where the selection criteria are those that the listener would have employed, no distortion is thus introduced by the intermediary. Where the selection intermediary uses criteria of discrimination that the listener would not have selected, the selection intermediary is undermining the establishment of a communicative relationship in a manner that restricts the freedom that both speaker and listener would otherwise have had.[35]

As will be seen, search engines, by the way they function, inevitably intervene in the communicative relationship between speaker and listener by interpreting user search queries and guiding the users to content.[36]

What emerges from this scenario is that the significance of search engines to democracy is their role in facilitating access to information.

---

[32] Ibid., para. I, 1. See also para 1.  [33] Chandler n. 21, p. 103.  [34] Ibid., p. 107.
[35] Ibid., p. 108.  [36] See discussion van Hoboken, n. 5, pp. 216–17.

However, as will be seen in Section 5.3, accessibility, although appearing to be a simple concept, does not translate seamlessly to the legal framework of free speech. Joris van Hoboken frames the societal role of search engines as one of *relative accessibility*, describing search engines as having conflicting ideals of providing universal access to the material on the web and prioritising valuable or less valuable information.[37] He posits, '[w]eb search engines, in particular, help construct the boundaries of accessibility in the new networked public information environment'.[38]

Search engines' functional, automated side has been cited as evidence that they don't fit with any of the traditional justifications for speech protection.[39] Such arguments largely come out of the United States, where freedom of expression, while given preferential weight in assessing competing rights compared to here in Europe, tends to be treated as a negative right.[40] The arguments, as Oren Bracha and Frank Pasquale noted, state that the speech engaged by search engines has no intrinsic value, that it does not encourage participation in the public sphere: '[w]hile having an undeniable expressive element, the prevailing character of such speech is performative rather than propositional. Its dominant function is not to express meaning but rather to "do things in the world"; namely, channel users to websites'.[41]

Their conclusion, like this author's, is that search itself is of free speech significance regardless of the content of the links. However, our approaches are couched in different historical views on the negative or positive duties of the state concerning freedom of expression. They frame the role of search engines as channelling information: 'search engine rankings play a central instrumental role in facilitating effective speech by others'.[42] However, they restrict the trigger for First Amendment scrutiny in the American tradition of negative treatment of free speech to situations in which search engines might be banned by governments or filter specific content – to the effect of the speech, not to the structure itself. In contrast, the argument here draws from the European Court of Human Rights (ECtHR) history of sometimes positive duties on the state to facilitate the exercise of the right to free speech and concludes that, as a macro-IIG, a search engine such as Google is of free speech significance

---

[37] Ibid., p. 227.    [38] Ibid., p. 195.

[39] In this regard, see O. Bracha and F. Pasquale, 'Federal Search Commission? Access, Fairness and Accountability in the Law of Search', *Cornell L. R.*, 93 (2008) 1149, pp. 1193–95.

[40] But see M. Ammori, 'First Amendment Architecture', *Wis. L. Rev.* (2012) 1.

[41] Bracha and Pasquale n. 39., p. 1193.    [42] Ibid., p. 1199.

on its own. Whether the state's responsibility is satisfied by encourage-ment of CSR frameworks or whether direct legal duties on states to regulate the industry are necessary is something explored further in Chapter 6. What is clear is that the state has a role to play, not necessarily in a legal sense, to shape access to information in the digital society.

This difficulty in identifying the nature of the relationship between search engines and free speech is explored by James Grimmelmann in the context of the United States. He identifies a tension between two theories of search: the *conduit theory*, which focuses on speech of the websites, on what search does, and the *editor theory* focusing on the speech of the search providers, on what search says.[43] As Grimmelmann notes, how-ever, these theories assume the user is a passive consumer of information rather than an active seeker; from a user's perspective, a search engine is a trusted advisor,[44] and he argues that the two theories are incomplete to this experience. The *advisor theory*, he posits, draws from and completes both the editor and conduit theories: '[i]t can promote *access* to search by enabling users to draw on the aid of search engines, and it can promote *loyalty* in search by preventing search engines from misleading users'.[45] Grimmelmann's advisor theory has two commitments:

> The advisor theory has two basic commitments. First, it puts users' interests first, rather than websites' or search engines': the goal of search is to help *users* find what they seek. And second, it defers to users' choices in defining those interests: the goal of search is to help users find what *they* seek.[46]

This shift in focus to the users and their active participation in the space can be seen in the gatekeeping model identified in Chapter 2.

In a European context, van Hoboken considers the interaction between search engines and free speech in its wider Article 10 European Convention on Human Rights (ECHR) context, where the right to freedom of expression can invite positive obligations on the state for its facilitation. He describes the societal legitimisation of knowl-edge in the Digital Age as taking place through the connection of information and ideas, a process van Hoboken describes as *opening up*. Search engines aid this process of connecting by making information accessible.[47] He continues,

---

[43] J. Grimmelmann, 'Speech Engines', University of Maryland Francis King Carey School of Law Legal Studies Research Paper No. 2014-11 (2014) 867, pp. 873, 889.

[44] Ibid., pp. 873-74.    [45] Ibid., p. 874.    [46] Ibid., p. 896.

[47] van Hoboken n. 5, pp. 195, 227-28.

> If one follows this logic [that search engines facilitate accessibility], the overarching public interest in the legal governance of Web search engines, from the ideals underlying the right to freedom of expression, lies in the establishment of a rich and robust societal infrastructure for the opening up of the Web.[48]

Often, people or businesses ranked low on search results or not ranked at all want to be highly ranked, whereas subjects of offensive, intrusive or defamatory information ranked highly on search indices want the information to be buried lower on search results or off the indices entirely. What Google decides to do in the face of such conflicts impacts the flow of information online. For example, in 2004, the search term 'Jew' returned an anti-Semitic site www.jewwatch.com at the top of the search results. In such a scenario, what can or should Google do? Should Google move such a result down further in the rankings or do nothing? Should it rely on a *Google bomb* (a term to be discussed shortly) to sort the problem out? In this particular case, Google took an approach that depended on domestic law. In the United Kingdom, a link was provided at the top of search results titled 'Offensive Search Results' with an explanation by Google condemning the site but not removing it from the search results.[49] In Germany, however, www.jewwatch.com was removed entirely from Google Germany's search results with a statement at the bottom of the search page indicating that a site was removed for legal reasons.[50]

The tension among the various potential rights of users, information providers and the search provider and the uncertainty in law concerning a search provider such as Google's duties and responsibilities challenges the legal system on various fronts. It challenges traditional debates about the limits of free speech, both in terms of theoretical foundations of free speech and its adequacy in reflecting a right of access to information, but it is also a challenge in terms of lack of engagement historically with the importance of mediums and forums of communication as an integral component of the right to free speech itself. It also challenges the limits of the reach of human rights to address the responsibilities of privately owned search providers. One can see situations in which human rights law has failed to hold search providers like Google to account for its rankings, but other areas of the law or public advocacy have been more successful. Often, free speech is addressed, rightly or wrongly, as

---

[48] Ibid., p. 228.    [49] See www.google.com/explanation.html (last visited 18 June 2014).
[50] See Grimmelmann n. 17, p. 948, which translates and discusses the German statement regarding this Google bomb.

a knock-on effect of discussions concerning neutrality and market dominance. We can see these sorts of dilemmas in four scenarios.

First, free speech issues arise concerning manipulation of Google's search rankings. Whereas businesses often purchase sponsored links which run alongside or at the top of the search results, businesses quite commonly attempt to play the system by capitalising on how Google's search algorithm works to push their business up the rankings or competitors down the rankings. Known as *search engine optimisation* (SEO), it attempts to manipulate the way Google's algorithm works. In its worst form, it creates artificial votes for a website by creating link farms, which are sites linking one site to the other to artificially boost the importance of a website in the eyes of the Googlebot, thereby securing a higher spot on Google's search results, or it uses other forms of manipulation based on the way Google's algorithms work. In its best form, SEO is an integral component of business marketing, such as collecting keyword data to understand why users visit your site or tailoring websites to capitalise on the evolution of Google's algorithms, such as Google Hummingbird, which understands conversational search terms, and Authorship, which links content with authors.[51] Should Google delete such SEO websites from its index? Manipulate the rankings to counteract it? Google has attempted to resolve the issue through its algorithm.[52] The difficulty is drawing the line between maintaining the integrity of the search results and punitive manipulations that are more properly acts of censorship.

Rankings have also been manipulated for political, humorous or hateful purposes – known as Google bombing – although changes to Google's algorithm in 2007 now make this much more difficult. The first such Google bomb was committed when Adam Mathes linked the term 'talentless hack' to his friend's website. The most famous Google bomb, however, was when the search term 'miserable failure' returned George Bush's official White House page. It took three years for it to be defused. Some Google bombs are arguably a tool for social mobilisation. In response to the search term 'Jew' returning the anti-Semitic site www.jewwatch.com, discussed earlier, users mobilised to counteract the offensive results. Led by Daniel Sieradski, a Google bomb was orchestrated to displace www.jewwatch.com from the top of Google's ranking

---

[51] See E. Enge, '6 major Google changes reveal the future of SEO' (30 December 2013), at http://searchenginewatch.com/article/2301719/6-Major-Google-Changes-Reveal-the -Future-of-SEO (last visited 25 May 2014).

[52] Google, 'Finding more high-quality sites in search', at http://googleblog.blogspot.com /2011/02/finding-more-high-quality-sites-in.html (last visited 18 June 2014).

and instead promote the Wikipedia definition of 'Jew'.[53] As Danielle Citron notes, '[s]ome Google bombs devolve into an arms race'.[54] In this case, Neo-Nazi sites successfully launched a counter Google bomb to return the anti-Semitic site to the top of search results.[55]

Second, legal issues arise concerning Google's autocomplete function. Autocomplete suggests terms to complete your search query, and, if you are signed into a Google account, this automated function personalises it to your search history.[56] Thus, if I input 'London', suggested completions are functional and localised, suggesting completions of my query with the terms 'underground', 'tube map' and 'weather'. These completions can have political and social significance. A search for the term 'Tories' suggests completion of the search query with 'are evil'. A search for the term 'UKIP' (UK Independence Party) suggests the completion term 'are racist'.[57] During the peak of the superinjunctions drama in the United Kingdom and the revelation that footballer Ryan Giggs was one of parties who sought this type of injunction, a search of his name suggested completion terms of 'Imogen', 'affair', 'super injunction' and 'wife'.[58] Although suggestions are automated, Google also has an automated blocking function (as much as is possible, otherwise requiring human review) for content that is hateful, violent, personally identifiable (i.e., phone number and social security number), pornographic or pirated. With regard to the latter, for example, the terms 'BitTorrent' and 'torrent' are unavailable as autocomplete terms.[59]

Google has been held liable for this autocomplete function in certain jurisdictions, such as Germany, France, Italy and Japan, although the reasoning of the courts on this issue has been inconsistent.[60] In France,

---

[53] C. Tatum, 'Deconstructing Google Bombs: A Breach of Symbolic Power or Just a Goofy Prank?', *First Monday*, 10(10) (2005) 1.

[54] D. K. Citron, *Hate Crimes in Cyberspace* (Cambridge, Mass.: Harvard University Press, 2014), p. 71.

[55] Ibid.

[56] This is its autocomplete or instant search function: see www.google.com/support/web search/bin/answer.py?hl=en&answer=106230 (last visited 18 June 2014).

[57] These were searched June 2014.

[58] This search was performed June 2011 on Google UK.

[59] K. Fiveash, 'Google disappears torrent terms from autocomplete search results' (27 January 2011), at www.theregister.co.uk/2011/01/27/google_bittorrent_terms_killed_on_au tocomplete/ (last visited 18 June 2014). See http://searchengineland.com/how-google-instant -autocomplete-suggestions-work-62592 (last visited 25 May 2014).

[60] See discussion of cases U. Kohl n. 8, p. 8. In the case of Germany, the Federal Supreme Court found Google liable for failing to remove the terms 'Scientology' and 'Betrug' (meaning fraud) from its autocomplete function in association with the Plaintiff

for example, Mr. X (the Plaintiff declined to be named) sued Google for defamation for its automated search suggestions. When users searched Mr. X's name, Google suggested completion terms of 'rape', 'rapist', 'Satanist' and 'prison'. At the time, the man was appealing a three-month suspended sentence for corrupting a minor. While initially successful at the court of first instance, the judgment was overturned on appeal on the basis that Google acted in good faith, which was affirmed by the *Cour de cassation* in 2013.[61] Are search engine results a private party's statement of opinion that it can censor and shape at will? This line of argument will be examined in Section 5.3.2. Or are there obligations as to neutrality, transparency or fairness that come into play? Regardless, the experience of using and running a search engine begins to reflect all of the complexities one is confronted with in any system of freedom of expression in the physical world.

SEO, bombing, autocomplete and manipulation of rankings illustrate the tension (and blurring of the lines) between the computer versus man forms of legal argument. The standard argument of Google is that it is neutral and therefore not legally liable; the search results page reflects a combination of community interests and algorithm. Since Google does not generally intervene to manually deselect or shift material in the rankings, it can be said to be neutral. The argument against this narrative of neutrality is that Google chooses the algorithms it uses, that these algorithms are really just 'organising principles' of the business and 'like other organizing principles they reflect biases towards some content over other content'.[62] This argument identifies the selectivity of the Google notion of neutrality – after all, even librarians as one of the more traditional forms of information gatekeepers select the books to shelve and where to shelve them.

businessman's name. The ruling imposed liability narrowly in circumstances where Google was made aware of the unlawful breach of personality rights and failed to remove the offending search term. This Court came to a different conclusion than previous rulings by other German lower courts: BGH decision of 14 May 2013 (case no VI ZR 269/12).

[61] *Cour de cassation, Civ 1ère, 19 juin 2013, Google Inc. c/ Société Lyonnaise de garantie*. In the United Kingdom, Google was found not liable for defamatory search snippets: *Metropolitan International Schools* v. *Designtechnica Corporation and Others* [2009] EWHC 1765 (QB), although this case is arguably distinguishable because Google was more clearly communicating the speech of others. See also *Budu* v. *BBC* [2010] EWHC 616 (QB), where the Court found that the BBC was not liable for, amongst other things, a search snippet on Google commenting, 'those who use Google search engines are well aware that such a snippet is merely a fragment of a larger whole (the underlying publication)': para. 75.

[62] Kohl n. 8, p. 3.

Utah Kohl further notes that the line between content creation and content organisation is blurry for Google when one considers the more diverse Google services such as Google News (aggregating online news) and Google Street View (street scene captures).[63] Relatedly, the concept of neutrality itself needs to be interrogated because there is an assumption on the part of Google and its ilk that automation translates to neutrality.[64] Rather, automation is not value free, and the design can create prejudices, assumptions or, in human rights terms, infringements. The case of *Fair Housing Council of San Fernando Valley* v. *Roommates. com*[65] illustrates this. Roommates.com lost its immunity under Section 230 of the Communications Decency Act (CDA)[66] because the questionnaire it created to match roommates, although executed automatically, had built-in bias due to questions about the preferred sexual orientation of roommates.[67]

Third, as mentioned earlier, many individuals and businesses wish to push unfavourable information about themselves down or entirely off the rankings. Sometimes it is simply embarrassing information, such as subjects of http://womenwhoeatontubes.tumblr.com. At other times, it is arguably defamatory or privacy-invasive information,[68] such as the subjects of www.cheaterville.com or http://thedirty.com and might involve some information being highly ranked but not other information, thereby creating a misleading story. For example, a name search might reveal a criminal charge against a person but not the subsequent dismissal of charges, or a complaint against a company might be highly ranked but not the dismissal of the complaint. Search engines can magnify harmful or embarrassing stories, whether through Google's autocomplete function or organic search results, and because its algorithm is based on popularity, the more links there are to such content, the higher the content will likely be ranked. In this way, Citron argues, '[s]earch engines contribute to the escalation of information cascades'[69]

---

[63] Ibid., p. 4.    [64] See discussion ibid., pp. 4–5

[65] (2008) 521 F.3d 1157 (9th Circ. USCA).    [66] 47 U.S.C.

[67] See discussion Kohl n. 8, pp. 4–5. Some American scholars argue that automation should not be treated as speech under the First Amendment. See T. Wu, 'Machine Speech', *U. PA. L. Rev.*, 161(6) (2013) 1495; and S. M. Benjamin, 'Algorithms and Speech', *U. PA. L. Rev.*, 161(6) (2013) 1445.

[68] See here *Doe* v. *Ciolli*, 3:2007CV00909 (D. Conn.), which settled in 2009. See B. Leiter, 'Cleaning Cyber-Cesspools: Google and Free Speech', in S. Levmore and M.C. Nussbaum (eds.), *The Offensive Internet* (Cambridge, Mass.: Harvard University Press, 2010) and Citron n. 54.

[69] Citron n. 54, p. 67.

in spreading abuse. Search engines create what Viktor Mayer-Schönberger calls (in the context of the internet more generally) an environment of perfect remembering – it is this which has underpinned his advocacy of a revival of forgetting.[70] These scenarios reflect the narrative force of search results. They tell a story about its subject, and the question is the extent to which individuals and businesses can control this narrative, as well as Google's discretionary rights to respond.

These issues have tended to be addressed not as part of more general debates on human rights, but more narrowly under the umbrella of a right to be forgotten. At a European level, a right to be forgotten has been a central feature in the debate concerning data protection reform, but talks were stalled by how best to balance such a right against free speech and in light of the Advocate General's opinion in *Google Spain SL, Google Inc.* v. *Agencia Espanola de Proteccion de Datos, Marios Costeja Gonzalez* (Google Spain) that Google is not a data controller within the meaning of the current Data Protection Directive.[71] However, the judgment of the Court of Justice of the European Union (CJEU)[72] came to a different conclusion than the Advocate General. The case involved Mr Costeja Gonzalez, who was the subject of insolvency proceedings in the 1990s. The proceedings were published in a newspaper at the time, and the article was later made available online. Mr Costeja Gonzalez asked the newspaper to delete the piece online on the basis that it was no longer relevant. The newspaper refused. He then asked Google to delete the link to the article from its search results. The Spanish Data Protection Authority also made this request of Google. Google contested the decision to a national court, which referred questions to the CJEU.

The CJEU in *Google Spain* makes several important pronouncements on data protection as it relates to search engines, not all of which are relevant for present purposes. With regard to search results, the CJEU held that the activities of search engines such as Google affect the fundamental right to privacy and to protection of personal data of those subject to searches.[73] Indeed, the Court held that inclusion on search engine

---

[70] See V. Mayer-Shönberger, *Delete: The Virtue of Forgetting in the Digital Age* (Princeton University Press, 2009).

[71] Directive 95/46/EC of the European Parliament and of the Council of 24 October 1995 on the protection of individuals with regard to the processing of personal data and on the free movement of such data. See Opinion of the Advocate General Jääskinen at http://curia.eu ropa.eu/juris/document/document_print.jsf?doclang=EN&text=&pageIndex=0&part=1& mode=lst&docid=138782&occ=first&dir=&cid=124792 (last visited 25 May 2014).

[72] (2014) Case C-131/12.     [73] Ibid., para. 38.

results 'constitute[s] a more significant interference with the data sub-ject's fundamental right to privacy than the publication on the web page'.[74] The CJEU held that where the data returned on search results as a result of a name search does not comply with Article 6(1)(c)–(e) of the Data Protection Directive – namely, the information is 'inadequate, irrelevant or no longer relevant, or excessive in relation to the purposes of the processing'[75] – then the link to the webpage should be removed from the results by Google for that name search. The information does not need to be prejudicial as a condition for its removal.[76] Unfortunately, the CJEU pushed this further and effectively rebalanced the relationship between free speech and privacy in the context of search engines in favour of privacy and data protection, with scant attention paid to free speech in the process:

> Those rights [Article 7 (privacy) and Article 8 (personal data)] override, as a rule, not only the economic interest of the operator of the search engine but also the interest of the general public in finding that information upon a search relating to the data subject's name. However, that would not be the case if it appeared, for particular reasons, such as the role played by the data subject in public life, that the interference with his fundamental rights is justified by the preponderant interest of the general public in having, on account of inclusion in the list of results, access to the informa-tion in question.[77]

The CJEU sidelined a holistic assessment of the right to freedom of expression in favour of the narrower concept of public interest. As Lorena Jaume-Palasi summarised the case, the Court held that 'the publicness of the data should not be amplified by a search engine'.[78] At the time of writing, it is unclear how free speech can be balanced against the tunnel vision of the CJEU judgment but, at the same time, advocates of free speech have tended to overlook the grave harm suffered by some who are victims of Google's algorithm. The problem in finding a balance,

---

[74] Ibid., para. 87.    [75] Ibid., para. 94.    [76] Ibid., para. 96.

[77] Ibid., para 97. Eric Schmidt, Google Chairman and former CEO, made a similar assess-ment, stating that the ruling was 'a collision between a right to be forgotten and a right to know. From Google's perspective that's a balance. Google believes, having looked at the decision, which is binding, that the balance that was struck was wrong': C. Arthur, 'Google faces deluge of requests to wipe details from search index' (4 May 2014), at www.theguard ian.com/technology/2014/may/15/hundreds-google-wipe-details-search-index-right-forg otten (last visited 18 June 2014).

[78] L. Jaume-Palasi, '"Google Spain case": court decision privatises the public sphere' (27 May 2014), at http://policyreview.info/articles/news/google-spain-case-court-decision-privat ises-public-sphere/291 (last visited 28 May 2014).

in the end, is the risk of abuse. Within days of this case, there were reports of requests to Google for removal of links by, for example, a man concerning a conviction for possession of child sexual abuse images, a doctor concerning a bad patient review and a politician for information on his actions in office.[79] Whether these reports were exaggerated or not is unknown. Within a few weeks, Google had received more than forty-thousand requests to remove content from its search results.[80] The question is which human right bears the burden of this risk. The CJEU, by examining solely data protection, implicitly foisted the burden onto freedom of expression, liberating privacy from the shackles of Google's algorithm.[81]

Fourth, to what extent is Google legally allowed to manipulate search results to favour its services over competitors in search results because such an act favours its own speech over the speech of others? Is Google allowed to penalise sites by effectively removing them from algorithmic consideration? At the heart of this inquiry is the extent to which search engines such as Google can and are neutral concerning the content they index and rank. A corollary issue is whether any intervention by Google to shift or delete content on the rankings, such as unlawful content, disrupts this neutrality. Google can be observed regularly intervening in natural search results to remove pirated material from search results or block hateful autocomplete terms. Arguments have been made against this notion of neutrality,[82] including this author arguing that search engines have public interest obligations,[83] but the minimal case law on the matter, mostly out of the United States, has held that the rankings, at least in America, are in fact statements of opinion protected by the First Amendment.[84] As Uta Kohl notes, this 'implicitly rejects the possibility of search neutrality',[85] but, equally, it acts as a powerful shield from any assessment of the space – because the results page are now the creative

[79] Arthur n. 77.

[80] J. Halliday, 'Google search results may indicate "right to be forgotten" censorship' (8 June 2014), at www.theguardian.com/technology/2014/jun/08/google-search-results-indicate-right-to-be-forgotten-censorship (last visited 9 June 2014).

[81] See Google's public response: https://support.google.com/legal/contact/lr_eudpa?product=websearch&hl=en (last visited 30 May 2014).

[82] See discussion by Grimmelmann, n. 43, in particular pp. 870–73. It is also discussed more implicitly through van Hoboken, n. 5.

[83] Laidlaw n. 28.

[84] *Search King, Inc.* v. Google *Technology, Inc.* (2003) Case No. CIV-02–1457-M (WD Okla); *Jian Zhang* v. *Baidu.com Inc.* (2014) 11 Civ. 3388 (DC SDNY).

[85] Kohl n. 8, p. 17.

output of Google alone. These cases will be discussed in more detail in Section 5.3.

This tension is identified for the reader because competition law has been more successful than other areas of the law in assessing search engine rankings, at least in the sense of going further with the analysis than has previously taken place.[86] At the time of writing, the European Commission (EC) is four years into its investigation of Google for anticompetitive behaviour related to its search indexing and ranking. In America, a similar anti-trust investigation by the Federal Trade Commission (FTC) concluded that there was not enough evidence to charge Google, although this followed a two-year investigation and settlement with Google whereby it agreed to make voluntary changes to its services.[87]

The European investigation was launched after complaints by Foundem (price comparison site), Ciao (shopping) and ejustice.fr (legal search) that Google was abusing its dominant position by lowering its rivals in its search rankings and favouring its own services. The EC's preliminary conclusion in 2012 was that there were four concerns that raised issues of abuse of dominance: (1) Google displays its vertical search services (specialised topics such as restaurants and news) differently than it does competitors' services; (2) Google copies content from competitor services, such as user reviews, and uses it on its own sites without prior authorisation; (3) agreements resulted in de facto exclusivity by obliging websites to obtain their online search advertisements from Google; and (4) contractual restrictions limit the extent to which advertising campaigns can be transferred from one platform to another.[88]

The EC gave Google the opportunity to propose a remedy, which remedy the EC then offered to the public for feedback.[89] The EC then advised Google that further improvements were needed, which were

---

[86] For analysis of market issues, see M. R. Patterson, 'Google and Search-Engine Market Power', *Harvard Journal Law and Technology Occasional Paper Series* (2013) 1.

[87] See Google, 'The Federal Trade Commission closes its antitrust review' (3 January 2013), at http://googleblog.blogspot.ca/2013/01/the-federal-trade-commission-closes-its.html (last visited 13 June 2014).

[88] J. Almunia Speech/12/372, 'Statement of VP Almunia on the Google antitrust investigation' (21 May 2012), at http://europa.eu/rapid/press-release_SPEECH-12-372_en.htm (last visited 18 June 2014).

[89] European Commission – IP/13/371, 'Antitrust: commission seeks feedback on commitments offered by Google to address competition concerns' (25 April 2013), at http://europa.eu/rapid/press-release_IP-13-371_en.htm (last visited 27 May 2014).

submitted to the EC in October 2013. One of the key commitments is that when Google promotes its specialised services in search engine results, it will list the services of three rivals in a way that is clearly visible to users.[90] The EC was satisfied with Google's proposal[91] but received such negative feedback from interested parties that, in September 2014, outgoing Competition Commissioner Joaquin Almunia reopened the investigation.[92] At the time of writing, the new European Competition Commissioner, Margrethe Vestager, has advised the European Parliament that she is 'deciding on next the steps'.[93]

These four dilemmas highlight that the impact of search engines reaches, expectedly, much wider than human rights law, particularly wider than the right to freedom of expression with which this book is engaged. In addition, they show that search providers are placed squarely at the centre of vexing legal questions concerning their rights and obligations in managing this 'critical pathway of communication'.[94] How the free speech impact of search engines would be treated under jurisprudence of the ECHR will be examined later in this chapter. As outlined in Chapter 3, such an analysis is important regardless of the public authority status of a search engine such as Google (and it will be shown that Google is quite clearly not a public authority). The issues come down to characterisation: are search results simply Google's marketing tool – Google's private forum for speech? Or are search engines critical communication tools for making any sensible use of the internet? The struggle to address this question and identify what responsibilities flow from its role as gatekeeper of information accessibility, it is argued, has stymied the potential development of CSR in this area, a point that we now explore further by reference to the regulatory and governance regime in the United Kingdom and, more broadly, in Europe.

---

[90] Ibid.

[91] European Commission – IP/14/116, 'Antitrust: commission obtains from Google comparable display of specialised search rivals' (5 February 2014), at http://europa.eu/rapid /press-release_IP-14-116_en.htm (last visited 27 May 2014).

[92] C. Arthur, 'European commission reopens Google antitrust investigation' (8 September 2014), at www.theguardian.com/technology/2014/sep/08/european-commission-reopens -google-antitrust-investigation-after-political-storm-over-proposed-settlement.

[93] European Commission – Statement, 'Statement by Commissioner Vestager on Google antitrust investigations at the European Parliament (ECON committee meeting)' (11 November 2014), at http://europa.eu/rapid/press-release_STATEMENT-14-1646_en.htm.

[94] Bracha and Pasquale n. 39, p. 1191.

## 5.2. Governance of search

The regulatory environment in which search engines operate is, as van Hoboken describes it, in its infancy.[95] This is partly due to the hybridity of search, making it difficult to apply current law to it. It is also partly due to the light-touch regulatory approach that has been taken in Western democracies to internet governance.[96] For example, one interesting comparison for search engines is mass media. Search engines as gatekeepers facilitate public discourse much the way that the media shape our understanding of the world, but search engines are not creators of the content. The question is whether search engines are creators of content in the sense of being publishers of the search engine results,[97] a point that will be explored later concerning the free speech rights of search providers. Equally, however, the role of search engines is functional, akin to transport services in creating the algorithms that 'route' information.[98] Thus, they are both powerful forces in shaping the information we consume and a logistically necessary infrastructure for internet navigation. The result, as Nico van Eijk states, is that search engines are effectively 'lost in law':[99]

> The limited legal attention devoted to search engines is, I believe, partly the result of the fact that the search engine is neither one thing nor the other: it concerns issues that are considered to fall within telecommunications law and partly – if not very much so – issues to do with content. Partly because of this, there is a legal vacuum: *the search engine does not have a place in law.*[100]

As a result of this hybridity, search engines continue to slip through the cracks of telecommunication regulations. This is because much of the law in this area was not drafted with search in mind.[101] The AudioVisual Media Services Directive,[102] for example, is aimed at regulating traditional television and video-on-demand services. The application of the

---

[95] van Hoboken, n. 5, p. 187.

[96] This is discussed in more detail in the previous chapter.

[97] E. Goldman argues this point in 'Search Engine Bias and the Demise of Search Engine Utopianism', *YJLT*, 8 (2005–6) 188.

[98] N. van Eijk, 'Search Engines: Seek and Ye Shall Find? The Position of Search Engines in Law', *Iris Plus*, 2 (2006) 1, p. 7.

[99] N. van Eijk, 'Search Engines, the New Bottleneck for Content Access', Amsterdam Law School Legal Studies Research Paper No. 2012–21, p. 150. Emphasis in original.

[100] van Eijk n. 98, p. 7.    [101] See discussion ibid., pp. 5–7.

[102] Directive 2010/13/EU of the European Parliament and of the Council of 10 March 2010 on the coordination of certain provisions laid down by law, regulation or administrative action in Member States concerning the provision of audiovisual media services.

Electronic Commerce Directive,[103] in particular the limitation of liability provisions in Articles 12–14 for information society services (ISS), which act as mere conduits, cache or host content, is uncertain.[104] The latter point requires elaboration.

Under the E-Commerce Directive, a search engine is an ISS. This is reflected in Recital 18 of the Directive[105] and was confirmed by the CJEU in *Google France, Google Inc. v. Louis Vuitton Malletier* (Google France),[106] although that case concerned Google's Adwords system (the sale by Google of sponsored links). More uncertain is whether Google, in its capacity as a provider of search services (namely, indexing and ranking of content) can benefit from the conditional limitations of liability in Articles 12–14. This is because the Directive does not explicitly include search engines within the safe harbour provisions for mere conduits, cache or hosts.[107] It was left to member states to decide how to treat search engines. This has led to divergent treatment of search engines amongst member states. Some states have explicitly extended the safe harbour, through legislation or the judicial application, to search engines by modifying the provisions for hosts or mere conduits.[108] This can be contrasted with the United States, where search engines are exempt from liability under the CDA Section 230[109] and more conditionally for copyright infringement, under Section 512(d) of the US Digital Millennium Copyright Act (DMCA).[110]

The United Kingdom does not provide an explicit exemption for search engines in the Electronic Commerce (EC Directive) Regulations[111] and,

---

[103] Directive 2000/31/EC of the European Parliament and of the Council of 8 June 2000 on certain legal aspects of information society services, in particular electronic commerce, in the Internet Market.

[104] See T. Verbiest et al., *Study on the Liability of Internet Intermediaries*, Markt/2006/09/E (November 2007), at http://ec.europa.eu/internal_market/e-commerce/docs/study/liability/final_report_en.pdf (last visited 4 November 2014), section E.

[105] E-Commerce Directive n. 103.

[106] (2010) C-236/08 (three conjoined cases C-236/08, C-237/08, and C-238/08), para. 110.

[107] E-Commerce Directive n. 103, Articles 12–14. See van Hoboken n. 5, where the author suggests that Article 21 of the E-Commerce Directive means that search engines are not covered by the intermediary liability regime: p. 249. Article 21 provides that 'in examining the need for an adaptation of this Directive, the report shall in particular analyse the need for proposals concerning the liability of providers of hyperlinks and location tool services'.

[108] See van Hoboken n. 5., section 9.3.4 discussing provisions in Spain, Portugal, Liechtenstein, Hungary and Poland. See also Metropolitan n. 59, paras. 85, 97–114

[109] CDA n. 66.

[110] 17 U.S.C., s. 512(d). For more on the United States, see section 9.3.3 in van Hoboken n. 5.

[111] 2002 No. 2013.

upon a review of the intermediary liability regime in 2006, declined to extend the safe harbour to search engines.[112] The UK courts have been relatively silent on the subject matter, although note the *obiter* comments of Justice Eady in *Metropolitan International Schools v. Designtechnica Corporation and Others*[113] that Google did not qualify as a mere conduit, cache or host of content. In his view, it was up to Parliament to extend the Regulations to cover search engines. The EC has encouraged development of such legal security for search providers.[114]

With regard to Article 14, the reader will recall from the previous chapter that Article 14 states that hosts of unlawful content are conditionally immune from liability as long as they did not know nor was it apparent that the content was unlawful, and, once they obtained such knowledge, acted expeditiously to remove or disable access to the content.[115] The CJEU in Google France considered whether the hosting safe harbour in Article 14 applied to Google in its capacity as seller and host of the AdWords programme. The Court concluded that Google's activities in storing the advertiser's keywords, links and commercial message brought Google within the scope of the Article 14 safe harbour, although left it to national courts to determine whether specific conduct was protected under the safe harbour. It is noteworthy that the CJEU focused on neutrality of the intermediary's role, stating that the activity would have to be 'of a mere technical, automatic and passive nature'[116] lacking in knowledge or control of the content. This has been criticised for

---

[112] The Department of Trade and Industry, *DTI Consultation Document on the Electronic Commerce Directive: The Liability of Hyperlinkers, Location Tools Services and Content Aggregators* (June 2005), at http://webarchive.nationalarchives.gov.uk/20090609003228/ http://www.berr.gov.uk/files/file13986.pdf (last visited 30 October). See also discussion in van Hoboken n. 5., p. 256.

[113] Metropolitan n. 59.

[114] Report from the Commission to the European Parliament, the Council and the European Economic and Social Committee – First Report on the Application of Directive 2000/31/ EC of the European Parliament and of the Council of 8 June 2000 on certain legal aspects of information society services, in particular electronic commerce, in the Internal Market (Directive on electronic commerce): 'whilst it was not considered necessary to cover hyperlinks and search engines in the Directive, the Commission has encouraged Member States to further develop legal security for internet intermediaries. It is encouraging that recent case-law in the Member States recognizes the importance of linking and search engines to the functioning of the internet. In general, this case-law appears to be in line with the Internal Market objective to ensure the provision of basic intermediary services, which promotes the development of the internet and e-commerce. Consequently, this case-law does not appear to give rise to any Internal Market concerns': para. 67.

[115] E-Commerce Directive n. 103.     [116] Google France n. 1–6, para. 113.

having further limited and confused the scope of intermediaries that can benefit from the safe harbour in the Directive.[117] However, this interpretation was reiterated by the Court in *L'Oreal* v. *eBay*.[118]

We may, of course, apply traditional law to the case of search engines with actions in, for example, intellectual property, contract, competition or data protection law. A body of cases and investigations is steadily growing, some of which were discussed earlier in this chapter. However, it is observed that these are all piecemeal approaches to the issues related to search governance, and none interrogates the question of how bodies with such significant social impact should be regulated. Equally, human rights law does not directly apply to search providers such as Google concerning how it manages its search results. In the UK, Google is not a public authority under the Human Rights Act (HRA).[119] It is a private, for-profit company without any of the features that might drive it to the murky arena of hybrid public authority, such as public funding, public function or special statutory powers.[120] If human rights law can be found to apply, it is indirectly[121] and through analogy to the media and their critical role in shaping democratic discourse. Additionally, a search provider such as Google is not subject to judicial review because it cannot be said to be a public body or carrying out a public function. As it stands at present, the law governing search engines is a mixed bag of 'maturing application of generally applicable laws a growing body of self-regulation, and in some jurisdictions a few search engine specific legal provisions such as the DMCA safe harbour for search engines'.[122] Given the otherwise light-touch approach to regulation of the internet in the United Kingdom and the rest of Europe, search providers have considerable room to develop their own governance framework.

---

[117] This interpretation relies on Recital 42, but critics have argued that Recital 42 applies to mere conduits and caching, not to hosts. See van Hoboken, n. 5, pp. 257–60.

[118] Case C-324/09 (July 2011) at para. 113. See discussion in van Hoboken n. 5., p. 260.

[119] 1998 c. 42. See previous chapter for discussion of public authority.

[120] See *YL* v. *Birmingham City Council* [2008] 1 AC 95. See discussion also in R. Clayton and H. Tomlinson, *The Law of Human Rights*, 2nd edn, vol. 1 (Oxford University Press, 2009), chapter five, particularly starting at 5.17 concerning hybrid public authorities. Note that search engines do not engage in activities that are public in their function, although they are of public interest, as argued in my earlier work, n. 28.

[121] See, for example, *Campbell* v. *MGN Ltd* [2004] UKHL 22, where the plaintiff grounded the claim in breach of confidence and then once before the Court argued infringement of Article 8 because the Court is a public authority. See also *Author of a Blog* v. *Times Newspapers Limited* [2009] EWHC 1358 (QB).

[122] Van Hoboken, n. 5, p. 187.

The significance of search engines to democracy and human rights has not, however, gone unnoticed. As discussed earlier, the CoE adopted a soft-law recommendation made by the Committee of Ministers on search engines (Recommendation).[123] In line with the Guiding Principles, it identifies the duties on member states to protect human rights impacted by search engines.[124] The Recommendation covers a variety of issues, including many covered by the investigation by the EC concerning anti-competitive behaviour.[125] Relevant here, the strategy makes recommendations on transparency, filtering and regulation.

First, it recommends increased transparency regarding the way that information is selected, ranked or removed, including any search bias such as geographic location services. Search providers should differentiate between natural search results and paid-for content and/or its own content. Second, it notes that filtering and blocking of content by search providers can be a violation of Article 10 and should only take place in limited circumstances. Importantly, the Recommendation teases out the difficulty in outsourcing this role to search providers. The language used is notable because although it retains the duty on member states, it also does not limit application of the principles to member states. This can be seen in the following provision (emphasis added):

> 15. Member States should:
> – ensure that any *law, policy or individual request* on de-indexing or filtering is enacted with full respect for relevant legal provisions, the right to freedom of expression and the right to seek, receive and impart information. The principles of due process and access to independent and accountable redress mechanisms *should also be respected in this context.*[126]

The Recommendation goes on to recommend that blocking of search results for specific keywords should *not* be something included in a self- and co-regulatory framework.

Third, it encourages member states to promote self- and co-regulatory mechanisms. It emphasises the need for due process with such mechanisms, stating that 'self- and co-regulation may amount to interference with the rights of others and should therefore be transparent, independent, accountable and effective, in line with Article 10 of the Convention'.[127] As will be seen, the CoE Recommendation can be used to inform a CSR model for search engines.

---

[123] Recommendation n. 31.    [124] Ibid., para. 7.    [125] Ibid., part II.
[126] Ibid., part III, para 15.    [127] Ibid., part IV para 17.

With this knowledge and against the legal backdrop discussed earlier, the purpose of the following section is to examine in more depth the freedom of speech issues posed by search engines against the backdrop of traditional human rights law. This serves two purposes. First, we must identify the limits of the legal model of human rights as applied to search engines. Second, as we have seen, traditional human rights principles can be extended via CSR to private bodies like Google. We must examine how ECHR jurisprudence can help shape and inform (and even confuse) a CSR framework. Having a better understanding of the free speech rights at stake concerning search engines and the legal status of such rights helps move the discussion forward concerning the viability of CSR as a governance tool. As will be shown, what freedom of expression entails in the context of search engines is unclear in the law, which makes it more difficult to identify with any specificity how CSR can add value beyond the legal framework or what it means for a company to respect free speech in this context.

### 5.3. Search engines and human rights law

Does Article 10 of the ECHR, as it has currently been interpreted, extend to accessibility of information and therefore bind the state to its facilitation? Not everything we utter is protected under the principles of freedom of expression and the accompanying human rights framework. Perjury, contractual promises or representations inducing contracts, competition, bribery or criminal threats, amongst others, are not forms of expression brought within the human rights framework.[128] The Universal Declaration of Human Rights (UDHR) defines the scope of freedom of expression as including the 'freedom to hold opinions without interference and to seek, receive and impart information and ideas through any media and regardless of frontiers'.[129] The language in the International Covenant on Civil and Political Rights (ICCPR) is similar but expands on the media that are protected to communicate the freedom. In its Article 19, it defines the scope of freedom of expression as including the 'freedom to seek, receive and impart information and ideas of all kinds, regardless of frontiers, either orally, in writing or in print, in the form of art, or through any other media of his choice'.[130] Article 10 of

---

[128] See discussion of E. Barendt in this regard: E. Barendt, *Freedom of Speech*, 2nd edn (Oxford University Press, 2005), p. 75. See also Bracha and Pasquale n. 39, pp. 1193–1995.
[129] 1948, Article 19.   [130] 1966, Article 19.

the ECHR does not mention a right to seek out information, although it is implicitly included. It asserts the 'freedom to hold opinions and to receive and impart information and ideas without interference by public authority and regardless of frontiers'. It is observed that accessibility per se is not provided for in any of these human rights frameworks.

Accessibility is a problematic concept in free speech discussions. Ideas of accessibility of information tend to be addressed through the right to freedom of information or what is sometimes termed the 'right to know'. Such a right tends to be reflected in freedom of information legislation entitling a right of access to information held by a government,[131] although it includes the wider notion of the right of the public to be informed, which is facilitated through other means such as the press.[132] With respect to the latter, the right to be informed can draw in other rights, such as the right of education.[133] The right has also been used to address broadcasting and information flows into a country.[134] Concerning digital matters, the right to know has tended to be addressed in the context of a right of access to the internet, although this right can also be found to build from other human rights as well, such as the right of assembly and education.[135] Discussions here are complicated by historically divisive debates in international forums on whether there should be freedom of international communication or a right to the free flow of information.[136] With regard to the former, this was debated in 2003 at the World Summit on the Information Society. The argument noted much of what has been stated here – that freedom of expression needs to reflect a wider notion of communication rights. This was controversial and

---

[131] See discussion D. Banisar, 'The Right to Information in the Age of Information', in R. F. Jørgensen (ed.), *Human Rights in the Global Information Society* (MIT Press, 2006).

[132] *Observer and Guardian v. UK*, No. 13585/88 (1991) 14 EHRR 153, para. 59. See discussion in W. Benedek and M. C. Kettemann, *Freedom of Expression and the Internet* (Strasbourg: Council of Europe Publishing, 2013), pp. 27–28.

[133] Benedek and Ketteman ibid., pp. 39–41.

[134] See discussion R. F. Jørgensen, *Framing the Net: The Internet and Human Rights* (Cheltenham: Edward Elgar, 2013), pp. 39–41.

[135] See *Ahmet Yildirim v. UK, Application no. 3111/10* (18 December 2012), para. 31; Benedek and Kettemann n. 132, pp. 41–44. See also discussion of Frank La Rue in chapter one.

[136] There were calls in the 1980s by Paul Sieghart (member of the UK Data Protection Committee) for an International Convention on the Flow of Information: see G. J. Walters, *Human Rights in an Information Age: A Philosophical Analysis* (University of Toronto Press, 2001), p. 19.

ultimately discarded on the basis that such a right was already covered by the ICCPR and other regional provisions such as Article 10.[137]

One cannot make use of the right to freedom of expression without access to some forum through which to express it, whether one is receiving or imparting the information. There is a long history in free speech jurisprudence concerning access to the media, town squares, parks and public halls for the circulation of information.[138] Search engines have characteristics drawn from both the public and private spheres. They have characteristics of media companies and their integral role in shaping our world views; they also have characteristics of public forums such as town squares, where people gather to circulate information and ideas. Yet they are owned, operated and spearheaded entirely by private companies. Thus, it becomes a private forum of public significance for which very little guidance is available as of yet in free speech jurisprudence. Scholarly work calls for a re-examination of these 'pseudo-public spaces' in law.[139]

We can find some guidance in the line of cases concerning access to private shopping malls,[140] in particular the emphasis of courts on whether alternative avenues for speech are available. In the case of search engines, as we saw, there are few alternatives to using search engines to access information online and a limited choice amongst search providers. Yet there is something altogether different between a shopping mall and a macro-IIG such as Google, and that is the extent of the ability to control the flow of information. In addition, whereas we can find guidance in cases concerning access to the media, particularly broadcasting cases, and the conflicting rights of the media themselves, such cases fail to encapsulate the infrastructure side of what search engines do.

---

[137] For discussion of WSIS and access to information, see K. Raseroka, 'Access to Information and Knowledge', in R. F. Jørgensen n. 131, and Benedek and Kettemann n. 132, pp. 32–33.

[138] For discussion of the United Kingdom, see Barendt n. 128. For the United States, see T. I. Emerson, *The System of Freedom of Expression* (New York: Random House, 1970).

[139] D. Mac Síthigh, 'Virtual Walls? The Law of Pseudo-Public Spaces', *Int. J.L.C.*, 8(3) (2012) 394. See Ammori n. 40. Although Ammori's focus is on America and the First Amendment, his arguments invite the same type of scrutiny to be undertaken concerning European jurisprudence. He challenges the account of the First Amendment as a negative-liberty model with a series of haphazard exceptions regarding spaces for such expression.

[140] See, for example, the previous chapter's discussion of *Appleby* v. *United Kingdom* (2003) 37 EHRR 38 and the American jurisprudence on shopping malls.

The ECtHR decision in *Yildirim* provides some guidance on the views of the Court regarding online forums of communication. It stated that Article 10 'applies not only to the content of information but also to the means of dissemination, since any restriction imposed on the latter necessarily interferes with the right to receive and impart information'.[141] In the case of *Yildirim*, the means of dissemination was a website hosted by Google. Google search results are arguably still one step removed from this framework of discussion. Indeed, Nico van Eijk cautions that Article 10 does not deal with what search engines do, which is to '*facilitate* access to information, but [they] do not offer access themselves'.[142] Search providers facilitate access to the search engine and to results produced from inputting a search term, but the information itself is obtained by linking from the search results to another page.

Search engines engage potentially three rights under traditional approaches to free speech: the rights of the users to receive information, the rights of the content providers to be listed on the rankings, and the rights of the search providers to publish their search results. The following section shows that, at the moment, the legal model is uncertain and arguably conflicts with the significance of search engines as facilitators of access to information. This shows a need to move beyond the jurisprudence to embed free speech responsibility into the governance of search engines.

### 5.3.1. *Users Rights*

The rights to receive and impart information are independent rights; the speaker has the right to express himself or herself, and the listener has the right to receive the expression. Thus, the enjoyment of the right to receive information is conditional on someone willing to impart that information. The law has interpreted this to mean that the right to receive information is a negative right – one cannot force a person to speak, and so the right to receive information simply means that where there is a willing speaker and listener, the government should not intervene to prevent the communication from taking place.[143] There is then no positive obligation on the state to facilitate receipt of information

---

[141] Yildirim n. 135, para. 50.    [142] van Eijk n. 98, p. 5.

[143] See discussion in Clayton and Tomlinson n. 120, paras. 15.248–15.249 and Barendt n. 128, pp. 105–11. As noted by Clayton and Tomlinson, and citing *R. v. Bow County Court, ex p Pelling*, [2001] 1 UKHRR 165, para. 36, '[a]dditional rights of access cannot be derived from Article 10 which the Court of Human Rights has consistently held does not

between private parties. In *Leander* v. *Sweden*, the ECtHR summarised the law as follows:

> The Court observes that the right of freedom to receive information basically prohibits a Government from restricting a person from receiving information that others wish or may be willing to impart to them. Article 10 does not, in the circumstances such as those of the present case, confer on an individual a right of access to a register containing information about his personal position, nor does it embody an obligation on the Government to impart such information to the individual.[144]

There are signs that the United Kingdom is moving towards a more expanded right of freedom of information, such as the greater weight being accorded to information of public interest in defamation cases.[145] Taking a narrow approach, however, it is difficult to argue that the state has a positive duty to facilitate access to search engine results.

There is greater chance of success if the users' rights are reframed as one of access to information. As discussed earlier, a narrow conception of this right frames it as a right of access to official information (such as medical records), and the United Kingdom has specifically legislated in this regard in the Freedom of Information Act.[146] The hesitation of developing the right of access to information too expansively is because, as Eric Barendt notes: '[r]ecognition of a right of access would impose a constitutional duty on government or other authority to provide information it did not want to disclose'.[147] UK cases concerning whether the government has an obligation to hold inquiries in public, for example, took different approaches.[148] Where such obligations are limited vis-à-vis the state, it can be concluded that it is even less likely that obligations will be found to apply to private companies with regard to the forums they provide. However, in such a situation, there is a willing speaker: the website owner or other provider of content on webpages that are then ranked on search results. The difficulty remains that the search results simply make the information more accessible.

include a general right to receive information in the absence of willingness to impart the information': para. 15.227.

[144] (1987) 9 EHRR 433, para. 74. Note that when an argument for access to information has been made successfully, it has largely been through Article 8 not Article 10: see *Gaskin* v. *United Kingdom* (1987) 12 EHRR 36.

[145] Defamation Act (2013) c. 26, s.4; *Reynolds* v. *Times Newspapers Ltd. and Others* [1999] UKHL 45.

[146] Freedom of Information Act 2000 c. 36.     [147] Barendt n. 128, p. 109.

[148] See *R* v. *Secretary of State for Health, ex p Wagstaff* [2001] 1 WLR 292, and *R (Persey)* v. *Secretary of State for the Environment, Food and Rural Affairs* [2002] EWHC 371.

However, recent years have seen an increasing recognition of a broader concept of a right of access to information. As we have seen, access to the internet is increasingly viewed as a precondition to the exercise of the right to freedom of expression online, thus making it a right unto itself.[149] There is by no means consensus on the issue. Vint Cert, for example, co-designer of TCP/IP protocol has argued that access to the internet is not a human right.[150] However, momentum of case law and international policy is in the direction of recognition of such a right. The ECtHR stated in *Yildirim* that the internet has become 'one of the principal means for individuals of exercising the right to freedom of expression and information'.[151] However, this does not seamlessly apply to search engines. As Daphne Keller, legal counsel for Google reminded at the Leveson Inquiry, 'Google is not the internet'.[152]

We can draw a right to freedom of expression for users from the general responsibilities imposed on media companies for their role in shaping public discourse. Judicial consideration of Article 10 shows an historic commitment to freedom of expression of the media reflected in the media's essential role in democratic society as public watchdog. In *Sunday Times* v. *United Kingdom* (No 1), it can be recalled, the EtCHR said, 'freedom of expression constitutes one of the essential foundations of a democratic society . . . [t]hese principles are of particular importance as far as the press is concerned'.[153] It goes on to state:

> [W]hilst the mass media must not overstep the bounds imposed in the interests of the proper administration of justice, it is incumbent on them to impart information and ideas concerning matters that come before the courts just as in other areas of public interest. Not only do the media have the task of imparting such information and ideas: the public also has a right to receive them.[154]

Freedom of expression in this instance involves a duty on the press to communicate information and ideas in the public interest and a corresponding right of the public to receive such information. Most of these media law cases, however, concern a specific article in the public interest

---

[149] See La Rue n. 29. See P. De Hert and D. Kloza, 'Internet (Access) as a New Fundamental Right. Inflating the Current Rights Framework?', *EJLT*, 3(3) (2012).

[150] V. Cerf, 'Internet access is not a human rights' (4 January 2012), at www.nytimes.com /2012/01/05/opinion/internet-access-is-not-a-human-right.html?_r=0 (last visited 18 June 2014).

[151] Yildirim n. 135, para. 54.

[152] See www.youtube.com/watch?v=9Q2L9fWnb8I (last visited 18 June 2014).

[153] (1979–80) 2 EHRR 245.          [154] Ibid.

that the newspaper or other media company has chosen to publish. For example, in *Fressoz* v. *France*, the article exposed the fact that the boss of Peugeot awarded himself a 45.9 per cent pay rise at a time when he refused to award employee pay rises.[155] *Thorgeirson* v. *Iceland*[156] involved a newspaper article calling for an independent investigation into allegations of police brutality. *Sunday Times* v. *UK*, quoted earlier, concerned a series of newspaper articles aimed at helping victims of the Thalidomide disaster to reach better settlements.

In contrast, search engines are not directly involved in the publication of the information, and certainly not all – in fact very little – of what is brought up on search results is in the public interest. The top search term in 2013 in the United States and United Kingdom was Paul Walker, an American actor who passed away that year.[157] Despite this, search engines continue to be some of the most visited websites on the internet and for good reason. Even if most searches are for inane matter, this simply reflects the general public's democratic participation in the real world. Not everyone reads newspapers, nor do such readers faithfully read every line of the news and politics sections, but they can be found more often reading lifestyle and entertainment sections that newspapers knowingly offer up to draw in such readers. This illustrates what is so unique about what search engines do. Visitors input search terms and search providers offer results. This immediately sets up a discourse between the visitor and the provider. The product of this discourse is a list of search results, ranked in order of purported relevance, which guides the user's attention.

Thus, it is not that a specific article is of public interest, but that simply search engines are of public interest because they now play an essential role in democratic society in structuring how we understand the informational world. This role is intimately tied with the roots of the protection of freedom of expression and the importance attached to the role of media in democratic society. Nico van Eijk argues along these lines that the main aim of search engines is to make information accessible: '[t]he functioning of a search engine therefore entails activities that are of crucial importance to making the actual perusal of information possible'.[158] The law that governs this role, van Eijk contends, can have

[155]  (2001) 31 EHRR 2.      [156]  (1992) 14 EHRR 843.
[157]  See Google Zeitgeist: www.google.com/intl/en/zeitgeist/
[158]  van Eijk n. 98, p. 5. See also his article n. 99.

implications to the right to receive and impart information and to access information.[159]

Thus, users arguably have a general right to receive information on search results, although there is uncertainty in the law concerning the scope of this right. One can identify a value of CSR in helping define the contours of user rights in a way that better captures search engines' role in facilitating access to information. However, it is arguable that state involvement is needed to identify what is expected of search providers, which is reflected in the CoE Recommendation. Whether what is needed would be better achieved by encouragement of industry codes or legal intervention is a question to be further explored in this chapter. One difficulty with further developing a user right is that it can conflict with the rights of content providers or search providers.

### 5.3.2. Content provider rights

Crafting a right of content providers to be ranked on search results and a corresponding duty on search providers to rank them is problematic because it imposes a right to communicate on a particular forum. Yet a forum is a necessary precondition to exercise any free speech right. As Barendt notes, '[p]olitical parties, other groups, and individuals cannot exercise their free speech rights without use of some property, whether a personal computer, printing press or broadcasting studio, a hall or park, or the streets'.[160] There are two potential avenues to argue such a right. First, it can be said that the rights of the content providers are rooted in historical rights of access to public streets and halls and other public forums for the exercise of freedom of expression. Although in the case of search engines the forum is privately owned, as will be shown, at times private places have been held to invite public rights, and it may be here the state's duty to facilitate access to it. Second, it is arguable that the right is akin to claims of access to various media of communication, such as rights of access to broadcast time or rights of reply in newspapers or to advertise on television.

Traditionally, the strongest arguments for rights of access to forums for speech have been to forums that have been quite clearly public areas – public halls, parks, streets – in contrast to enclosed buildings such as

---

[159] van Eijk n. 98, p. 5.
[160] Barendt n. 128, p. 274. See generally on this topic, chapter eight. Indeed, it is the notion of a right to spaces for speech that is at the heart of Ammori's article n. 37.

schools and halls where someone would have to specifically make the space available to be used. The appropriate analogy then becomes those cases concerning access to private places of public appeal, such as shopping malls. As discussed in the previous chapter, one sees a variation in the United States, where the Federal Court has found that there is no constitutional right to free speech in privately owned shopping malls, although some states have interpreted their state constitutions as conferring such a right. The ECtHR in *Appleby* v. *UK*, discussed at length in the previous chapter, held that freedom of expression did not necessarily grant rights of entry to private property such as shopping malls, particularly when there were alternative venues available to exercise the expression, such as in the old town centre or through door-to-door calls.[161] This was despite the fact that the shopping mall had only recently been privatised, had been partially publicly financed and functioned like a town centre. It stretches the case law too far to interpret this to mean that the state might have a duty to facilitate freedom of speech on search engines.

Search engines like Google, although places of discursive significance, are private, for-profit companies that simply make information more accessible. Accessibility is critical on the internet, as we have seen and concerning users rights, but this does not translate into a right of content providers to be ranked. The content provider's information is still available on the internet, and alternative avenues are available to bring their websites' attention to consumers (e.g., advertising campaigns, online or off, word-of-mouth and mail). Furthermore, it would impose free speech obligations on an algorithm to ensure that all content is ranked.[162] This becomes a form of imposed innovation, although cases such as France's *LICRA et UEJF* v. *Yahoo! Inc.*[163] and the CJEU's Google Spain case,[164] discussed earlier, indicate a willingness of some courts to do just that. However, in framing the responsibilities of providers to manage their forums fairly and proportionately, this shifts the human rights discussion away from the concern of the algorithm to discussions of due process and transparency.

The second possible avenue to argue is that being ranked is the equivalent of rights of reply in newspapers or rights of access to broadcasting to communicate one's views. However, obligations on the state to

---

[161] *Appleby* n. 140.
[162] For a discussion of the First Amendment in the context of algorithms, see Wu n. 66 and Benjamin n. 66.
[163] Ordonnance Refere, TGI Paris, 20 November 2000.     [164] Google Spain n. 72.

provide for a right of reply have only arisen over specific incidents,[165] which is different from the categorical, automated nature of search results. A general right to be ranked cannot be drawn from such cases. It might arise for the searched, however, for those that are the subject of searches which they believe to be defamatory or the like. Scholars such as Pasquale have explored this avenue, arguing that there should be a right of reply in certain circumstances on search engines.[166]

An argument can be made that users' rights to be ranked on search results are analogous to claims for access to broadcasting. For example, in the ECtHR case *Vgt Verein gegen Tiefabriken* v. *Switzerland*, Swiss law banned the broadcast of political advertisements and thus a Swiss television station refused to air a commercial against cruelty to pigs, which was prepared in response to an ad for meat. The ECtHR held that the law banning political advertising contravened Article 10 because it didn't apply to other media and denied the opportunity to reach a wide audience.[167] ECtHR rulings concerning access to broadcasting media have not been consistent, with a later ruling upholding the ban on religious advertising in Ireland.[168] In the United Kingdom, the House of Lords controversially upheld a ban on an anti-abortion party election broadcast.[169] All such cases involve state action and are rooted in the historical scarcity of available broadcasting channels, as well as in arguments that broadcasting is especially pervasive in one's home, that it is monopolised by a few, and that there is a need for pluralism of views because of television's powerful role in society. In this regard, search engines have similar power to shape information flows, although such power is far more subtle than with broadcasting. However, search engines are altogether more functional and automated than the editorial and publishing role played by broadcasters that drives the regulatory environment here, and search engine operations are further removed from the state than was the situation in these cases.

---

[165] See *Melnychuk* v. *Ukraine* (28743/03), Decision of 5 July 2005. In *Melnychuk* v. *Ukraine*, HRCD, 15 (2004–2005) 1051, it summarised: '[w]hilst as a general principle private media should be free to exercise editorial discretion in deciding whether to publish or not letters of private individuals, there could be exceptional circumstances in which a newspaper could legitimately be required to publish a retraction or apology': pp. 1051–52.

[166] See F. Pasquale, 'Rankings, Reductionalism and Responsibility', *Clev. St. L. Rev.*, 54 (2006) 115; and, more recently, F. Pasquale, 'Asterisk Revisited: Debating a Right of Reply on Search Results', *J. Bus. & Tech. L.*, 3 (2008) 61.

[167] *VgT Verein gegen Tierfabriken* v. *Switzerland* (2002) 34 EHRR 4.

[168] *Murphy* v. *Ireland* (2004) 38 EHRR 13.

[169] *R.* v. *British Broadcasting Corporation ex parte ProLife Alliance* [2003] UKHL 23.

An attempt was made to apply broadcasting laws to search engines in the United States in *Langdon* v. *Google*,[170] where the Delaware District Court was tasked with determining whether the broadcasting 'must carry' rule applied to Google's advertisements. Langdon ran two internet websites, www.NCJusticeFraud.com, which he alleged exposed fraud perpetrated by North Carolina government officials, and www.ChinaIs Evil.com, which he alleged discussed atrocities committed by the Chinese government. Langdon sought paid advertising placement of his websites on Google, Microsoft, Yahoo! and AOL and was refused. Various reasons were given by the providers for refusing to run his ads. Google advised that it does not run ads that advocate against an individual, group or organisation, Yahoo advised it does not run ads for websites it does not host and Microsoft simply did not reply.

Langdon alleged,[171] *inter alia*, breach of his rights to free speech, stating that the Defendants should have placed his ads in prominent places and 'honestly' ranked his websites, which he felt they did not do. Google argued that search results are protected speech[172] and that doing what the Plaintiff wished was compelled speech and 'would prevent Google from speaking in ways that [the] Plaintiff dislikes'.[173] The Court agreed with Google, holding the relief sought would breach the Defendants' First Amendment rights akin to newspapers' rights to refuse to print editorials or to run advertisements based on their content.[174]

Additionally, the Plaintiff tried to argue a right of access to search engines akin to a user right discussed earlier in Section 5.3.1. Langdon argued that search engines are public forums in the way that shopping malls have occasionally been held to be, but the Court rejected this argument, finding that although the Defendants have speech rights, they are not subject to the Constitution: 'Defendants are private, for profit companies, not subject to constitutional free speech guarantees. . . . They are internet search engines that use the internet as a medium to conduct business'.[175] Langdon's argument that he had no alternative to advertising on the Defendants' search engines

---

[170] (2007) Civ. Act. No. 06–319-JJF (D. Del. February 20, 2007)
[171] Note that the Plaintiff was self-represented.
[172] Relying on *Search King* n. 84 discussed in the next section.
[173] *Langdon* n. 170, p. 12.
[174] Ibid., pp. 12–13. Bracha and Pasquale argue that the Court in *Langdon* extended the principle concerning compelled speech too far for the line of cases it was relying on: n. 39, pp. 1196–98.
[175] *Langdon* n. 170, p. 17.

was promising, but was also rejected by the Court citing alternatives such as 'mail, television, cable, newspapers, magazines, and competing commercial online services'.[176] In the end, the Court dismissed all claims against the Defendants in this preliminary motion, upholding only the continuance of the breach of contract claim against Google.

In the United Kingdom, although there cannot be said to be a specific right of content providers to be ranked on search results, the fact that search engines themselves have speech significance might invite positive obligations on the state to ensure that the search provider manages its affairs in a fair, transparent and proportionate manner consistent with Article 10. Although there is no general right of access to broadcast time, the ECtHR, for example, has held that the decision-making process must be even-handed, as in *Haider* v. *Austria*,[177] where the Court gave the example of one political party but not another being excluded from broadcasting, or in *Vereinigung Demokratischer Soldaten Osterreichs and Gubi* v. *Austria*,[178] where the state was held to have breached Article 10 for failing to be balanced in its provision of assistance to information providers.[179] Even if the state has no positive duties as such, this provides guidance on the soft-law obligations of search engines and is in keeping with the CoE's Recommendation. Thus, while the content provider has no right to be ranked per se, Google has an obligation to manage the rankings against Article 10 principles. Such an approach accords with the Guiding Principles advocating access to forums of remediation.

Thus far, we have established search engines as places of democratic significance inviting general free speech scrutiny and that users arguably thus have the right to receive information on search results. Evident, however, are limits in the traditional legal model of free speech as applied to search engines, showing potentially the need to extend ECHR principles for deployment in CSR frameworks. We are left with a key conflict in the development of CSR frameworks along these lines, however, and that is the legal free speech rights of search providers such as Google. Up until now, we have been looking at how a legal model can inform a CSR model, but, as will be shown, the legal rights of search providers conflict with any CSR commitments sought to be imposed.

---

[176] Ibid., p. 19    [177] (1995) 85 DR 66.    [178] (1994) 20 EHRR 55.
[179] See general discussion in Clayton and Tomlinson n. 120, para. 15.251.

### 5.3.3. Search provider rights

In contrast to the preceding case study, where determinations by the Internet Watch Foundation (IWF) of the content that is blacklisted arguably engages directly the HRA, the issue of search engine rankings raises the murkier issue of the legal rights of the search providers themselves.[180] Thus, any CSR model that might be developed immediately comes into conflict with legal duties. In the United States, case law thus far has favoured the speech rights of the search provider over the users. While such cases are specific to its First Amendment context, they are the only cases for which this issue has been litigated thus far and provide guidance on the issues that might be argued in Europe if a similar case arises here.

The seminal case in this regard is *Search King Inc.* v. *Google Technology*, a preliminary injunction by the District Court for the Western District of Oklahoma.[181] Search King is a search engine optimisation company. In 2002, it introduced PR Ad Network (PRAN) to arrange for their clients advertisements to be placed on third-party sites, effectively a link farm. Link farms violate Google's Webmaster Guidelines.[182] Google's toolbar shows a webpage as having a PageRank between 1 and 10, the most popular having a rank of 10. In 2002, Search King's website dropped from a PageRank of 8 to 4, and PRAN dropped from 2 to being eliminated from the ranking entirely. Search King sued for tortious interference with contractual relations arguing that Google intentionally decreased the PageRank of Search King and PRAN, the result being an indeterminate adverse impact on their business opportunities because their exposure on Google's search engine was limited.

Although Judge Miles La Grange agreed that the drop in rankings was intentional on the part of Google, she concluded, 'there was no meaningful way to determine whether any lost business is directly related to the lower PageRank'.[183] Most important for our purposes, the judge was

---

[180] For such an argument, see E. Volokh and D. M. Falk, 'First Amendment protection for search engine search results' (white paper commissioned by Google) (2012), at http://papers.ssrn.com/sol3/papers.cfm?abstract_id=2055364 (last visited 18 June 2014).

[181] *Search King* n. 84. For a reanalysis of the case, see Grimmelmann n. 43, starting at p. 912.

[182] See Google, 'Link schemes', at www.google.com/support/webmasters/bin/answer.py?answer=66356 (last visited 18 June 2014); and Google, 'Webmaster guidelines', at www.google.com/support/webmasters/bin/answer.py?answer=35769 (last visited 18 June 2014).

[183] *Search King* n. 84, p. 6.

persuaded by Google's arguments and held that search results are opinions and accordingly protected speech:

> [A] PageRank is an opinion – an opinion of the significance of a particular web site as it corresponds to a search query. Other search engines express different opinions, as each search engine's method of determining relative significance is unique. There is no question that the opinion relates to a matter of public concern. Search King points out that 150 million searches occur every day on Google's search engine alone. ... A statement of relative significance, as represented by the PageRank, is inherently subjective in nature. Accordingly, the Court concludes that Google's PageRanks are entitled to First Amendment protection.[184]

Since then, a case concerning a specialised search engine on a website that ranked and rated lawyers was held to be constitutionally protected speech.[185] A similar case arose over an alleged drop in rankings in *Kinderstart.com LLC et al.* v. *Google Inc.*,[186] and although the judge dismissed the case in a strongly worded judgment critical of Kinderstart, the case is highly revealing of Google's view of its search results. Following in the footsteps of *Search King*, Google's Brief to the Court characterised its search engine as the expression of opinion of a private business about the importance of websites.[187] It framed its function as essentially a promotional device for companies, as 'a private forum for Google's speech',[188] highlighting particularly well the tension between legal and CSR models of human rights:

> Over the years, authors who felt their books belonged on bestseller lists, airlines who thought their flights should be featured more prominently in airline flight listings, bond issuers dissatisfied with their ratings, and even website owners angry about Google's ranking on their sites, have turned to litigation seeking to override such judgments. Each time, the courts have rejected such claims, recognizing that private businesses have a right to express these opinions freely.[189]

In *Jian Zhang et al.* v. *Baidu.com Inc.*,[190] a group of New York residents sued Baidu, a large company running the most popular search engine in China, contending that Baidu unlawfully blocks articles and information concerning democracy in China from its search results in the United States. The issue in this motion by Baidu for judgment on the pleadings

---

[184] Ibid., p. 9.   [185] *Browne* et al. v. *Avvo* (2007) Case No. 2:2007cv00920 (W.D. Wash.).
[186] (2007) Case 5:06-cv-02057-JF (DC NCAL).
[187] Google's Notion of Motion and Motion to Dismiss the First Amended Complaint, and Memorandum of Points, 2006 WL 1232481, p. 8.
[188] Ibid., p. 10.   [189] Ibid., p. 6.   [190] Baidu n. 84.

was whether the First Amendment protects search results as speech. District Court Judge Furman granted Baidu's motion concluding that search results are protected speech of the search providers.

Judge Furman went further than previous decisions in analysing the scope and extent of this right. He framed search engine results as editorial judgments, drawing analogy to the editorial function of newspapers and decisions by website owners on which stories to link to or display prominently.[191] In this way, we can analogise search engines to the media as gatekeepers. He avoided making a pronouncement on the free speech status of search results in all circumstances, rather limiting application to the facts of this case.[192] This is rather unfortunate because a wider analysis of the media, for example, reveals that free speech protections of the press are also accompanied by public interest obligations because of their critical role in keeping the public informed.

In this case, the Court held that the very argument made by the Plaintiffs was their downfall. By arguing Baidu disfavoured expression on certain political topics, the Plaintiffs could not argue that Baidu was merely a platform delivering content in a neutral way. The judge rather framed the case as the Plaintiffs seeking to punish Baidu for a conscious decision it made on how to design its search algorithms, which would be an affront to a speaker's 'autonomy to choose the content of his own message'.[193]

Despite the narrow application of his ruling, the judge ventured an opinion on the argument that search engines should have must-carry obligations akin to cable. He concluded that it is 'debatable' whether search engines are mere conduits, and the fact that Baidu interferes with rankings shows it is not a mere conduit.[194] Underlying the court's argument seems to be the idea that a search provider's failure to comply with neutrality, even boldly for censorship purposes and even when the provider otherwise purports to be neutral, is the very thing that protects it from scrutiny. Regardless of whether one finds compelling arguments for search neutrality or not, the reasoning of the Court weakens public interest arguments of users or content providers concerning fairness in the way search engine results are managed. The Court concluded,

---

[191] Ibid., p. 7.
[192] The Court acknowledges arguments of authors such as Brach and Pasquale discussed earlier (n. 39), but states '[t]his Court, however, need not resolve the scholarly debate in order to decide the present motion because, whether or not the First Amendment shields all search engines from lawsuits based on the content of their search results, it plainly shields Baidu from the Plaintiffs' claims in this lawsuit'. Baidu n. 84, p. 10.
[193] Ibid., p. 11 quoting from *Hurley*, 515 U.S. (1995) at 573.    [194] Baidu ibid., pp. 11–12

In short, Plaintiffs' efforts to hold Baidu accountable in a court of law for its editorial judgments about what political ideas to promote cannot be squared with the First Amendment. There is no irony in holding that Baidu's alleged decision to disfavour speech concerning democracy is itself protected by the democratic ideal of free speech. ... [T]he First Amendment protects Baidu's right to advocate for systems of government other than democracy (in China or elsewhere) just as surely as it protects Plaintiffs' rights to advocate for democracy.[195]

*Baidu* has been followed-up with *S. Louis Martin* v. *Google Inc.*,[196] which was a claim by coastnews.com, a San Francisco tourism site, that Google engaged in unfair and deceptive business practices; namely, that coastnews.com ranked highly for certain keywords on Yahoo! and Bing, but not on Google.[197] Google successfully brought a motion to dismiss on the basis that it was a strategic lawsuit against public participation (SLAPP), and legislation allows such cases to be dismissed if they were initiated to stifle speech. The SLAPP element, Google creatively claimed, was that the plaintiff was seeking to silence Google's constitutional right to free expression as to its search engine rankings. The California Superior Court agreed, stating that the 'Defendant has met its burden of showing the claims asserted against it arise from constitutionally protected activity'.[198] The combined force of American case law indicates little chance of success in the United States for users or content providers who wish to dispute search rankings.

In Europe, we do not have any similar cases draw from,[199] but the Court's reasoning in a case like *Baidu* would be less likely to be sustainable because Article 10 of the ECHR provides for legitimate interference to facilitate the exercise of speech by others, such as the positive obligation on states to promote pluralism. We are returned to the initial argument, one rooted in free speech principles: it is not so much the speech of search engines that emerges as particularly critical, but the public importance of the space to democracy. Therefore, the space is one of free speech significance inviting responsibilities on the search providers to manage the forum in a manner compliant with human rights principles. Although there is no direct duty under human rights law, this shows the need to extend ECHR principles for deployment in CSR

---

[195] Ibid., pp. 15–16.    [196] (November 2014) Case No. CGC-14-539972 (Cal Sup SF).
[197] The Statement of Claim is available at http://digitalcommons.law.scu.edu/cgi/viewcontent.cgi?article=1761&context=historical (last visited 19 November 2014).
[198] *Martin* n. 196.
[199] There are the cases concerning autocomplete (see n. 61), but these are a narrower engagement with the issues.

frameworks. However, here the legal system, at least in America, hampers the potentiality of CSR because any extension of search providers duties and responsibilities through CSR conflicts with the provider's right to free speech. In such a situation, it is difficult to convince search companies to take on further and conflicting responsibilities.

By emphasising the speech rights of search providers, rankings are effectively removed from free speech scrutiny. The issue is further complicated by the type of gatekeeping position Google occupies: as well as possessing its own speech rights, Google is forced into a pseudo-judicial role. It fields complaints by those offended by search results (prejudicial content as with www.jewwatch.com), those unsatisfied with their ranking or lack thereof (*Search King, Kinderstart* etc.), those seeking removal of defamatory or otherwise personally prejudicial material (rights of the searched to be forgotten) and those seeking advertising placement (rights of access to a commercial forum). In such a situation, Google is sometimes a party to the complaint whilst simultaneously carrying out a judicial role. At other times, Google acts purely in a pseudo-judicial capacity, negotiating the dispute between third parties. The situation is compounded by the role the search algorithm plays in the dispute because, inevitably, a complaint concerning search has an algorithmic component.

We are faced then with a body engaged in a complicated and sometimes conflicting gatekeeping role, one that clearly engages free speech issues, but for which the law is unclear on how this translates into specific responsibilities. This puts pressure on the governance structure of search engines because it is this private sphere that becomes the vehicle through which freedom of expression is administered. This governance directly engages the Guiding Principles as relevant to a determination of their human rights compliance. As we saw in the previous chapter, however, human rights principles can be found to grow out of traditional ECHR jurisprudence, and therefore a consideration of the ECHR is necessary to understand what a commitment to human rights entails and to identify the limits of the legal model. The CoE adopted this type of approach in its Recommendation when it encouraged search providers 'to discard search results only in accordance with Article 10, paragraph 2 of the Convention'.[200] With this in mind, we now look more closely at Google's governance framework, to see whether it has any of the elements identified in the Guiding

---

[200] Recommendation n. 31, para. 8.

Principles, and at the CoE's Recommendation, namely, the presence of due diligence processes such as monitoring and tracking of performance, mitigation strategies and due process through independent redress mechanisms.

This analysis begins with Google's terms of service (ToS), wherein we must be mindful of two things. First, ToS are specific contractual relationships search providers enter into and do not encapsulate the wider governance relationship between the search provider and society. The ToS, however, do impact, even if often indirectly, the relationships among search providers, users and content providers. Second, ToS do not operate in a legal vacuum, of course, and are subject to the wider law. For example, there are questions about whether any limitation of liability in a ToS are enforceable, given the authority of *Thornton v. Shoe Lane Parking Limited*,[201] in which it was decided that there must be communication of these terms before the contract is concluded. Most of the public uses search engines without ever having seen the ToS. In addition, the provisions might be in breach of the Unfair Terms in Consumer Contracts Regulations 1999 (UTCCR).[202] The UTCCR applies to contracts that have not been individually negotiated to protect weaker parties (with little or no bargaining power) from the enforceability of unfair terms.[203] Such legal issues raise interesting questions about the legal enforceability of these terms, but we are concerned here with the significance of these provisions through a human rights lens. Furthermore, without an understanding of the human rights aspects of these ToS, it is difficult to identify a harm or imbalance against which these consumer protection provisions can be applied.

---

[201] [1970] EWCA Civ 2.

[202] The Unfair Terms in Consumer Contracts Regulations 1999 No. 2083 implementing Directive 93/13/EEC of 5 April 1993 on unfair terms in consumer contracts. See also the Consumer Rights Directive: Directive 2011/83/EU of 25 October 2011 of the European Parliament and of the Council of 25 October 2011 on consumer rights, amending Council Directive 93/13/EEC and Directive 1999/44/EC of the European Parliament and of the Council and repealing Council Directive 85/577/EEC and Directive 97/7/EC of the European Parliament and of the Council. For more on such contracts, see C. Riefa and J. Hornle, 'The Changing Face of Electronic Consumer Contracts in the Twenty-First Century: Fit for Purpose?', in L. Edwards and C. Waelde (eds.), *Law and the Internet*, 3rd edn (Oxford: Hart Publishing, 2009), in particular Part B.

[203] Regulation 5 says a term is unfair if 'contrary to the requirement of good faith, it causes a significant imbalance in the parties' right and obligations arising under the contract, to the detriment of the consumer'.

### 5.3.4. Google's corporate governance framework

Google's ToS[204] apply to any of Google's services, which would include its search engine, being its primary service. With regard to management of search results, Google does not specifically address the issue in the ToS, but rather couches its legal rights and responsibilities in sweeping terms as regards generalised matter. This is problematic, given the diversity of Google services. For example, one clause states:

> When you upload, submit, store, send or receive content to or through our Services, you give Google (and those we work with) a worldwide licence to use, host, store, reproduce, modify, create derivative works (such as those resulting from translations, adaptations or other changes that we make so that your content works better with our Services), communicate, publish, publicly perform, publicly display and distribute such content. The rights that you grant in this licence are for the limited purpose of operating, promoting and improving our Services, and to develop new ones.[205]

It is unclear whether this provision applies to what ordinary users do with Google's search engine; namely, whether the act of inputting search terms and selecting links from the results involves submitting, storing, sending or receiving content. If so, by using Google's search engine, a user grants Google the right to do a variety of things with their search data.

The Google ToS have evolved in recent years from more formal, legal language to everyday language. Although this makes the ToS more accessible, in terms of understanding for the general public, it also has the effect of being less clear in law. This can be observed by comparing the old clause concerning removal of content from its services to the new clause. The old clause provided:

> 8.3 Google reserves the right (but shall have no obligation) to pre-screen, review, flag, filter, modify, refuse or remove any or all Content from any Service. For some of the Services, Google may provide tools to filter out explicit sexual content. These tools include the SafeSearch preference settings (see http://www.google.co.uk/help/customize.html#safe). In addition, there are commercially available services and software to limit access to material that you may find objectionable.[206]

---

[204] 'Google terms of service', at www.google.co.uk/intl/en-GB/policies/terms/regional.html (last visited 18 June 2014).

[205] Ibid.

[206] Google, 'Google terms of service', at www.google.co.uk/intl/en-GB/policies/terms/arch ive/20070416/ (last visited 18 June 2014).

The content to which it refers was defined in the then Section 8.1 as 'all information (such as data files, written text, computer software, music, audio files or other sounds, photographs, videos or other images) which you may have access to as part of, or through your use of, the Services'.[207] The implication of these provisions was that Google could remove content from its search service at will. The new clause provides:

> Our Services display some content that is not Google's. This content is the sole responsibility of the entity that makes it available. We may review content to determine whether it is illegal or violates our policies, and we may remove or refuse to display content that we reasonably believe violates our policies or the law. But that does not necessarily mean that we review content, so please do not assume that we do.[208]

This indicates that Google might or might not review content and may remove content that violates its policies or the law.

Google retains sole discretion to stop, suspend or limit its Services, including stopping the provision of Services to just one person or to adding/removing functionalities or features on its Services.[209] The terms 'features' and 'functionalities' are not defined (there is, in fact, no definitions section given the informal nature of the ToS). Are links on its search results 'features', for example, thereby granting Google sole discretion to remove links at will? In this regard, the ToS are unclear because, although Google's search engine would clearly be covered by the ToS, it is not clear that the results are. The results would logically be the output of the Services and if so, then, despite their significance, they are not covered by the ToS.

The ToS only serve to exempt Google from liability. Google advises that its services are provided 'as is'. This allows Google to avoid liability for any failures to deliver its services, such as search reliability. Google further insulates itself by stating that it is not 'responsible for lost profits, revenues or data, financial losses or indirect, special, consequential, exemplary or punitive damages'.[210] A company disappearing from the index, for example, might be a side effect of changes to the search algorithm, and this provision would exclude Google from liability for this. This occurred in October 2010, when certain high-profile sites such as www.cnn.com were not listed for several days.[211] The ToS further

---

[207] Ibid.      [208] 'Using our services', in Terms of Service n. 204.
[209] 'Modifying and terminating our services', ibid.      [210] Ibid.
[211] Note that www.cnn.com was available as long as the user knew its URL. It was simply not listed on Google's rankings.

limits its liability, when permitted by law, to 'the amount that you paid us to use the Services',[212] which, in the case of using search engines (and in fact many Google Services) is zero. Given that Google's primary vehicle for remuneration is advertising, for which user data is collected and used for this purpose, perhaps a valuation of personal data is warranted as a determination of the amount paid for the Service. Such an analysis is outside the scope of this book.

There is the additional problem that we simply do not know what is being removed from search results. Google's search algorithm is protected as a trade secret, and, on a day-to-day basis, it does not reveal the reasons for manual manipulation of rankings. Whereas protection of the algorithm is necessary for this business model and to ward off SEO and other such manipulations, it forces the user to have faith that what is happening behind the scenes is fair, proportionate and nondiscriminatory. The need for transparency of processes was one of the points emphasised by the CoE in its Recommendation.

Google expands on its approach to removal of content from search results not in the ToS, but in its Frequently Asked Questions, Removal Policies and on its blog http://googleblog.blogspot.com.[213] The FAQ focuses on advising how a person can remove information about him- or herself from Google's search results. It advises the user to contact the webmaster of the site with the offending content to have it removed, and '[o]nce the content has been removed and Google has noted the update, the information will no longer appear in Google's search results'.[214]

Google has improved its transparency concerning removal of content in recent years. The Removal Policies is relatively new, offering transparency of processes unavailable before, although the next question is whether there are accountability mechanisms such as audits to check appropriate execution of such a policy. The Removal Policies provide that, upon request, Google will remove two types of content.[215] First, it

---

[212] 'Liability for our services', in Terms of Service n. 204.

[213] A proposal was raised at a 2007 Annual Shareholders Meeting to create a Human Rights Committee, but the Board voted against it. What was proposed was: '[t]here is established a Board Committee on Human Rights, which is created and authorized to review the implications of company policies, above and beyond matters of legal compliance, for the human rights of individuals in the US and worldwide': Google Proxy Statement, Proposal 5, at http://investor.google.com/documents/2008_google_proxy_statement.html #rom98719_69 (last visited 18 June 2014).

[214] 'Removal policies', at http://www.google.co.uk/intl/en-GB/policies/faq/ (last visited 18 June 2014).

[215] Ibid.

will remove personal information that might subject the individual to harms such as identity theft or financial fraud (i.e., credit card number, national identification numbers). Second, it will remove offensive content when it contains child sexual abuse images and for other legal reasons, such as for copyright infringement under the DMCA.[216] It will also remove images or videos or prevent them from showing if they contain pornographic content, content showing bodily functions, vulgar words, graphic content, animal cruelty or violence. Google also encourages users to make use of SafeSearch[217] to filter pornographic images. Google is also a member of the IWF. In addition to receiving a list of URLs from the blacklist, as discussed in Chapter 4, the IWF can provide its members with a list of keywords associated with child sexual abuse material and criminally obscene content, which members such as Google can then filter.[218] The IWF states that the benefit of such a service, amongst other things, is that 'it can improve the quality of search returns'.[219] It is not known whether Google makes use of this service.[220]

If a person wishes to have content removed from search results, therefore, there are two steps to the process. First, the user contacts the webmaster to have the content removed from the source. The webmaster then contacts Google, using its removal tool to have the content removed from Google cache (or it can simply request that particular content is not indexed on Google search results). Second, if the webmaster does not respond to the user's request, he or she can use the removal tool on Google https://support.google.com/websearch/troubleshooter/3111061. The complaint is forwarded to a team in Mountain View, California, which then assesses it in accordance with UK law.[221]

Google at times has addressed its removal of content on its blog, although its posts mainly have focused on how it handles government requests that breach international human rights principles. But, in the process, it also explains Google's approach to its own services. Although not binding on the company the way that ToS would be, it can be evidentiary support in an action in tort or for breach of contract. With regard to search, its policy is to remove 'content from search globally in narrow circumstances, like child pornography, certain links to

---

[216] DMCA n. 110.

[217] See https://support.google.com/websearch/answer/510 (last visited 28 May 2014).

[218] See 'What services can IWF offer you', at www.iwf.org.uk/join-us/services (last visited 12 November 2014).

[219] Ibid.     [220] See discussion in van Hoboken n. 5., pp. 244–45.

[221] See Leveson, n. 148.

copyrighted material, spam, malware and results that contain sensitive personal information like credit card numbers. Specifically, we do not engage in political censorship'.[222] With regard to removal of content in Europe, it states,

> Some democratically-elected governments in Europe and elsewhere do have national laws that prohibit certain types of content. Our policy is to comply with the laws of these democratic governments – for example, those that make pro-Nazi material illegal in Germany and France – and remove search results from only our local search engine (for example, www.google.de in Germany). We also comply with youth protection laws in countries like Germany by removing links to certain material that is deemed inappropriate for children or by enabling Safe Search by default, as we do in Korea. Whenever we do remove content, we display a message for our users that X number of results have been removed to comply with local law and we also report those removals to chillingeffects.org, a project run by the Berkman Center for Internet and Society, which tracks online restrictions on speech.[223]

What does it mean if you dispute information on Google's search results? If you have personal information that you do not want indexed, you can contact the website owner directly to remove the offending page and have the owner contact Google to tell them not to crawl or index that page or to remove the cached copy. If the webmaster is unresponsive, you can contact Google directly for the content to be assessed for removal.[224] If you are unhappy with a drop in rankings, there are not many options available. Such an issue is not specifically provided for in the Removal Policies. You can sue, but, as the cases discussed show, courts are struggling when trying to assess the application of traditional law to search engines, and such lawsuits take a long time at significant expense.

In addition, there is no remedial mechanism within the company or through industry through which to address issues of rankings. Google has implemented a discursive approach to issues of removal of content, framing it in technical rather than legal terms as 'troubleshooting problems'. It seems particularly striking that human rights is approached as an issue of troubleshooting, perhaps reflecting the difficulties with engineers shaping so much of the experience of rights in the digital

---

[222] Google Blog, 'Controversial content and free expression on the web: a refresher', at http://googleblog.blogspot.com/2010/04/controversial-content-and-free.html (last visited 18 June 2014).
[223] Ibid.     [224] This should be read in light of CJEU Google Spain n. 72.

environment.[225] For removal of content, a user answers a questionnaire for advice on how to proceed. For general problems with search, a user can answer a similar questionnaire or ask questions in a Google Search Forum.[226] A search for 'sudden drop in ranking' revealed several such posts, and users were advised to consult the Webmaster Central, which has a Crawling, Indexing and Ranking subforum.[227]

However, there is no formalised grievance or appeal mechanism akin to those used by, for example, the IWF (however flawed), eBay or the domain name registrar Nominet. The informal nature of Google's ToS combined with the informal nature of its complaints mechanism result in there being very little structure, at least internally, to how Google is governed. Certainly, the lack of any formalised grievance mechanism means that a key component of the Guiding Principles is missing in Google's governance structure. This informality infiltrates even the most well-meaning aspects of its governance. Instead of a human rights policy that might inform a more formalised grievance mechanism, it has a public policy blog that comments on human rights matters.[228] There can be seen to be processes regarding certain aspects of its free speech impact, namely with regard to removal of content, however critical I am of its informality. However, the discursive nature of its troubleshooting of problems in this arena is insufficient to be the type of grievance mechanism needed because it is difficult to identify precisely when the company can be said to be failing to comply with its policies or blog posts. Indeed, there are not any of the principles of due process or access to an independent redress mechanism necessary for a macro-IIG with such an impact on participation in democratic culture. Access to a grievance mechanism has been emphasised consistently in the Guiding Principles, the work of UN Special Rapporteur Frank La Rue and the CoE Recommendation on search engines.

The question is whether Google's governance is supported by a commitment to any general or industry CSR frameworks that mend the problems in its internal governance structure. Specific to Germany,

---

[225] See interesting discussion J. Rosen, 'The delete squad' (29 April 2013), at www.new republic.com/article/113045/free-speech-internet-silicon-valley-making-rules (last visited 18 June 2014).

[226] See https://productforums.google.com/forum/#!forum/websearch (last visited 28 May 2014).

[227] See https://productforums.google.com/forum/#!categories/webmasters/crawling-index ing-ranking (last visited 28 May 2014).

[228] It makes posts such as this: http://googlepublicpolicy.blogspot.ca/2011/10/technology -and-human-rights.html (last visited 28 may 2014).

Google is a signatory to a Subcode of Conduct for Search Engine Providers (Code).[229] This Code is rooted in co-regulation because it is a creature of the *Freiwillige Selbstokontrolle Multimedia-Diensteanbieter* (Association for the Voluntary Self-Monitoring of Multimedia Service Providers), which is part of a framework of regulated self-regulation of media in Germany.[230] The Code's purpose is protection of consumers and young people, and the duties of signatories include voluntary removal of search results based on a government-administered blacklist. The Code has been criticised by scholars such as van Hoboken for being of mere 'symbolic value'[231] because it lacks transparency and consistency and is arguably ineffective because German users can search for black-listed terms such as stormfront.org using non-German-specific Google sites, such as google.ca or google.com.[232] Ultimately, the goals of the Code are too narrow for the purposes here, but the Code serves as a warning in crafting a CSR framework that, in order to encourage inter-nalisation of the commitments at an operational level, accountability mechanisms such as transparency must be in place and monitored.

Google has not signed on to international CSR frameworks such as the UN Global Compact. Google is, however, a founding member of the Global Network Initiative (GNI). The difficulty is that the GNI has limited impact on regulation of search rankings, although the wider impact of Google's involvement with the GNI might have a knock-on effect on the same. The GNI was discussed in more detail in Chapter 3, and therefore a discussion of its strengths and weaknesses as a general CSR instrument will not be repeated here. Rather, analysis here will focus on its application in the context of management of search engine index-ing and ranking. Furthermore, its sufficiency can be assessed against the sorts of criteria identified by the CoE in its Recommendation. The Recommendation identifies the following as key to regulation of search engines: transparency concerning the way that information is selected, ranked and removed, removal or blocking of content only pursuant to Article 10(2) principles and respect for the right to due process and access to independent and accountable redress mechanisms.[233]

The GNI is a corporate responsibility framework for information and communication technologies (ICT) companies concerning freedom of expression and privacy, so seems at first blush to be ideal to address the

---

[229] See www.fsm.de/voluntary-commitments/search-engines (last visited 12 November 2014). See discussion generally in Laidlaw n. 28, p. 142; van Hoboken n. 5., s. 9.2.2.
[230] van Hoboken ibid., p. 238.     [231] Ibid., p. 239.     [232] Ibid., pp. 239–43.
[233] Recommendation n. 31.

sorts of free speech dilemmas posed by search engine rankings identified so far.[234] However, as discussed in Chapter 3, its strength is in guiding companies concerning their conduct in countries where local laws conflict with international human rights principles, rather than concerning the elusive nature of internet governance in Western states, where companies often are simply encouraged to govern themselves. This elusiveness is particularly the case for search engines, which, as we have seen, operate in an environment where the regulatory framework is still evolving.

The scope of the GNI is more relevant to the removal of references from search results than to issues of the selection and ranking of these references. The GNI's Principles state '[p]articipating companies will respect and protect the freedom of expression of their users by seeking to avoid or minimize the impact of government restrictions on freedom of expression'.[235] This focus on conduct in the face of government demands can be seen as well in the Implementation Guidelines.[236] Such a focus on government interferences risks sidelining an issue such as search engine rankings, although it is applicable concerning government-mandated removal of search references.

The applicability of the GNI to search rankings is further diminished by the lack of detail in the GNI concerning the scope of freedom of expression as it relates to what member businesses do. None of the GNI's Principles, Implementation Guidelines or Governance, Accountability and Learning Framework identify precisely the business activities that impact freedom of expression. Although such a broad-strokes approach is appropriate to allow for it to develop as a living, breathing instrument and respond to the changing landscape of ICT business, it becomes problematic when examining a scenario at the borders of free speech engagement, such as search engine rankings. For example, the Principles state that companies should respect and protect free speech against 'government demands, law and regulations to suppress freedom of

---

[234] The GNI was inspired by the Sullivan Principles, a code of conduct for businesses engaged in apartheid South Africa, which is telling. See discussion A. Wales, *Big Business, Big Responsibilities* (Basingstoke: Palgrave Macmillan, 2010), and Colin Maclay, 'Protecting Privacy and Expression Online: Can the Global Network Initiative Embrace the Character of the Net?', in R. Deibert et al., *Access Controlled: The Shaping of Power, Rights, and Rule in Cyberspace* (MIT Press, 2010), p. 92.

[235] See 'Principles', at www.globalnetworkinitiative.org/principles/index.php#18 (last visited 28 May 2014).

[236] See 'Implementation guidelines', at http://globalnetworkinitiative.org/implementation guidelines/index.php (last visited 28 May 2014).

expression'.[237] This provides minimal guidance concerning the regulatory lacunae in which search engine rankings are managed.

The Principles state that '[p]articipating companies will identify circumstances where freedom of expression and privacy may be jeopardized or advanced and integrate these Principles into their decision making in these circumstances'.[238] GNI Implementation Guidelines state that companies should 'employ human rights impact assessments to identify circumstances when freedom of expression and privacy may be jeopardized or advanced, and develop appropriate mitigation strategies'.[239] It is quite easy for search engines to state that the way that search results are produced is a proprietary algorithm protected as a trade secret and an expression of opinion of the search provider. Google has stated just this in the instances where it has been sued by content providers who believe their drop in rankings have been illegitimate.[240]

The GNI published its first complete independent assessment (Assessment) of Google in January 2014. It had been hoped that it might independently assess the businesses' self-assessment of what they identify as their free speech or privacy impacts. In this sense, it could highlight for Google, for example, where it has a free speech impact that is not reflected in its operational structure. Unfortunately, the remit was limited to an assessment of how Google (and Microsoft and Yahoo!) responded to government requests implicating freedom of expression and privacy.[241] Within this narrow remit, however, the assessment evidences awareness and robust engagement by the companies' employees with the free speech issues related to governmental requests for content removal from search engine results[242] although not necessarily through a formalised framework.

The Assessment was at times quite generalised, despite the use of case studies, with the effect that, at least for public consumption, it acted as a reassurance device rather than a targeted accountability tool. This effect might have been partly because of the broad focus on three companies and the anonymising of specific company names and other details in the case studies and recommendations.[243] It therefore lacked the direct engagement of their human rights impact in the way that the IWF

---

[237]  Principles n. 235.     [238]  Ibid.     [239]  Implementation Guidelines n. 236.
[240]  See discussion of Search King n. 84 and Langdon n. 170.
[241]  Independent Assessment, at http://globalnetworkinitiative.org/sites/default/files/GNI%20Assessments%20Public%20Report.pdf (last visited 28 May 2014), p. 3.
[242]  Ibid., pp. 17–20.
[243]  See, for example, the broad-strokes summaries of the companies, ibid., pp. 13–16.

Human Rights audit achieved. Behind the scenes with the companies, of course, the Assessment might have prompted some productive conversations. However, CSR accountability entails public accountability. Indeed, the role of the public in CSR is an important regulatory tool.

The Assessment did acknowledge that disclosure was limited in certain situations, for example, to maintain user privacy, attorney-client privilege or protect trade secrets.[244] The sensitivity of particular information, including political sensitivity concerning disclosure of government requests, arguably leads to such anonymising of information in the Assessment. How to overcome this difficulty to make this an effective governance tool is problematic, although it should be noted that one way that Google has sought to resolve issues of lack of specific disclosure is through its participation in the Chilling Effects program and in its spearheading of the Transparency Reporter, both of which disclose information about requests for content removal, which will be discussed later.[245]

This analysis shows that Google has arguably failed to do enough to embed human rights considerations concerning search indexing and rankings into its structure at an operational level on more than an informal basis. The way the GNI is structured is broad. This is compounded by the voluntary nature of the regime and the fact that it is industry-led (even if multiple stakeholders participate), with the result that businesses have ample wiggle room to sidestep those human rights issues they wish to avoid. If they are forced to, they can simply refuse to join, citing whatever public relations statement suits the purpose best, or quit, using much the same rhetoric.[246] For example, Facebook, in a letter to The Honourable Richard J. Durbin, the Chairman of the US Subcommittee on Human Rights and the Law, stated that one of the reasons it did not join the GNI was that Facebook is a resource-strained start-up.[247] It assured, however, that it admires the GNI and that it has 'embodied' its principles in its governance documents.[248] Facebook has

---

[244] Ibid., pp. 11–12.

[245] See Google's 'Transparency report', at www.google.com/transparencyreport/ (last visited 30 October 2014); and Chilling Effects, at www.chillingeffects.org (last visited 30 October 2014).

[246] The letters are available on Senator Dick Durbin's website under 'Related Files': http://durbin.senate.gov/public/index.cfm/pressreleases?ID=c3078a7d-bfd9-4186-ba86-2571e 0e05ec8 (last visited 18 June 2014).

[247] Letter, Timothy Sparipini, Director Public Policy, Facebook to the Honourable Richard Durbin (27 August, 2009), p. 2. Available from Durbin's site, ibid.

[248] Ibid.

since joined the GNI. Twitter, in its letter to Durbin, stated it simply had not had the time to evaluate GNI and that 'it is our sense that GNI's draft policies, processes and fees are better suited to bigger companies who have actual operations in sensitive regions'.[249]

Despite these drawbacks, the very fact that Google is a founding member of such a CSR initiative is promising, although it needs to be extended to more clearly govern the core of what search engines do, namely indexing and ranking. Frank La Rue commended the GNI as an example of good corporate practice.[250] Such participation highlights that Google, and indeed other search engines, have turned their attention to their impact on freedom of expression and have worked to create a CSR framework to address this impact. At present, however, most governance of search rankings is limited to Google's contractual ToS and soft commitments in its policies and blogs.

As discussed in Chapter 3, the GNI's greatest strength might be as advocate for ICT businesses on free speech and privacy matters, and this has wider regulatory impact.[251] Membership in the GNI has also led to innovative solutions to human rights dilemmas, such as the Google Transparency Report tool, with which Google details worldwide requests by governments for content removal and sharing of data about users and requests by copyright owners to remove webpages from search results.[252] Admittedly, the Snowden revelations that companies like Google were compelled to collect and share data on users with Western governments, something that was not revealed to the GNI through consultations or the audits, makes the GNI seem rather irrelevant to the task of rights protection. This led the Electronic Frontier Foundation (EFF) to resign from the organisation.[253] This illustrates the limits of CSR governance tools for human rights, a point made in the Assessment in its call for broader reform that includes governmental and non-state actors:

---

[249] Letter, Alexander Macgillvray, General Counsel, Twitter to Senator Richard Durbin, p. 2. Available from Durbin's site, ibid.

[250] La Rue n. 29, paras. 46–47.

[251] See, for example, the compelling commentary of Mark Stephens, the Independent Chair of its Board of Directors, on the recent Google Spain CJEU decision: 'Only the powerful will benefit from the "right to be forgotten"' (18 May 2014), at www.theguardian.com /commentisfree/2014/may/18/powerful-benefit-right-to-be-forgotten (last visited 28 May 2014).

[252] 'Transparency report', at www.google.com/transparencyreport/ (last visited 28 May 2014).

[253] See 'GNI resignation letter', at www.eff.org/document/gni-resignation-letter (last visited 14 March 2014).

Given that all three companies could not even confirm whether or not they had been subject to national security surveillance demands by the U.S. government under FISA, much less provide any details had they received such a request, carrying out an assessment of the companies' response to such requests was not possible. This reinforces our conviction – what we believe to be a broad consensus – that reform is necessary.[254]

The space to watch is development of the GNI's remedial mechanism. It designed a complaints procedure with the help of Shift, a nonprofit organisation, which is being piloted in 2014.[255]

From a human rights perspective, in Google, we have a company whose activities significantly impact participation in democratic culture, and yet, in Europe at least, the reach and applicability of Article 10 to govern the rights of users, content providers and search providers is evolving in the law and therefore currently uncertain. The GNI in its current form does not provide clear guidance concerning search engine indexing and ranking, although it is stronger in providing guidance concerning content removal. Google's ToS and related policies may or may not breach consumer protection or contract laws.[256] Although Google likely has internal policies governing issues of free speech, and employee awareness of issues was clear in the GNI Assessment, the focus here is on the public-facing governance framework. Certainly its ToS and other policies indirectly engage with human rights such as freedom of expression, but it is done so informally that it fails to even be the semblance of a framework against which the activities of Google can be judged, much less have the power to embed principles into its operational structure. There are no processes of due diligence or mitigation strategies built into how it is governed and no avenue for remediation.

What does this mean, then, for the capacity of CSR to be the regime for governance of search engines concerning freedom of expression? This case study shows that current governance of search engine indexing and ranking fails to be a human rights-compliant regulatory structure. The

---

[254] Independent Assessment n. 241, pp. 5–6.

[255] See discussion in its Annual Report 2012, at http://globalnetworkinitiative.org/sites/de fault/files/GNI%20Annual%20Report%202012.pdf (last visited 13 March 2014), p. 7.

[256] The enforceability of Google ToS from this perspective was not examined in detail here. Note, however, cases such as Landgericht (Berlin) (Google) (15 O 402/12) Unreported November 19, 2013 (Germany), wherein the Berlin County Court held that several clauses of Google's ToS were void because they were unclear and were unreasonably disadvantageous to users: see discussion. C. Seyfert, '25 Clauses of Google's Privacy Policy and Terms of Service Are Legally Void', E.C.L. Rep., 14(1) (2014), 23.

question is why that is, because this answers the question of the potentiality of CSR for governance of this gatekeeper. In the case of Google, the hurdle to developing CSR here might be in part the views of Google on what it is. Google's CSR webpage talks about CSR as a form of philanthropy stating, '[s]ince its founding, Google has been firmly committed to active philanthropy',[257] citing in support its work concerning China, earthquake relief and grants it awarded.[258] It also has its nonprofit project www.google.org, discussed earlier, which does such things as track flu trends. This view of CSR is relatively archaic, reflecting the approaches of business executives in the eighteenth and nineteenth centuries (discussed in Chapter 3), who treated it as a form of charity. To move forward, there is a need here to separate CSR from philanthropy. Socially responsible management of the company is different from its charitable activities, and interchanging the two risks whitewashing otherwise socially irresponsible conduct.

Furthermore, the absence of attention to search results in the governance frameworks, with the exception of government requests for content removal, highlights one of the weaknesses commonly identified with pure-CSR frameworks: their voluntariness. Although such voluntariness has advantages, as identified in Chapter 3, such as flexibility, innovativeness and commitment, it also allows important issues calling for regulatory attention to go unattended. Such is the case with search indexing and ranking. However, there is more than simple inattention going on here. When confronted with the dilemma of search rankings, indexing and content removal, the search providers are being asked to grapple with complicated, conflicting questions of law and then undertake responsibilities therefrom. The GNI Assessment showed that Google employees were acutely aware of the balance they were being asked to assess. There is a tension here, however, that is not reflected in such industry reports, and that is the tension between legal and CSR models of human rights, an issue area which needs to be unpicked.

For the purposes of corporate governance, for the moment, the legal model has helped shut down that avenue for development. It is difficult to bring business to the table and convince them that they have responsibilities the courts have ruled they don't have, and it would be unwise for a

---

[257] 'Corporate social responsibility', at www.google.com/intl/zh-CN/corporate/responsibili ty_en.html (last visited 28 May 2014).
[258] For a criticism of www.google.org. see S. Strom and M. Helft, 'Google finds it hard to reinvent philanthropy', at www.nytimes.com/2011/01/30/business/30charity.html?_r=1 (last visited 28 May 2014).

business to act differently. This is evident with the GNI, where cases such as *Baidu* and *Search King* have limited the scope of free speech consideration. It becomes clear, therefore, that government leadership is needed in setting the expectations of search providers' responsibilities for search rankings.[259]

## 5.4. Conclusion

Search engines play a critical role in democratic culture by making information accessible. They sort through the clutter and present information in a consumable, searchable shape and thereby become macro-IIGs to the flow of information online. This bestows great power on search providers. Without clear acknowledgement by search providers that they shape democratic culture by defining how and what information is sent, received and presented on the internet, a situation results in which '[f]reedom is contained while retaining the illusion of total freedom'.[260]

The governance environment of search engines in Europe is complex and uncertain, comprising the application of general law, self-regulatory instruments and soft-law guidance. This is compounded by uncertainty concerning the free speech rights triggered by search engine activities and how Article 10 applies. As we saw, search engines engage potentially three rights under traditional approaches to free speech: the rights of the users to receive information, the rights of the content providers to be listed on the index and the rights of the search providers to publish their search results. We do not have any case law in Europe concerning Article 10 and search rankings; however, case law out of the United States, such as *Search King* and *Baidu*, favour the rights of search providers.

We are faced, then, with a body engaged in a complicated and sometimes conflicting gatekeeping role, one that clearly engages free speech issues, but for which the law is unclear on how this translates into specific responsibilities. This environment would seem ripe for CSR to flourish, but it hasn't. Case law out of the United States potentially hampers any value CSR can add to search governance because any extension of search providers duties and responsibilities through CSR conflicts with the provider's right to free speech. This shows a need to move beyond the

---

[259] The need for government leadership was a point emphasised in the Recommendation n. 31.
[260] S. Vegh, 'Profit over Principles: The Commercialization of the Democratic Potentials of the Internet', in K. Sarikakis and D. K. Thussu (eds.), *Ideologies of the Internet* (Cresskill, New Jersey: Hampton Press, 2006), p. 72.

jurisprudence to embed free speech responsibility into the governance of search engines.

The significance of the findings in this case study will be examined in the following chapter although can be briefly outlined as follows. The unclear relationship between search engines and freedom of expression and the complicated pseudo-judicial role that search engines undertake concerning content assessment and removal has made it difficult for search providers to confidently craft out their responsibilities for freedom of expression. This was observed in the analysis of Google's ToS and related policies, where free speech was engaged informally and indirectly, and processes of due diligence and grievance mechanisms were either insufficiently developed or, in the case of the latter, nonexistent.

Yet, the transnational nature of search engines makes the need for government leadership more complicated and the need for alternative governance structures such as CSR more compelling. Thus, CSR has a role to play concerning search governance, but government leadership is necessary to tease out what this role should be, indicating that a pure-CSR model of governance would likely be ineffective to address the issues explored here. In addition, the piecemeal regulatory environment in Europe shows the need for coherence, which can potentially be achieved by building complementarity between the various forms and approaches to regulation.[261] It is argued that search engines are the forums to exercise the right to information access online. The responsibilities that flow from this, not necessarily as a matter of law, are that search providers such as Google should commit to processes of due diligence and transparency and provide grievance mechanisms for failures to satisfy these terms. Such criteria is reflected in the CoE Recommendation, thus making it a useful model to guide industry.

Drawing from the case studies, we have two macro-IIGs critical to participation in democratic culture operating in vastly different regulatory environments concerning freedom of expression. In the case of ISPs, the industry did come together to create a governance framework for filtering, but, until 2013, the IWF simply failed to account for human rights in any aspect of its structure. In the case of search engines, the sometimes indirect nature of their free speech impact and the potentially conflicting rights of users, content providers and search providers has

---

[261] See discussion in Chapter 3 of articulated regulation, proposed by P. Utting in 'Rethinking business regulation: from self-regulation to social control', Technology, Business and Society Programme Paper Number 15, United Nations Research Institute for Social Development (2005).

arguably stymied the potential of CSR to address free speech. The next chapter draws this book to a close and asks, based on the findings presented herein, whether CSR adds sufficient value in the context of regulating the free speech impact of IIGs. The value can be assessed based on its potential to facilitate or protect freedom of expression on the internet. An alternative corporate governance model will be proposed that can serve as a template for approaching governance of human rights on the internet, one that may serve to mend the deficiencies present in current approaches.

# 6

## A corporate governance model
## for the Digital Age

When the Kimberly Process was established to provide companies and governments with an international diamond certification scheme to prevent the supply of blood diamonds, corporate social responsibility (CSR) was celebrated as having coming of age.[1] It was a triumph of leadership and corporate commitment to end the violence associated with diamond mines in Africa. Years later and the regime is in tatters, its legitimacy and accountability questioned even by its own drafters.[2] The public are hard pressed to see that the Kimberly Process made a difference, with authors such as Oladiran Bello warning that without governance-enhancing reform, it 'risks sleep-walking into irrelevance'.[3] Other frameworks seem to have fared better, whether because they are generalised and aspirational, such as the Global Sullivan Principles[4] and the United Nations Global Compact,[5] or more targeted and instrumental

[1] Kimberley Process, at http://www.kimberleyprocess.com (last visited 19 June 2014). See Global Witness, 'The Kimberley Process', at www.globalwitness.org/campaigns/conflict /conflict-diamonds/kimberley-process (last visited 19 June 2014).

[2] See J. Melik, 'Diamonds: does the Kimberley Process work?' (28 June 2010), at www.bbc .co.uk/news/10307046 (last visited 19 June 2014); and S. Nyaira, 'Kimberley Process in turmoil after chairman clears Zimbabwe diamond sales' (23 March 2011), at www.voa news.com/zimbabwe/news/Kimberley-Process-In-Turmoil-After-Chairman-Allows-Zi mbabwes-Marange-Gems-Trade-118509874.html (last visited 19 June 2014).

[3] O. Bello, 'The Kimberley Process risks becoming irrelevant to cogent concerns' (28 October 2013), at www.saiia.org.za/opinion-analysis/the-kimberley-process-risks-becom ing-irrelevant-to-cogent-concerns (last visited 8 April 2014).

[4] The Global Sullivan Principles, at http://www.thesullivanfoundation.org/The-Global-Sul livan-Principles.htm (last visited 19 June 2014). Note however, that Sullivan of the Sullivan principles has since criticised the principles as not going far enough. See discussion of academic Larry Downes in Forbes about the GNI: L. Downes, 'Why no one will join the Global Network Initiative' (20 March 2011), at http://blogs.forbes.com/larrydownes/2011 /03/30/why-no-one-will-join-the-global-network-initiative/ (last visited 19 June 2014).

[5] United Nations Global Compact, 'The Ten Principles', at www.unglobalcompact.org/About TheGC/TheTenPrinciples/index.html (last visited 19 June 2014).

and therefore more capable of being operationalised, such as the Forest Stewardship Council.[6] What, then, of the corporate responsibility instruments used for the protection of freedom of expression on the internet? As we have seen in this book, CSR has failed to be enough to facilitate the internet's potential as a force in democratic culture, but it is not irrelevant to this vision either.

This book has examined corporate governance of a particular type of gatekeeper, the internet information gatekeeper (IIG). A gatekeeper, drawing from network gatekeeper theory (NGT),[7] is an entity that exercises information control by, for example, selecting the information to publish, channelling information through a channel, deleting information or shaping information into a particular form. A simple gatekeeper is elevated to an internet information gatekeeper (IIG) when, as a result of this control of the flow of information, it gatekeeps deliberation and participation in democratic culture. Where a particular IIG fits on the scale of responsibility in this environment, whether as a macro-gatekeeper, authority gatekeeper or micro-gatekeeper, depends on the extent to which (1) the information has democratic significance and (2) the reach or structure of the communicative space.

It is the impact of these gatekeepers on participation in democratic culture that raises the free speech questions that are central to this book. It asks: what value can CSR add in the context of regulating the impact of IIGs on the exercise of the right to free speech on the internet? Is this value sufficient to the goal of facilitating and protecting freedom of expression? The information society is upon us. Access to the internet and participation in discourse on the internet has become an integral part of our democratic life, and facilitation of this democratic potential critically relies on a governance structure supportive of free speech.[8] Since IIGs control the services that make this discourse possible, we inevitably rely on these companies for the realisation of the internet's democratic potential. A decision by an IIG that affects our engagement in the information society affects our democratic life. This puts pressure on companies to have in place governance structures supportive of free

---

[6] The Forest Stewardship Council, at www.fsc.org/ (last visited 19 June 2014).
[7] See discussion in Chapter 2; and see K. Barzilai-Nahon, 'Network Gatekeeping Theory', in S. Erdelez et al. (eds.), *Theories of Information Behavior: A Researcher's Guide* (Medford, New Jersey: Information Today, 2005) and K. Barzilai-Nahon, 'Toward a Theory of Network Gatekeeping: A Framework for Exploring Information Control', *JASIST*, 59(9) (2008) 1493.
[8] See T. I. Emerson, *The System of Freedom of Expression* (New York: Random House, 1970).

speech. At the moment, as Chapters 4 and 5 showed, the regulatory environment is uncertain and evolving, and companies have been largely left alone to address issues of free speech through CSR frameworks such as in-house codes of conduct seen in terms of service (ToS) and other company policies, through the work of regulatory bodies such as the Internet Watch Foundation (IWF), and through industry initiatives such as the Global Network Initiative (GNI). This reflects a shift in the locations of regulation, away from the state and to private nodes of governance.[9]

The regulation in the United Kingdom, and indeed in the Western World, has been relatively light touch, and, where contributions have been made in Europe, it has been soft-law guidance or recommendations for internet service providers (ISPs) and search engines from bodies such as the Council of Europe.[10] The direct application of Article 10 to the activities of such gatekeepers has been uncertain, and it strains the horizontal reach of Article 10 when the experience of human rights online is increasingly between private parties. Although the European Convention on Human Rights (ECHR) has considerable leeway for its application to private parties, the focal point nevertheless remains on government. The focus on governmental responsibility for human rights is particularly the case in the UK Human Rights Act (HRA),[11] which, as we saw in Chapter 4, limits its direct application to public authorities.[12] The law, therefore, seems increasingly inconsequential to the reality of human rights governance on the internet. This has fractured the administrative structure of free speech[13] between free speech as a legal concept

---

[9] See, in particular, section 4 of R. Lambers, 'Code and Speech. Speech Control through Network Architecture', in E. Dommering and L. Asscher (eds.), *Coding Regulation* (Cambridge University Press, 2006), where Lambers describes this as 'tilting'. Julia Black's work describes this as 'decentring': J. Black, 'Decentring Regulation: Understanding the Role of Regulation and Self-Regulation in a "Post-Regulatory" World', *CLP*, 54 (2001) 103.

[10] As was discussed in Chapters 4 and 5; see Council of Europe and European Internet Service Providers Association, 'Human rights guidelines for Internet service providers', at www.coe.int/t/informationsociety/documents/HRguidelines_ISP_en.pdf (15 November 2014); Council of Europe, *Recommendation CM/Rec(2008)6 of the Committee of Ministers to member states on measures to promote the respect for freedom of expression and information with regard to internet filters* (March 2008); Council of Europe, Recommendation CM/Rec(2012)3 of the Committee of Ministers to Member States on the protection of human rights with regard to search engines.

[11] 1998 Ch. 42.      [12] Ibid., s. 6.

[13] J. M. Balkin talks about the notion of the infrastructure of free speech in 'The Future of Free Expression in the Digital Age', *Pepp. L. Rev.*, 36: N (2008) 101. See also T. Emerson's discussion of the administrative structure of free speech in Emerson n. 8, chapter one.

and as an experienced concept. It is in this fissure that CSR has grown and taken shape. The result is a system of private governance running alongside the law without any of the human rights safeguards one normally expects of state-run systems, such as principles of accountability, predictability, accessibility, transparency and proportionality. As Jack Balkin states concerning the United States,

> At the very moment that our economic and social lives are increasingly dominated by information technology and information flows, the First Amendment seems increasingly irrelevant to the key free speech battles of the future . . . the most important decisions affecting the future of freedom of speech will not occur in constitutional law; they will be decisions about technological design, legislative and administrative regulations, the formation of new business models, and collective activities of end-users.[14]

What is needed to remedy this mismatch is to pay closer attention to the administrative structure of free speech protection in the digital world, which requires more than pure-CSR or voluntary codes. One can discuss generalised commitments of Twitter to human rights and its role in furthering democratic discourse, the commitment of Google to making information accessible, and of ISPs to connecting users in the first place. The problem is not a commitment, real or facile, to free speech. No company says it is against human rights in general or free speech in particular. The breakdown happens when moving from these generalised commitments to the operationalisation of these commitments – to the rules that give effect to them. Yet it would be equally a disservice to treat businesses as akin to states in their capacities and duties – although, as we have seen with the IWF, the regulatory bodies that these businesses help create can be treated in this way. The businesses, however, are commercial enterprises and should not incur governmental responsibilities.

Drawing on regulatory and human rights traditions, this chapter will propose a new corporate governance model, one that embraces the legal and extralegal, public and private, dimensions involved in the process of protecting the right to freedom of expression. The conclusion of this author is that increased reliance on pure-CSR codes has been insufficient to the task of facilitating the internet's democratic potential. Equally, top-down legal controls are a blunt tool for the tricky arena of business and human rights, as was identified in Chapter 3. What is needed is a framework that works with the governance environment of the internet by

---

[14] Balkin ibid., p. 101. He sees free expression being subsumed under an even larger set of concerns that he frames as 'knowledge and information policy': ibid., p. 102.

building complementarity between the various systems of regulation. This is challenging on multiple levels, as will be seen. Furthermore, this framework needs to facilitate the provision of dispute resolution services, which will be shown to be particularly critical when top-down legal controls are bypassed for more open-ended regulatory approaches.

What we can take away is that the model needs to be responsive and participative, have standard-setting appeal but be flexible and bespoke. Can any one framework be all of these things? It is suggested here that it can, but only if it is approached as a theoretical framework that is more or less formalised for a particular body depending on its scale of responsibility as a gatekeeper (as identified in Chapter 2). This will be further explored in the next section. As Aurora Voilescu describes this kind of governance, it is 'interactive voluntarism', in which a governance regime originates with government or is underpinned by regulatory interventions.[15] It underscores the seriousness of the issues without rigidifying the framework (and rendering it quickly out of date). This also allows discussion to be lifted from the voluntary versus binding debate to reflect the web of networks that govern the internet.

The corporate governance model proposed takes the form of an Internet Rights Governance Model (Governance Model). This model's value is in creating a standard framework for addressing human rights matters both internal to the organisation and external to it through the creation of a Commission. The latter is particularly controversial as it is argued that a special body is needed because, in the end, the responsibility for protection of free speech and furtherance of a human rights culture is a duty of the state, a duty that it has wholly neglected by outsourcing our rights through encouragement of corporate governance without additional guidance in the form of policies or rules. If we are serious about a human rights culture in the United Kingdom, and we are serious about the democratising potential of the internet, it is something that must be so chosen and facilitated by building human rights compliance into the governance structures of the internet. At a legal level, this means creating a governance framework that supports and furthers human rights.

The focus in this chapter – and, indeed, in this book – is to craft a solution for the United Kingdom. Thus, when the government is discussed in this chapter, it is with reference to the UK government.

---

[15] See discussion in Chapter 3. A. Voilescu, 'Changing Paradigms of Corporate Criminal Responsibility: Lessons for Corporate Social Responsibility', in D. McBarnet et al. (eds.), *The New Corporate Accountability: Corporate Social Responsibility and the Law* (Cambridge University Press, 2007), p. 373.

However, the issues raised are of global concern. Combined with the transnational nature of many of the companies that qualify as IIGs, as well as the transnational nature of internet communications, there is an inevitable outward focus to any model proposed to solve the issues raised here. However, the United Kingdom is responsible for its own human rights culture, and, because the conclusion is that the solution is a governmental responsibility, the external aspect of the model is tailored to the UK jurisdiction. The model proposed, however, is offered as a template to be used to address other human rights engaged by the activities of IIGs, such as issues of privacy and freedom of association, and to be used, modified as necessitated by domestic laws and culture, in other countries in the Western World.

This last chapter is split into two parts. In this first part, I will examine the common failures of CSR as revealed by the case studies and the significance of these failures. Drawing from these findings, the second part of the chapter will outline the details of the Governance Model, addressing how this model can mend the weaknesses evident in the current corporate governance approach.

## 6.1. A fractured system

In the second chapter, I outlined three types of IIGs – macro-gatekeepers, authority gatekeepers and micro-gatekeepers – and identified their differences as related to democracy. It was in this context that Chapters 4 and 5 focused on macro-gatekeepers, those gatekeepers we inevitably must engage to participate online and which incur the strongest human rights obligations. In Chapter 4, the role of ISPs in governing the filtering of content was examined, and the industry regulator, the IWF, was shown to have evolved into a hybrid public authority under the HRA and arguably operating in breach of Article 10. In Chapter 5, the role of search engines in controlling indexing and rankings on search results was examined; what was found in examining Google was a lack of sufficient consideration of human rights in its governance structure that monitors this aspect of its role. The problems identified by these case studies were found to go to the very core of the purposes of freedom of expression, and the way CSR was used as a governance framework to address these problems was found to be insufficient to be human rights-compliant. This section will synthesise the findings from these case studies into points of analysis concerning the sufficiency of CSR as a governance tool for IIGs. Two key differences were found between the case studies, whereas four common problems with CSR were identified. The cumulative effect of these findings is that government leadership is needed to set the expectations of companies regarding their human rights responsibilities.

### 6.1.1. Where the case studies diverged

The first of the divergences between the case studies was the role CSR plays in regulating conduct. In the case of search engines, whose impact on free speech can be more subtle because they guide and channel information flows indirectly, the regulatory environment is young, comprising a mix of generally applicable law, soft-law guidance and self-regulatory and CSR codes. This has created uncertainty concerning the duties and responsibilities of a provider such as Google, which is further complicated by the tension between the potential free speech rights of users, information providers and search providers. Although Europe does not have a case concerning Article 10 and search engine rankings, case law out of the United States has favoured the rights of search providers. The lack of clarity on how the right to freedom of expression, and Article 10 more specifically, applies to search engine activities has put pressure on the private governance structures of search providers. Bodies such as the GNI have been created, but despite praise from governments[16] and John Ruggie,[17] amongst others, few companies have taken up the initiative. And, in any event, the regime fails to explicitly address governance of search engine rankings. The failure to address rankings in the GNI illustrates the difficulty in identifying the free speech issues concerning online gatekeepers. The inherent murkiness of free speech means that unless sufficiently powerful forces compel attention to an issue, it can be overlooked or avoided.

This shift in the free speech impact away from the state and to private forces reflects a very traditional decentring of power. A governance gap has been created, one that has largely been filled by private governance

---

[16] See Congressional Hearings of Dick Durbin, 'Global internet freedom, corporate responsibility and the rule of law' (2008), at http://www.judiciary.senate.gov/meetings/global-internet-freedom-corporate-responsibility-and-the-rule-of-law (last visited 29 June 2014), and 'Global internet freedom and the rule of law, part II' (2010), at http://www.judiciary.senate.gov/meetings/global-internet-freedom-and-the-rule-of-law-part-ii (last visited 19 June 2014).

[17] J. Ruggie, 'Business and human rights: towards operationalizing the "protect, respect and remedy" framework' (2009), at www2.ohchr.org/english/bodies/hrcouncil/docs/11session/A.HRC.11.13.pdf (last visited 19 June 2014), p. 18.

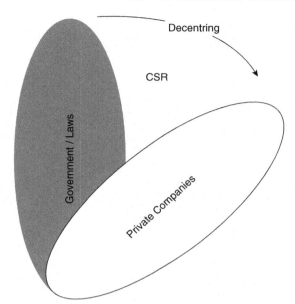

**Figure 6.1.** Decentring of human rights governance.

structures, such as in-house codes of conduct and ToS, which govern the day-to-day expressive opportunities of the public on search services. This can be seen in Figure 6.1. In this circumstance, the role of CSR in filling this gap is a rickety, insufficient and incoherent framework that has only served to delay the development of much needed policy and law.

In contrast, the case of ISPs and filtering technologies and the creation of the IWF in the United Kingdom reflects the formalisation of a corporate governance structure. As a result of the steering hand of government, industry take-up of the IWF and the passage of time, filtering in the United Kingdom has become standardised, and the IWF has thereby become entrenched and legitimised. The effect of this is quite different from the case of search engines. It has recentred the administrative structure of free speech. This is reflected in Figure 6.2.

This realignment has had two effects. First, as discussed in Chapter 4, the IWF has accepted that it is a public authority and thus directly bound by the HRA. Therefore, the attention needed concerning governance of filtering isn't additional laws, but a clarification of the applicability of existing laws. As will be recalled, the IWF historically tended to view itself in different terms, describing membership in the organisation as 'a

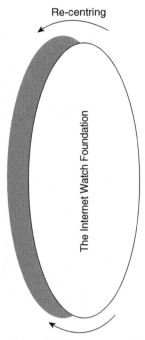

**Figure 6.2.** Recentring of human rights governance.

visible, tangible and valuable means of demonstrating corporate social responsibility'.[18] Here, CSR is a linguistic tool, the effect of which, intentionally or unintentionally, helped obscure the public authority status of the IWF for a long time and delayed much-needed attention to bring the body in line with the law.

The second effect of this realignment is to illustrate the risks associated with more formalised governance codes. The more formalised a CSR framework, the more human rights principles are operationalised, the more likely it will be a public authority and thus bound by the HRA. The very act of strengthening the administrative structure of free speech risks dissuading companies or industries from addressing free speech concerns for fear of incurring direct liability.[19] The GNI is wrestling with this problem. In the process of drafting the

---

[18] See www.iwf.org.uk/members/membership-benefits (last visited 19 June 2014).
[19] Here the results of *Choc* v. *Hudbay Minerals Inc.* 2013 ONSC 1414 potentially will have a significant impact.

GNI, the structure was rendered weaker and more flexible to draw companies to the table, but this also drove away human rights organisations that saw the GNI as being too flimsy to be called a human rights framework.[20] And here is the rub: the notion of a framework of responsibilities, even a weakened one, has prevented businesses from signing on.[21] Although they cite their involvement with other CSR frameworks such as the Electronic Industry Citizenship Coalition (EICC)[22] or simply reassure that the company is committed to freedom of speech,[23] the fact is that few companies have joined. The result is a framework that neither side is satisfied with. At a Senate Hearing in the United States on Global Internet Freedom, GNI board member Rebecca McKinnon opined,

> What is holding these companies back? It does seem in part a fear of acknowledging that human rights is part of their business, that telecommunications and internet companies no matter how you slice it have implications for free expression, privacy and human rights. And I think a lot of companies are afraid of even having that conversation for fear that people will then hang charges on them of various kinds, and that they'd rather just avoid having the conversation at all. And I think what we saw with Google, Yahoo!, and Microsoft was an evolution of self-awareness

[20] See M. D'Jaen, 'Global Initiative to Protect Net Privacy and Freedoms Launched', *E-Commerce Law & Policy* (December 2008), p. 11. Also see commentary of Colin Maclay, 'Protecting Privacy and Expression Online: Can the Global Network Initiative Embrace the Character of the Net?' in R. Deibert et al., *Access Controlled: The Shaping of Power, Rights, and Rule in Cyberspace* (MIT Press, 2010), p. 98; the Electronic Frontier Foundation (letter), at www.eff.org/files/filenode/gni/signon_letter.txt (last visited 19 June 2014); and see Amnesty's criticisms, discussed in B. Johnson, 'Amnesty criticises Global Network Initiative for online freedom of speech' (30 October 2008), at www.guardian.co.uk/technology/2008/oct/30/amnesty-global-network-initiative (last visited 19 June 2014).

[21] See Global Internet Freedom Part II n. 16.

[22] Electronic Industry Citizenship Coalition, at www.eicc.info/ (last visited 19 June 2014). Apple cited its membership in the EICC in its letter to Senator Durbin (27 August 2009), further citing the focus of the GNI on networks rather than its main business of the provision of devices, as the reasons for not joining the GNI. Apple states that, internally, it has a 'comprehensive and principled approach to address human rights around the world': p. 1. A review of Apple's Supplier Code of Conduct attached to the letter reveals no provisions concerning freedom of expression as discussed in this book. Facebook has since joined the GNI.

[23] See Letter, Timothy Sparipini, Director Public Policy, Facebook to the Honourable Richard Durbin (27 August, 2009), or Letter, Alexander Macgillvray, General Counsel, Twitter to Senator Richard Durbin. Both available from Durbin's site: http://durbin.sen ate.gov/public/index.cfm/pressreleases?ID=c3078a7d-bfd9-4186-ba86-2571e0e05ec8 (last visited 19 June 2014).

and a coming out of recognising it is ok to have this conversation, it is ok to have responsibility, and if you hold yourself accountable it is good for business.[24]

The second divergence between the case studies is that CSR is forced to accommodate two different focuses: human rights impact at an international level, where CSR in its purest form is of most use, and human rights impact at a national level, where there is greater capacity for government and/or judicial control. For example, the decision of a country and/or its companies and their industry body on what information to filter is ultimately a question of national concern based on the laws that govern the boundaries of free speech in that country. The issue can, in effect, be localised, because determinations have local effect. Whereas a website hosted abroad might infringe the United Kingdom's Protection of Children Act[25] by publishing images of child sexual abuse, the United Kingdom cannot in this instance censor the speaker without international cooperation, whether informally through information sharing or more formally through legal mechanisms. Yet the United Kingdom can directly address access to the material within its borders either by prosecuting those residing in the United Kingdom who access such material (if they can be discovered) and/or by employing filtering mechanisms.[26]

Search engines, on the other hand, are far more international from the outset. A company such as Google uses geolocation techniques to tailor search results to a user's country or city, and it uses such techniques to filter results to comply with local law. Consider the examples in the case study, such as the filtering of Google search results in China or the different responses to the anti-Semitic site www.jewwatch.com. Regardless of the ability to localise search results, the major search engine providers such as Google, Bing and Yahoo! are transnational with a

---

[24] See Global Internet Freedom Part II n. 16, evidence of Rebecca McKinnon. See also V. G. Kopytoff, 'Sites like Twitter absent from free speech pact' (6 March 2011), at www.ny times.com/2011/03/07/technology/07rights.html (last visited 19 June 2014).

[25] 1999 c. 14.

[26] The boundary is not always so clear-cut. This is exemplified in the famous Yahoo! case in which Yahoo! hosted an auction site on which third parties sold Nazi memorabilia. The sale of such material is illegal in France, yet the host of the content, as well as the source of the content, originated in America. After hearing evidence from experts, the Court imposed on Yahoo! the obligation to block access to the material by French users: *LICRA et UEJF* v. *Yahoo! Inc.*, Ordonnance Refere, TGI Paris, 20 November 2000. This then led to an action in the United States by Yahoo! seeking a declaration that the judgment was unenforceable because it conflicted with the First Amendment: *Yahoo! Inc.* v. *La Ligue Contre Le Racisme et L'Antisemitisme* (2001) 169 F Supp 2d 1181 (N.D. Cal.).

firmly international focus. The waters become further muddied by the more subtle way that search engines shape information flows. A decision to filter a webpage is a more obvious act of censorship because it removes that webpage from public circulation. However, a search engine's rankings, the ordering of answers to search queries, are less obviously a free speech concern. Yet it is equally as effective in clamping down on avenues of democratic discourse, particularly in light of users' reliance on search engines to navigate the Web and their tendency to only click on links from the top search results.[27]

The combination of the transnational nature of search engines and the subtle way they can impact free speech challenges the boundaries of state law. It makes it more difficult for the UK government to address the free speech impact of search engines domestically. This drives search into the international arena, where free speech protections are hotly contested. Western states are unable to agree on the scope of free speech protection, particularly concerning issues of hate speech, pornography and obscenity. This proves problematic when it comes to setting any standards for search engine providers. For example, the miserable failure of the negotiations for a hate speech provision in the Convention on Cybercrime[28] only served to highlight the differences between the American approach to hate speech and other Western democracies. The American constitutional system prevents the United States from signing international accords that conflict with the US Constitution. Given the US approach to hate speech under the First Amendment, their negotiators were hamstrung from agreeing to a provision in the Convention to address hate speech, and so all other parties to the Convention were forced to address the issue of hate speech in the First Additional Protocol.[29] In such an environment, there is a much greater role to play by companies in coming together to commit to codes of conduct to govern issues of free speech because nation-states can at times be hard-pressed to cope.

Apart from these two differences in the case studies, most of the findings concerning the viability of CSR as a governance tool were similar. Four common failures with CSR as it is currently used to regulate IIGs emerged from the case studies. The commonality of the failures show that the breakdown comes from two directions. It comes from the

---

[27] B. Edelman and B. Lockwood, 'Measuring bias in "organic" web search', at http://www
.benedelman.org/searchbias/ (last visited 19 June 2014).
[28] 23.XI.2001.    [29] First Protocol to Convention on Cybercrime, 23.XI.2001.

state in failing to fulfil its positive obligation to protect freedom of expression by promoting a human rights culture in the United Kingdom, and it is a failure of businesses to respect freedom of expression. One way that these two can come together to address the human rights impact of IIGs on democratic culture is through operationalisation of the Governance Model.

### 6.1.2. Identifying the problem

First, a common concern in the field of CSR is that imposing human rights duties, whether direct duties via legislative enactment or the obligation to respect outlined in the Guiding Principles, risks disrupting the market and chilling innovation. In some cases, the argument goes, it might be a breach of fiduciary duty to the stakeholders, particularly when the human rights-driven decisions impact a company's income stream. This concern is also common in the technology industry where many a start-up began in someone's garage. A lot of the leading information technology (IT) businesses we know today, such as Google, Microsoft, Apple and Facebook, were all small-scale start-ups that might have been affected by overly legalised human rights obligations. In the end, these are profit-making institutions, and, although we want the institution to be governed in a human rights-compliant way, this is not the end goal of the institution. It is not necessarily the case that human rights obligations will chill innovation, but simply that imposing state-like human rights obligations might burden a company without the capital to accommodate them.

Such a concern, however, misses the point. Imposing human rights obligations on business, whether formalised through laws or indirectly through incentives, audits or public praising/shaming *will* disrupt the market. In fact, that is the point. The purpose is to disrupt the market to realign business conduct along human rights-compatible terms. The goal is simply to narrowly tailor the obligations to minimise disruptions beyond the intended purpose of encouraging human rights compliance. Furthermore, disruption is not necessarily a bad thing if the goal and effect is to give companies more certainty about the nature of their responsibilities, which are otherwise litigated piecemeal through the courts. Or worse, the uncertainty might lead to overly censorial decisions by companies fearful of being sued. For example, Microsoft stopped offering a series of discussion groups in 2003–2004 because of fears of hosting illegal content and the associated uncertainty and expense of moderating.[30] BT, in implementing the UK government-mandated opt-in filter for legal pornographic content, elected to execute it under a framework of parental controls, whereby users must now opt-in to view a wide variety of content, ranging from obscene content, to content featuring nudity, drugs and alcohol, self-harm and dating sites.[31]

We must remember that IIGs, particularly macro-IIGs, are different from 'ordinary' companies. As discussed in Chapter 2, such companies control the flow of information in a way that facilitates or hinders participation in democratic culture, and macro-IIGs are gatekeepers we inevitably engage to go online, whether literally or figuratively. In carrying out a role integral to the facilitation of the internet's democratic potential, macro-gatekeepers and some authority gatekeepers, it is contended, are more akin to the 'democratic public interest' institutions adverted to by Ruggie and discussed in Chapter 3.[32] There are certain institutions, Ruggie concluded, that are a special class of company and might invite additional corporate responsibilities beyond the duty to respect outlined in his framework. Thus, although fears of market disruption are real, they are abated by the narrow focus on companies going to the heart of democratic discourse online. Imposition of special regulations on companies, such as media companies and public utilities, have a long history, particularly those industries that are integral to the functioning of democracy.[33]

The second problem with CSR identified by the case studies is that CSR is ill-suited to oversight of the IIGs' gatekeeping role. IIGs are often not the originator of human rights abuses and rather are forced into a pseudo-judicial role weighing competing human rights interests and making determinations of the merit of complaints and the information that should be filtered. This dilemma is universal to the online gatekeeper, whether one is a search engine such as Google, an industry body such as the IWF, Apple in gatekeeping the apps that are available with its

---

[30] D. Tambini et al., *Codifying Cyberspace* (London: Routledge, 2008), p. 294.

[31] S. Curtis, 'BT forces porn filter choice' (16 December 2013), at www.telegraph.co.uk/technology/internet-security/10520537/BT-forces-porn-filter-choice.html (last visited 19 June 2014).

[32] J. Ruggie, 'Protect, respect and remedy: a framework for business and human rights: report of the Special Representative of the Secretary General on the issue of human rights and transnational corporations and other business enterprises' (2008), at www.reports-and-materials.org/Ruggie-report-7-Apr-2008.pdf (last visited 19 June 2014), p. 16.

[33] Justifications of media regulation often centre on the media's role in public discourse: see M. Feintuck and M. Varney, *Media Regulation, Public Interest and the Law* (Edinburgh University Press, 2006).

products, YouTube in removing offensive videos, a message board operator removing scurrilous comments or simply a blogger removing contributions made to its comments section. All are tasked with assessing the
lawfulness of content that, although within their control, they did not
create. Whereas the US approach is to exempt such gatekeepers from
liability under section 230(c) of the Communications Decency Act
(CDA),[34] and the European approach is less far-reaching, providing a
safe harbour to certain intermediaries that are then regulated at a
national level,[35] both the European and US systems are aimed at encouraging businesses to privately regulate their affairs. Thus, we have a system
of private governance running alongside the law, with its own rules, often
variable and unknown, concerning what is acceptable and not acceptable
speech.

When the rules are set down in company policies, sometimes in the
company's ToS, the rights of the business are always framed broadly in
order to avoid potential liability. Often, many businesses are stuck in the
middle, forced into the role of proxy censor[36] by the guiding hand of
government. This is particularly the case with ISPs, which are increasingly being pressurised by government (apart from the IWF) to filter a
more expansive range of material. Such a pseudo-judicial role is challenging to the promise of CSR. It also distinguishes IIGs from other types of
businesses for which CSR has been more successful in holding businesses
to account. It is easier to frame environmental responsibilities when the
companies are the perpetrators, but less clear how to define pseudo-
judicial responsibilities in the face of conflicting local speech laws. The
natural aversion to taking on such responsibilities, combined with the
complexity of fleshing out what the rule structure would be, has arguably
impeded the development of CSR in this area. What becomes clear is that
government guidance on what these responsibilities should be is crucial
to move corporate governance forward.

Third, one of the key weaknesses in current corporate governance of
IIGs is the lack of sufficient remedial mechanisms. The need for such
mechanisms was shown in the case studies and has been identified by

---

[34] 47 U.S.C.; see the Digital Millennium Copyright Act 1998 Pub. L. No. 105–304, 112 Stat.
2860 (Oct. 28, 1998) for specific provisions in the copyright context.

[35] Directive 2000/31/EC of the European Parliament and of the Council of 8 June 2000 on
certain legal aspects of information society services, in particular electronic commerce, in
the Internal Market.

[36] See S. F. Kreimer, 'Censorship by Proxy: First Amendment, Internet Intermediaries, and
the Problem of the Weakest Link', U. Pa. L. Rev., 155 (2006–2007) 11.

Ruggie as a touchstone of his framework. As Ruggie summarises, the aim of such a mechanism is 'to counteract or make good any human rights harms that have occurred'.[37] What is clear from the case studies is that core democratic rights of free speech are being engaged by the activities of IIGs, and yet there is little available to users to address potential or actual infringements of such rights through corporate governance mechanisms. It is asserted that 'public signalling'[38] from government is needed to advise companies on what is expected of them. In the case of search engines, there is nothing available. There is no internal adjudicative process available through, for example, Google to address complaints. In the case of ISPs and the regulatory body the IWF, there is a remedial mechanism, but it is insufficient to be called human rights-compliant. Its recent human rights audit has identified ways to mend these weaknesses. In both case studies, there were none of the criteria identified in the Guiding Principles as important for a human rights-compliant grievance mechanism of legitimacy, accessibly, predictability, equitability, rights-compatibility, transparency or dialogue with stakeholders.[39]

The IWF does not notify website owners that their sites are being blocked, and although it encourages ISPs to notify consumers trying to access such sites of the block, it is not, at present, mandatory. Thus, from the outset, a body like the IWF is plagued with issues of transparency and legitimacy. If a person finds out his or her site has been blocked or access to such a site blocked, there are a set of procedures the IWF must follow to handle complaints. However, the procedures are hardly an adjudicative process because the complainant has no access to make representations to the decision makers or to hear the case being made against him or her. Thus, the process is not accessible, predictable or transparent. Without access to make representations or knowledge of the reasons for decisions, then the decision-making body has ample room to make inequitable and rights-infringing decisions, and we are none the wiser. As a public authority under the HRA Section 6, much work is needed to reshape the body to be compliant with Article 10. Unlike search engines,

---

[37] J. Ruggie, 'Guiding principles on business and human rights: implementing the United Nations "protect, respect and remedy" framework' (March 2011), at www.business-hu manrights.org/media/documents/ruggie/ruggie-guiding-principles-21-mar-2011.pdf (last visited 19 June 2014), p. 21.

[38] See Ruggie evidence, Joint Committee on Human Rights, *Any of Our Business? Human Rights and the UK Private Sector* (First Reports of Session 2009–10), vol. II, p. 12.

[39] For an explanation of what these criteria mean, see Ruggie n. 37.

however, which operate in a more uncertain regulatory environment, the task with the IWF is to bring it in line with its legal obligations.

Fourth, there is a fundamental problem with voluntariness, which is at the heart of many corporate governance regimes and is prevalent in the area of internet governance. This is a tricky arena because CSR is not per se restricted to voluntary codes, as we saw in Chapter 3. There is a difference, however, between corporate governance as a broader notion, which includes within it well-developed self-regulatory frameworks, legislation, government cooperation and industry codes, and pure-CSR in the form of voluntary industry or in-house codes or commitments. The Joint Committee on Human Rights Report identified the issue of voluntariness as one of the key criticisms of the UK government in this area, commenting that the government unduly favours voluntary initiatives and lacks policy coherence and leadership.[40] The European Commission (EC) and the United Kingdom have begun to shift towards a mixed approach to CSR, advocating a model of corporate-led responsibility underpinned by government activity.[41] Such an approach more closely matches the legal and extralegal dimensions of human rights governance. It is both of these dimensions that the Governance Model seeks to harness as the governance solution.

Pure-CSR codes simply lack the standard-setting appeal and oversight necessary to the structure of a free speech system. Such codes are too reliant on the whims or commitments of management; they are thus susceptible to change over time and unreliable as a public signal of the expectations of company conduct. A change in management, for example, can lead to a change in the business's human rights policies or, more insidiously, lead to no change in policy, but a change in the seriousness with which human rights matters are treated. The work of the Private Sector and Human Rights Project found that the commitment of particular leaders in a company was the 'dominant driver for engaging with human rights'.[42] The finding was particularly the case for companies that operated outside the public sector and industry regulation,[43] which would be the case for most macro-IIGs such as ISPs and search engines. The problem inherent in this situation is exacerbated by the fact that IT companies, in terms of their democratic impact, are changeable, and the

---

[40] Joint Committee on Human Rights, *Any of Our Business? Human Rights and the UK Private Sector* (First Reports of Session 2009–10), vol. I, p. 53.
[41] See Chapter 3, Section 3.2.
[42] Twentyfifty, *The Private Sector and Human Rights in the UK* (October 2009), p. 42.
[43] Ibid., p. 52.

internet environment is unstable. This leaves the public hopelessly confused and offers none of the characteristics of due process needed to be a governance framework. Most important, it makes it more difficult to establish and sustain human rights standards.

In the case of IIGs, such codes are too heavily burdened with the task of delineating the nature of their judicial role. In the case of human rights, voluntary frameworks generally only draw in those already committed to human rights, and initiatives like the GNI are plagued by a lack of take-up by key gatekeepers of democratic discourse, such as Twitter.[44] Businesses become stuck in the middle, reluctant to take on the burden of adjudicating on human rights, both in terms of resources and effort whilst the government outsources the obligation through the back door of public pressure. This is not an arena where government pressure alone will suffice. As Ruggie states, '[a]t the end of the day, therefore, the promotion of voluntary approaches by governments often differs very little from *laissez-faire*'.[45] We need to stop thinking about CSR as something extralegal and start thinking of this simply as one of the various tools that we need to use to address the issues of business and human rights, some legal and some extralegal.[46] For this, we need government leadership.

If the commitment is to the democratising potential of the internet and a human rights culture in the United Kingdom, then positive steps must be taken to secure this system, which voluntariness cannot on its own enable. In the context of IIGs, leadership is needed to retain a focus on digital free speech issues because otherwise it is easily relegated to the back seat, behind issues of discrimination and labour that more urgently and readily capture the attention of policy makers. The result is that the government has positive obligations to frame something that has both legal and extralegal dimensions. Why not, then, discard CSR entirely in favour of top-down legal controls? It is the legal and extralegal dimensions of the subject matter of digital free speech for which voluntariness has a key role to play and that makes CSR a crucial component of any governance solution that is finally arrived at.

---

[44] See recent criticism of Kopytoff n. 24, and see evidence in Global Internet Freedom Part I and II, n. 16.

[45] Joint Committee on Human Rights vol. II n. 38, p. 8.

[46] Ruggie describes it as follows: '[t]he human rights policies of states in relation to business need to be pushed beyond their narrow institutional confines. Governments need actively to promote a corporate culture respect of human rights at home and abroad': Joint Committee on Human Rights, ibid., p. 61. He suggests such things as clearer guidance for businesses and reforms to legislation such as the Companies Act and to approaches to Export Credit Guarantees.

Voluntariness arguably brings businesses to the negotiating table, involving them in the process of defining their roles and responsibilities and thereby has more potential to capture the spirit of commitment on the part of companies. This is particularly important in the field of human rights, where its moral force is often of greater weight and value than its legal dimension. Furthermore, it has greater potential to realise free speech values without as readily chilling innovation and has more potential to prompt a culture change, which is needed to truly embed human rights into everyday internet governance by business. Additionally, CSR has greater potential to address responsibilities of transnational companies at an international level when there are variations in national law, allowing them to carve out a path of responsibility and create standards. As Daniel Weitzner commented at the Global Internet Freedom Senate Hearings in 2010,

> Some part of the way that we can come together in an environment where the Internet can actually function globally. . . . We should have a basic expectation of due process. National rules may vary but when they become arbitrary I think we all have a concern. That is most concern for the individual rights at stake. By the same token transparency and pre-dictability of these rules wherever they fall on the spectrum and however that spectrum evolves over time are essential if we are going to have a viable commercial environment.[47]

What clearly won't work in this arena is legislation that regulates indirectly by encouraging take-up of CSR policies through the back door. Such legislation includes, for example, the UK Companies Act, which under Section 417(5) requires companies to provide information on their CSR policies in their annual directors' report.[48] Such creative legislating helps uptake of CSR codes, but it does not provide the policy framework needed for the murky arena of free speech protection. How would such legislation help advise ISPs on the information to be filtered or social networking sites or blog providers on the information to be taken down? The combination of this type of legislation without guidance on how to go about it might have the opposite effect and paralyse companies,

---

[47] Global Internet Freedom Part II n. 16, testimony of Daniel J. Weitzner, finishing at 70:34.

[48] Companies Act 2006 c. 46, s. 417. Note that the requirement is narrowed to the extent that information provided must only be 'to the extent necessary for an understanding of the development, performance or position of the company's business' (s. 417(5)). The Director, however, is required to have regard to the company's impact on the community and environment under s. 172. See also discussion, Joint Committee on Human Rights vol. I n. 40, pp. 74–75.

preventing them from moving forward for fear of falling foul of widely drawn codes in ways that they cannot predict. Such legislation fails to provide the coherence and standards needed for facilitation of the internet's democratic potential. Likewise, promotion of generic risk assessment tools, as promoted by the UK National Contact Point (NCP),[49] does not solve the issues raised by IIGs. There is something more fundamental about IIGs, in particular macro-IIGs, that cannot be addressed by a risk assessment tool.

## 6.2. Framing the solution

The literature tends to be split on the optimal framework to address business and human rights. One group sees the proper role and responsibilities of businesses in the arena of human rights to mirror the obligations of the state or, at minimum, to be a product of government policies. Such groups often see pure-CSR policies as not doing enough to remedy or prevent human rights abuses and argue for more structured, stringent governance frameworks and remedial mechanisms that are, for the most part, legally binding.[50] Evidence by several witnesses before the Joint Committee on Human Rights favoured CSR frameworks 'underpinned' by a legally binding framework of human rights.[51] The other group argues for the value of voluntary company codes and the use of alternative measures to ensure respect for human rights. Such measures include the encouragement of human rights impact assessments and independent audits and mediation services, and they emphasise the ability of voluntary codes to better capture the spirit of commitment than legal benchmarks.[52] This split is unnecessary. There is room to

---

[49] See information on the UK NCP at www.gov.uk/uk-national-contact-point-for-the-orga nisation-for-economic-co-operation-and-development-oecd-guidelines-for-multination al-enterprises (last visited 19 June 2014).

[50] See, for example, A. Ganesan, 'Viewpoint: why voluntary initiatives aren't enough', *Leading Perspectives*, (Spring 2009), at www.bsr.org/reports/leading-perspectives/2009 /LP_Spring_2009_Voluntary_Initiatives.pdf (last visited 19 June 2014). Also see International Council on Human Rights Policy, *Beyond Voluntarism: Human Rights and the Developing International Legal Obligations of Companies* (February 2002), at www .ichrp.org/files/reports/7/107_report_en.pdf (last visited 19 June 2014).

[51] Joint Committee on Human Rights vol. I n. 40, pp. 39–40. The Committee recommended something less legislative, arguing that government should adopt the Ruggie framework and explain clearly what the responsibility to 'respect' on the part of businesses entails: ibid., p. 40.

[52] See evidence at Joint Committee on Human Rights vol. II n. 38.

accommodate both, and, as Chapters 4 and 5 showed, both approaches are needed to address the governance of internet gatekeepers.

### 6.2.1. Theoretical basis of the model

What is needed is a framework that builds human rights safeguards into the governance structure. Any communication occurs in an environment of rules.[53] The challenge, as articulated by Damian Tambini et al., is 'to ensure that rules are democratically set at the necessary minimum, procedurally fair, accountable and in the public interest'.[54] The Governance Model proposed here has both an external element in the form of a regulatory body independent of IIGs and an internal element integrating the model into an IIG's internal operations and due diligence. Although the general framework remains the same for its external and internal role, they differ on the scale and formality of responsibility. The unifying aspect is the model itself.

This book has shown the increasingly complex environment in which these businesses operate, one where CSR as it has been used has shifted from largely voluntary initiatives, which I termed pure-CSR, to more accountability-based initiatives, characterised by monitoring, reporting, codes of conduct and support through law and policy. It is further complicated by what I described earlier as the decentring of the regulatory structure of rights in cyberspace from between citizens and the state to between citizens and the private sector. Combined with the challenges to governance posed by the transnational nature of internet communications, certain observations can be made.

To protect human rights online, we need to work with the regulatory environment rather than against it. To be certain, reform is needed to incorporate human rights considerations into information and communication technology (ICT) regulation, however, reform will be best achieved by enabling the environment through mainstreaming of human rights codes. Perhaps, down the road, these codes will lead to legalistic standards or international norms. Some of this depends on a political environment the assessment of which is beyond the scope of this book. Indeed, as Peter Utting comments, 'it seems clear that any

---

[53] See here the work of J. A. Chandler, discussed in earlier chapters, arguing that free speech protection revolves around protecting the communicative aspect of speech: J. A. Chandler, 'A Right to Reach an Audience: An Approach to Intermediary Bias on the Internet', *Hofstra L. Rev.*, 35(3) (2007) 101.

[54] Tambini n. 30, p. 294.

significant advance in relation to both mainstream CSR or the more transformative corporate accountability agenda would require a more conducive structural and political environment'.[55] The goal is to draw from the moral underpinning that links human rights and CSR as identified in Joseph Lozano's grid in Chapter 3.[56]

In addition, we must be mindful that human rights is always at risk of being neglected by a regulator in favour of a cost-benefit analysis. After all, a human rights-based decision often requires a business to look beyond the bottom line. Tony Prosser explores this issue, identifying impact assessments as a mechanism to monitor human rights, but one that is still difficult to quantify. The avenue through this, he suggests, is regulation of the regulators, such as the role of parliamentary committees in monitoring the human rights obligations of regulators.[57] It will be argued here that this requires an independent body to regulate digital human rights issues, which is the external element of the Governance Model.

The path forward is in harnessing what Bronwen Morgen describes as the role of regulation in being the machinery for monitoring and enforcing human rights.[58] The task in a multinodal regulatory environment such as the internet is to link these various forms and approaches to regulation in a complementary, mutually reinforcing way, something Utting describes as articulated regulation. Such links, Utting argues, include, amongst others, legislation requiring that companies report on human rights issues in their annual reports, encouragement through taxation, subsidies or threats of regulation and enabling through international human rights laws or sequentially by voluntary frameworks 'paving the way' for hard laws.[59] Indeed, it is this complex narrative of rights protection that is reflected in the Guiding Principles, and the power of the Guiding Principles, as we saw in Chapter 3, is in providing a common conceptual language for framing the business and human

---

[55] P. Utting, 'Rethinking business regulation: from self-regulation to social control', Technology, Business and Society Programme Paper Number 15, United Nations Research Institute for Social Development (2005), p. 21.

[56] See discussion in Chapter 3 concerning J. M. Lozano et al., *Governments and Corporate Social Responsibility: Public Policies beyond Regulation and Voluntary Compliance* (Basingstoke: Palgrave Macmillan, 2008).

[57] T. Prosser, *The Regulatory Enterprise: Government, Regulation, and Legitimacy* (Oxford University Press, 2010), p. 218–20.

[58] See B. Morgan (ed.), *The Intersection of Rights and Regulation: New Directions in Sociolegal Scholarship* (Aldershot: Ashgate, 2007), chapter one.

[59] Utting n. 55, pp. 10–11.

rights debate. Chapters 4 and 5 revealed two key areas where complementarity can be facilitated: a common policy framework for addressing human rights issues and complementary dispute resolution mechanisms. These can be seen to be two of the three main features of the Governance Model discussed herein. The other feature, as will be seen, is the need for a framework that is dynamic and responsive to the changing environment of the internet and businesses that operate within it.

At the external level, what is needed is a partnership, but one with the government firmly at the lead. This will better institute the legal and extralegal dimension of human rights. What is not advocated is multistakeholderism because what is sought is operational in nature, which multistakeholderism struggles to achieve.[60] Rather, what is proposed is an avenue to operationalise free speech commitments. The partnership envisioned here places the government in a meta-regulatory capacity or in a position to engage in the legal regulation of self-regulation, an arrangement wherein a government body has oversight of industry and in-house corporate governance in the arena of human rights.[61] For certain industries of the information society, the optimal approach will be reflexive in that well-defined processes are used to underpin open and undefined outcomes.[62] Although this might appear too woolly for furtherance of free speech online, it is not without enforcement effect. For example, communicating these policies to the public becomes itself a benchmark against which companies are judged, framing the public conversation and public expectation.[63] Thus, whereas simple encouragement by government is insufficient, we must remember than the law can be a blunt instrument, and we must not turn to it as the panacea. In other situations, more well-defined legal frameworks will be required, such as

---

[60] *Multistakeholderism* here refers to how it has been used in forums such as the Internet Governance Forum and discussed by academics such as Wolfgang Kleinwachter. The IGF thus far has been unable to move beyond platforms of discussion of principles to rules or plans of actions.

[61] For a discussion of the concept of meta-regulation and CSR, see Chapter 3 with reference to C. Parker, 'Meta-Regulation: Legal Accountability for Corporate Social Responsibility', in ibid.; and C. Scott, 'Reflexive Governance, Meta-Regulation, and Corporate Social Responsibility: The Heineken Effect', in N. Boeger et al. (eds.), *Perspectives on Corporate Social Responsibility* (Cheltenham: Eward Elgar, 2008).

[62] Scott ibid., pp. 174–75. Not everything discussed by Scott concerning reflexive governance and CSR is advocated as applicable here. Also see here the work of A. Murray on symbiotic regulation: 'Symbiotic Regulation', *J. Marshall J. of Computer & Info. L.*, 26(2) (2009) 207.

[63] This would be a type of alternative meta-regulation discussed by C. Scott in his article, ibid.

in the case of filtering, where the decision of the company or industry body has an immediate censorship effect on the circulation of information. The unifying factor in this is that a single body in the United Kingdom oversees issues of business and human rights for the information society. The state duty to protect would be realised through creation of such a body to set out the structure of obligations and, through this, better frame the realisation of a company's duty to respect.

The challenge will be to convince the UK government that such a body is needed. After all, a more generalised body to address issues of human rights, business and the environment has been suggested and so far has not been taken up by the government.[64] Yet it is the narrow focus on the information society and human rights that makes such a body compelling. A commission tasked with business and human rights is a wide mandate, yet a body focused on companies in the information society, namely ICT companies, is focused on their human rights responsibilities as they relate to communication. The focus of this book has been more narrowly on freedom of expression. Indeed, the examples explored later are interrogated from the perspective of free speech. However, the body is presented more generally because it is contended that the Governance Model has relevance concerning other human rights, such as the right to privacy and freedom of association.

In addition, there is an existing model in this area, one found in the Information Commissioner's Office (ICO). The ICO is a product of the Data Protection Act[65] to oversee safeguarding of personal data, and, since then, its responsibilities have expanded to include oversight of access to information held by public authorities under the Freedom of Information Act and the Environmental Information Regulations.[66] The ICO will be discussed in more detail later. In addition, in 2012, the Protection of Freedoms Act received royal assent,[67] which creates a Surveillance Camera Commissioner to oversee a Code of Practice for CCTV systems.[68] The Digital Rights Commission proposed here would

---

[64] Joint Committee on Human Rights vol. I n. 40, pp. 4, 89–90. Note in 2010 that the government axed 192 such bodies: The BBC, 'Quango list shows 192 to be axed' (14 October 2010), at www.bbc.co.uk/news/uk-politics-11538534 (last visited 19 June 2014).

[65] Directive 95/46/EC of the European Parliament and of the Council of 24 October 1995 on the protection of individuals with regard to the processing of personal data and on the free movement of such data.

[66] See generally, www.ico.gov.uk (last visited 19 June 2014). And see www.ico.gov.uk/what_we_cover.aspx (last visited 19 June 2014). For history, see www.ico.gov.uk/about_us/our_organisation/history.aspx (last visited 19 June 2014).

[67] 2012 c. 9.   [68] Ibid., part 2, chapter one.

be focused on gatekeepers of the internet because they are the choke-points to democratic participation.

We must be mindful of the risks of capture, which is particularly pressing when tasking a body to govern human rights as applied to the private sector.[69] Perhaps the most egregious example of capture in the field of communications is the defunct Press Complaints Commission (PCC).[70] The PCC was the self-regulatory body for the press in the United Kingdom. Its failure to take seriously the hacking claims against the News of the World[71] is one of the events that prompted the Leveson Inquiry into press reform in 2011–2012. Lord Justice Leveson concluded that the PCC had failed, and a new regulatory body was needed. He stated that the PCC could not even be described as a regulator, but rather as a complaints handling body, and its failings were profound: lack of independence, voluntary nature of membership, concentration of power and inadequate remedial powers, to name a few.[72] Lord Justice Leveson's proposal for reform can be seen in many ways to parallel the proposals here. He argues for a self-regulatory body for the press underpinned by legislation. The legislation would not establish the regulatory body nor deal with day-to-day disputes. Rather, the legislation, in addition to enshrining freedom of the press, would provide an independent process to recognise the body so as to ensure independence and effectiveness, and it would validate the standards and arbitral system the regulator create and thus allow the legal standards to flow through the process.[73] Thus, much as here, the legislation would be directed at the process and legitimacy of the body, with allowance for undefined and open outcomes.

The risk of a Digital Rights Commission being created with power over business and little accountability or legitimacy is of concern, in particular

---

[69] Note that risks of capture exist for any body taking on a regulatory role: see discussion of capture in R. Baldwin and M. Cave, *Understanding Regulation: Theory, Strategy, and Practice* (Oxford: Oxford University Press, 1999), pp. 24–25.

[70] See www.pcc.org.uk (last visited 19 June 2014).

[71] See criticism, such as that by M. Cain, 'Why does the PCC pretend it can do something about phone hacking?' (31 January 2011), at http://pccwatch.co.uk/why-does-the-pcc -pretend-about-phone-hacking/ (last visited 19 June 2014). See history of hacking treatment in the news: Reuters, 'PCC clears Murdoch paper over hacking claim' (9 November 2009), at www.independent.co.uk/news/media/press/pcc-clears-murdoch -paper-over-hacking-claim-1817573.html (last visited 19 June 2014); and J. Robinson, 'PCC to re-examine News of the World phone-hacking evidence', at www.guardian.co .uk/media/2010/sep/21/phone-hacking-news-of-the-world (last visited 19 June 2014).

[72] For a summary on the PCC, see The Leveson Inquiry, *An Inquiry into the Culture, Practices and Ethics of the Press (Executive Summary)* (November 2012), paras. 41–46.

[73] Ibid., paras. 47–76.

because this too can disrupt the market and chill innovation. There is a real risk with tasking a body to define the obligations of profit-making institutions for human rights if it is not legislatively set. The powers, duties and scope of such a body would have to be clearly and narrowly defined by government, and particular care would have to be taken concerning the makeup of the Commission Board who oversee policy and adjudicate complaints.

The final point to be made about the external element of the Governance Model is an acknowledgement. The source of funding for such a body is not the focus of this chapter, but I would be remiss were I not to flag for the reader that the creation of such a body requires a lot of resources, whether raised privately or publicly. While there are options available, such as membership fees or industry levies, the economics of such a body is beyond the scope of this book. What this book does is set out an area where there exists a governance gap and for which governance is needed to be human rights-compliant, and it then sets out a model framework to satisfy human rights principles for which funding options can then be explored.

At an internal level, the Governance Model will be the blueprint for a business fulfilling its corporate responsibility to respect human rights. By using the same framework as the external body, it creates policy coherence and links these different systems of regulating. It also allows for a more open-ended regulatory regime, one in which the Commission sets the regulatory environment but leaves it open-ended as to how a business fulfils its human rights responsibilities. It also facilitates dialogue between businesses and the Commission, a necessary ingredient in the fluid environment that is the technology industry. In this way, the model can be seen to be responsive in that the regulatory strategy seeks to respond to differing industry behaviours and structures.[74] The difference between a business's role and that of the Commission, and indeed the difference between various types of businesses, is the scale of responsibility.

As the reader will recall, the scale of responsibility of gatekeepers was articulated in Chapter 2. In Figure 2.4, three types of gatekeepers were identified.

Based on this model, macro-gatekeepers would be at the top end of the scale of responsibility as an IIG because of the extent to which (1) the information has democratic significance and (2) the reach or structure of the communicative space. Applying it to the Governance Model, the

---

[74] See I. Ayres and J. Braithwaite, *Responsive Regulation: Transcending the Deregulation Debate* (Oxford University Press, 1992).

greater the scale of responsibility, the more formalised and integrated into the businesses operations would have to be the Governance Model. Sliding down the scale to content moderators, which would have less responsibility for human rights, their commitment thereto would be more intuitive and informal (if at all in some cases such as an individual's personal blog). An IIG that is a macro-gatekeeper would have greater responsibilities to more formally implement the Governance Model, whereas an authority gatekeeper would be further down the scale, allowing for more informal engagement, and a micro-gatekeeper would require mere informal engagement if at all.

This is in keeping with the evolving approach to CSR and human rights, although these instruments are more focused on differentiating between the responsibilities of small and medium-sized enterprises (SMEs) versus transnational companies (TNCs), whereas the gatekeeping model here is more focused on the scale of the impact of the particular gatekeeper. In practice, an IIG will most likely be a TNC, like Google, Twitter or Facebook, or, at minimum, a large-scale national enterprise, such as an ISP. The EC Communication on CSR, for example, identifies SMEs as having more informal, intuitive obligations and larger TNCs as having more formalised commitments set down through recognised international frameworks such as the Organisation for Economic Co-operation and Development (OECD) Guidelines, the UN Global Compact and the Guiding Principles.[75]

The Guiding Principles differentiate between TNCs and SMEs on a similar sliding scale, although they make clear that the responsibility for human rights applies to all businesses regardless of their size. The difference lies simply in how that responsibility is met:

> The means through which a business enterprise meets its responsibility to respect human rights will be proportional to, among other factors, its size. Small and medium-sized enterprises may have less capacity as well as more informal processes and management structures than larger companies, so their respective policies and processes will take on different forms. But some small and medium-sized enterprises can have severe human rights impacts, which will require corresponding measures regardless of their size. Severity of impacts will be judged by their scale, scope and irremediable character.[76]

---

[75] European Commission, 'A Renewed EU strategy 2011–14 for Corporate Social Responsibility', *COM*(2011) 681, p. 6. 'For most small and medium-sized enterprises, especially micro-enterprises, the CSR process is likely to remain informal and intuitive': ibid.

[76] Ruggie n. 37, p. 14.

Indeed, the Equality and Human Rights Commission (EHRC) notes that SMEs make up 99 per cent of the businesses in the United Kingdom, and, therefore, their observance of human rights is crucial.[77] The EC has also published a guidance for SMEs in applying the Guiding Principles.[78] The ICT Sector Guidance, discussed in Chapter 3, frames its approach as applicable to the entire ICT industry but provides bespoke approaches for SMEs where appropriate, noting that SMEs 'will typically have simpler management systems and need less complex human rights due diligence processes'.[79] The Guidance notes the dilemma captured in the gatekeeping model just described, that 'even small ICT companies can have a large and diverse customers or end-user base with the potential for a variety of impacts to occur'.[80]

From this, certain basic requirements of the Governance Model can be identified. First, we cannot treat all forms of CSR and all forms of situations the same. IIGs are varied, not only in terms of the types of businesses and their impact on democracy, but in terms of their size and resources. Thus, any body created must be able to accommodate such variations. In fact, the variety involved brings home the need for a singular body to set policy and the standards against which the activities of these companies are judged.

Second, rules set down in codes of conduct or policies are needed. The case studies revealed that the failure of international CSR initiatives was in moving from generalised principles to rules of operation.[81] It is easy enough for the UN Global Compact to advise companies to respect Article 19 of the Universal Declaration of Human Rights (UDHR), but another thing entirely to advise companies on how to do this. Here lies

---

[77] See Equality and Human Rights Commission, *A Guide to Business and Human Rights* (March 2013), at www.equalityhumanrights.com/private-and-public-sector-guidance/or ganisations-and-businesses/businesses/human-rights-matter (last visited 19 June 2014). The UK government has identified the need to develop guidance for SMEs regarding human rights: HM Government, *Good Business: Implementing the UN Guiding Principles on Business and Human Rights* (September 2013), p. 14.

[78] European Commission, *My Business and Human Rights: A Guide to Human Rights for Small and Medium-Sized Enterprises*, at http://ec.europa.eu/enterprise/policies/sustain able-business/files/csr-sme/human-rights-sme-guide-final_en.pdf (last visited 19 June 2014).

[79] European Commission, *ICT Sector Guide on Implementing the UN Guiding Principles on Business and Human Rights* (drafted by Shift and the Institute for Human Rights and Business), p. 16.

[80] Ibid.

[81] This was identified as a general problem with the respect framework as well: Joint Committee on Human Rights vol. I n. 40, p. 36.

the problem, and it is particularly complex for IIGs as a result of their pseudo-judicial role. Bodies such as the Forest Stewardship Council[82] have been successful in encouraging more responsible forestry, but the goal with such a body is increased take-up of such responsibility; therefore voluntariness and the spirit of commitment feed the legitimacy and success of such a body. In the case of IIGs, it is unclear what a responsibility for free speech entails, particularly when the responsibility is triggered by a complaint that content a gatekeeper hosts is, for example, offensive, bullying or other acts of hate or that the content conflicts with the rights of the providers themselves to make editorial decisions. On a case-by-case basis, some of the acts might be illegal, at other times offensive or cruel; at other times, the result depends on weighing one right of free speech against another right of free speech or privacy.

Above all, due process is needed in the administration of free speech. Unifying the system of free speech governance of ICTs under one body will solve most of the problems of due process, at least in the United Kingdom, because it will provide a focal point, and decisions of the body would be expected to be made in a manner that is not arbitrary, discriminatory, unreasonable or unfair. This can then be integrated into an IIG's internal operations and due diligence. Linked with this notion is the need for the body – and the businesses – to be accountable to the public.[83] The rules that are then instituted need to be predictable, accessible, transparent and proportionate, and businesses and the public must be educated about their rights and how to access the system. This fits well with Ruggie's criteria for nonjudicial grievance mechanisms that they be legitimate, accessible, predictable, transparent, rights-compatible and involve learning and engagement with stakeholders.[84]

---

[82] FSC n. 6.

[83] See definitions of accountability in C. Scott, 'Accountability in the Regulatory State', *Journal of Law and Society*, 27(1) (2000) 38, where he describes accountability as referring to giving account of one's actions.

[84] Note that Ruggie's criteria are focused on those of a remedial mechanism, whereas it is argued here that such criteria have broader application to the governance framework. The list also has similarities to the principles of good regulation. Pre-Coalition, BERR identified five principles of good regulation: that it was transparent, accountable, proportionate, consistent and targeted: http://www.berr.gov.uk/whatwedo/bre/index.html (no longer available). D. Tambini et al., identified guidelines for self-regulation in cyberspace as external involvement creating the framework, stakeholder involvement, independence from industry, consumer representation, known rules and complaints procedure, keeping the scheme up to date and reporting requirements: n. 30, pp. 282–85. C. Maclay, in talking about the GNI, noted the following as underlying values for success: efficacy, adaptability, scalability, transparency, legitimacy, neutrality and sustainability: n. 20, pp. 102–103.

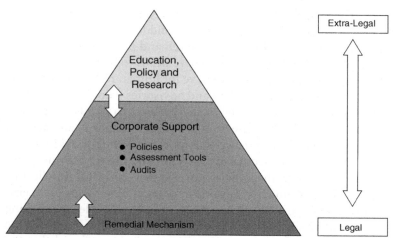

**Figure 6.3.** Internet rights governance model.

### 6.2.2. A new model for corporate governance

The Governance Model will be presented first in its more formalised context external to businesses through creation of a Digital Rights Commission (the Commission), and then its application internal to businesses will be explained.

The Governance Model has three layers: (1) education, research and policy; (2) company support in the form of policies, assessment tools and auditing and advisory services; and (3) rule-setting and adjudication. See Figure 6.3 for a model of this governance framework. The key value in this framework is that it has legal and extralegal dimensions, with the bottom layer forming primarily legal dimensions, the top layer focused on extralegal dimensions and the middle layer working to bring the two together.[85] In human rights terms, the various layers can be seen in Table 3.2 in Chapter 3 differentiating among the state duty to protect, indirect legal obligations and pure-CSR. What sets the Governance Model apart from other frameworks is the responsive nature of the interplay between these layers of regulation.[86] The aim of this interplay is to facilitate integration of human rights within a business's operations.

---

[85] These various aspects at work also harken back to J. M. Lozano's grid discussed in Chapter 3: Lozano n. 56.

[86] See Ayres and Braithwaite n. 74.

For the sake of clarity, the top and bottom layers will be elucidated first to better contextualise the key work of the middle layer.

At the top layer is the education, research and policy arm. The public need to be educated in two respects. There needs to be better awareness about the responsibilities businesses have for human rights. Information in the form of publications, updates and advisories would help translate the confusing arena of human rights and business to points of communication for the public. The Intellectual Property Office is an excellent example in this regard, with its website www.ipo.gov.uk providing educative information on intellectual property law and the services the Office provides in its role as the official government body for intellectual property. The ICO is similarly valuable in advocating on issues concerning data protection through its membership in the Article 29 Working Party and through its issuance of reports and good practice guides for the public and businesses.[87] However, Lord Justice Leveson found that the ICO did not do enough in educating the press about data protection laws, in particular pinpointing the need for comprehensive good practice guidelines.[88] At the moment, for the internet industry, this work is largely undertaken by nongovernmental organisations (NGOs), such as the excellent work of the Institute for Human Rights and Business and Privacy International.[89] At an internal level, for macro-gatekeepers, this work can be more formalised, with businesses such as Google having a well-developed policy unit (arguably lobbying unit), and for micro-gatekeepers, it can be internalised more intuitively through preparation of annual reports of the company and human rights audits.

There also needs to be awareness of the remedial mechanisms available to consumers who feel they have had their rights infringed. Part of this education will come once we have a better understanding of what these responsibilities are and once we have created a remedial mechanism. But, once this work is done, it is of no use unless the public and businesses are aware of its substance. Such a responsibility will be ongoing for the Commission, particularly in continually educating the public concerning

---

[87] Look at the documents produced by the ICO: www.ico.gov.uk/tools_and_resources/doc ument_library.aspx (last visited 19 June 2014).

[88] See Leveson n. 72, paras. 58–66 (part H). The ICO is drafting such a Code. See Information Commissioner's Office, *Data Protection and the Press – Framework Consultation on Proposed ICO Code of Practice*, at http://ico.org.uk/news/blog/2013/~/media/docu ments/library/Data_Protection/Research_and_reports/framework-consultation-summary -of-responses.pdf (last visited 20 June 2014).

[89] See www.ihrb.org (last visited 27 March 2014) and www.privacyinternational.org (last visited 27 March 2014).

human rights issues that develop and change with technological change. The businesses need to be educated as well. The Private Sector and Human Rights project found that most businesses associate human rights only with their overseas operation, and where focused on at a national level, the issue was treated not as human rights, but as a workplace issue regarding, for example, labour standards.[90]

Part of this educative arm is the Commission and businesses educating themselves on human rights issues. There is a research component to this area that sorely needs attention. This need is particularly acute for the information society where there are so many varied industries intersecting online; thus, tailored solutions and policies are needed. Sweeping up the area of human rights, business and technology into broader areas of corporate governance or human rights is a risk. It might simply regurgitate the facile treatment of the subject thus far, wasting resources and time and bringing us no further towards responsible business treatment of human rights in the technology sector. What is missing from this arena is engagement with the issues in any depth. We can take cues from the Danish Institute for Human Rights[91] in this respect: it has a research department that works in cooperation with academic institutions, as well as a business and human rights project that draws from the work of researchers to develop methodologies to address business issues.[92] However, bear in mind the Danish Institute's scope is much broader than advocated here.

At the base layer of the model is the remedial and rule-making arm of the Commission. This layer applies to all IIGs. A key governance gap identified in my book is the lack of a sufficient remedial mechanism for internet users impacted by the activities of businesses. As shown in Chapters 4 and 5, those whose businesses suffer as a result of inexplicable drops in rankings or whose websites have been blocked for unknown or arguably unjustifiable reasons have had their right to participate in democratic discourse impacted and require access to a forum to resolve the dispute. Moving down the scale to authority gatekeepers, the impact on the right to freedom of expression is just as serious. Users of social networking sites such as Facebook are at the mercy of the business's assessment of what is and is not acceptable speech and the inevitable imperfection in this assessment for a company that receives 2 million

---

[90] Twentyfifty n. 42, pp. 4–5.

[91] See The Danish Institute for Human Rights, www.humanrights.dk/ (last visited 19 June 2014).

[92] See www.humanrightsbusiness.org/ (last visited 19 June 2014).

requests per week for content removal.[93] This mechanism is the bedrock of the Commission's governance framework underpinning any CSR frameworks companies might devise. If instituted properly, the mechanism will allow for escalation of a dispute, with more informal and softer mechanisms to resolve disputes as a first step and with more formalised and stricter enforcement mechanisms as the dispute escalates.[94] It may be that in accessing this forum a complainant is found to have not suffered any free speech infringement, but it is the access to a forum for remediation that is the key to building the much-needed administrative structure of free speech online.

Concerns have been expressed by CSR bodies such as the GNI that remedial mechanisms will cause a deluge of complaints that will tax the resources of the body.[95] These are valid concerns. One option is to build disincentives into the framework to dissuade the casual complainer. First, instituting a formal complaint will require time and effort on the part of the complainant. Second, there should be an initial investigative stage by the Commission to assess the substantiality of a claim to weed out trivial or abusive claims. Such substantiality has found its way into defamation law[96] and can be drawn from to create an initial hurdle for a claim to proceed. A complainant would be able to appeal such a finding, which again would indicate seriousness on the part of a complainant that would weed out some of the more casual complainers. Last, a financial

---

[93] See J. Rosen, 'The delete squad' (29 April 2013), at www.newrepublic.com/article/11304 5/free-speech-internet-silicon-valley-making-rules (last visited 18 June 2014). The examples concerning Facebook are numerous, given the social nature of the space. They include complaints about rape joke groups, anorexia groups and removal of photos of women breastfeeding.

[94] See Ayres and Braithwaite n. 74 enforcement pyramid pp. 35–51. The model proposed here is presented in the opposite manner of the enforcement pyramid, with remedial mechanisms forming the bedrock of the model. However, the remedial mechanism itself draws from the enforcement pyramid.

[95] See discussion of complaints mechanism by Maclay n. 20, pp. 100–101. Amnesty International pulled out of the GNI after viewing the final draft of the principles. It stated, '[f]ollowing careful consideration of these documents Amnesty International has come to the conclusion that, while they represent a degree of progress in responding to human rights concerns, they are not yet strong enough to allow Amnesty International to endorse them': Amnesty International Public Statement, 'Amnesty International involvement with the internet multi stakeholder initiative' (29 October 2008), at www.amnesty.org/ar/library /asset/POL30/009/2008/es/1c327fdf-a67c-11dd-966b-0da92cc4cb95/pol300092008en.pdf (last visited 19 June 2014).

[96] This was initially set down in *Jameel (Yousef)* v. *Dow Jones [2005] EWCA Civ 75*. A similar concept can be seen in the new requirement of serious harm in s. 1(1) of the Defamation Act 2013(2013) c. 26.

disincentive can be built into the framework, such as a financial penalty if the complaint is found to be frivolous or vexatious at the appeals stage.[97] It must also be borne in mind that some of the issues adverted to concerning remedial mechanisms simply reflect the wider problems faced by the legal system, which are then exacerbated when the framework is nonjudicial in nature.[98]

In designing the dispute resolution framework of the Commission, guidance can be sought from the United Kingdom's Nominet Dispute Resolution model,[99] and the World Intellectual Property Organisation Arbitration and Mediation Centre.[100] Suggested procedural steps in a complaint are as follows.[101] First, a complaint is assessed for substantiality, a low-level threshold to weed out trivial or abusive claims. Second, assuming a complaint passes this threshold, the complainant and business will have the option to engage in mediation to resolve the dispute. This author is hesitant to impose mandatory mediation because, in certain circumstances, mediation will quite obviously not be able to resolve the dispute, and then the process becomes a burden on time and money and a simple hurdle to get to the adjudicative process.[102] Third, the complaint would be adjudicated with opportunities for the complainant and business to make representations and hear the case being made in opposition to theirs. One of the failures of the IWF's structure was the lack of transparency concerning the adjudicative process. It purportedly existed, but those embroiled in the dispute had no real access to it.

Fourth, the Commission in adjudicating a case must have the power to award damages to the complainant for a breach of what will be called at this stage 'the rules', or, at minimum, the Commission must have the power to impose a fine on the offending business. The human rights compliance of self-regulatory bodies such as the PCC is in doubt ever

---

[97] The sum could be held as a bond when the initial complaint is launched with the Commission.

[98] See discussion, Joint Committee on Human Rights vol. I n. 40, p. 87.

[99] Nominet's Dispute Resolution Service, at www.nominet.org.uk/disputes/drs/ (last visited 19 June 2014).

[100] World Intellectual Property Organization, Arbitration and Mediation Center, at www.wipo.int/amc/en/index.html (last visited 19 June 2014).

[101] Here, guidance can be sought regarding dispute resolution frameworks such as ICANN's Uniform Domain-Name Dispute-Resolution Policy, at www.icann.org/en/udrp/udrp.htm (last visited 19 June 2014), or Nominet's Dispute Resolution Service n. 95.

[102] Mediation is mandatory for a Nominet dispute, but not for a WIPO dispute.

since *Peck v. United Kingdom*,[103] where the European Court of Human Rights (ECtHR) held that the lack of domestic remedy through the PCC and the predecessors to the Office of Communications (Ofcom), the Broadcasting Standards Council and the Independent Television Commission, breached the right to a remedy under Article 12. Without the legal power to award damages to the complainant, something the Court noted to be different from the power to fine, such bodies did not provide an effective remedy under law.[104] The UK government has somewhat ignored this ruling in its subsequent set-up of Ofcom, limiting its power to the imposition of fines. What we can conclude from this is that the power to fine will make such a body compliant with the views of the UK government, but the power to award damages will be needed to be ECHR compliant; thus, the optimal framework will allow for the awarding of damages. Through the enforcement mechanism, this provides the element of bindingness needed to create legitimacy for the body.[105]

Without, at minimum, the power to fine, the body proposed here would be hamstrung from protecting and promoting digital human rights. This need was recognised in the United Kingdom concerning privacy violations. In the face of a series of egregious breaches of the data protection principles,[106] such as Google gathering personal information from Wi-Fi networks via its Streetview cars,[107] the government recognised the need for the Information Commissioner to have the power to fine organisations.[108] The extent of the fine or damages awarded

---

[103] (2003) 36 EHRR 41. See discussion of significance of the case in H. Fenwick and Gavin Phillipson, *Media Freedom under the Human Rights Act* (Oxford University Press, 2006), pp. 862–71.

[104] *Peck* ibid). The Court clearly noted that the ITC's power to fine did not qualify as an award of damages as required. Also note the finding that the United Kingdom's approach to judicial review was not an effective remedy concerning Convention rights. The bar was so high that no assessment under the ECHR was then possible (i.e., pressing social need, proportionality). Judges must be able to assess for themselves whether there had been a breach of Convention rights. See discussion of this in *R v. Secretary of State for the Home Department, Ex p Daly* [2001] 2 AC 532.

[105] See here discussion of J. Nolan, 'The Corporate Responsibility to Respect Human Rights: Soft Law or Not Law?', in S. Deva and D. Bilchitz (eds.), *Human Rights Obligations of Business: Beyond the Corporate Responsibility to Respect* (Cambridge University Press, 2013), p. 157.

[106] Data Protection Act 1998 c. 29.

[107] See J. Oates, 'ICO reopens Google Street View privacy probe' (25 October 2010), at www .theregister.co.uk/2010/10/25/ico_google_probe/ (last visited 20 June 2014).

[108] Criminal Justice and Immigration Act 2008 c. 4. See discussion: Out-Law.com, 'Information Commissioner gets power to fine for privacy breaches', at www.out-law.com /page-9110 (last visited 20 June 2014).

would depend ultimately on the type of gatekeeper and seriousness of harm on the scale of responsibility discussed earlier. The Commission should also have the power to make orders, although care would have to be taken in defining the extent of this power. Just as Nominet has the power to revoke ownership of a domain name deemed fraudulently or otherwise illegally obtained, the Digital Rights Commission should have the power to, for example, order the removal of URLs from the IWF's blacklist. At its core, it is about creating incentives that make the companies comply with human rights. The e-commerce sector has developed the use of trustmarks or quality labels to indicate, for example, which companies comply with good commercial practices, security standards or dispute resolution mechanisms.[109]

Fifth, access to this remedial framework can be either the first step in the remedial process or the appeal mechanism, although an institution that has properly integrated the Governance Model will have a remedial mechanism in-house. If an institution has a remedial mechanism in-house or through an industry association, this would be the first stop for an individual, but such a decision would be reviewable by the Digital Rights Commission for human rights compliance. If, however, no remedial mechanism exists, as is the case with search engines, then individuals can access the remedial mechanism of the Digital Rights Commission as a first step. The steps in the remedial process are summarised in Figure 6.4.

At an internal level, companies can look to the e-commerce sector, where private dispute resolution frameworks have been functioning for the past fifteen years. Certainly, there is a cleanness to the kinds of disputes managed by the e-commerce sector that do not translate seamlessly to the human rights area, where decisions have to be made about, for example, whether to take down a rape joke group on Facebook.[110] The value from this sector is that there has been a recognition by businesses from the early days of electronic commercial transactions that there needs to be a mechanism to resolve disputes, and it is this recognition that needs to be transferred to these businesses' human rights impact. At

---

[109] P. Cortes and F. E. De la Rosa, 'Building a Global Redress System for Low-Value Cross-Border Disputes', *Intl. & Comp. L.Q.*, 62(2) (2013) 407, pp. 424–25, 433–34.

[110] See initial coverage with L. Davies, 'Facebook refuses to take down rape joke pages' (30 September 2011), at www.theguardian.com/technology/2011/sep/30/facebook-refuses -pull-rape-jokepages (last visited 17 June 2014), then the change in policy in M. Bennett-Smith, 'Facebook vows to crack down on rape joke pages after successful protest, boycott' (29 May 2013), at www.huffingtonpost.com/2013/05/29/facebook-rape-jokes-pro test_n_3349319.html (last visited 17 June 2014).

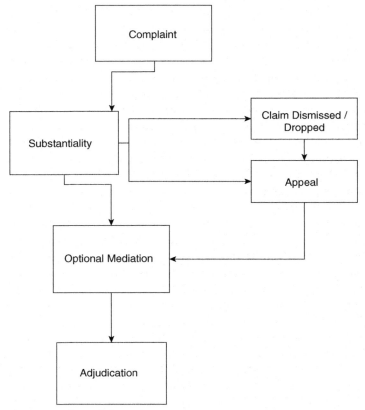

**Figure 6.4.** Remedial process.

the moment, the United Nations Commission for International Trade Law (UNCITRAL) is finalising rules on Online Dispute Resolution for Cross-border Electronic Transactions,[111] but they do not provide any guidance to human rights disputes. The focus appears to be quite narrow, focusing on high-volume, low-value cross-border disputes, including a proposal to limit the scope to simple fact-based claims.[112]

Within the firm, guidance can be sought from dispute resolution models such as eBay's resolution centre and use of mediator

---

[111] See www.uncitral.org/uncitral/commission/working_groups/3Online_Dispute_Resolu tion.html (last visited 27 March 2014).

[112] See Cortes and De la Rosa n. 109. See also 'Proposal for a Directive on Alternative Dispute Resolution for Consumer Disputes', *COM*(2011) 793 final.

Squaretrade or Amazon's Buyer Dispute Programme. The formality of the framework will depend on the type of gatekeeper involved, although even micro-gatekeepers with minimal impact must have in place some method for hearing complaints and resolving disputes. The Guiding Principles note the value of such mechanisms in not only resolving disputes, but also in pinpointing and resolving human rights issues before they escalate. The Office of the High Commissioner of Human Rights interprets the Guiding Principles as being open-ended as to the process of remediation, but that, in many instances, the most effective process is the more formalised operational-level grievance mechanism – much as set out earlier – in which 'an individual can raise concerns about the impact an enterprise has on them'.[113] The need for the Commission detailed herein to facilitate an understanding of what this means is evident because the enterprise might not always be the subject of the complaint, but be instead the adjudicator.

The question is then the system of rules against which institutions are judged. A generalised code concerning the duty of companies to respect human rights against principles from the UDHR, as seen in the UN Global Compact and the Guiding Principles, is a necessary if generalised first step. This initial commitment is important to spell out for companies their duty to respect human rights, and it locates the source of duties for companies. These rules accompany the remedial mechanism in the base layer of the corporate governance model because they are applicable to all IIGs and draw from such international instruments 'transnational stamp of legitimacy'.[114] A body such as the IWF, for example, could not only turn to the Commission in its advisory role, but could act as partner with the Commission in carrying out the dispute resolution aspect of the IWF's operation. This is when the work of the second layer of governance is engaged, as policies specific to the various ICTs can be crafted here.

This second layer, the 'corporate support' layer, is the most promising yet complicated layer of the corporate governance model because it joins the legal and extralegal arms together. This layer includes formalised policies and codes, whether drafted by the Commission or external to the Commission itself but approved by the Commission. It also includes auditing and advisory services, issuances of opinions and help in the form

---

[113] United Nations Office of the High Commissioner for Human Rights, *The Corporate Responsibility to Respect Human Rights: An Interpretive Guide* (2012), section c, Q70.

[114] M. Rundle and M. Birdling, 'Filtering and the International System: A Question of Commitment', in R. Deibert et al. (eds.), *Access Denied: The Practice and Policy of Global Internet Filtering* (MIT Press, 2008), p. 97.

of assessment tools. Here you see the link between the more formalised role of the Commission applying the Governance Model and the operational level application of the model by businesses. For example, an advisory by such a body that it considers the IWF to be a public authority for the purposes of the HRA would have been helpful, if anything, to spur the body to revisit its own governance structure. With regard to the GNI, for example, its framework of principles can form the basis against which a GNI member might be reviewed by the Commission.[115] In addition, this layer becomes the arena for taking the ideas from the research and education layer above and operationalising them. This might be in the form of policies for a particular industry or toolkits for businesses to engage in human rights risk assessments.

Two duties emerge as key for this second layer. First, for a specific industry such as search engines or ISPs, or for specific human rights such as privacy, a coherent package should be available, with policies against which a company will be judged laid clear in the form of codes of practice (internal or industry) and toolkits and guidance mechanisms to help companies operationalise these duties to prevent abuses of rights. This is the legal and extralegal arms working together in its purest form. As was evident in the case studies, finding common ground with these contentious disputes is not easy nor always possible, but by focusing on a package of responsive strategies to different behaviours, complementarity can be identified and allowances made for undefined outcomes. Second, the Commission must have the capacity to independently audit such companies for their human rights compliance as a step to prevent human rights abuses or, at minimum, prevent the escalation of abuses, a role that the Information Commissioner's Office has evolved into.[116] Related to this, the Commission must act as a helpline to companies, providing advice where they are uncertain of how to handle a given situation.

The value in this approach is that it encourages and brings within its ambit CSR codes, which run alongside it. Such codes can help inform the policies of the Commission, and, likewise, the Commission's work can

---

[115] If there are concerns that judging a company on the basis of rules created by another body is beyond such a body's remit, these voluntary rules form the basis of judgments by courts for breach of contract or standards of care in tort and likewise can form the basis of human rights judgments of such a commission.

[116] The ICO's responsibilities now include conducting audits under the Privacy and Electronic Communications Regulations 2003 and the Environmental Information Regulations 2004.

help frame the legitimacy and content of such codes. As a helpline, such a service is familiar to such bodies as law societies, which have advisory services for lawyers concerned about an ethical dilemma they are facing with a client. Likewise, a company such as Google can seek out the advice of such a Commission on how to handle a pseudo-judicial-type decision it is forced to make in the United Kingdom. This would not only help Google, but would also help a body such as the Commission in gathering information that would feed its policy development role.

One of the key problems faced by companies is a failure to recognise what is and what is not a human rights issue. This is particularly so for free speech. Google is one of the key participants in the GNI, yet, as we have seen, even it fails to recognise the free speech significance of its core business, arguing rather the opposite in cases such as *Search King Inc.* v. *Google Technology, Inc.*,[117] that the rankings are the search providers free speech right. This principle was confirmed in *Zhang* v. *Baidu.com*.[118] A body such as the one being suggested here is needed to identify those areas in which IIGs are responsible for human rights, to predict future areas of human rights significance and thereby build human rights into technological design and policy. We are in the midst of a human rights explosion in the arena of mobile telephony, and such a body could work with industry at the ground level to define the contours of their human rights responsibilities. Thus, such a body would not only serve a remedial role for human rights abuses, but would also help to guide companies in avoiding abuses in the first place.[119] In this role, the Commission pushes CSR principles outside the law and also discharges the state's duty to protect free speech at the same time.

The Governance Model also becomes a lens through which a company can identify gaps in its human rights governance. In looking at the macro-gatekeepers examined in the case studies, one observes that the IWF, for example, has an insufficient remedial arm and engages in some research and education, but, until the human rights audit in 2013, there was minimal engagement with the middle layer of the Governance Model. By developing work in this area, it would be better positioned to translate work on research and education into corporate support, and this in turn would inform a more robust grievance mechanism. In the case of search engines such as Google, one can see that the work of the

---

[117] (2003) Case No. CIV-02–1457-M (W.D.Okla.).     [118] 11 Civ. 3388 (JMF).
[119] Ruggie suggests this type of thing internal to companies, saying it allows one to address problems earlier, before things escalate: Ruggie n. 37, p. 25.

GNI engages all elements of this Governance Model. However, the informal nature of Google's governance structure means that, at an internal level, Google engages minimally with the Model. This shows a need to embed human rights governance into its operational structure in a way it has not yet done. The use of this Model in this fashion is not limited to macro-gatekeepers. It can be applied to gatekeepers further down the scale of responsibility, such as social networking providers, which the reader will recall from Chapter 2 are authority gatekeepers because their impact on democratic culture is significant, but their use is not an inevitable aspect of using the internet.[120] Having examined the Governance Model, the pressing question that emerges is where to house the external arm of this governance model, the proposed Digital Rights Commission.

### 6.2.3.  The need for a new commission

As Eve Darian-Smith and Colin Scott state, 'growing nonstate regulatory power requires either an acceptance of diminished rights or the elaboration of a new rights narrative which more effectively embraces private power'.[121] As we have seen in this book, reliance on CSR codes has often differed little from an acceptance of diminished rights. This risks the internet's democratic potential. We need a self-standing Digital Rights Commission to set the framework of a new rights narrative for ICTs; as will be shown, this is too important and too cross-cutting to be slotted into the machinery of existing bodies.

We must, however, look more closely to these bodies to identify why they are of limited appeal to satisfy the vision articulated here. Looking at the United Kingdom, the technical particularities of this industry compel the need for something specialised, which presents difficulties from the outset as to the appropriateness of looking to existing regulatory bodies, such as the ICO, Ofcom, the EHRC or the OECD NCP in the UK Department for Business, Innovation and Skills (BIS). Their mandates are too broad-based to handle the complexity of what is going on here without, at minimum, the creation of a subcommission or executive agency to handle it. The EHRC is a specialist in human rights without

---

[120]  For a discussion of this, see my slides from a presentation at a conference on The Legal Challenges of Social Media to Freedom of Expression at the University of Leicester in December 2013: www.laidlaw.eu/2014/06/what-is-a-joke-the-role-of-social-media-provid ers-in-regulating-speech/ (last visited 20 June 2014).

[121]  E. Darian-Smith and C. Scott, 'Regulation and Human Rights in Socio-Legal Scholarship', *Law and Policy*, 31(3) (2009) 271, p. 276.

knowledge specific to the ICT industry, whereas Ofcom is a specialist in media and new media with no human rights specialism, and BIS specialises in business and growth, not human rights or ICTs. The ICO would seem the natural choice, given the characteristics sought in this Commission; however, the ICO has struggled to handle its expanding remit as is and is focused more properly on data protection and data access issues than on freedom of expression. What is needed is a realignment of thinking on the part of government concerning the importance of the internet to democratic discourse through the creation of a Commission aimed at specialising in all three: business, human rights and ICTs. It is this lacuna in governance that has been the main theme running through this book, one that the state has a duty to fill.

First, the power to fine or award damages identified as necessary in the base layer of the governance model dismisses BIS and the OECD NCP from consideration. The idea of a fine requires that something is identified as prohibited. This would require either (a) laws setting down the act as prohibited or (b) voluntary agreement of the members that they be subject to fines. Thus, a body such as Ofcom finds authority to fine under Section 237 of the Communications Act.[122] The press, on the other hand, as members of the PCC, did not agree to be fined for a breach of the Code of Practice.[123] The new regulator established by Royal Charter has the power to fine, and the money thus collected will be reinvested in the arbitration unit to be set up to address smaller libel and privacy claims.[124] The model proposed here is not entirely voluntary, and thus we cannot rely on agreement by businesses to be fined: we are reliant on laws setting down the power to fine. In this case, legislative enactment of this duty on the body would be necessary.

Regardless, BIS is ill-suited to take on the role envisioned here. BIS only serves an information and guidance role, thus its power to develop policies binding on businesses and to offer remediation services is more limited. If BIS were found to be the proper home for this Commission, it should be as an Executive Agency to BIS akin to the setup of the Intellectual Property Office.[125] In BIS's capacity as the NCP for the

---

[122] 2003 c. 21. See also Ofcom, 'Penalty guidelines', at www.ofcom.org.uk/codes_guidelines /penalty (last visited 19 June 2014).
[123] The PCC n. 71.
[124] Royal Charter on Self-Regulation of the Press, at www.gov.uk/government/uploads/sys tem/uploads/attachment_data/file/254116/Final_Royal_Charter_25_October_2013_clean __Final_.pdf (last visited 20 June 2014).
[125] See www.ipo.gov.uk/about/whatwedo.htm (last visited 20 June 2014).

OECD Guidelines, there is more promise, but the NCP role in the United Kingdom is still relatively toothless. The UK NCP was reformed in 2006 after complaints about its operation and structure, but its lack of remedial powers against companies and for victims continues to be a pressing problem.[126] The reader will recall the example given in Chapter 3 concerning the investigation into Vedanta Plc regarding its mining operations in Orissa, India. Vedanta simply refused to participate in the mediation, and the UK NCP did not have any powers to compel participation beyond expressing disappointment.[127]

In 2007, Global Witness accused Afrimex of financing armed conflict in the Democratic Republic of Congo (DRC) by paying tax to a rebel group RCD-Goma, as well as by buying minerals from mines with horrific working conditions. The UK NCP attempted to mediate a solution, but Afrimex pulled out of the process and refused to continue to cooperate. The NCP then engaged in its own investigation, concluding that Afrimex was indeed supporting armed conflict and failed to implement supply chain due diligence regarding working conditions. Afrimex later stated that it no longer trades minerals from the DRC. Global Witness argued, 'the Afrimex case highlights a key problem: when an NCP issues recommendations to a company that has breached the Guidelines, the NCP's inability or unwillingness to monitor adherence allows companies simply to ignore the statement and continue business as usual with absolutely no consequences'.[128] Too much work would be needed to flesh out the NCP role to take on what is needed for the Commission envisioned here.

The ICO is equally problematic, at least in its current form in the United Kingdom. The ICOs of other countries, such as Canada, are more comfortable with the role of investigator and advocate as set out in the top layer of the model and thus better suited to taking on the role envisioned by the body proposed here.[129] Canada's model is not

---

[126] Joint Committee on Human Rights vol. I n. 40, pp. 28–29. Other complaints were that the UK NCP was not independent from government and there was a lack of sufficient guidance for companies on the standards they were to meet: ibid., p. 28.

[127] Ibid., pp. 28–29.

[128] OECD Watch, *10 Years On: Assessing the Contribution of the OECD Guidelines for Multinational Enterprises to Responsible Business Conduct*, p. 37.

[129] See The Office of the Information Commissioner of Canada, at www.oic-ci.gc.ca/eng/ (last visited 20 June 2014). It was an investigation of the Canadian Information Commissioner that revealed the data breach by Google concerning its Streetview cars: J. Halliday, 'Google Street View broke Canada's privacy law with Wi-Fi capture' (20 October 2010), at www.guardian.co.uk/technology/2010/oct/19/google-street-view-privacy-canada (last visited 20 June 2014).

advocated as the ideal, however, because the private-sector privacy leg-islation in Canada provides weak enforcement power for the Office of the Privacy Commissioner.[130] With regard to the United Kingdom, the ICO is a creature of statute, and its focus thus far, as indicated earlier, is narrowly on issues of data protection and data access. It would have difficulty accommodating the more amorphous issues pertaining to free-dom of expression on the internet. The history of the ICO dates to 1984, with the enactment of the Data Protection Act and its eight principles of good practice. A Data Protection Register was created to oversee the Act and manage registration of data controllers.[131] Over the years, its role has expanded. It fields questions and complaints, educates the public and businesses, participates in policy discussions and now can impose sub-stantial fines.[132] It took on its current form as ICO in 2000, when it was tasked with also overseeing the Freedom of Information Act, and its remit was further expanded to cover the Privacy and Electronic Communications Regulations 2003,[133] the Environmental Information Regulations 2004[134] and the INSPIRE Regulations 2009.[135]

As it stands, the ICO is a cautionary tale of what can go wrong with the type of model proposed here. Bodies such as Privacy International are deeply critical of the ICO for being toothless and failing to engage properly in the advocacy work it purports to undertake, with the effect of diverting attention away from important matters of privacy.[136] This is illustrated in the Google Streetview case discussed briefly earlier, in which Google's Streetview cars collected sensitive personal information includ-ing emails, passwords and URLs.[137] The ICO's initial position was that it

---

[130] Canada's former Privacy Commissioner, Jennifer Stoddart, wrote a report advocating for reform of the Personal Information Protection and Electronic Documents Act (PIPEDA) S.C. 2000, c. 5. She called for greater enforcement power of PIPEDA, amongst other recommendations: Office of the Privacy Commissioner, 'The case for reforming the Personal Information Protection and Electronic Documents Act' (May 2013), at https://www.priv.gc.ca/parl/2013/pipeda_r_201305_e.pdf (last visited 21 November 2014).

[131] See ICO n. 66.

[132] J. Halliday, 'Google Street View: information commissioner shackled by Data Protection Act' (28 October 2010), at www.guardian.co.uk/technology/2010/oct/28/google-street -view-information-commissioner (last visited 20 June 2014).

[133] No. 2426.    [134] No. 3391    [135] No. 3157.

[136] Privacy International, 'Civil liberties groups say UK Information Commissioner's Office is not "fit for purpose"' (3 November 2010), at www.privacyinternational.org/article/civil -liberties-groups-say-uk-information-commissioner%E2%80%99s-office-not-fit-purpose (last visited 23 September 2011); Privacy International, 'Cultural dysfunction', at www .privacyinternational.org/reports/the-uk-information-commissioners-office-lets-bury -our-bad-news-on-a-busy-news-day/cultural (last visited 20 June 2014).

[137] Halliday n. 130.

was not a breach of the Data Protection Act, which led the Metropolitan Police to decide to stop investigating the matter. The ICO's view was hasty and wrong, and it was forced to reverse its position later. The ICO further cemented the weakness of its bite, even when exercised, when it imposed a flimsy fine of £1000 on Andrew Crossley, the sole operator of ACS: Law, for the leaking of the personal information of thousands of file sharers.[138] The most thoughtful and rigorous analysis of the ICO is by Lord Justice Leveson, although the ICO was not the focus of the inquiry. He recommended that the ICO be reconstituted as a Commission led by a Board of Commissioners and with expanded duties and powers,[139] a proposal the Justice Committee has recommended that the government reject.[140] At the time of writing, the government is considering the recommendations of Leveson and the Justice Committee on 'the future power, governance and accountability arrangements of the ICO'.[141] If reconstituted as a Commission, then the ICO may be a worthwhile body to explore to incorporate the Governance Model proposed here. However, as it stands, the ICO has a lot of work sorting out its current role concerning data protection and privacy before expanding to accommodate what is needed here.[142]

The EHRC has more promise, but ultimately only serves to show the importance of a self-standing Digital Rights Commission. It is the United

---

[138] Information Commissioner's Office News Release, 'ICO fines former ACS Law boss for lax IT security', at www.ico.gov.uk/~/media/documents/pressreleases/2011/monetary _penalty_acslaw_news_release_20110510.ashx (last visited 19 June 2014). The reason for the decision to award such a low fine was that ACS: Law ceased trading, but this arguably is now the route businesses like ACS: Law will take when staring down the pipe at a hefty fine from the ICO.

[139] Leveson n. 72, Part H, chapter six, para. 4.9. For ICO response to Leveson inquiry, see http://ico.org.uk/news/~/media/documents/consultation_responses/ico_response_to _leveson_report_012013.ashx (last visited 2 April 2014). For an excellent discussion of this, see House of Commons, Justice Committee, *The Functions, Powers and Resources of the Information Commissioner, Ninth Report of Session 2012–13* (12 March 2013), at www.publications.parliament.uk/pa/cm201213/cmselect/cmjust/962/962.pdf (last visited 2 April 2014).

[140] Ibid.

[141] Rt Hon Lord McNally (letter), *The Functions, Powers and Resources of the Information Commissioner: Government Response to the Committee's Ninth Report of Session 2012–13* (30 June 2013), www.publications.parliament.uk/pa/cm201314/cmselect/cmjust/560/560 04.htm (last visited 2 April 2014).

[142] Furthermore, the government in rejecting and reconstituting it as a Commission also discussed the financial pressure the ICO is under with an ever-expanding remit, making it difficult to expand its remit as it is currently modelled to govern other human rights issues: n. 134.

Kingdom's National Human Rights Institution (NHRI). Ruggie has identified NHRIs as promising bodies for the implementation of his Protect, Respect, Remedy framework, describing NHRIs as potential 'lynchpins' in the system of grievance mechanisms for companies and human rights because they can provide 'culturally appropriate, accessible, and expeditious' remedies, and, when they can't, they can provide information.[143] Although the idea of NHRIs goes back to period just after the Second World War and the adoption of the UDHR in 1948,[144] they gained a focal point with the drafting of the UN Paris Principles,[145] a set of guidelines for local human rights institutions that was adopted by the UN General Assembly in 1993.[146] The same year, at the Second International Conference, the International Coordinating Committee of NHRIS (ICC) was created to coordinate the activities of NHRIs and created a subcommittee to accredit NHRIs that complied with the Paris Principles. Currently, seventy NHRIs are accredited with A status, including the United Kingdom's EHRC.[147]

The EHRC is the product of legislative enactment through the Equality Act 2006. It took over the Commission for Racial Equality, the Equal Opportunities Commission and the Disability Commission.[148] Due to its history, it is more deeply rooted in issues of equality than in rights such as freedom of expression or privacy, a problem that persists today and is problematic to tasking the body with the commission work proposed here. The EHRC has the scope to do the work articulated in this chapter by its generalised mandate to address human rights in the United Kingdom as the anointed NHRI. The EHRC, however, has been quite timid in the few years since its creation in expanding beyond its focus on equality and yet has managed to be plagued by issues of in-fighting, with six commissioners resigning in 2009.[149]

---

[143] Ruggie (2008) n. 32, p. 25.

[144] See B. G. Ramcharan (ed.), *The Protection Role of National Human Rights Institutions* (Leiden: Martinus Nijhoff Publishers, 2005), introduction.

[145] Principles Relating to the Status of National Institutions (The Paris Principles), at www.ohchr.org/EN/ProfessionalInterest/Pages/StatusOfNationalInstitutions.aspx (last visited 19 June 2014).

[146] United Nations General Assembly, National institutions for the promotion and protection of human rights, GA Res. *48/134 of 20 December 1993*, paras. 11–12.

[147] See Office of the High Commissioner for Human Rights, *Chart of the Status of National Institutions (as of 28 January 2014)*, at www.ohchr.org/Documents/Countries/NHRI/Chart_Status_NIs.pdf (last visited 4 April 2014).

[148] See discussion, Joint Committee on Human Rights, *Equality and Human Rights Commission* (Thirteenth Report of Session 2009–10), p. 8.

[149] See discussion ibid., starting at p. 15.

Academics such as Francesca Klug have argued that, at a most basic level, the EHRC is simply 'not providing us with a credible vision of what human rights are'.[150] Whereas there is recognition of the need for institutional stability by the creation of such a Commission, many question whether the EHRC is doing much to further a human rights culture in Britain.[151]

With regard to the issue of business and human rights, the EHRC has been even more timid. In the Joint Commission hearings, the EHRC was cautious about assuming additional responsibilities, stating that it was new and 'still finding its feet' concerning business and human rights.[152] Furthermore, the EHRC's work in the private sector has been focused, once again, primarily on issues of equality, specifically elimination of discrimination and achieving equality in the workplace,[153] not on its broader mandate of human rights. It identified business and human rights as a commitment in its 2009–2012 action plan[154] but framed it unhelpfully as 'we will build business and public awareness of the key human rights issues in the private sector'.[155] However, since 2012, the EHRC has started to pay closer attention to business and human rights matters. This is at a time when the business and human rights debate has received greater attention in the press and by government.[156] Its 2012–2015 action plan focuses on smaller businesses and the provision of good practice and standards.[157] For example, in March 2013, it published a guide for small businesses on human rights.[158]

As it stands, the EHRC is a disappointment. It would require a much larger undertaking on the part of the EHRC to do what it would need to in order to satisfy the requirements of the body proposed here.[159] Given

---

[150] Ibid., p. 11.

[151] To see more, see the oral and written evidence available at Joint Committee on Human Rights vol. II n. 38.

[152] Joint Committee on Human Rights vol. I n. 40, p. 83.

[153] Equality and Human Rights Commission, Submission to the 10th International Conference of NHRIs (Session 6 on 9 October 2010), *The Corporate Responsibility to Respect Human Rights*, p. 3.

[154] Joint Committee on Human Rights vol. I n. 40, pp. 83–84.

[155] Joint Committee on Human Rights n. 148, p. 13.    [156] See UK government n. 77.

[157] Equality and Human Rights Commission, *Strategic Plan 2012-2015*, at www.equalityhumanrights.com/about-us/about-commission/our-vision-and-mission/strategic-plan-2012-2015 (last visited 19 June 2014).

[158] Equality and Human Rights Commission n. 77.

[159] Note that if the EHRC is the body tasked with the role set out here, then guidance can be sought from NRHIs like Denmark's Danish Institute for Human Rights, which has an education and research mandate as well. With regard to the private sector, it has an HR

that the EHRC's budget has fallen from £70 million in 2007 to £26.8 million by the end of 2015,[160] the EHRC is challenged in fulfilling its current remit, a matter that has led it to refocus on its enabling role of rights and on fewer but high-impact activities.[161] Many of the issues examined in this book would take the back seat to what are seen at present by the EHRC as more pressing human rights issues, and it is questionable whether the Governance Model can be strengthened as needed, in particular with reference to the remedial role sought by the Model, not to mention the cash infusion required.

The framework proposed is much more targeted than the current broad-strokes approach of the EHRC, so without significant changes to the EHRC, it seems ill-fitting. Rather, the ICO is better placed to address wider issues of rights in the information society, particularly if the government elects to reconstitute it as a Commission. What is missing concerning business and human rights in the digital age is not wider commitments to human rights, but operationalisation of these commit-ments. Thus, a more targeted regulatory body such as Ofcom might seem better suited to this task. However, this is also the weakness of Ofcom, and ultimately its downfall because its targeted, regulatory focus comes without a wider human rights remit. This helps identify what is so meaningful about the corporate governance model proposed. What the Digital Rights Commission offers is an avenue for the state to fulfil its duty to protect human rights and, through this frame, businesses' duty to respect human rights.

Ofcom is the United Kingdom's communications regulator, regulating 'TV and radio sectors, fixed line telecoms and mobiles, and the airwaves over which wireless devices operate'.[162] It is a creature of statute; its remit, duties and responsibilities are set out in the Communications Act 2003.[163] Under the Act, its principal duties are to further the interests of citizens concerning communications matters and further the interests of consumers through promotion of competition in the marketplace.[164] There has been, unsurprisingly, tension between these two duties.[165] Its remit has been legislatively expanded since then, for example, to address

---

programme with tools and consultancy services on offer to businesses to help them with HR impact assessments and other strategic advice.
[160] ECHR Strategic Plan n. 157, p. 6, para. 6.    [161] Ibid.
[162] See www.ofcom.org.uk/about/what-is-ofcom/ (last visited 19 June 2014).
[163] Ofcom was established as a body corporate by the Communications Act 2002 c. 11.
[164] Ibid., s. 3.    [165] A case study by T. Prosser n. 54, chapter eight, examines this tension.

the framework for handling illegal file sharers by ISPs.[166] It has been reported that it has more than 263 different statutory duties.[167] Thus, there is a line of progressive expansion that a human rights commission can latch onto if the government sees fit.

Ofcom has been quite a controversial regulator in its few short years of service.[168] Putting aside such matters, Ofcom can be seen to engage all three layers of the Governance Model, although it is weak at the middle layer. As the United Kingdom's communications regulator with the power to receive and investigate complaints, resolve disputes, revoke licenses and fine businesses, it engages the base layer. Its consultation work with industry engages the middle layer, such as its Draft Code of Practice for file sharing. However, it goes no further to engage the other criteria of the middle layer identified earlier. Ofcom engages the top-layer education, policy and research arm through its extensive research and consultation work.

The difficulty with Ofcom is that its ethos is simply at odds with a human rights-driven framework. Its regulatory principles are tailored to minimal intervention and support of free market principles. For example, it cites as one of its regulatory principles, 'Ofcom will intervene when there is a specific statutory duty to work towards a public policy goal which markets alone cannot achieve'.[169] Its principles of intervention align with the generally accepted principles of regulatory regimes – principles advocated here – specifically principles of proportionality, consistency, accountability and transparency.[170] In this respect, Ofcom has more clarity than the human rights-based bodies discussed earlier concerning how to regulate. Since the remedial regime forms the core base of the corporate governance model, knowledge and leadership on this aspect is crucial.

Ofcom does not operate divorced from human rights consideration. It has incorporated human rights principles into its operation in order to

---

[166] Digital Economy Act 2010 c. 24. Under the DEA, Ofcom was given duties to draft and enforce a code of practice. See the Draft Code here, although implementation is delayed: 'Online Infringement of Copyright and the Digital Economy Act 2010: Draft Initial Obligations Code', at http://stakeholders.ofcom.org.uk/binaries/consultations/copyright -infringement/summary/condoc.pdf (last visited 19 June 2014).

[167] Prosser n. 57, p. 158.

[168] For a history of the creation of Ofcom, see P. Smith, 'The Politics of UK Television Policy: The Making of Ofcom', *Media Culture & Society*, 28(6) (2006) 929.

[169] See www.ofcom.org.uk/about/what-is-ofcom/statutory-duties-and-regulatory-princi ples/ (last visited 19 June 2014).

[170] Ibid.

fulfil its duty to further the interests of citizens. For example, the revision of the Broadcast Code in 2004–2005 included reference to the right to free speech and privacy.[171] Human rights can be seen to infiltrate Section 2 on harm and offence, in particular the guidance on taking into account the context of a broadcast, such as the time of day it was broadcast, the service it was on, the programmes before and after and the chance of stumbling on the material unaware.[172] These incorporate notions of minimal interference and proportionality, as seen in Article 10. However, Ofcom is not a human rights specialist, and the risk is that human rights concerns would be minimised in the face of technical and logistical issues that draw more readily on its expertise. There is a risk that human rights would be turned into a mere regulatory issue, one to be codified and applied, which would either overregulate business on terms more akin to the state or underregulate business and leave the lacuna in the law unfilled. The soft law of corporate governance is crucial to engender human rights commitments by business and instigate a cultural shift, which a regulator such as Ofcom, strictly speaking, cannot do.

The examination of these four bodies shows the need to further explore the viability of an independent Digital Rights Commission. Ofcom is far too regulatory in its orientation to take on a corporate governance role, and BIS and the ICO cannot provide the strength of structure proposed for this Commission. The EHRC or a subcommission thereof is struggling to find its footing at a time when its leadership in building a human rights culture in Britain is desperately needed. Something self-standing is potentially the only way through the intractability of this dilemma. An examination of these existing bodies brings home the importance of facilitating a human rights culture both online and off, and a new Commission built around the Governance Model identified herein is one way to potentially achieve this goal.

## 6.3. Conclusion

It seems almost trite to proclaim that the internet's democratic potential is dependent on a system of free expression. Social networking sites such

---

[171] Prosser n. 57, p. 165. See Ofcom, 'Citizens, communications and convergence' (2008), at http://stakeholders.ofcom.org.uk/binaries/consultations/citizens/summary/discussion paper.pdf (last visited 20 June 2014) for a discussion of its role in furthering the interests of citizens.

[172] Broadcasting code, at http://stakeholders.ofcom.org.uk/broadcasting/broadcast-codes /broadcast-code/harmoffence/ (last visited 2 April 2014).

as Twitter and Facebook have played important roles in protests across the world, spreading information and mobilising participants.[173] In the case of the protests in Africa and the Middle East, governments, seeing the power internet communications were enabling, sought to block access to mobile and internet services.[174] This shows both the democratising potential of internet-empowered communications and the susceptibility to control that the networks face. Although we may dismiss these issues as singular to historically human rights-oppressive regimes, the struggle for online freedoms is a pressing fight in the Western World as well. It is just taking place more insidiously and quietly in the private sphere, dressed in the language of freedom – free market, free speech and freedom of choice.

The internet is the conduit for communication in the digital age, making it the heart of any system of free expression. The problem is that digitisation has fractured the system, separating the legal system of free expression from the experience. This gap has been filled by CSR mostly in the form of encouragement by government of voluntary codes or, in the case of the IWF, the formalisation of a corporate governance framework to the point that the HRA directly applies. Both approaches have been insufficient for the protection of freedom of expression online and have differed little from an acceptance of diminished rights in cyberspace. In the case of search engines, the complicated and conflicting regulatory environment has meant that free speech, when it is engaged through CSR, has been informal and indirect, and the core of what search engines do, namely, indexing and ranking, has been overlooked. In the case of the IWF, CSR historically was a linguistic tool obscuring its public authority status.

What is needed to mend the fracture is to focus on the administrative structure of speech protection. The structure needed is particular to the information society and the concerns posed by digitisation, and the only way through this minefield is through a partnership between business and government. Let us be clear, however: the argument of this book is that governments are very much tasked with leading this project, and, in the case of the United Kingdom, the government has wholly neglected its positive human rights obligations to further a free speech culture by its laissez-faire approach. The government does not relinquish its

---

[173] See discussion in Chapter 1, Section 1.3.

[174] In January 2011, during the Egyptian protests, Google traffic reflected what was being reported: that internet access was being blocked in Egypt: Google, 'Transparency report', at www.google.com/transparencyreport/traffic/ (last visited 20 June 2014).

obligations under international human rights just because it contracts or legislates the obligation to business.[175] We need government to be involved in creating a governance framework at a national level because, in the end, the experience of a system of freedom of expression is localised.

The task in a dynamic and multinodal regulatory environment such as the internet is to link the various approaches to regulation in ways that are complementary, mutually reinforcing and responsive. This is particularly challenging for establishing and sustaining human rights standards. This book showed two ways in which this can be facilitated: a common policy framework to address human rights issues and complementary dispute resolution mechanisms. What is needed is a governance model that focuses on the administration of free speech, whereby the processes are well defined but allow for open and undefined outcomes. It is suggested that this can be achieved with the Governance Model outlined in this chapter. It has both an external and internal arm: external in creating an independent body in the form of the Digital Rights Commission and internal by integrating the Governance Model into an IIG's operational structure. This allows a state to discharge its human rights duties whilst providing a blueprint for businesses to fulfil their corporate responsibility respect. The unifying aspect between the external and internal arms is the model itself. This three-layered model creates a framework of research, education and policy underpinned by a regulatory remedial mechanism. The goal of this model is to facilitate work between the legal and extralegal dimensions of the human rights problems engaged online.

---

[175] Ruggie (2011) n. 37, p. 9.

# CONCLUDING REMARKS

When I started this project years ago the subject of human rights and the internet was still in its infancy, and it was at times through vision more than example that its potential as a democratising force was articulated. Questions about corporate social responsibility (CSR) of internet companies were even further removed from public concern, particularly in the United Kingdom. Now, the subject matter has come of age. Scandals surrounding the mass surveillance by governments using data gathered and shared by companies, the role of technology in facilitating and hindering protests and management of social networking for issues of offensiveness (such as rape joke groups on Facebook) and abuse (such as cyberbullying) have served to draw attention to the critical role private companies play in facilitating or hindering human rights online.

Since 2010, we have seen a paradigm shift at an international level in the recognition of human rights in cyberspace. As this book has described, access to the internet as a fundamental right received the United Nations (UN) stamp of approval in a report by Frank La Rue, the Special Rapporteur on the promotion and protection of the right to freedom of opinion and expression.[1] In 2012, the UN Human Rights Council passed a resolution affirming internet freedom as a basic human right, in particular the right to freedom of expression.[2] At a European level, we have seen the Court of Justice of the European Union and the European Court of Human Rights issue judgments with strong rights-based arguments directed at the activities of information and

---

[1] Report of the special rapporteur on the promotion and protection of the right to freedom of expression, Frank La Rue to the United Nations General Assembly, 16 May 2011, at http://www2.ohchr.org/english/bodies/hrcouncil/docs/17session/A.HRC.17.27_en.pdf (last visited 20 June 2014).

[2] UN Human Rights Council A/HRC/20/L.13, at www.regeringen.se/content/1/c6/19/64/51 /6999c512.pdf (last visited 16 June 2014).

communication technologies (ICT) companies. This can be seen in cases such as *Scarlet* v. *SABAM*[3] followed by *Sabam* v. *Netlog*[4] regarding internet service provider (ISP) filtering, *Ahmet Yildirim* v. *Turkey*[5] regarding hosts and *SL, Google Inc.* v. *Agencia Espanola de Proteccion de Datos, Marios Costeja Gonzalez*[6] regarding a right to be forgotten on search engines.

At the same time, the business and human rights agenda has been a focal point of international governance discussions, most importantly with the work of John Ruggie in drafting the United Nations Guiding Principles.[7] They were endorsed by the UN in 2011 and have been widely praised by governments, businesses and nongovernmental organisations (NGOs). They have been incorporated into many agendas on CSR, as seen in Europe[8] and the United Kingdom,[9] and have formed the basis of industry CSR codes and guides, such as the European Commission Guidance for ICTs[10] and the Global Network Initiative.[11] The discussion, however, is far from over. There continue to be calls for a treaty-based governance regime for the human rights obligations of businesses; the Human Rights Council has established a working group to negotiate such a treaty,[12] but this book has shown the limited appeal of such a model for the ICT industry.

In the arena of internet regulation, understanding of cyberspace regulation has developed significantly since the early conception of the

---

[3] *Scarlet Extended SA* v. *Société belge des auteurs, compositeurs et éditeurs SCRL* (2011) Case C-70/10.

[4] *Belgische Vereniging van Auteurs, Componisten en Uitgevers CVBA (SABAM)* v. *Netlog NV* (2012), Case C-360/10.

[5] *Application no. 3111/10* (18 December 2012). [6] Case C-131/12 (2014).

[7] J. Ruggie, 'Guiding principles on business and human rights: implementing the United Nations "protect, respect and remedy" framework' (March 2011), at www.business-hu manrights.org/media/documents/ruggie/ruggie-guiding-principles-21-mar-2011.pdf (last visited 19 June 2014).

[8] European Commission *A Renewed EU Strategy 2011–14 for Corporate Social Responsibility* COM(2011) 681.

[9] HM Government, *Good Business: Implementing the UN Guiding Principles on Business and Human Rights* (September 2013).

[10] European Commission, *ICT Sector Guide on Implementing the UN Guiding Principles on Business and Human Rights* (drafted by Shift and the Institute for Human Rights and Business).

[11] See www.globalnetworkinitiative.org (last visited 20 June 2014).

[12] Human Rights Council, 'Elaboration of an international legally binding instrument on Transnational Corporations and other Business Enterprises with respect to Human Rights' (A/HRC/26/L.22), at http://daccess-dds-ny.un.org/doc/UNDOC/LTD/G14/064 /48/PDF/G1406448.pdf?OpenElement (last visited 31 October 2014).

internet by cyberlibertarians as a separate place outside the reach of the law. This evolution is both in our understanding of the regulatory models at work in this environment, but also reactionary in the sense that responses to new technologies and efforts to control the uses of such technologies have themselves spurred regulatory responses, often from unexpected sources, such as from the users of the technology. The modalities of regulation are now understood to be often overlapping or conflicting and come from state and non-state sources. Indeed, internet regulation debates can now be seen to be predominantly concerned with two things: the interaction between these regulatory forces and public/private forms of governance.[13] These issues are playing out most significantly concerning human rights issues, such as freedom of expression, privacy and freedom of assembly.

How do we then address the responsibilities of internet information gatekeepers (IIG) when human rights laws do not directly apply to them? This book sought to move the conversation forward towards a governance model to address issues of human rights regulation in cyberspace. To do so requires an extension of the internet regulatory debate to take account of CSR, which up until now has been either unaccounted for in the regulatory discussion or folded too simply within the notion of self-regulation. This has made it difficult for the discussion of human rights issues to be wholly addressed by existing models because they fall short of capturing the nonlegal element of the human rights system that relies so often, as we have seen, on moral force. Equally, however, the human rights system is currently in a time of flux because the system in its legal form has been largely focused on the human rights obligations of the state, whereas the impact of human rights can be seen increasingly to come from the private sector. The role and power of private companies as regulatory forces is something with which cyberregulatory theorists are well-acquainted, with authors such as Joel Reidenberg, Lawrence Lessig, Jonathan Zittrain and Andrew Murray identifying their regulatory role early on. This book showed that CSR is the link that has been missing from discussions of internet regulation to address human rights issues, bridging the extralegal dimension of human rights with the rule-making arm of the law. As we saw, it is in this grey area between legal and social responsibility that many IIGs operate.

---

[13] See discussion, J. G. Palfrey, 'Four Phases of Internet Regulation', *Social Research*, 77(3) (Fall 2010).

The task in the internet environment is finding ways to link the various models of regulation in ways that are complementary and responsive and that can sustain human rights standards. What we found in this book and through the case studies was that the best path forward in framing a governance model is to focus on the administrative structure of free speech. This helps lift debates from the standoff seen between advocates of legal versus nonlegal models of governance and rules aimed at the state versus rules of more general application. Thus, the Governance Model outlined in Figure 6.3 of Chapter 6 is both a tweak in the way the relationships among human rights, CSR and the law is viewed and a model governance regime for going forward.

Although the Model has three layers of remedial mechanisms – corporate support, education, policy and research – the core of the model can be said to comprise two things: a common policy framework to address human rights issues and complementary dispute resolution mechanisms. Thus, this Model has both an external and internal arm: external in creating an independent body in the form of the Digital Rights Commission and internal by integrating the Governance Model into an IIG's operational structure. This allows a state to discharge its human rights duties whilst providing a blueprint for businesses to fulfil their corporate responsibility respect. Although this book has focused on what the United Kingdom can do to address this matter, the Model proposed in Chapter 6 is intended to have wider application. It serves as a template for the increasingly common use of non-state-based models of governance to address human rights and businesses issues in the technology sector.

There is more work to be done. The next step is to begin testing this model through further case studies in relation to other macro-IIGs such as mobile operators or in relation to authority gatekeepers such as social networking providers. It is expected that the model's application will be tweaked and loosened the further one slides down the scale of responsibility identified in Chapter 2. For example, there are questions about whether voluntariness has a greater role to play the further we slide down the gatekeeping scale, where standardisation across industry might be less necessary and the engendering of a commitment to human rights is vitally so. In addition, this book focused on freedom of expression, and work is required to test this Model against other human rights. In particular, it is a natural extension to examine application of this Governance Model to the regulatory structures that govern privacy. Finally, the case studies in this book focused on the public-facing governance aspects of these businesses. Further empirical work examining the internal structures, both formal and informal, of such businesses would help identify not only what should be reformed internal to the organisations, but also what aspects of such frameworks more appropriately should be developed as part of a public accountability framework.

# BIBLIOGRAPHY

## Codes, terms of service, guidelines and audits

AccountAbility 1000S (AA1000S), at www.accountability.org/

Advertising Standards Authority, at www.asa.org.uk

Agenda 21, at www.unep.org/Documents.Multilingual/Default.asp?documentid=52

Beijing Delcaration, at www.un.org/womenwatch/daw/beijing/platform/declar.htm

The Ceres Principes, at www.ceres.org/about-us/our-history/ceres-principles

Council of Europe, Recommendation CM/Rec(2012)3 of the Committee of Ministers to member States on the protection of human rights with regard to search engines

Electronic Industry Code of Conduct, at www.eicc.info/eicc_code.shtml

Equality and Human Rights Commission, *A Guide to Business and Human Rights* (March 2013), at www.equalityhumanrights.com/private-and-public-sector-guidance/organisations-and-businesses/businesses/human-rights-matter

European Commission, *ICT Sector Guide on Implementing the UN Guiding Principles on Business and Human Rights* (drafted by Shift and the Institute for Human Rights and Business)

European Commission, *My Business and Human Rights: a guide to human rights for small and medium-sized enterprises*, at http://ec.europa.eu/enterprise/policies/sustainable-business/files/csr-sme/human-rights-sme-guide-final_en.pdf

Facebook's 'Community Standards', at www.facebook.com/communitystandards

The Forest Stewardship Council, at www.fsc.org/

*Freiwillige Selbstokontrolle Multimedia-Diensteanbieter* (Association for the Voluntary Self-Monitoring of Multimedia Service Providers), 'Subcode of Conduct for Search Engine Providers'

The Global e-Sustainability Initiative, at http://gesi.org

The Global Network Initiative, at www.globalnetworkinitiative.org/

The Global Network Initiative, *Independent Assessment* (2014), at http://globalnetworkinitiative.org/sites/default/files/GNI%20Assessments%20Public%20Report.pdf

The Global Reporting Initiative, at www.globalreporting.org/Home
The Global Sullivan Principles, at www.thesullivanfoundation.org/The-Global
    -Sullivan-Principles.htm
Google, Blogger Terms of Service, at www.blogger.com/terms.g
Google, 'Google terms of service', at www.google.co.uk/intl/en-GB/policies/terms
    /regional.html
Google, 'Removal policies', at www.google.co.uk/intl/en-GB/policies/faq/
ICANN, Uniform Domain-Name Dispute-Resolution Policy, at www.icann.org
    /en/udrp/udrp.htm
The International Labour Organisation, at www.ilo.org/global/lang–en/index.htm
International Standards ISO/DIS 26000, *Social Responsibility*, at www.iso.org/obp
    /ui/#iso:std:iso:26000:ed-1:v1:en
ISPA, Code of Practice, at www.ispa.org.uk/about-us/ispa-code-of-practice/
ISPA, Best Current Practice on Blocking and filtering of Internet Traffic, at
    www.ispa.org.uk/home/page_327.html
IWF Code of Practice, at www.iwf.org.uk/members/funding-council/code-of
    -practice
IWF, *Content Appeal Process*, at www.iwf.org.uk/accountability/complaints/con
    tent-assessment-appeal-process#3
Kimberley Process, at www.kimberleyprocess.com/home/index_en.html
Lord Macdonald of River Glaven, QC, 'A human rights audit of the Internet Watch
    Foundation', available at www.iwf.org.uk/accountability/human-rights-audit
Memorandum of Understanding between the Crown Prosecution Service (CPS)
    and the Association of Chief Police Officers (ACPO) concerning Section 46
    Sexual Offences Act 2003
Nominet's Dispute Resolution Service, at www.nominet.org.uk/disputes/drs/
OECD Guidelines for Multinational Enterprises, at www.oecd.org/document/28
    /0,3343,en_2649_34889_2397532_1_1_1_1,00.html
Ofcom, *Broadcasting code*, at http://stakeholders.ofcom.org.uk/broadcasting/broad
    cast-codes/broadcast-code/harmoffence/
Ofcom, Customer Codes of Practice for handling complaints and resolving
    disputes (May 2005)
Ofcom, 'Online Infringement of Copyright and the Digital Economy Act 2010:
    Draft Initial Obligations Code', at http://stakeholders.ofcom.org.uk/binaries
    /consultations/copyright-infringement/summary/condoc.pdf
Principles for Responsible Investment, at www.unpri.org
Social Accountability 8000, at www.sa-intl.org/index.cfm?fuseaction=Page.View
    Page&PageID=937
The Telecommunications Industry Dialogue on Freedom of Expression and
    Privacy, Guiding Principles, version 1 (March 6 2013), at www.telecomindustry
    dialogue.org/sites/default/files/Telecoms_Industry_Dialogue_Principles_Version
    _1_-_ENGLISH.pdf

Twitter, 'The Twitter Rules', at https://support.twitter.com/articles/18311-the
-twitter-rules

United Nations Global Compact, 'The Ten Principles', at www.unglobalcompact
.org/AboutTheGC/TheTenPrinciples/index.html

World Intellectual Property Organization, Arbitration and Mediation Center, at
www.wipo.int/amc/en/index.html

## Personal communications

Emails between Emily Laidlaw and Lene Nielsen, Communications Executive and
Webmaster Internet Watch Foundation (March–April 2010), on file with the
author.

## Court briefs

Google's Notion of Motion and Motion to Dismiss the First Amended Complaint,
and Memorandum of Points, 2006 WL 1232481 for *Kinderstart.com LLC et al.* v.
*Google Inc.*, Case 5:06-cv-02057-JF (2007) (DC N.Cali).

## Hearings

The U.S. Senate Subcommittee on Human Rights and the law, 'Global Internet
Freedom and the Rule of Law, Part II' (2010).

The U.S. Senate Subcommittee on Human Rights and the law, 'Global Internet
Freedom: Corporate Responsibility and the Law' (2008).

## Inquiries

The Leveson Inquiry, *An Inquiry into the Culture, Practices and Ethics of the Press*
(November 2012).

Leveson Inquiry, evidence of Daphne Keller, at www.youtube.com/watch?v=9
Q2L9fWnb8I

### Secondary sources

## Books

Akdeniz, Y. *Internet Child Pornography and the Law* (Aldershot: Ashgate, 2008).

Auletta, K. *Googled: The End of the World as We Know It* (London: Virgin Books,
2010).

Ayres, I., and J. Braithwaite. *Responsive Regulation: Transcending the Deregulation
Debate* (Oxford University Press, 1992).

Baldwin, R., and M. Cave. *Understanding Regulation: Theory, Strategy, and Practice* (Oxford: Oxford University Press, 1999).

Balkan, J. *The Corporation: The Pathological Pursuit of Profit and Power* (London: Constable and Robinson Ltd., 2005).

Barendt, E. *Freedom of Speech*, 2nd edn (Oxford University Press, 2005).

Benedek, W., and M. C. Kettemann. *Freedom of Expression and the Internet* (Strasbourg: Council of Europe Publishing, 2013).

Benkler, Y.*The Wealth of Networks: How Social Production Transforms Markets and Freedom* (Yale University Press, 2006).

Bernal, P. *Internet Privacy Rights: Rights to Protect Autonomy* (Cambridge University Press, 2014).

Blowfield, M., and A. Murray. *Corporate Responsibility: A Critical Introduction* (Oxford University Press, 2008).

Braithwaite, J., and P. Drahos. *Global Business Regulation* (Cambridge University Press, 2000).

Brand, S. *The Media Lab: Inventing the Future at MIT* (New York: Penguin Group, 1987).

Castells, M. *The Internet Galaxy: Reflections on the Internet, Business, and Society* (Oxford University Press, 2001).

Castells, M. *The Rise of the Network Society*, 2nd edn (Oxford: Blackwell, 2000).

Citron, D. K. *Hate Crimes in Cyberspace* (Cambridge, Mass.: Harvard University Press, 2014).

Clapham, A. *Human Rights in the Private Sphere* (Oxford: Clarendon Press, 1993).

Clayton, R., and H. Tomlinson. *The Law of Human Rights*, 2nd edn, vol. 1 (Oxford University Press, 2009).

Coffee, J. C. *Gatekeepers: The Role of the Professions in Corporate Governance* (Oxford University Press, 2006).

Dahl, R. A. *Democracy and Its Critics* (Yale University Press, 1989).

Donnelly, J. *Universal Human Rights in Theory and Practice*, 2nd edn (Cornell University Press, 2002).

de Sola Pool, I. *Technologies of Freedom* (Cambridge, Mass.: Belknap Press, 1983).

Emerson, T. I. *The System of Freedom of Expression* (New York: Random House, 1970).

Feintuck, M., and M. Varney. *Media Regulation, Public Interest and the Law* (Edinburgh University Press, 2006).

Fenwick, H., and Gavin Phillipson. *Media Freedom under the Human Rights Act* (Oxford University Press, 2006).

Fiske, J. *Television Culture* (London: Routledge, 1987).

Friedman, M. *Capitalism and Freedom* (University of Chicago Press, 1962).

Gearty, C. *Principles of Human Rights Adjudication* (Oxford University Press, 2004).

Habermas, J. *Between Facts and Norms* (MIT, 1996).

Habermas, J., *Justification and Application: Remarks on Discourse Ethics* (Cambridge: Polity Press, 1993).

Habermas, J. *Moral Consciousness and Communicative Action* (Translated Cambridge: Polity Press, 1990).

Habermas, J. *The Structural Transformation of the Public Sphere* (Translated Cambridge: Polity Press, 1989).

Harris, D. J. et al. *Law of European Convention on Human Rights*, 2nd edn (Oxford University Press, 2009).

Heald, M. *The Social Responsibilities of Business: Company and Community, 1900–1960* (Cleveland, OH: Press of Case Western Reserve University, 1970).

Jørgensen, R. F. *Framing the Net: The Internet and Human Rights* (Cheltenham: Edward Elgar, 2013).

Keen, A. *The Cult of the Amateur* (London: Nicholas Brealey Publishing, 2007).

Lessig, L. *Code: Version 2.0* (New York: Basic Books, 2006).

Lessig, L. *Code and other Laws of Cyberspace* (New York: Basic Books, 1999).

Lord Lester of Herne Hill et al. *Human Rights Law and Practice* (London: Butterworths, 1999).

Lozano, J. M. et al. *Governments and Corporate Social Responsibility: Public Policies beyond Regulation and Voluntary Compliance* (Basingstoke: Palgrave Macmillan, 2008).

Mackay, H. et al, *Investigating the Information Society* (London: Routledge, 2001).

MacKinnon, R. *Consent of the Networked: The Worldwide Struggle for Internet Freedom* (New York: Basic Books, 2012).

Marsden, C. *Internet Co-Regulation: European Law, Regulatory Governance and Legitimacy in Cyberspace* (Cambridge University Press, 2011).

Mayer-Shönberger, V. *Delete: The Virtue of Forgetting in the Digital Age* (Princeton University Press, 2009).

Morgan, B., and K. Yeung. *An Introduction to Law and Regulation: Text and Materials* (Cambridge University Press, 2007).

Morozov, E. *The Net Delusion: The Dark Side of Internet Freedom* (New York: Public Affairs, 2011).

Morsink, J. *The Universal Declaration of Human Rights: Origins, Drafting & Intent* (Philadelphia: University of Pennsylvania Press, 1999).

Murray, A. *Information Technology Law: The Law and Society* (Oxford University Press, 2010).

Negroponte, N. *Being Digital* (New York: Vintage Books, 1995).

Norris, P. *Digital Divide: Civic Engagement, Information Poverty, and the Internet Worldwide* (Cambridge University Press, 2001).

Prosser, T. *The Regulatory Enterprise: Government, Regulation, and Legitimacy* (Oxford University Press, 2010).

Richter, J. *Holding Corporations Accountable: Corporate Conduct, International Codes, and Citizen Action* (London: Zed Books Ltd, 2001).

Ruggie, J. *Just Business: Multinational Corporations and Human Rights* (New York: W. W. Norton & Company, 2013).

Shoemaker, P. *Gatekeeping (Communication Concepts)* (Newbury Park, CA: Sage, 1991).

Shoemaker, P. *Gatekeeping Theory* (New York: Routledge, 2009).

Smith, R. K. M. *International Human Rights* (Oxford University Press, 2007).

Sunstein, C. R. *Infotopia* (Oxford University Press, 2006).

Sunstein, C. R. *Republic.com* (Princeton University Press, 2001).

Sunstein, C. R. *Republic.com 2.0* (Princeton University Press, 2007).

Tambini, D. et al. *Codifying Cyberspace* (London: Routledge, 2008).

van Hoboken, J. *Search Engine Freedom: On the Implications of the Right to Freedom of Expression for the Legal Governance of Web Search Services* (Amsterdam: Kluwer Law International, 2012).

Wales, A. *Big Business, Big Responsibilities* (Basingstoke: Palgrave Macmillan, 2010).

Walters, G. J. *Human Rights in an Information Age: A Philosophical Analysis* (University of Toronto Press, 2001).

Weaver, R. L. *From Gutenberg to the Internet: Free Speech, Advancing Technology, and the Implications for Democracy* (Durham: Carolina Academic Press, 2013).

Weber, R. H. *Shaping Internet Governance: Regulatory Challenges* (Berlin: Springer-Verlag, 2010).

Webster, F. *Theories of the Information Society*, 2nd edn (London, Routledge, 2002).

Zittrain, J. *The Future of the Internet and How to Stop It* (Yale University Press, 2008).

## Unpublished dissertations

Klang, M. *Disruptive Technology* (Doctoral Dissertation, unpublished, 2006).

## Edited books

Allison, J. E. (ed.). *Technology, Development, and Democracy: International Conflict and Cooperation in the Information Age* (Albany: State University of New York Press, 2002).

Boeger, N. et al. (eds.). *Perspectives on Corporate Social Responsibility* (Cheltenham, Eward Elgar, 2008).

Brownsword, R., and K. Yeung (eds.). *Regulating Technologies: Legal Future, Regulatory Frames and Technological Fixes* (Oxford: Hart Publishing, 2008).

Calhoun, C. (ed.). *Habermas and the Public Sphere* (MIT Press, 1992).

Crane, A. et al. (eds.). *The Oxford Handbook of Corporate Social Responsibility* (Oxford University Press, 2008).

Dahl, R. A. et al. (eds.). *The Democracy Sourcebook* (MIT Press, 2003).

Deibert, R. et al. (eds.). *Access Controlled: The Shaping of Power, Rights, and Rule in Cyberspace* (MIT Press, 2010).

Deibert, R. et al. (eds.). *Access Denied: The Practice and Policy of Global Internet Filtering* (MIT Press, 2008).

De Sousa Santos, B., and C. A. Rodriguez-Garavito (eds.). *Law and Globalization from Below: Towards a Cosmopolitan Legality* (Cambridge University Press, 2005).

Deva, S., and D. Bilchitz (eds.). *Human Rights Obligations of Business: Beyond the Corporate Responsibility to Respect* (Cambridge University Press, 2013).

Dommering, E., and L. Asscher (eds.). *Coding Regulation* (Cambridge University Press, 2006).

Dyzenhaus, D. (ed.). *Recrafting the Rule of Law* (Oxford: Hart Publishing, 1999).

Edwards, L., and C. Waelde (eds.). *Law and the Internet*, 3rd edn (Oxford: Hart Publishing, 2009).

Erdelez, S. et al. (eds.). *Theories of Information Behavior: A Researcher's Guide* (Medford, New Jersey: Information Today, 2005).

Feenberg, A., and D. Barney (eds.). *Community in the Digital Age: Philosophy and Practice* (Oxford: Rowman & Littlefield Publishers, 2004).

Jørgensen, R. F. (ed.). *Human Rights in the Global Information Society* (MIT Press, 2006).

Klang, M., and A. Murray (eds.). *Human Rights in the Digital Age* (London: Cavendish Publishing, 2005).

Levmore, S., and M. C. Nussbaum (eds.). *The Offensive Internet* (Cambridge: Harvard University Press, 2010).

MacKenzie, D., and J. Wajcman (eds.). *The Social Shaping of Technology*, 2nd edn (Buckingham: Open University Press, 1999).

McBarnet, D. et al. (eds.). *The New Corporate Accountability: Corporate Social Responsibility and the Law* (Cambridge University Press, 2007).

Morgan, B. (ed.). *The Intersection of Rights and Regulation: New Directions in Sociolegal Scholarship* (Aldershot: Ashgate, 2007).

Nissebaum, H., and M. E. Price (eds.). *Academy & Internet* (New York: Peter Lang Publishing, 2004).

Ramcharan, B. G. (ed.). *The Protection Role of National Human Rights Institutions* (Leiden, The Netherlands: Martinus Nijhoff Publishers, 2005).

Sarikakis, K., and D. K. Thussu (eds.). *Ideologies of the Internet* (Cresskill, New Jersey: Hampton Press, 2006).

Shane, P. M. (ed.). *Democracy Online: The Prospects for Political Renewal through the Internet* (New York: Routledge, 2004).

Sullivan, R. (ed.). *Business and Human Rights: Dilemmas and Solutions* (Greenleaf, 2003).

Walker, C., and R. L. Weaver (ed.). *Free Speech in an Internet Era* (Durham: Carolina Academic Press, 2013).

Webb, K. (ed.). *Voluntary Codes: Private Governance, the Public Interest and Innovation* (Carleton Research Unit for Innovation, Science and Environment, 2004).

Webster, F. (ed.). *The Information Society Reader* (London: Routledge, 2004).

## Chapters in edited books

Agre, P. E. 'The Practical Republic: Social Skills and the Progress of Citizenship', in A. Feenberg and D. Barney (eds.), *Community in the Digital Age: Philosophy and Practice* (Oxford: Rowman & Littlefield Publishers, 2004).

Banisar, D. 'The Right to Information in the Age of Information', in R. F. JØrgensen (ed.), *Human Rights in the Global Information Socie'ty* (MIT Press, 2006).

Barzilai Nahon, K. 'Network Gatekeeping Theory', in S. Erdelez et al. (eds.), *Theories of Information Behavior: A Researcher's Guide* (Medford, New Jersey: Information Today, 2005).

Bilchitz, D. 'A Chasm between "Is" and "Ought"? A Critique of the Normative Foundations of the SRSG's Framework and the Guiding Principles', in S. Deva and D. Bilchitz (eds.), *Human Rights Obligations of Business: Beyond the Corporate Responsibility to Respect* (Cambridge University Press, 2013).

Bohman, J. 'Expanding Dialogue: The Internet, Public Sphere, and Transnational Democracy', in P. M. Shane (ed.), *Democracy Online: The Prospects for Political Renewal through the Internet* (New York: Routledge, 2004).

Campbell, T. 'The Normative Grounding of Corporate Social Responsibility: A Human Rights Approach', in D. McBarnet et al. (eds.), *The New Corporate Accountability: Corporate Social Responsibility and the Law* (Cambridge University Press, 2007).

Carroll, A. B. 'A History of Corporate Social Responsibility: Concepts and Practices', in A. Crane et al. (eds.), *The Oxford Handbook of Corporate Social Responsibility* (Oxford University Press, 2008).

Deibert, R. J., and N. Villeneuve. 'Firewalls and Power: An Overview of Global State Censorship of the Internet', in M. Klang and A. Murray (eds.), *Human Rights in the Digital Age* (London: Cavendish Publishing, 2005).

Esler, B. W. 'Filtering, Blocking and Rating: Chaperones and Censorship', in M. Klang and A. Murray (eds.), *Human Rights in the Digital Age* (London: Cavendish Publishing, 2005).

Faris, R., and N. Villeneuve. 'Measuring Global Internet Filtering', in R. Deibert et al. (eds.), *Access Denied: The Practice and Policy of Global Internet Filtering* (MIT Press, 2008).

Freeman, J. 'Private Parties, Public Functions and the New Administrative Law', in D. Dyzenhaus (ed.), *Recrafting the Rule of Law* (Oxford: Hart Publishing, 1999).

Froomkin, A. M. 'Technologies for Democracy', in P. M. Shane (ed.), *Democracy Online: The Prospects for Political Renewal through the Internet* (New York: Routledge, 2004).

Glinski, C. 'Corporate Codes of Conduct: Moral or Legal Obligation', in D. McBarnet et al. (eds.), *The New Corporate Accountability: Corporate Social Responsibility and the Law* (Cambridge University Press, 2007).

Johnson, D., and B. Bimber. 'The Internet and Political Transformation Revisited', in A. Feenberg and D. Barney (eds.), *Community in the Digital Age: Philosophy and Practice* (Oxford: Rowman & Littlefield Publishers, 2004).

Kahn, R., and D. Kellner. 'Virtually Democratic: Online Communities and Internet Activism', in A. Feenberg and D. Barney (eds.), *Community in the Digital Age: Philosophy and Practice* (Oxford: Rowman & Littlefield Publishers, 2004).

Kedzie, C. R., and J. Aaragon. 'Coincident Revolutions and the Dictator's Dilemma: Thoughts on Communication and Democratization', in J. E. Allison (ed.), *Technology, Development, and Democracy: International Conflict and Cooperation in the Information Age* (Albany: State University of New York Press, 2002).

Kinley, D. et al. ' "The Norms Are Dead! Long Life the Norms!" The Politics behind the UN Human Rights Norms for Corporations', in D. McBarnet et al. (eds.), *The New Corporate Accountability: Corporate Social Responsibility and the Law* (Cambridge University Press, 2007).

Lambers, R. 'Code and Speech. Speech Control through Network Architecture', in E. Dommering and L. Asscher (eds.), *Coding Regulation* (Cambridge University Press, 2006).

Leiter, B. 'Cleaning Cyber-Cesspools: Google and Free Speech', in S. Levmore and M. C. Nussbaum (eds.), *The Offensive Internet* (Cambridge: Harvard University Press, 2010).

Lopez, C. 'The "Ruggie Process": From Legal Obligations to Corporate Social Responsibility?', in S. Deva and D. Bilchitz (eds.), *Human Rights Obligations of Business: Beyond the Corporate Responsibility to Respect* (Cambridge University Press, 2013).

McBarnet, D. 'Corporate Social Responsibility beyond Law, through Law, for Law: The New Corporate Accountability', in D. McBarnet et al. (eds.), *The New Corporate Accountability: Corporate Social Responsibility and the Law* (Cambridge University Press, 2007).

Maclay, C, 'Protecting Privacy and Expression Online: Can the Global Network Initiative embrace the character of the Net?', in R. Deibert et al. (eds.), *Access Controlled: The Shaping of Power, Rights, and Rule in Cyberspace* (MIT Press, 2010).

McIntyre, T., and C. Scott. 'Internet Filtering: Rhetoric, Legitimacy, Accountability and Responsibility', in R. Brownsword and K. Yeung (eds.), *Regulating Technologies: Legal Future, Regulatory Frames and Technological Fixes* (Oxford: Hart Publishing, 2008).

Morrison, A., and K. Webb. 'Bicycle Helmets and Hockey Helmet Regulations: Two Approaches to Safety Protection', in K. Webb (ed.), *Voluntary Codes: Private Governance, the Public Interest and Innovation* (Carleton Research Unit for Innovation, Science and Environment, 2004).

Muchlinski, P. 'The Development of Human Rights Responsibilities for Multinational Enterprises', in R. Sullivan (ed.), *Business and Human Rights: Dilemmas and Solutions* (Greenleaf, 2003).

Murdoch, S. J., and R. Anderson. 'Tools and Technology of Internet Filtering', in R. Deibert et al. (eds.), *Access Denied: The Practice and Policy of Global Internet Filtering* (MIT Press, 2008).

Nolan, J. 'The Corporate Responsibility to Respect Human Rights: Soft Law or Not Law?', in S. Deva and D. Bilchitz (eds.), *Human Rights Obligations of Business: Beyond the Corporate Responsibility to Respect* (Cambridge University Press, 2013).

Noveck, B. S. 'Unchat: Democratic Solution for a Wired World', in P. M. Shane (ed.), *Democracy Online: The Prospects for Political Renewal through the Internet* (New York: Routledge, 2004).

Parker, C. 'Meta-Regulation: Legal Accountability for Corporate Social Responsibility', in D. McBarnet et al. (eds.), *The New Corporate Accountability: Corporate Social Responsibility and the Law* (Cambridge University Press, 2007).

Pinter, A., and T. Oblak. 'Is There a Public Sphere in This Discussion Forum?', in K. Sarikakis and D. K. Thussu (eds.), *Ideologies of the Internet* (Cresskill, New Jersey: Hampton Press, 2006).

Riefa, C., and J. Hornle. 'The Changing Face of Electronic Consumer Contracts in the Twenty-First Century: Fit for Purpose?', in L. Edwards and C. Waelde (eds.), *Law and the Internet*, 3rd edn (Oxford: Hart Publishing, 2009).

Rosenzweig, R. 'How Will the Net's History Be Written? Historians and the Internet', in H. Nissebaum and M. E. Price (eds.), *Academy & Internet* (New York: Peter Lang Publishing, 2004).

Rowland, D. 'Free Expression and Defamation', in M. Klang and A. Murray (eds.), *Human Rights in the Digital Age* (London: Cavendish Publishing, 2005).

Raseroka, K. 'Access to Information and Knowledge', in R. F. Jørgensen (ed.), *Human Rights in the Global Information Society* (MIT Press, 2006).

Rundle, M., and M. Birdling. 'Filtering and the International System: A Question of Commitment', in R. Deibert et al. (eds.), *Access Denied: The Practice and Policy of Global Internet Filtering* (MIT Press, 2008).

Scott, C. 'Reflexive Governance, Meta-Regulation, and Corporate Social Responsibility: The Heineken Effect', in N. Boeger et al. (eds.), *Perspectives on Corporate Social Responsibility* (Cheltenham, Eward Elgar, 2008).

Shamir, R. 'Corporate Social Responsibility: A Case of Hegemony and Counter-Hegemony', in B. De Sousa Santos and C. A. Rodriguez-Garavito (eds.), *Law and*

*Globalization from Below: Towards a Cosmopolitan Legality* (Cambridge University Press, 2005).

Vegh, S. 'Profit over Principles: The Commercialization of the Democratic Potentials of the Internet', in K. Sarikakis and D. K. Thussu (eds.), *Ideologies of the Internet* (Cresskill, New Jersey: Hampton Press, 2006).

Vick, D. 'Regulating Hatred', in M. Klang and A. Murray (eds.), *Human Rights in the Digital Age* (London: Cavendish Publishing, 2005).

Voilescu, A. 'Changing Paradigms of Corporate Criminal Responsibility: Lessons for Corporate Social Responsibility', in D. McBarnet et al. (eds.), *The New Corporate Accountability: Corporate Social Responsibility and the Law* (Cambridge University Press, 2007).

Webb, K. 'Understanding the Voluntary Codes Phenomenon', in K. Webb (ed.), *Voluntary Codes: Private Governance, the Public Interest and Innovation* (Carleton Research Unit for Innovation, Science and Environment, 2004).

Webb, K., and A. Morrison. 'The Law and Voluntary Codes: Examining the "Tangled Web"', in K. Webb (ed.), *Voluntary Codes: Private Governance, the Public Interest and Innovation* (Carleton Research Unit for Innovation, Science and Environment, 2004).

Weber, L. M., and S. Murray. 'Interactivity: Equality, and the Prospects for Electronic Democracy: A Review', in K. Sarikakis and D. K. Thussu (eds.), *Ideologies of the Internet* (Cresskill, New Jersey: Hampton Press, 2006).

Winner, L. 'Do Artifacts Have Politics?', in the D. MacKenzie and J. Wajcman (eds.), *The Social Shaping of Technology*, 2nd edn (Buckingham: Open University Press, 1999).

## Journal articles

Akdeniz, Y. 'To Block or Not to Block: European Approaches to Content Regulation, and Implications for Freedom of Expression', *CLSR*, 26 (2010) 260.

Ammori, M. 'First Amendment Architecture', *Wis. L. Rev.* (2012) 1.

Balkin, J. M. 'The Future of Free Expression in the Digital Age', *Pepp. L. Rev.* 36 (2008) 101.

Balkin, J. M. 'Digital Speech and Democratic Culture: A Theory of Freedom of Expression for the Information Society', *NYULR*, 79(1) (2004) 1.

Barber, B. R. 'Three Scenarios for the Future of Technology and Strong Democracy', *PSQ*, 113(4) (1998–99) 573.

Barber, B. R. 'Which Technology for Which Democracy? Why Democracy for Which Technology?', *IJCLP*, 6 (2001) 1.

Barzilai-Nahon, K. 'Gatekeeping Revisited: A Critical Review', *Annual Review of Information Science and Technology*, 43 (2009) 1.

Barzilai-Nahon, K. 'Toward a Theory of Network Gatekeeping: A Framework for Exploring Information Control', *JASIST*, 59(9) (2008) 1493.

Barzilai-Nahon, K. 'Gatekeepers, Virtual Communities and the Gated: Multidimensional Tensions in Cyberspace', *Int'l J. Comm. L. & Pol'y*, 11(9) (2006) 1.

Ben-Ishai, S. 'Corporate Gatekeeper Liability in Canada', *Tex. Intl. L. J.*, 42 (2007) 443.

Benjamin, S. M. 'Algorithms and Speech', *U. PA. L. Rev.* 161(6) (2013) 1445.

Benkler, Y. 'From Consumers to Users: The Deeper Structures of Regulation Toward Sustainable Commons and User Access', *Fed. Comm. L. J.* 52 (2000) 561.

Benkler, Y. et al. 'Social Mobilization and the Networked Public Sphere: Mapping the SOPA-PIPA Debate' (July 2013), The Berkman Center for Internet & Society Research Publication Series No. 2013–16.

Bergman, M. 'The Deep Web: Surfacing Hidden Value', *J. Electron. Publ.*, 7(1) (2001) 1.

Black, J. 'Decentring Regulation: Understanding the Role of Regulation and Self-Regulation in a "Post-Regulatory" World', *CLP*, 54 (2001) 103.

Bracha, O., and F. Pasquale. 'Federal Search Commission? Access, Fairness and Accountability in the Law of Search', *Cornell L. R.* 93 (2008) 1149.

Chandler, J. A. 'A Right to Reach an Audience: An Approach to Intermediary Bias on the Internet', *Hofstra L. Rev.* 35(3) (2007) 101.

Cortes, P., and F. E. De la Rosa. 'Building a Global Redress System for Low-Value Cross-Border Disputes', *Intl. & Comp. L. Q.* 62(2) (2013) 407.

Dahlberg, L. 'Democracy via Cyberspace', *New Media & Society*, 3(2) (2001) 157.

Dahlgren, P. 'The Internet, Public Spheres, and Political Communication: Dispersion and Deliberation', *Political Communication*, 22 (2005) 147.

Darian-Smith, E., and C. Scott. 'Regulation and Human Rights in Socio-Legal Scholarship', *Law and Policy*, 31(3) (2009) 271.

De Hert, P., and D. Kloza. 'Internet (Access) as a New Fundamental Right. Inflating the Current Rights Framework?', *EJLT*, 3(3) (2012).

Doane, D. 'The Myth of CSR: The Problem with Assuming That Companies Can Do Well While Also Doing Good Is That Markets Don't Really Work That Way', *SSIR*, 3(3) (2005) 23.

Edwards, L. 'From Child Porn to China, in One Cleanfeed', *Script-ed*, 3(3) (2006) 174.

Elkin-Koren, N. 'Let the Crawlers Crawl: On Virtual Gatekeepers and the Right to Exclude Indexing', *U. Dayton L. Rev.* 26 (2000) 179.

Froomkin, A. M. 'Habermas@Discourse.Net: Towards a Critical Theory of Cyberspace', *HLR*, 116(3) (2003) 751.

Garnham, N. 'Information Society Theory as Ideology' (1998) 21(1) *Loisir et Societe* 97.

Gasser, U. 'Responsibility for Human Rights Violations, Acts or Omissions, within the "Sphere of Influence" of Companies', Working Paper Series (December 2007).

Goldman, E. 'Search Engine Bias and the Demise of Search Engine Utopianism', *YJLT*, 8 (2005–6) 188.

Grimmelmann, J. 'The Google Dilemma', *N. Y. L. School L. Rev.*, 53 (2008/2009) 939.

Grimmelmann, J. 'Speech Engines', *U. Md. Francis King Carey School of Law Legal Studies Research Paper* No. 2014–11 (2014) 867.

Habermas, J. 'Human Rights and Popular Sovereignty: The Liberal and Republican Versions', *Ratio Juris*, 7(1) (1994) 1.

Habermas, J. 'Political Communication in Media Society: Does Democracy Still Enjoy an Epistemic Dimension? The Impact of Normative Theory on Empirical Research', *Communication Theory*, 16 (2006) 411.

Halcli, A., and F. Webster. 'Inequality and Mobilization in the Information Age' (2000) 3(1) *European Journal of Social Theory* 67.

Heverly, R. 'Breaking the Internet: International Efforts to Play the Middle against the Ends: A Way Forward', *Georgetown J. of Intl. L.* 42(4) (2011) 1083.

Heverly, R. A. 'Law as Intermediary', *Mich. St. L. Rev* (2006) 107.

Hildebrandt, M., and B. Koops. 'The Challenges of Ambient Law and Legal Protection in the Profiling Era', *MLR*, 73(3) (2010) 428.

Howard, P. N., and M. M. Hussain. 'The Upheavals in Egypt and Tunisia: The Role of Digital Media', *Journal of Democracy*, 22(3) (2011) 35.

Johnson, D. R., and D. G. Post. 'Law and Borders – The Rise of Law in Cyberspace' (1996), at www.temple.edu/lawschool/dpost/Borders.html.

Julia-Barcelo, and K. J. Koelman, 'Intermediary Liability in the E-Commerce Directive: So Far So Good, But It's Not Enough', *CLSR*, 16(4) (2004) 231.

Katyal, S. K. 'Semiotic Disobedience', *Wash. U. L. Rev.* 84(2) (2006) 489.

Kohl, U. 'Google: The Rise and Rise of Online Intermediaries in the Governance of the Internet and Beyond (Part 2)', *IJILT*, 21(2) (2013) 187.

Kohl, U. 'The Rise and Rise of Online Intermediaries in the Governance of the Internet and Beyond – Connectivity Intermediaries', *IRLCT* 26(2) (2011) 185.

Kraakman, R. H. 'Corporate Liability Strategies and the Costs of Legal Controls', *Yale L. J.* 93 (1983–1985) 857.

Kraakman, R. H. 'Gatekeepers: The Anatomy of a Third-Party Enforcement Strategy', *J. L. Econ. & Org.* 2 (1986) 53.

Kreimer, S. F. 'Censorship By Proxy: First Amendment, Internet Intermediaries, and the Problem of the Weakest Link', *U. Pa. L. Rev.* 155 (2006–2007) 11.

Laidlaw, E. B. 'A Framework for Identifying Internet Information Gatekeepers', *IRLCT*, 43(3) (2010) 263.

Laidlaw, E. B. 'Private Power, Public Interest: An Examination of Search Engine Accountability', *IJLIT*, 17 (1) (2009) 113.

Laidlaw, E. 'The Responsibilities of Free Speech Regulators: An Analysis of the Internet Watch Foundation', *IJILT*, 20(4) (2012) 312.

Lewin, K. 'Frontiers in Group Dynamics', *Human Relations*, 1(2) (1947) 143.

Lievens, E. et al. 'The Co-Protection of Minors in New Media: A European Approach to Co-Regulation', *U. C. Davis J. Juv. L. & Pol'y*, 10 (2006) 98.

Longford, G., and S. Patten. 'Democracy in the Age of the Internet', *UNBLJ*, 56 (2007) 5.

Mac Síthigh, D. "App Law Within: Rights and Regulation in the Smartphone Age', *IJILT*, 21(2) (2013) 154.

Mac Síthigh, D. 'The Fragmentation of Intermediary Liability in the UK', *JIPLP*, 8(7) (2013) 521.

Mac Síthigh, D. 'Virtual Walls? The Law of Pseudo-Public Spaces', *Int. J. L. C.* 8(3) (2012) 394.

Mann, R. J., and S. R. Belzley. 'The Promise of Internet Intermediary Liability', *W. M. & Mary L. Rev.* 47 (2005) 239.

Manokha, I. 'Business Ethics and the Spirit of Global Capitalism: Moral Leadership in the Context of Global Hegemony', *Journal of Global Ethics*, 2(1) (2006) 27.

Manokha, I. 'Corporate Social Responsibility: A New Signifier? An Analysis of Business Ethics and Good Business Practice', *Politics*, 24(1) (2004) 56.

McCorquodale, R. 'Corporate Social Responsibility and International Human Rights Law', *Journal of Business Ethics*, 87 (2009) 385.

McCorquodale, R., and R. Fairbrother. 'Globalization and Human Rights', *Hum. Rts. Q.* 21(3)) (1999) 735.

Metoyer-Duran, C. 'Information Gatekeepers', *Annual Review of Information Science and Technology*, 28 (1993) 111.

Murray, A. 'Nodes and Gravity in Virtual Space', *Legisprudence*, 5(2) (2011) 195.

Murray, A. 'Symbiotic Regulation', *J. Marshall J. of Computer & Info. L.* 26(2) (2009) 207.

Murray, A., and C. Scott. 'Regulating New Media', *MLR*, 65 (2002) 491.

Okoye, A. 'Theorising Corporate Social Responsibility as an Essentially Contested Concept: Is a Definition Necessary?', *J. Bus. Ethics*, 89 (2009) 613.

Orgad, S. 'The Cultural Dimensions of Online Communication: A Study of Breast Cancer Patients' Internet Spaces', *New Media & Society*, 8(6) (2006) 87.

Palfrey, J. G. 'Four Phases of Internet Regulation', *Social Research*, 77(3) (Fall 2010).

Papacharissi, Z. 'The Virtual Sphere: The Internet as a Public Sphere', *New Media & Society*, 4(1) (2002) 9.

Pasquale, F. 'Asterisk Revisited: Debating a Right of Reply on Search Results', *J. Bus. & Tech. L.* 3 (2008) 61.

Pasquale, F. 'Rankings, Reductionalism and Responsibility', *Clev. St. L. Rev.* 54 (2006) 115.

Patterson, M. R. 'Google and Search-Engine Market Power', *Harvard Journal Law and Technology Occasional Paper Series* (2013) 1.

Picciotto, S. 'Rights, Responsibilities and Regulation of International Business', *Columbia Journal of Transnational Law*, 42 (2003) 131.

Pitts, C., and J. Sherman. 'Human Rights Corporate Accountability Guide: From Laws to Norms to Values', Working Paper No. 51, Corporate Social Responsibility Initiative (December 2008).

Price, V. et al. 'Does Disagreement Contribute to More Deliberative Opinion?', *Political Communication*, 19(1) (2002) 95.

Reidenberg, J. R. 'Lex Informatica: The Formulation of Information Policy Rules through Technology', *Tex. L. R.* 76(3) (1998) 553.

Rowbottom, J. 'To Rant, Vent and Converse: Protecting Low Level Digital Speech', CLJ, 71(2) (2012) 355.

Scherer, A. G., and G. Palazzo. 'Toward a Political Conception of Corporate Social Responsibility: Business and Society Seen from a Habermasian Perspective', *Academy of Management Review*, 32(4) (2007) 1096.

Schulz, W. et al. 'Search Engines as Gatekeepers of Public Communication: An Analysis of the German Framework Applicable to Internet Search Engines Including Media Law and Anti Trust Law', *German Law Journal*, 6(1) (2005) 1419.

Scott, C. 'Accountability in The Regulatory State', *Journal of Law and Society*, 27(1) (2000) 38.

Seyfert, C. '25 Clauses of Google's Privacy Policy and Terms of Service Are Legally Void', *E. C. L. Rep.* 14(1) (2014), 23.

Sheehy, B. 'Understanding CSR: An Empirical Study of Private Self-Regulation', *Monash Law Review*, 38(2) (2011) 1.

Shoemaker, P. et al. 'Individual and Routine Forces in Gatekeeping', *J&MC Quarterly*, 78(2 (2001) 233.

Smith, P. 'The Politics of UK Television Policy: The Making of Ofcom', *Media Culture & Society*, 28(6) (2006) 929.

Sutter, G. '"Nothing New under the Sun": Old Fear and New Media', *IJLIT*, 8 (2000), 338.

Van Couvering, E. 'Is Relevance Relevant? Market, Science, and War: Discourses of Search Engine Quality', *J. Comput.-Mediat. Comm.* 12(3) (2007) 866.

van Eijk, N. 'Search Engines: Seek and Ye Shall Find? The Position of Search Engines in Law', *Iris plus*, 2 (2006) 1.

Votaw, D. 'Genius Became Rare: A Comment on the Doctrine of Social Responsibility Pt 1', *Calif. Manage. Rev.* 15(2) (1972) 25.

Wu, T. 'Machine Speech', *U. PA. L. Rev.* 161(6) (2013) 1495.

Zittrain, J. 'A History of Online Gatekeeping', *Harv. J. L. & Tech.* 19(2) (2006) 253.

Zittrain, J. 'Internet Points of Control', *B. C. L. Rev.* 44 (2002) 653.

## Reports, conference papers, opinions and other research papers

Ahlert, C. et al. 'How "liberty" disappeared from cyberspace: the mystery shopper tests internet content self-regulation', at http://pcmlp.socleg.ox.ac.uk/sites/pcmlp.socleg.ox.ac.uk/files/liberty.pdf.

Bayer, J. 'Liability of internet service providers for third party content', *Victoria University Wellington Working Paper Series*, 1 (2008) 1.

Best, M. L., and K. W. Wade. 'The internet and democracy: global catalyst or democratic dud' (Research Publication No. 2005–12: Berkman Center, 2005).

Brown, I. 'Internet self-regulation and fundamental rights', *Index on Censorship*, 1 (2010) 98.

Brown, I., and D. Korff. 'Digital freedoms in international law: practical steps to protect human rights online' (June 2012) (report commissioned by the Global Network Initiative).

Business Leaders Initiative on Human Rights, United Nations Global Compact and the Office of the High Commissioner for Human Rights. 'A guide for integrating human rights into business management I'.

Business Leaders Initiative on Human Rights, United Nations Global Compact and the Office of the High Commissioner for Human Rights. 'A guide for integrating human rights into business management II'.

Canadian Centre for Child Protection. *Child sexual abuse images: an analysis of websites by cybertip.ca* (November 2009).

Lord Carter. *Digital Britain final report* (June 2009), at http://webarchive.nation alarchives.gov.uk/±/http://www.culture.gov.uk/images/publications/digital britain-finalreport-jun09.pdf.

Communication. 'Implementing the Partnership for Growth and Jobs: Making Europe a Pole of Excellence on Corporate Social Responsibility', *COM* (2006) 136.

Council of Europe. 'Building a Free and Safe Internet', Submission to the Internet Governance Forum, Rio de Janeiro, Brazil, 12–15 November 2007.

Council of Europe and European Internet Service Providers Association. 'Human rights guidelines for Internet service providers', at www.coe.int/t/information society/documents/HRguidelines_ISP_en.pdf.

Council of Europe and the Interactive Software Federation of Europe. 'Human rights guidelines for online game providers', at www.coe.int/t/information society/documents/HRguidelines_OGP_en.pdf.

Council of Europe. *Recommendation CM/Rec(2008)6 of the Committee of Ministers to member states on measures to promote the respect for freedom of expression and information with regard to internet filters* (March 2008).

Clayton, R. 'Failures in a hybrid content blocking system', at www.cl.cam.ac.uk /~rnc1/cleanfeed.pdf.

Clayton, R. 'Technical aspects of censoring Wikipedia', at www.lightbluetouchpa per.org/2008/12/11/technical-aspects-of-the-censoring-of-wikipedia/.

The Department of Trade and Industry. *DTI Consultation Document on the Electronic Commerce Directive: The Liability of Hyperlinkers, Location Tools Services and Content Aggregators* (June 2005), at http://webarchive.national archives.gov.uk/20090609003228/http://www.berr.gov.uk/files/file13986.pdf.

Edelman, B., and B. Lockwood. 'Measuring bias in "organic" web search', at www.benedelman.org/searchbias/.

Equality and Human Rights Commission. *Strategic Plan 2012–2015*, at www.equality humanrights.com/about-us/about-commission/our-vision-and-mission/strategic -plan-2012-2015.

Equality and Human Rights Commission. Submission to the 10th International Conference of NHRIs (Session 6 on 9 October 2010), *The Corporate Responsibility to Respect Human Rights.*

European Commission. *Communication on Internet Policy and Governance Europe's role in shaping the future of Internet Governance* COM/2014/072.

European Commission. 'A Coherent Framework for Building Trust in the Digital Single Market for E-Commerce and Online Services', *COM*(2011) 942.

European Commission. 'A Renewed EU strategy 2011–14 for Corporate Social Responsibility', *COM*(2011) 681.

European Commission. 'European Governance: A White Paper',*COM*(2001) 428 (25 July 2001).

*European Multi-Stakeholder Forum on CSR: Final Results and Recommendations* (29 June 2004).

Frankental, P., and F. House. 'Human Rights – Is It Any of Your Business?' (2000) *Amnesty International.*

Global Network Initiative. Annual Report 2012, at http://globalnetworkinitiative .org/sites/default/files/GNI%20Annual%20Report%202012.pdf.

Green Paper. 'Promoting a European Framework for Corporate Social Responsibility', *COM* (2001) 366.

HM Government. *Corporate Responsibility Report* (BERR, February 2009).

HM Government. *Corporate Social Responsibility: A Government Update* (DTI, May 2004).

HM Government. *Good Business: Implementing the UN Guiding Principles on Business and Human Rights* (September 2013).

House of Commons, Justice Committee. *The Functions, Powers and Resources of the Information Commissioner, Ninth Report of Session 2012–13* (12 March 2013), at www.publications.parliament.uk/pa/cm201213/cmselect/cmjust/962/962.pdf.

Human Rights Council. 'Elaboration of an international legally binding instrument on Transnational Corporations and other Business Enterprises with respect to Human Rights' (A/HRC/26/L.22), at http://daccess-dds-ny.un.org/doc/UNDOC /LTD/G14/064/48/PDF/G1406448.pdf?OpenElement.

Information Commissioner's Office. *Data Protection and the Press – Framework Consultation on Proposed ICO Code of Practice*, at http://ico.org.uk/news /blog/2013/~/media/documents/library/Data_Protection/Research_and_reports /framework-consultation-summary-of-responses.pdf.

Information Commissioner's Office. *The Information Commissioner's Response to the Leveson Report*, at http://ico.org.uk/news/~/media/documents/consultation _responses/ico_response_to_leveson_report_012013.ashx (last visited 2 April 2014).

International Council on Human Rights Policy. *Beyond Voluntarism: Human Rights and the Developing International Legal Obligations of Companies* (February 2002), at www.ichrp.org/files/reports/7/107_report_en.pdf.

Internet Watch Foundation. *Annual and Charity Report* 2013, at www.iwf.org.uk /accountability/annual-reports/2013-annual-report.

Internet Watch Foundation. 2012 *Annual and Charity Report*, at www.iwf.org.uk /accountability/annual-reports/2011-annual-report (last visited 27 June 2014).

Internet Watch Foundation. 2010 *Annual and Charity Report*, at www.iwf.org.uk /assets/media/annual-reports/Internet%20Watch%20Foundation%20Annual %20Report%202010%20web.pdf.

Internet Watch Foundation. 2008 *Annual and Charity Report*, at www.iwf.org.uk /accountability/annual-reports/2008-annual-report.

Internet Watch Foundation, *Annual and Charity Report* 2006.

Joint Committee on Human Rights. *Any of Our Business? Human Rights and the UK Private Sector* (First Reports of Session 2009–10), vol. I.

Joint Committee on Human Rights. *Any of Our Business? Human Rights and the UK Private Sector* (First Reports of Session 2009–10), vol. II.

Joint Committee on Human Rights. *Equality and Human Rights Commission* (Thirteenth Report of Session 2009–10).

Joint Committee on Human Rights. *Tenth Report* (2007), at www.parliament.the -stationery-office.com/pa/jt200607/jtselect/jtrights/81/8105.htm.

Laidlaw, E. 'Unraveling Intermediary Liability', presented at *British and Irish Law, Education and Technology* (University of East Anglia, April 2014), at www.laid law.eu/2014/06/unraveling-intermediary-liability/.

Laidlaw, E. 'What is a joke? The role of social media providers in regulating speech', presented at *The Legal Challenges of Social Media to Freedom of Expression* (University of Leicester, December 2013), at www.laidlaw.eu/2014 /06/what-is-a-joke-the-role-of-social-media-providers-in-regulating-speech/.

McIntyre, T. J. 'Intermediaries, Invisibility and the Rule of Law', *BILETA Conference Paper* (2008).

Monash University Castan Centre for Human Rights Law. *Human Rights Translated: A Business Reference Guide.*

Nahon, K. et al. 'Information flows in events of political unrest' at www.ideals .illinois.edu/bitstream/handle/2142/39165/259.pdf?sequence=4.

Ntoulas, A. et al. 'Downloading hidden content', at http://oak.cs.ucla.edu/~cho /papers/ntoulas-hidden.pdf.

OECD Watch. *10 Years On: Assessing the Contribution of the OECD Guidelines for Multinational Enterprises to Responsible Business Conduct.*

Office of the Privacy Commissioner. 'The case for reforming the Personal Information Protection and Electronic Documents Act' (May 2013), at https://www.priv.gc.ca/parl/2013/pipeda_r_201305_e.pdf.

Office of the United Nations Commissioner for Human Rights. *Business and Human Rights: A Progress Report* (2000), at www2.ohchr.org/english/about /publications/docs/business.htm.

Opinion of the Advocate General Jääskinen, at http://curia.europa.eu/juris/document /document_print.jsf?doclang=EN&text=&pageIndex=0&part=1&mode=lst&docid =138782&occ=first&dir=&cid=124792.

Palfrey, J. G. Jr. 'Reluctant Gatekeepers: Corporate Ethics on a Filtered Internet', in *Global Information Technology Report* (World Economic Forum: 2006–2007).

Promoting a European Framework for corporate social responsibility, Green Paper (Employment & Social Affairs, 2001).

Report from the Commission to the European Parliament, the Council and the European Economic and Social Committee. First Report on the Application of Directive 2000/31/EC of the European Parliament and of the Council of 8 June 2000 on certain legal aspects of information society services, in particular electronic commerce, in the Internal Market (Directive on electronic commerce).

Report of the special rapporteur on the promotion and protection of the right to freedom of expression, Frank La Rue to the United Nations General Assembly, 16 May 2011, at www.ohchr.org/Documents/Issues/Opinion/A.66.290.pdf.

Rt Hon Lord McNally. Letter. *The Functions, Powers and Resources of the Information Commissioner: Government Response to the Committee's Ninth Report of Session* 2012–13 (30 June 2013), at www.publications.parliament.uk /pa/cm201314/cmselect/cmjust/560/56004.htm.

Ruggie, J. 'Business and human rights: Further steps towards the operationalization of the "protect, respect and remedy" framework' (April 2010), at www.reports -and-materials.org/Ruggie-report-2010.pdf (last visited 5 August 2011).

Ruggie, J. 'Business and human rights: towards operationalizing the "protect, respect and remedy" framework' (2009), at www2.ohchr.org/english/bodies /hrcouncil/docs/11session/A.HRC.11.13.pdf.

Ruggie, J. 'Guiding principles on business and human rights: implementing the United Nations "protect, respect and remedy" framework' (March 2011), at www.business-humanrights.org/media/documents/ruggie/ruggie-guiding-prin ciples-21-mar-2011.pdf.

Ruggie, J. 'Protect, respect and remedy: a framework for business and human rights: Report of the Special Representative of the Secretary General on the issue of human rights and transnational corporations and other business enterprises' (2008), at www.reports-and-materials.org/Ruggie-report-7-Apr-2008.pdf.

Ruggie, J. 'State obligations to provide access to remedy for human rights abuses by third parties, including business: an overview of international and regional provisions, commentary and decisions' (Addendum) (2009), at www.reports-and -materials.org/Ruggie-addendum-15-May-2009.doc.

*Safer Children in a Digital World: The Report of the Byron Review* (Crown copyright, 2008).

Twentyfifty. *The Private Sector and Human Rights in the UK* (October 2009).

UK Government. 'Corporate Social Responsibility: A Government Update' (DTI, May 2004).

United Nations Office of the High Commissioner for Human Rights. *The Corporate Responsibility to Respect Human Rights: An Interpretive Guide* (2012).

United Nations Global Compact. *Corporate Citizenship in the World Economy* (October 2008).

Utting, P. 'Rethinking business regulation: from self-regulation to social control', Technology, Business and Society Programme Paper Number 15, United Nations Research Institute for Social Development (2005).

van Eijk, N. *Search Engines, the New Bottleneck for Content Access*, Amsterdam Law School Legal Studies Research Paper No. 2012–21.

Verbiest, T. et al. *Study on the Liability of Internet Intermediaries*, Markt/2006/09/E (November 2007), at http://ec.europa.eu/internal_market/e-commerce/docs/study /liability/final_report_en.pdf.

Volokh, E., and D. M. Falk. 'First Amendment protection for search engine search results' (white paper commissioned by Google) (2012), at http://papers.ssrn .com/sol3/papers.cfm?abstract_id=2055364.

Walker, C., and Y. Akdeniz. 'The governance of the Internet in Europe with special reference to illegal and harmful content', at www.cyber-rights.org/documents /CrimLR_ya_98.pdf.

Westminster eForum. Transcript. *Taming the Wild Web? – Online Content Regulation* (London: 11 February 2009).

Wild, L. *Democracy in the Age of Modern Communications: An Outline* (2008) Paper for Freedom of Expression Project, Global Partners & Associates.

## Interview

Interview with Stephen Fry, at http://www.videojug.com/interview/stephen-fry -web-20 (last visited 22 July 2011).

## Articles, commentaries and posts

Agence France-Press. 'Russia censors media by blocking websites and popular blog' (4 March 2014) at www.theguardian.com/world/2014/mar/14/russia -bans-alexei-navalny-blog-opposition-news-websites.

Alexander, A. 'Internet role in Egypt's protests' (9 February 211), at www.bbc.co .uk/news/world-middle-east-12400319.

Almunia, J. Speech/12/372, 'Statement of VP Almunia on the Google antitrust investigation' (21 May 2012), at http://europa.eu/rapid/press-release_SPEECH -12-372_en.htm.

Amnesty International. Public statement. 'Amnesty International involvement with the internet multi stakeholder initiative' (29 October 2008), at www.amnesty.org /ar/library/asset/POL30/009/2008/es/1c327fdf-a67c-11dd-966b-0da92cc4cb95 /pol300092008en.pdf.

Anderson, S. et al. 'Top 200: the rise of corporate global power' (4 December 2000), at http://corpwatch.org/article.php?id=377.

Annan, K. A. 'Break the technology barrier – the world information summit' (9 December 2003), at (9 December 2003), at www.nytimes.com/2003/12/09 /opinion/09iht-edannan_ed3_.html.

Arthur, C. 'European commission reopens Google antitrust investigation' (8 September 2014), at www.theguardian.com/technology/2014/sep/08/european -commission-reopens-google-antitrust-investigation-after-political-storm-over -proposed-settlement.

Arthur, C. 'Google faces deluge of requests to wipe details from search index' (4 May 2014), at www.theguardian.com/technology/2014/may/15/hundreds-google-wipe -details-search-index-right-forgotten.

Barlow, J. P. 'Selling wine without bottles: economy of mind on the global net' (March 1994), at http://virtualschool.edu/mon/ElectronicFrontier/WineWithout Bottles.html.

Barrett, T. 'To censor pro-union website, Telus blocked 766 others' (4 August 2005), at www.labournet.net/world/0508/canada2.html.

The BBC. 'Child abuse "big business online"' (13 May 2010), at http://news.bbc.co .uk/1/hi/technology/10108720.stm.

The BBC. 'Internet access is a "fundamental rights"' (8 March 2010), at http://news .bbc.co.uk/1/hi/technology/8548190.stm.

The BBC. 'Luminaries look to the future web', at http://news.bbc.co.uk/1/hi /7373717.stm.

The BBC. 'Online pornography to be blocked by default, PM announces' (22 July 2013), at www.bbc.co.uk/news/uk-23401076.

The BBC. 'Quango list shows 192 to be axed' (14 October 2010), at www.bbc.co.uk /news/uk-politics-11538534.

Beckett, C. 'SuperMedia: the future as "networked journalism"' (10 June 2008), at www.opendemocracy.net/article/supermedia-the-networked-journalism-future.

Beckett, C. 'State 2.0: a new front end?' (7 September 2009), at www.opendemocracy .net/article/state-2-0-a-new-front-end.

Bello, O. 'The Kimberley Process risks becoming irrelevant to cogent concerns' (28 October 2013), at www.saiia.org.za/opinion-analysis/the-kimberley-process -risks-becoming-irrelevant-to-cogent-concerns.

Bennett-Smith, M. 'Facebook vows to crack down on rape joke pages after successful protest, boycott' (29 May 2013), at www.huffingtonpost.com/2013 /05/29/facebook-rape-jokes-protest_n_3349319.html.

Berners-Lee, T. et al. 'The Semantic Web' (17 May 2001), at www.scientificamer
ican.com/article.cfm?id=the-semantic-web.

Cain, M. 'Why does the PCC pretend it can do something about phone hacking?'
(31 January 2011), at http://pccwatch.co.uk/why-does-the-pcc-pretend-about
-phone-hacking/.

Cameron, D. Prime Minister's speech. 'The internet and pornography: Prime
Minister calls for action' (22 July 2013), at www.gov.uk/government/speeches
/the-internet-and-pornography-prime-minister-calls-for-action.

Cerf, V. 'Internet access is not a human rights' (4 January 2012), at www.nytimes
.com/2012/01/05/opinion/internet-access-is-not-a-human-right.html?_r=0.

Change.org. 'We need women on British banknotes', at www.change.org/en-GB
/petitions/we-need-women-on-british-banknotes.

CNN World. '"Neda" becomes rallying cry for Iranian protests' (21 June 2009), at
http://articles.cnn.com/2009-06-21/world/iran.woman.twitter_1_neda-peaceful
-protest-cell-phone?_s=PM:WORLD.

comScore. 'ComScore releases January 2014 U. S. search engine rankings' (18
February 2014), at www.comscore.com/Insights/Press_Releases/2014/2/com
Score_Releases_January_2014_US_Search_Engine_Rankings.

Crete-Nishihata, M. 'Egypt's internet blackout: extreme example of just-in-time
blocking' (28 January 2011), at http://opennet.net/blog/2011/01/egypt%E2%80
%99s-internet-blackout-extreme-example-just-time-blocking.

Curtis, S. 'BT forces porn filter choice' (16 December 2013), at www.telegraph.co
.uk/technology/internet-security/10520537/BT-forces-porn-filter-choice.html.

Davies, L. 'Facebook refuses to take down rape joke pages' (30 September 2011),
at www.theguardian.com/technology/2011/sep/30/facebook-refuses-pull-rape
-jokepages.

Davies, C. J. 'The hidden censors of the Internet', *Wired Magazine* (June 2006), at
www.wired.co.uk/wired-magazine/archive/2009/05/features/the-hidden-censors
-of-the-internet.aspx?page=all.

D'Jaen, M. 'Global Initiative to protect net privacy and freedoms launched',
*e-commerce law & policy* (December 2008), at www.perkinscoie.com/files/uplo
ad/PRIV_09-01_Article_Jaen.pdf.

Downes, L. 'Why no one will join the Global Network Initiative' (30 March 2011), at
www.forbes.com/sites/larrydownes/2011/03/30/why-no-one-will-join-the-global
-network-initiative/.

Electronic Frontier Foundation. Commentary. 'Everyone who's made a Hitler
parody video, leave the room' (20 April 2010), at www.eff.org/deeplinks/2010
/04/everyone-who-s-made-hitler-parody-leave-room.

Electronic Frontier Foundation. 'GNI resignation letter', at www.eff.org/document
/gni-resignation-letter.

Electronic Frontier Foundation. Letter, at www.eff.org/files/filenode/gni/signon
_letter.txt.

Enge, E. '6 Major Google changes reveal the future of SEO' (30 December 2013), at http://searchenginewatch.com/article/2301719/6-Major-Google-Changes-Reveal -the-Future-of-SEO.

European Commission. IP/14/116, 'Antitrust: commission obtains from Google comparable display of specialised search rivals' (5 February 2014), at http:// europa.eu/rapid/press-release_IP-14-116_en.htm.

European Commission. IP/13/371, 'Antitrust: commission seeks feedback on commitments offered by Google to address competition concerns' (25 April 2013), at http://europa.eu/rapid/press-release_IP-13-371_en.htm.

European Commission. Statement, 'Statement by Commissioner Vestager on Google antitrust investigations at the European Parliament (ECON committee meeting)' (11 November 2014), at http://europa.eu/rapid/press-release_STATE MENT-14-1646_en.htm.

Facebook. 'How to report things', at www.facebook.com/help/181495968648557.

Fallows, D. 'Election newshounds speak up: newspaper, TV, and internet fans tell how and why they differ', *The Pew Research Center* (6 February 2007), at http://pewresearch.org/pubs/406/election-newshounds-speak-up.

Feigenbaum, L. et al. 'The semantic web in action', *Scientific American* (Dec 2007), reproduced with permission, at www.thefigtrees.net/lee/sw/sciam/semantic-web -in-action.

Fiveash, K. 'Google disappears torrent terms from autocomplete search results' (27 January 2011), at www.theregister.co.uk/2011/01/27/google_bittorrent_terms _killed_on_autocomplete/.

Galperin, E., and D. O'Brien. 'Russia blocks access to major independent news sites' (13 March 2014), at www.eff.org/deeplinks/2014/03/russia-blocks-access -major-independent-news-sites.

Ganesan, A. 'Viewpoint: why voluntary initiatives aren't enough', *Leading Perspectives* (Spring 2009), at www.bsr.org/reports/leading-perspectives/2009 /LP_Spring_2009_Voluntary_Initiatives.pdf.

Global Witness. 'The Kimberley Process', at www.globalwitness.org/campaigns/con flict/conflict-diamonds/kimberley-process.

Google. 'A new approach to China' (12 January 2010), at http://googleblog.blog spot.com/2010/01/new-approach-to-china.html.

Google. 'A quick note about music blog removals' (10 February 2010), at http:// buzz.blogger.com/2010/02/quick-note-about-music-blog-removals.html.

Google. 'Corporate social responsibility', at www.google.com/intl/zh-CN/corpo rate/responsibility_en.html.

Google. 'Controversial content and free expression on the web: a refresher' (19 April 2010), at http://googleblog.blogspot.com/2010/04/controversial-content and-free.html.

Google. 'The Federal Trade Commission closes its antitrust review' (3 January 2013), at http://googleblog.blogspot.ca/2013/01/the-federal-trade-commission -closes-its.html.

Google. 'Finding more high-quality sites in search' (24 February 2011), at http://googleblog.blogspot.com/2011/02/finding-more-high-quality-sites-in .html.

Google. 'Let the music play' (26 August 2009), at http://buzz.blogger.com/2009/08 /let-music-play.html.

Google. 'Link schemes', at www.google.com/support/webmasters/bin/answer.py ?answer=66356.

Google. 'Making search more secure', at http://googleblog.blogspot.com/2011/10 /making-search-more-secure.html.

Google. 'Search more securely with encrypted Google web search' (21 May 2010), at http://googleblog.blogspot.com/2010/05/search-more-securely-with-encrypted. html.

Google. 'Some weekend work that will (hopefully) enable more Egyptians to be heard' (31 January 2011), at http://googleblog.blogspot.com/2011/01/some-we ekend-work-that-will-hopefully.html.

Google. 'Transparency report', at www.google.com/transparencyreport/traffic/.

Google. 'Webmaster guidelines', at www.google.com/support/webmasters/bin /answer.py?answer=35769.

Google Blog. 'Controversial content and free expression on the web: a refresher', at http://googleblog.blogspot.com/2010/04/controversial-content-and-free.html.

Grossman, W. 'IWF reforms could pave way for UK net censorship: who is watching the watchers?' (29 December 2006), at www.theregister.co.uk/2006 /12/29/iwf_feature/page3.html.

Grossman, W. 'IWF: what are you looking at?' (25 March 2002), at www.independent .co.uk/news/business/analysis-and-features/iwf-what-are-you-looking-at-655425 .html.

The Guardian. 'Occupy protests around the world: full list visualised', at www .theguardian.com/news/datablog/2011/oct/17/occupy-protests-world-list-map.

Halfacree, G. 'Government extends porn filter to "extremist" content' (29 November 2013), at www.bit-tech.net/news/bits/2013/11/29/extremism-filter/1.

Halliday, J. 'Google search results may indicate "right to be forgotten" censorship' (8 June 2014), at www.theguardian.com/technology/2014/jun/08/google-search -results-indicate-right-to-be-forgotten-censorship.

Halliday, J. 'Google Street View: information commissioner shackled by Data Protection Act' (28 October 2010), at www.guardian.co.uk/technology/2010/oct /28/google-street-view-information-commissioner.

Halliday, J. 'Google Street View broke Canada's privacy law with Wi-Fi capture' (20 October 2010), at www.guardian.co.uk/technology/2010/oct/19/google-street -view-privacy-canada.

Hudson, A. 'Turkey lifts its ban on YouTube-agency' (30 October 2010), at http://uk.reuters.com/article/2010/10/30/oukin-uk-turkey-youtube-idUKTRE 69T1JE20101030.

The Huffington Post. 'Neda video wins Polk Award: Iran protest death video first anonymous winner of journalism prize' (16 February 2010, at www.huffington post.com/2010/02/16/neda-video-wins-polk-award_n_463378.html.

Information Commissioner's Office. News release. 'ICO fines former ACS Law boss for lax IT security', at www.ico.gov.uk/~/media/documents/pressreleases /2011/monetary_penalty_acslaw_news_release_20110510.ashx.

ISPreview. *Top 10 UK ISPs*, at www.ispreview.co.uk/review/top10.php.

ISPreview. 'UK government seeking to expand website blocking remit through IWF' (9 June 2011), at www.ispreview.co.uk/story/2011/06/09/uk-government -seeking-to-expand-website-blocking-remit-through-iwf.html.

Jaume-Palasi, L. '"Google Spain case": court decision privatises the public sphere' (27 May 2014), at http://policyreview.info/articles/news/google-spain-case -court-decision-privatises-public-sphere/291.

Jeffries, S. 'A rare interview with Jürgen Habermas', *The Financial Times* (30 April 2010), at www.ft.com/cms/s/0/eda3bcd8-5327-11df-813e-00144feab49a.html.

Johnson, B. 'Amnesty criticises Global Network Initiative for online freedom of speech' (30 October 2008), at www.guardian.co.uk/technology/2008/oct/30 /amnesty-global-network-initiative.

Kain, E. 'Reddit makes headlines boycotting GoDaddy over online censorship bills' (26 December 2011), at www.forbes.com/sites/erikkain/2011/12/26/reddit -makes-headlines-boycotting-godaddy-over-online-censorship-bills/.

Kiss, J. 'Facebook's 10th birthday: from college dorm to 1.23 billion users' (4 February 2014), at www.theguardian.com/technology/2014/feb/04/face book-10-years-mark-zuckerberg.

Kopytoff, V. G. 'Sites like Twitter absent from free speech pact' (6 March 2011), at www.nytimes.com/2011/03/07/technology/07rights.html.

Kravets, D. 'What's fueling Midest protests? It's more than Twitter' (28 January 2011), at www.wired.co.uk/news/archive/2011-01/28/middle-east-protests-twitter ?page=all.

Letsch, C., and D. Rushe. 'Turkey blocks YouTube amid "national security" concerns' (28 March 2014), at www.theguardian.com/world/2014/mar/27/google -youtube-ban-turkey-erdogan.

MacAskill, E. 'Wikileaks website pulled by Amazon after US political pressure', at www.guardian.co.uk/media/2010/dec/01/wikileaks-website-cables-servers -amazon.

Marsden, C. 'Corporate responsibilities in times of civil unrest: the case of Egypt and Vodafone' (July 2011), at www.networkedcranfield.com/doughty /Document%20Library/Hot%20Topics/Corporate%20Responsibilities%20in %20Times%20of%20Civil%20Unrest%20the%20case%20of%20Egypt%20and %20Vodafone.pdf.

Melik, J. 'Diamonds: does the Kimberley Process work?' (28 June 2010), at www .bbc.co.uk/news/10307046.

Metz, C. 'Google's "Musicblogocide" – blame the DMCA' (11 February 2010), at www.theregister.co.uk/2010/02/11/google_musicblogocide_2010/.

Metz, C. 'IWF confirms Wayback Machine porn blacklisting' (14 January 2009), at www.theregister.co.uk/2009/01/14/iwf_details_archive_blacklisting/.

Michaels, S. 'Google shuts down music blogs without warning' (11 February 2010), at www.guardian.co.uk/music/2010/feb/11/google-deletes-music-blogs.

Morton, G. 'Muslim leader drops Ezra Levant cartoon complaint' (12 February 2008), at www.nationalpost.com/news/canada/story.html?id=303895.

Mulholland, H. 'Government targets extremist websites' (17 January 2008), at www.guardian.co.uk/politics/2008/jan/17/uksecurity.terrorism.

Nakashima, E. 'Sexual threats stifle some female bloggers' (30 April 2007), at www.washingtonpost.com/wp-dyn/content/article/2007/04/29/AR2007042901555.html.

Netmarketshare. 'Search engine market share', at www.netmarketshare.com/search-engine-market-share.aspx?qprid=4&qpcustomd=0.

Noman, H. 'Saudi Arabia to impose restrictions on online content production, including on YouTube' (3 December 2013), at https://opennet.net/blog/2013/12/saudi-arabia-impose-restrictions-online-content-production-including-youtube.

Nyaira, S. 'Kimberley Process in turmoil after chairman clears Zimbabwe diamond sales' (23 March 2011), at www.voanews.com/zimbabwe/news/Kimberley-Process-In-Turmoil-After-Chairman-Allows-Zimbabwes-Marange-Gems-Trade-118509874.html.

Oates, J. 'ICO reopens Google Street View privacy probe' (25 October 2010), at www.theregister.co.uk/2010/10/25/ico_google_probe/.

Ofcom. 'Identifying appropriate regulatory solutions: principles for analysing self- and co-regulation' (10 December 2008), at http://stakeholders.ofcom.org.uk/binaries/consultations/coregulation/statement/statement.pdf.

Office of National Statistics. 'Internet access – households and individuals, 2013', at www.ons.gov.uk/ons/rel/rdit2/internet-access—households-and-individuals/2013/stb-ia-2013.html.

Office for National Statistics. 'Internet access 2010', at http://www.statistics.gov.uk/pdfdir/iahi0810.pdf.

O'Reilly, T. 'What is Web 2.0' (30 September 2005), at http://www.oreillynet.com/pub/a/oreilly/tim/news/2005/09/30/what-is-web-20.html.

Out-Law. 'Super-injunction Twitter user in contempt of court if tweets were true' (10 May 2011), at www.theregister.co.uk/2011/05/10/super_injunctions_tweeter_in_trouble_if_its_true/.

Out-Law.com. 'Why the IWF was wrong to lift its ban on a Wikipedia page' (11 December 2008), at www.out-law.com/page-9653.

Out-Law.com. 'Information Commissioner gets power to fine for privacy breaches' (12 May 2008), at www.out-law.com/page-9110.

Palfrey, J. 'Testimony on internet filtering and surveillance' at http://jpalfrey.and over.edu/2008/05/20/testimony-on-internet-filtering-and-surveillance/.

Pauli, D. 'Australia's Web blacklist leaked' *Computer World* (19 March 2009), at www.computerworld.com.au/article/296161/australia_web_blacklist_leaked/.

Petley, J. 'Web Control', *Index on Censorship*, 38(1) (2009) 78.

Pew Research Center. 'Internet use over time' (September 2013), at www.pewinter net.org/data-trend/internet-use/internet-use-over-time/.

Press Association. 'Two face jail over Twitter abuse of banknote campaigner' (24 January 2014), at www.theguardian.com/technology/2014/jan/24/two-face -jail-twitter-abuse.

Privacy International. 'Cultural dysfunction', at www.privacyinternational.org /reports/the-uk-information-commissioners-office-lets-bury-our-bad-news-on-a -busy-news-day/cultural.

Privacy International. 'Civil liberties groups say UK information commissioner's office is not "fit for purpose"' (3 November 2010), at www.privacyinternational .org/article/civil-liberties-groups-say-uk-information-commissioner%E2%80 %99s-office-not-fit-purpose.

Rainey, J. 'Barack Obama can thank "citizen journalist" for "bitter" *tempest*' (15 April 2008), at http://articles.latimes.com/print/2008/apr/15/nation/na-bitter15.

Reporters Without Borders. 'Why reporters without borders is not endorsing the global principles on freedom of expression and privacy for ICT companies operating in internet-restricting countries' (28 October 2008), at http://en.rsf .org/why-reporters-without-borders-is-28-10-2008,29117.html.

Reuters. 'PCC clears Murdoch paper over hacking claim' (9 November 2009), at www.independent.co.uk/news/media/press/pcc-clears-murdoch-paper-over -hacking-claim-1817573.html.

Rhoads, C., and G. A. Fowler. 'Egypt shuts down internet, cellphone services', *The Wall Street Journal* (29 January 2011), at http://online.wsj.com/article/SB1000142 4052748703956604576110453371369740.html?mod=googlenews_wsj.

Robinson, J. 'PCC to re-examine News of the World phone-hacking evidence', at www.guardian.co.uk/media/2010/sep/21/phone-hacking-news-of-the-world.

Rosen, J. 'The delete squad' (29 April 2013), at www.newrepublic.com/article/113 045/free-speech-internet-silicon-valley-making-rules.

Ruggie, J. 'The past as prologue? a moment of truth for UN business and human rights treaty' at www.ihrb.org/commentary/past-as-prologue.html#_edn2.

Salkowitz, R. 'Politicans seek "new" new media for 2012 run' (21 April 2011), at www.internetevolution.com/author.asp?section_id=697&doc_id=205850&f_src =internetevolution_gnews%3Cbr%20/%3E.

Science Daily. 'Google flu trends estimates off, study finds', at www.sciencedaily .com/releases/2010/05/100517101714.htm (last visited 27 July 2011).

Sky News. 'Paedophiles target virtual world' (31 October 2007), at http://news.sky .com/home/article/1290719.

Starr, S. 'Internet Freedom', *New Humanist*, 117(1) (2002).

StatCounter. 'Search engine market share as at April 2014' from http://theeword
.co.uk/seo-manchester/february_2014_uk_search_engine_market_share_stats
.html.

Statistic Brain. 'Google annual search statistics', at www.statisticbrain.com/google
-searches/.

Stephens, M. 'Only the powerful will benefit from the 'right to be forgotten''
(18 May 2014), at www.theguardian.com/commentisfree/2014/may/18/powerful
-benefit-right-to-be-forgotten.

Strom, S., and M. Helft. 'Google finds it hard to reinvent philanthropy', at
www.nytimes.com/2011/01/30/business/30charity.html?_r=1.

*Telegraph*. 'Hitler downfall parodies: 25 worth watching' (6 October 2009), at www.
telegraph.co.uk/technology/news/6262709/Hitler-Downfall-parodies-25-worth
-watching.html.

Tripathi, S. 'How businesses have responded in Egypt' (7 February 2011), at
www.ihrb.org/commentary/staff/how_businesses_have_responded_in_egypt
.html.

Tripathi, S. 'How should internet and phone companies respond in Egypt?'
(4 February 2011), at www.ihrb.org/commentary/staff/internet_providers_in
_egypt.html.

UN News Centre. 'UN Human Rights Council endorses principles to ensure
businesses respect human rights' (16 June 2011), at www.un.org/apps/news/story
.asp?NewsID=38742&Cr=human±rights&Cr1=.

Villelabeitia, I. 'Turkey reinstates YouTube ban' (3 November 2010), at www.reuters
.com/article/2010/11/03/us-turkey-youtube-idUSTRE6A227C20101103.

Wearden, G. 'Bank of England turns to Google to shed light on economic trends'
(13 June 2011), at www.guardian.co.uk/business/2011/jun/13/bank-of-england
-google-searches?intcmp=239.

WorldWideWebSize. 'The size of the World Wide Web', at www.worldwideweb
size.com/.

## Online resources

Barack Obama 2012, at www.barackobama.com/get-involved.

The British Board of Film Classification, at www.bbfc.co.uk.

Business & Human Rights Resource Centre, at www.business-humanrights.org
/Home.

Canadian Centre for Child Protection Inc. at www.cybertip.ca/app/en/.

Center for Justice and Accountability, at http://cja.org/article.php?id=435.

Change.org, at www.change.org.

Chilling Effects, at www.chillingeffects.org.

CorpWatch, at www.corpwatch.org.

Creative Commons, at http://creativecommons.org/.

The Danish Institute for Human Rights, at www.humanrights.dk/.

Darfur Is Dying, at www.darfurisdying.com/.

Department for Business, Innovation and Skills, at www.bis.gov.uk/.

Dick Durbin, at http://durbin.senate.gov/public/index.cfm/.

Electronic Frontiers Australia, at www.efa.org.au/category/censorship/manda
tory-isp-filtering/.

Electronic Frontier Foundation, at www.eff.org.

Electronic Industry Citizenship Coalition, at www.eicc.info/.

E-petitions, at http://epetitions.direct.gov.uk/.

European Digital Rights (EDRI), at www.edri.org/.

Freedom of Information (Archive), at www.foi.gov.uk.

Global Business Initiative on Human Rights, at www.global-business-initiative
.org.

Global Movement for a Binding Treaty at www.treatymovement.com.

Google.org Initiative, at www.google.org.

Institute for Human Rights and Business, at www.ihrb.org.

Information Commissioner's Office, at www.ico.gov.uk/.

The Intellectual Property Office, at www.ipo.gov.uk.

International Answer, at www.answercoalition.org.

International Standards Organization, at www.iso.org/iso/home.htm.

Internet Live Stats, at www.internetlivestats.com.

Internet Rights and Principles Coalition, at http://internetrightsandprinciples.org/.

The Internet Service Providers' Association, at www.ispa.org.uk/.

Internet Watch Foundation, at www.iwf.org.uk.

mySociety, at www.mysociety.org.

Nominet, at www.nominet.org.

Office of Communication (Ofcom), at www.ofcom.org.uk/about/.

The Office of the High Commissioner for Human Rights, at www.ohchr.org/.

Office of the Information Commissioner of Canada, at www.oic-ci.gc.ca/eng/.

The Press Complaints Commission, at www.pcc.org.uk/.

Privacy International, at www.privacyinternational.org.

Roger Darlington's website, at www.rogerdarlington.co.uk/iwf.html#Introduction.

Search Engine History, at www.searchenginehistory.com.

Social Accountability International, at http://www.sa-intl.org/.

True Vision, at www.report-it.org.uk/home.

United for Peace and Justice, at www.unitedforpeace.org.

The United Kingdom National Contact Point, at www.gov.uk/uk-national-con
tact-point-for-the-organisation-for-economic-co-operation-and-development
-oecd-guidelines-for-multinational-enterprises.

United Nations Global Compact, at www.unglobalcompact.org.

Virtual Global Task Force, at www.virtualglobaltaskforce.com/what-we-do/.

Lightning Source UK Ltd.
Milton Keynes UK
UKOW05f2144260217
295343UK00022B/1342/P